4-98

The Living U.S. Constitution

The Living U.S. Constitution

Completely Revised and Enlarged

Presented with Historical Notes

by Saul K. Padover

MERIDIAN BOOKS
The World Publishing Company
New York and Cleveland

For Peggy, as always

I wish to thank my friend and colleague,
Professor Jacob Landynski,
for his many wise suggestions.

A MERIDIAN BOOK

Published by The World Publishing Company
2231 West 110th Street, Cleveland, Ohio 44102
Published simultaneously in Canada by
Nelson, Foster & Scott Ltd.

First Meridian Printing—April, 1969
Reprinted by arrangement with The New American Library, Inc.

Manufactured at World Publishing Press, a division of
The World Publishing Company, Cleveland, Ohio
Library of Congress Catalog Card Number: 76–37

PRINTED IN THE UNITED STATES OF AMERICA

Contents

PART I

THE CONSTITUTION

PART II

THE UNITED STATES SUPREME COURT

Part I

The Constitution

Chapter I

The Story of the Making of the Constitution

ITS WORLD SIGNIFICANCE:

The formation of the Constitution, which British Prime Minister Gladstone once described as "the most wonderful work ever struck off at a given time by the brain and purpose of man," is a story of great historic drama. Its significance transcends the boundaries of the United States, for it offers a lesson and example to peoples throughout the world. The American Constitution has turned out to be perhaps the most successful example in history of a legal instrument that has served both as a safeguard of individual freedom and as a ligament of national unity. Today, several generations after it was put into shape, it is still a living document, meeting the needs, as it always has done, of a great, growing, powerful, technologically advanced, self-governing republic. In duration, flexibility, and underlying democratic wisdom, there is nothing quite like it anywhere else in the world.

THE DELEGATES:

The gentlemen who met in the State House at Philadelphia in May, 1787, to draw up the Constitution, represented some of the best talents in America. Fifty-five delegates had been chosen by twelve of the thirteen states, but not all of them attended the sessions, which continued for nearly four months. In the end only thirty-nine signed the completed document. The aim of the delegates was the construction of a political framework that would both protect property against revolutionary expropriation and secure liberty from a potentially tyrannical government. What they wanted, in other words, was a government that would have power, but not exercise it capriciously or cruelly. How they finally accomplished this is one of the marvels of history.

Among the delegates were men with wide experience in government and business. They were merchants from New England, judges from the middle states, planters from the South. Half of them were lawyers or government officials trained in law. More than two-thirds had served in the Continental Congress. Some were governors. Many were highly educated and were scholars. Half of them were college graduates. The average age was forty-two, the oldest, Benjamin Franklin, being eighty-one, and the youngest, Jonathan Dayton, twenty-seven. Eight of them had signed the Declaration of Independence eleven years before. Their viewpoints ranged all the way from the tough conservatism of Alexander Hamilton, who thought that the best government was an aristocracy, to the warm democracy of James Wilson, who was dedicated to the idea of government by the people. But in spite of the immense diversity of outlook, the delegates shared a common American culture, a common language, and a common respect for law against the whims of personal tyranny. Above all, most of them shared the great eighteenth-century belief in reason and regard for the individual. As reasonable men they could argue vehemently for their particular points of view, and as cultured gentlemen they were bound to come to a working compromise.

WASHINGTON:

The fame of some of the delegates was world-wide. Foremost among them, in both reputation and greatness, were the granite-charactered General George Washington and the sage Benjamin Franklin. The sheer presence of General Washington was almost a guarantee of the convention's success. A silent, big, square-shouldered gentleman with a face molded in chill dignity, Washington had few intimates, but inspired universal respect mixed with awe.

FRANKLIN:

Almost opposite in every way was Benjamin Franklin, then eighty-one years old and spry enough to walk to and from the sessions whenever the weather permitted. He was the wisest, the wittiest, the most mellow, humane, and—if the truth be told—the most garrulous man of his age, known throughout the civilized world as an inventor, scientist, and philosopher. He had a way with him, and with the ladies, too. When he was American Minister in Paris, even the haughty Marie Antoinette liked him. He was one of those men who trailed glory and affection. In Paris, when Thomas Jefferson came to succeed him and presented his credentials to the French Foreign Minister, the latter asked: "It is you who replace Monsieur Franklin?"

Jefferson replied quickly: "No one can replace him, Sir. I am only his successor."

Benjamin Franklin was also a famous wit. During the Revolutionary War Franklin commanded a company of soldiers of which Rev. Charles Beatty, a Presbyterian minister, was chaplain. Mr. Beatty complained to Franklin that the men did not attend prayers. They had been promised upon enlistment a half-pint of rum a day, half of it served in the morning and half in the afternoon. For the rum they came punctually, but for the prayers they did not. Franklin, thinking about this, said: "It is perhaps below the dignity of your profession to act as steward for the rum; but if you were to distribute it just after prayers, you would have them all about you." Beatty did it—and never were prayers more punctually attended.

Of the other important men at the convention, the men who not only shaped the Constitution of the United States, but also the early days of the Republic, let us mention only, first, Alexander Hamilton and, second, James Madison.

Hamilton:

Alexander Hamilton is one of the earliest American "success stories." His is a veritable Horatio Alger story with a tragic finish. Foreign-born and of illegitimate birth, he not only married into the American aristocracy, but also occupied high public office. He was one of the most brilliant men in America, a friend of George Washington, and one of the architects of the American Republic.

His background helps, perhaps, to explain his personal ambition and drive. Like so many Americans—let us recall that 10 per cent of all distinguished Americans listed in the *Dictionary of American Biography* and in *Who's Who* are foreign-born—Hamilton was born abroad. His parentage is uncertain. He was the illegitimate child of a Scottish father. He may also have had French blood in him. At any rate, whatever the precise measure of genes in Hamilton, he was apparently well mixed—and thus a real American.

At the ripe age of fifteen he came to New York and attended King's College (now Columbia University). In those days Hamilton was what we would call a "liberal" today. As a political writer he attracted attention with his brilliant polemics against the British crown. When the Revolutionary War broke out, he joined the militia, and a year later General Washington appointed him his aide-de-camp with the rank of lieutenant-colonel. He came out of the war a hero and a political conservative. His conservatism—some would call it extreme reaction—was deepened when he married into the bluest of New York's blue-blooded families. Hamilton was twenty-three years old and already a famous man when he married Elizabeth, daughter of General Philip Schuyler. For an immigrant boy this marital alliance was no mean achievement.

He had a powerful mind and he rose to the top rank of the legal profession. In 1787, at the age of thirty, he was already important enough to be one of the delegates to the Constitutional Convention. General Washington was deeply attracted to the swift-minded, brilliant Hamilton, and he made him his Secretary of the Treasury in the first American administration. At thirty-two, Alexander Hamilton was to be the youngest member of the Cabinet in American history.

Hamilton's later achievements as Secretary of the Treasury, though bitterly criticized by the Jeffersonian democrats of the day, must be ranked as epochal. His hard, tough, unsentimental mind gave to the weak young Republic the guidance it desperately needed. Hamilton established the national credit, stabilized the currency, encouraged manufactures, and above all he attracted the moneyed and propertied classes to the Republic.

Hamilton did this with sharp realism. He reasoned that only the wealthy and well-educated—many of whom had only contempt for democracy and entertained doubts as to the efficacy of a republic—could give the young government both prestige and cohesion. To tie them to the unrespected, struggling Republic, Hamilton later attracted them with chains of gold. He did this with calculated cynicism, for he had but a low opinion of most of mankind. Viewing his tactics and analyzing his philosophy, one cannot escape the conclusion that Hamilton used low means for high ends.

Contemporary democrats hated and feared him, for Hamilton was an honest and a blunt man and he did not conceal his opinions. He said that the people were a "great beast." At the convention he blurted out: "Take mankind in general, they are vicious." Of course, he did not mean the aristocratic mankind; he meant the poor portion of mankind. I cannot refrain from quoting a characteristic passage from one of his speeches at the Federal Convention:

> Take mankind as they are, and what are they governed by? Their passions. . . . One great error is that we suppose mankind more honest than they are. Our prevailing passions are ambition and interest; and it will ever be the duty of a wise government to avail itself of those passions, in order to make them subservient to the public good. . . . All communities divide themselves into the few and the many. The first are the rich and well-born, the other the mass of the people. The voice of the people has been said to be the voice of God; and, however generally this maxim has been quoted and believed, it is not true in fact. The people are turbulent and changing; they seldom judge or determine right. Give, therefore, to the first class a distinct, permanent share in the government. They will check the unsteadiness of the second, and, as they cannot receive any advantage by a change, they therefore will ever maintain good government. . . . Nothing but a permanent body can check the imprudence of democracy. Their turbulent and uncontrollable disposition requires checks.

Had Hamilton had his way, the United States might have become an aristocratic republic; but fortunately his views did not prevail. Instead he gave the Constitution and later the new Republic the benefit of his penetrating mind and brilliant ability. Whatever his shortcomings, he was one of the great men of the American Republic, his cold skepticism serving as a balance, especially after the government was set up, against the warm idealism of a Jefferson.

MADISON:

James Madison, delegate from Virginia and future president of the United States, was then thirty-six years old and deeply learned in history and politics, both ancient and contemporary. He knew more about American affairs than probably any man present. He was a powerful and lucid debater. Despite his youth, his greatness was universally acknowledged. A disciple of Jefferson, whose lifelong friend he was to become, Madison was a middle-of-the-road statesman, conservative in economic matters and liberal in civil liberties. He was humane and yet skeptical. Unlike Jefferson, Madison was not given to illusions about human nature, but, on the contrary, considered man as a self-interested creature capable of evil, although not necessarily always evil. Since history taught him that humanity was nearly always its own enemy and that governments in the past had usually ended in tyranny, Madison visualized the creation of a new type of government that would not have the power or temptation to tyrannize over the citizens. This required careful and delicate safeguards that would be built into the governmental structure and become an integral part of it.

In one of the profoundest paragraphs on politics that was ever written, Madison thus summarized his basic skeptical views of government in general:

> It may be a reflection on human nature, that such devices should be necessary to control the abuses of government. But what is government itself, but the greatest of all reflections on human nature? If men were angels, no government would be necessary. If angels were to govern men, neither external or internal controls on government would be necessary. In framing a government which is to be administered by men over men, the great difficulty lies in this: you must first enable the government to control the governed; and in the next place oblige it to control itself. A dependence on the people is, no doubt, the primary control on the government; but experience has taught mankind the necessity of auxiliary precautions.

This, in a nutshell, may be said to be the underlying philosophy of the American Constitution, for which Madison, more than any other single individual, was mainly responsible. It was Madison who gave the Constitution its basic shape, its essential conservatism, and yet flexibility sufficient to meet the changing needs of future times.

BEGINNINGS:

In the middle of May, 1787, as the delegates were beginning to arrive in Philadelphia, Benjamin Franklin gave a dinner for them in his new dining room, which could seat twenty-four. It was a fine dinner, particularly since Franklin had just received shipment of a barrel of porter. "The cask," he tells, "was broached, and its contents met with the most cordial reception and universal approbation. In short, the company agreed unanimously that it was the best porter they had ever tasted."

The first act of the convention was to elect a president. There were many eminent candidates available—Governor Edmund Randolph of Virginia, Justice Oliver Ellsworth of Connecticut, General Thomas Mifflin of Pennsylvania, to mention but a few. But only two, Washington and Franklin, commanded universal approval. Pennsylvania's Robert Morris nominated General Washington. "The nomination," wrote James Madison, "came with particular grace from Pennsylvania, as Doctor Franklin alone could have been thought of as a competitor. The Doctor was himself to have made the nomination of General Washington, but the state of the weather and his health confined him to his house."

Washington was unanimously elected president of the convention. He rose and thanked the gentlemen for their confidence and apologized for his inexperience in such matters, but hoped, he said, that he would not make too many mistakes. A committee was then appointed to draw up the rules for the convention and the delegates adjourned for the weekend.

THE RULES:

They reassembled on Monday, May 28, and adopted the rules. These were strict and businesslike. One of the rules shows that the convention had a high regard for its dignity. The rule required that "Every member, rising to speak, shall address the President; and whilst he shall be speaking, none shall pass between them, or hold discourse with another, or read a book, pamphlet or paper, printed or manuscript." The tight-lipped George Washington, who could freeze the boldest with a look, saw to it that this was severely enforced.

Another rule demanded absolute secrecy of the proceedings: "that nothing spoken in the House be printed, or otherwise published or communicated." This was a wise regulation, for the country was in a pitch of excitement, and the wildest kind of gossip—for instance that the Duke of York was being invited to become king of the United States—was being repeated. The press, too, was irresponsible and factional, given to vitriolic personal attacks and political character assassination. In order, therefore, to safeguard the debates and to guarantee the fullest freedom of speech on the floor, it was essential not to let anything leak out. An iron curtain thus hung over the convention, and for thirty-two years the secret of what went on inside was kept from the American public. Not until 1819, in the Administration of President Monroe, was the first *Journal* of the convention printed.

The fear of Washington's wrath kept the members careful. When an important project was being debated, copies of it were made and distributed to every member. One morning a delegate accidentally dropped his copy; it was picked up by General Mifflin, who handed it over to the president. Washington put it in his pocket and said not a word. He waited until the debates of the day were over and then he stood up and spoke coldly:

"Gentlemen—I am sorry to find that some member of this Body has been so neglectful of the secrets of the Convention as to drop a copy . . . I must entreat Gentlemen to be more careful, lest our transactions get into the News Papers, and disturb the public repose by premature speculations. I know not whose Paper it is, but there it is"—he threw it on the table—"let him who owns it take it."

Then he bowed, picked up his hat and, in the words of one of the delegates, "quitted the room with a dignity so severe that every Person seemed alarmed." No member ever dared claim that copy.

MADISON'S NOTES:

Most of what we know of what happened in the convention is due to James Madison. By common consent young Madison became the more or less official recorder of the convention. He sat out in front, his back to Washington, facing the delegates. "In this favorable position for hearing all that passed," he tells, "I noted in terms legible and in abbreviations and marks intelligible to myself what was read from the Chair or spoken by the members; and losing not a moment . . . I was enabled to write out my daily notes during the session or within a few finishing days after its close." At the same time he participated vigorously in the debates and contributed greatly to the clarification of many issues. Evenings he would check up with the delegates to make sure that his shorthand record was accurate. It was a grueling task which, Madison said years later, almost killed him, for he was small and frail. His notes, which were not published until after his death, constitute the most complete and priceless record of the convention.

THE DEBATES:

The debates were opened by Governor Edmund Randolph of Virginia. He started out with a vigorous attack on the Articles of Confederation, that makeshift constitution under which the states then maintained an ineffectual union, and then he moved a series of fifteen carefully prepared (mostly by Madison) resolutions. This so-called Virginia Plan became the basis of the whole subsequent discussion. It called for a strong *national* government, consisting of an executive, a judiciary, and a legislature; the latter was to have two branches, one elected by freemen and the other chosen by the state legislatures.

On this the debate got into high gear and rolled along for two weeks. Reduced to its essentials, the great arguments centered around the two issues of democracy and states' rights. Should the people elect their representatives? Could the people be trusted with self-government? If they were permitted to vote, was there not a danger that the numerous poor would outvote the few rich, and, therefore, property would no longer be safe? Was it not better that gentlemen of social position, wealth, and education do the ruling? These were the most hotly debated questions. Then there was the matter of the states. What should be the relation between the big and the little ones? Was it right that tiny Delaware should have as many representatives as populous Virginia or Massachusetts? And were not the little states in danger of being swallowed up by the Big Three?

DEMOCRACY:

On the question of democracy a large number of the delegates were outright skeptical and even hostile. The distinguished-looking Randolph started the debate with an attack on the dangers of democracy and the need to curb the people. Massachusetts' rich Elbridge Gerry (from whom we get the word *gerrymander*) remarked: "The evils we experience flow from the excess of democracy." His colleague Rufus King agreed with him.

Pennsylvania's wealthy and brilliant Gouverneur Morris said: "The people never act from reason alone," but are the "dupes of those who have more knowledge."

New York's Alexander Hamilton spoke contemptuously of

the "imprudence of democracy," because "the people seldom judge or determine right."

Democracy had few champions, three or four at most. Old George Mason, aristocratic Virginia liberal (who used to refer to George Washington in the old days as "that damned young surveyor"), observed philosophically that the upper classes had always been selfish and indifferent to human needs, and he warned against going to extremes. "We ought to attend," he said, "to the rights of every class of people."

Scottish-born James Wilson, a signer of the Declaration of Independence and an eminent jurist, argued strenuously for a broadening of the franchise and insisted that at least one branch of the legislature be elected by the people. "No government," he reminded the delegates, "could long subsist without the confidence of the people."

James Madison talked in the same way. "The great fabric to be raised," he said, "would be more stable and durable if it should rest on the solid foundation of the people themselves."

Finally there was Benjamin Franklin, who was not afraid of the people, who believed in full democracy, in giving everybody the right to vote and elect the government. "It is of great consequence," he said, "that we should not depress the virtue and public spirit of our common people; of which they displayed a great deal during the war, and which contributed principally to the favorable issue of it." This was a diplomatic way of reminding the assembled gentlemen that if the common people were good enough to fight in the Revolution, which they won, they were also good enough to govern themselves.

POSITION OF THE STATES:

The bitterest arguments, which led to weeks of deadlock, concerned the position of the individual states within any federal framework. Big states like Virginia, Pennsylvania, and Massachusetts naturally favored representation in Congress according to population; the little states were terrified that this would swamp them. William Paterson of New Jersey proposed a plan whereby each state, regardless of size, would have the same representation in the national legislature. This was, of course, unfair and undemocratic, but Paterson, speaking for the small states, ridiculed the whole idea of numbers.

"What, pray," he cried angrily, "is representation founded on numbers? If State sovereignty is to be kept up, shall I submit the welfare of New Jersey with five votes in a council where Virginia has sixteen?" This, he said, would lead to autocracy. "Neither my State nor myself will ever submit to despotism or to tyranny."

THE GREAT COMPROMISE:

After weeks of wrangling which, in the Philadelphia summer heat, produced ragged tempers, Connecticut brought in the Great Compromise. According to this, the national legislature would consist of two branches—a Senate in which every state, regardless of size, would have an equal vote, and a House of Representatives, in which representation would be based on the numbers of the free population plus three-fifths of the slaves. This was actually a double compromise, for the House was to be more or less democratically elected, and the Senate, appointed by the state legislatures, was to serve as a check on democratically inspired legislation.

THE SENATE:

The Senate idea was a victory for both the small states and the conservative interests. When Jefferson returned from France he had a visit with George Washington and asked him critically why he had favored the Senate in the convention. "Why," countered General Washington, "did you pour that coffee into your saucer?"

"To cool it," said Jefferson.

"Even so," replied Washington, "we pour legislation in the Senatorial saucer to cool it."

The Senate, in other words, was to serve as the balancing wheel in the governmental mechanism. Its members enjoying a six-year term of office and not being subject to popular election, it was designed to be the stabilizing force in the new government. The makers of the Constitution, it is clear, took no undue chances. They were cautious about indulging in too much democracy, fearing that the common people, who were then mostly without education, and even illiterate, would not have sufficient wisdom and knowledge to govern themselves intelligently. Nevertheless, in order to maintain a balance between conservatism and liberalism, the House of Representatives was made subject to popular and direct election by the people.

FRANKLIN'S CONCLUDING SPEECH:

After the fundamental problems were finally settled, a committee "on stile," headed by Gouverneur Morris, drew up the completed document of the Constitution. On September 17, after sixteen weeks of continuous work, the convention met for the last time. The Constitution lay on the table for signature. There were several minutes of silence. Then Benjamin Franklin stood up, holding a paper, but his voice was too weak, and he handed it to James Wilson to read for him. Franklin's words best summarize the mood of that historic moment:

> Mr. President, I confess that there are several parts of this Constitution which I do not at present approve, but I am not sure I shall never approve them. For, having lived long, I have experienced many instances of being obliged, by better information or fuller consideration, to change opinions, even on important subjects, which I once thought right, but found to be otherwise. It is therefore that, the older I grow, the more apt I am to doubt my own judgment, and to pay more respect to the judgment of others. Most men, indeed, as well as most sects in religion, think themselves in possession of all truth, and that wherever others differ from them, it is so far error. Steele,* a Protestant, in a dedication, tells the Pope, that the only difference between our churches, in their opinions of the certainty of their doctrines, is, "the Church of Rome is infallible, and the Church of England is never in the wrong." But though many private persons think almost as highly of their own infallibility as of that of their sect, few express it so naturally as a certain French lady, who, in a dispute with her sister, said, "I don't know how it happens, sister, but I meet with nobody but myself that is always in the right—*il n'y a que moi qui a toujours raison.*"
>
> In these sentiments, sir, I agree to this Constitution, with all its faults, if they are such; because I think a general government necessary for us, and there is no form of government, but what may be a blessing to the people if well administered; and believe further, that this is likely to be well administered for a course of years, and can only end in despotism, as other forms have done before it, when the people shall become so corrupted as to need despotic government, being incapable of any other. I doubt, too, whether any other convention we can obtain may be able to make a better constitution. For, when you assemble a number of men to have the advantage of their joint wisdom, you inevitably assemble with those men all their prejudices,

* Sir Richard Steele (1672-1729), the famous British essayist.

their passions, their errors of opinion, their local interests, and their selfish views. From such an assembly can a perfect production be expected? It therefore astonishes me, sir, to find this system approaching so near to perfection as it does; and I think it will astonish our enemies, who are waiting with confidence to hear that our councils are confounded, like those of the builders of Babel, and that our States are on the point of separation, only to meet hereafter for the purpose of cutting one another's throats. Thus I consent, sir, to this Constitution, because I expect no better, and because I am not sure that it is not the best. The opinions I have had of its errors I sacrifice to the public good. I have never whispered a syllable of them abroad. Within these walls they were born, and here they shall die. If every one of us, in returning to our constituents, were to report the objections he has had to it, and endeavor to gain partisans in support of them, we might prevent its being generally received, and thereby lose all the salutary effects and great advantages resulting naturally in our favor among foreign nations, as well as among ourselves, from our real or apparent unanimity. Much of the strength and efficiency of any government, in procuring and securing happiness to the people, depends on opinion—on the general opinion of the goodness of the government, as well as of the wisdom and integrity of its governors. I hope, therefore, that for our own sakes, as a part of the people, and for the sake of posterity, we shall act heartily and unanimously in recommending this Constitution (if approved by Congress and confirmed by the conventions) wherever our influence may extend, and turn our future thoughts and endeavors to the means of having it well administered. . . .

On the whole, sir, I cannot help expressing a wish that every member of the Convention, who may still have objections to it, would with me, on this occasion, doubt a little of his own infallibility, and, to make manifest our unanimity, put his name to this instrument.

While the members were signing, Franklin, looking at the president's chair, on the back of which a sun was painted, said: "I have, often and often, in the course of the session, and the vicissitudes of my hopes and fears as to its issue, looked at that behind the president, without being able to tell whether it was rising or setting; but now, at length, I have the happiness to know that it is a rising, and not a setting sun."

Chapter II

Conflict over the Constitution and Some Opinions about It

Class divisions:

As soon as the Constitution was submitted to the states for ratification, there broke out an intense and often bitter conflict over its adoption. Article VII of the Constitution provided that nine out of the thirteen states would be needed to ratify it. For a while it looked as if this could not be achieved. A considerable portion of public opinion—especially in the big and populous states like New York and Virginia—seemed to be against the Constitution. Both the defenders and opponents of the Constitution girded for a tough fight.

The struggle produced at least two first-rate publications in the field of political literature. One, defending the Constitution, was *The Federalist,* a series of eighty-five essays mostly written by Madison and Hamilton. The other, criticizing the Constitution as being undemocratic, was Richard Henry Lee's *Letters from the Federal Farmer to the Republican.*

In general, the battle was drawn along class lines. Propertied and educated people as a rule favored the Constitution; the poor and nonprivileged usually opposed it. There was, in addition, a middle-of-the-road group which found in the Constitution some good things and some bad ones. Members of this group objected mainly because the Constitution, while providing for every measure to safeguard property, contained no bill of rights for the protection of individual liberties.

Arguments of those who favored the Constitution:

The most outspoken and searching opinions about the

Constitution were expressed by members—often ordinary farmers—of the state ratification conventions. This was especially true of the conventions of Massachusetts, New York, and Virginia. Other opinions were stated in private letters by leading individuals. The Constitution's defenders generally followed the line (1) that it was the best that could be had in an imperfect world, (2) that if it had undesirable features, there were means of amending them, and (3) that, in the last analysis, it did provide for a government by the people.

Some of America's ablest men defended the Constitution.

The following are a few samples of letters and speeches of the Constitution's supporters:

George Washington
Letter to Colonel David Humphreys, October 10, 1787

The Constitution that is submitted [to the states for ratification], is not free from imperfections, but there are as few radical defects in it as could well be expected, considering the heterogeneous mass of which the Convention was composed and the diversity of interests that are to be attended to. As a Constitutional door is opened for future amendments and alterations, I think it would be wise in the People to accept what is offered to them and I wish it may be by as great a majority of them as it was by that of the Convention. . . . Much will depend however upon literary abilities, and the recommendation of it by good pens should be openly, I mean, publickly afforded in the Gazettes.

George Washington
Letter to Bushrod Washington, November 10, 1787

The warmest friends and the best supporters the Constitution has, do not contend that it is free from imperfections; but they found them unavoidable, and are sensible, if evil is likely to arise therefrom, the remedy must come hereafter; for in the present moment it is not to be obtained; and, as there is a constitutional door open for it, I think the people (for it is with them to judge), can, as they will have the advantage of experience on their side, decide with as much propriety on the alterations and amendments which are necessary, as ourselves. I do not think we are more inspired, have more wisdom, or possess more virtue, than those who will come after us.

The power under the Constitution will always be in the people. It is intrusted for certain defined purposes, and for a certain limited period, to representatives of their own choosing; and, whenever it is executed contrary to their interest, or not agreeable to their wishes, their servants can and undoubtedly will be recalled. It is agreed on all hands, that no government can be well administered without powers; yet the instant these are delegated, although those, who are intrusted with the administration are no more than the creatures of the people, act as it were but for a day, and are amenable for every false step they take, they are, from the moment they receive it, set down as tyrants. . . .

Dr. Benjamin Rush
Letter to John Coakley Lettsom, September 28, 1787

Our new federal government is very acceptable to a great majority of our citizens and will certainly be adopted immediately by *nine* and in the course of a year or 18 months by *all* the States. When this shall happen, *then* to be a citizen of the United States *with all its consequences* will be to be a citizen of the freest, purest, and happiest government upon the face of the earth. It contains all the theoretical and practical advantages of the British Constitution without any of its defects or corruptions. While the nations of Europe have waded into order through seas of *blood,* you see we have traveled peaceably into order only through seas of *blunders.*

Dr. Benjamin Rush
Letter to David Ramsay, March or April, 1788

The objections which have been urged against the federal Constitution, from its wanting a bill of rights, have been reasoned and ridiculed out of credit in every state that has adopted it. There can be only two securities for liberty in any government, viz., representation and checks. By the first the rights of the people, and by the second the rights of representation, are effectually secured. Every part of a free constitution hangs upon these two points; and these form the two capital features of the proposed Constitution of the United States. Without them, a volume of rights would avail nothing; and with them, a declaration of rights is absurd and unnecessary; for the people, where their liberties are committed to an equal representation and to a compound legislature such as we observe in the new government, will always be the sovereigns of their rulers and hold all their rights in their own hands. To hold them at the mercy of their servants is disgraceful to the dignity of freemen. Men who call for a bill of rights have not recovered from the habits they acquired under the monarchical government of Great Britain.

I have the same opinion with the Antifederalists of the danger of trusting arbitrary power to any single body of men, but no such power will be committed to our new rulers. Neither the House of Representatives, the Senate, or the President can perform a single legislative act by themselves. An hundred principles in man will lead them to watch, to check, and to oppose each other should an attempt be made by either of them upon the liberties of the people. If we may judge of their conduct by what we have so often observed in all the state governments, the members of the federal legislature will much oftener injure their constituents by voting agreeably to their inclinations than against them.

But are we to consider men entrusted with power as the receptacles of all the depravity of human nature? By no means. The people do not part with their full proportions of it. Reason and revelation both deceive us if they are all wise and virtuous. Is not history as full of the vices of the people as it is of the crimes of the kings? What is the present moral character of the citizens of the United States? I need not describe it. It proves too plainly that the people are as much disposed to vice as their rulers, and that nothing but a vigorous and efficient government can prevent their degenerating into savages or devouring each other like beasts of prey.

A simple democracy has been very aptly compared by Mr. Ames of Massachusetts to a volcano that contained within its bowels the fiery materials of its own destruction. A citizen of one of the cantons of Switzerland, in the year 1776, refused in my presence to drink "the commonwealth of America" as a toast, and gave as a reason for it "that a simple democracy was the devil's own government." The experience of the American states under the present confederation has in too many instances justified these two accounts of a simple popular government.

It would have been a truth, if Mr. Locke had not said it, that where there is no law there can be no liberty; and nothing deserves the name of law but that which is certain and universal in its operation upon all the members of the community.

To look up to a government that establishes justice, insures order, cherishes virtue, secures property, and protects from every species of violence, affords a pleasure that can only be exceeded by looking up, in all circumstances, to an overruling providence. Such a pleasure I hope is before us and our posterity under the influence of the new government.

The dimensions of the human mind are apt to be regulated by the extent and objects of the government under which it is formed. Think, then, my friend, of the expansion and dignity the American mind will acquire by having its powers transferred from the contracted objects of a state to the more unbounded objects of a national government!—A citizen and a legislator of the free and united states of America will be one of the first characters in the world.

I would not have you suppose, after what I have written, that I believe the new government to be without faults. I can see them—yet not in any of the writings or speeches of the persons who are opposed to it. But who ever saw anything perfect come from the hands of man? It realizes notwithstanding, in a great degree, every wish I ever entertained in every state of the Revolution for the happiness of my country.

Mr. Smith, in Massachusetts Constitutional Convention, January-February, 1788

I am a plain man, and get my living by the plough. I am not used to speak in public, but I beg your leave to say a few words to my brother ploughjoggers in this house. . . .

I formed my own opinion, and was pleased with this Constitution. My honorable old daddy there [pointing to Mr. Singletary] won't think that I expect to be a Congress-man, and swallow up the liberties of the people. I never had any post, nor do I want one. But I don't think the worse of the Constitution because lawyers, and men of learning, and moneyed men, are fond of it. I don't suspect they want to get into Congress and abuse their power. I am not of such a jealous make. They that are honest men themselves are not apt to suspect other people. . . . I think those gentlemen, who are so very suspicious that as soon as a man gets into power he turns rogue, had better look at home.

Zachariah Johnson, in Virginia Constitutional Convention, June, 1788

It is my lot to be among the poor people. The most that I can claim or flatter myself with, is to be of the middle rank. . . . But I shall give my opinion unbiased and uninfluenced, without erudition or eloquence . . . ; and in so doing I will satisfy my conscience. If this Constitution be bad, it will bear equally as hard on me as on any other member of the society. It will bear hard on my children. . . . Having their felicity and happiness at heart, the vote I shall give in its favor can only be imputed to a conviction of its utility and propriety. When I look for responsibility, I full find it in that paper [Constitution]. When the members of the government depend on ourselves for their appointment, and will bear an equal share of the burdens imposed on the people . . . , I conceive there can be no danger. . . . When one of them sees that Providence has given him a numerous family, he will be averse to lay taxes on his own posterity. . . . They will be as liable to be taxed as any other persons in the community. Neither is he sure that he shall enjoy the place again, if he breaks his faith. When I take these things into consideration, I think there is a sufficient responsibility.

ARGUMENTS AGAINST THE CONSTITUTION:

Those who opposed the Constitution, known as the Anti-federalists, had some able spokesmen on their side, too. Perhaps the most eloquent opponent was Patrick Henry in Virginia. The opposition argued (1) that the Constitution was undemocratic, (2) that it threatened the people's liberties by providing for a too-strong central government, and (3) that it was an instrument of the rich for the oppression of the poor.

The following extracts, which have a special flavor, are from speeches against the adoption of the Constitution:

Patrick Henry, in Virginia Constitutional Convention, June, 1788

I have the highest veneration for those gentlemen [who attended the Philadelphia Constitutional Convention]; but, sir, give me leave to demand, What right they had to say, *We, the people?* . . . Who authorized them to speak the language of, *We, the people,* instead of *We, the States?* . . . The people gave them no power to use their name. . . . I wish to hear the real, actual, existing danger, which should lead us to take those steps, so dangerous in my conception. . . . The federal Convention ought to have amended the old system; for this purpose they were solely delegated. . . .

The principles of this system [the Constitution] are extremely pernicious, impolitic, and dangerous. . . . It is not a democracy, wherein the people retain all their rights securely. . . . The rights of conscience, trial by jury, liberty of the press, all your immunities and franchises, all pretensions to human rights and privileges, are rendered insecure, if not lost, by this change [of government]. . . . Is this tame relinquishment of rights worthy of freemen? Is it worthy of that manly fortitude that ought to characterize republicans?

William Grayson, in Virginia Constitutional Convention, June, 1788

Will this Constitution remedy the fatal inconveniences of the clashing state interests? . . . Will the liberty and property of this country be secure under such a government? What, sir, is the present Constitution? A republican government founded on the principles of monarchy, with the three estates. Is it like the model of Tacitus or Montesquieu? Are there checks in it, as in the British monarchy? There is an executive fetter in some parts, and as unlimited in others as a Roman dictator. A democratic branch marked with the strong features of aristocracy, and an aristocratic branch with all the impurities and imperfections of the British House of Commons, arising from the inequality of representation and want of responsibility. . . . Are not all defects and corruption founded on the inequality of representation and want of responsibility . . . ? We have asked for bread, and they have given us a stone.

Mr. Randall, in Massachusetts Constitutional Convention, January-February, 1788

I hope, sir, these great men of eloquence and learning will not try to *make* arguments to make this Constitution go down, right or wrong. An old saying, sir, is, that a "good thing don't need praising"; but, sir, it takes the best men in the state to gloss this Constitution, which they say is the best that human wisdom can invent. In praise of it we hear the reverend clergy, the judges of the Supreme Court, and the ablest lawyers, exerting their utmost abilities. Now, sir, suppose all this artillery turned the other way, and these great men would speak half as much against it, we might complete our business and go home in forty-eight hours.

Amos Singletary, in Massachusetts Constitutional Convention, January-February, 1788

We contended with Great Britain . . . because they claimed a right to tax and bind us in all cases whatever. And does not this Constitution do the same? Does it not take away all we have—all our property? Does it not lay *all* taxes, duties, imposts, and excises? . . . They tell us Congress won't lay dry taxes upon us, but collect all the money they want by impost. I say . . . they won't be able to raise money enough by impost, and then they will lay it on the land, and take all we have got. These lawyers and men of learning and moneyed men, that talk so finely, and gloss over matters so smoothly, to make us poor illiterate people swallow down the pill, expect to be the manager of this Constitution, and get all the power and all the money into their own hands, and then they will swallow up all us little folks, like the great Leviathan, Mr. President; yes, just as the whale swallowed up Jonah. This is what I am afraid of.

Thomas Tredwell, in New York Constitutional Convention, June-July, 1788

In this Constitution, sir, we have departed widely from the principles and political faith of '76, when the spirit of liberty ran high, and danger put a curb on ambition. Here we find no security for the rights of individuals, no security for the existence of our state governments; here is no bill of rights, no proper restriction of power; our lives, our property, and our consciences, are left wholly at the mercy of the legislature, and the powers of the judiciary may be extended to any degree short of almighty. . . .

Is this, sir, a government for freemen? Are we thus to be duped out of our liberties? I hope, sir, our affairs have not yet arrived to that long-wished-for pitch of confusion, that we are under the necessity of accepting such a system of government as this. . . .

We are told, sir, that a government is like a mad horse, which, notwithstanding all the curb you can put upon him, will sometimes run away with his rider. The idea is undoubtedly a just one. Would he not, therefore, justly be deemed a mad man, and deserve to have his neck broken, who should trust himself on this horse without any bridle at all?

JEFFERSON'S CRITICISM OF THE CONSTITUTION:

Jefferson was the most cogent spokesman of the middle group, that is, those who thought the Constitution had good features but needed some fundamental amending.

Thomas Jefferson to James Madison, December 20, 1787

I like much the general idea of framing a government, which should go on of itself, peaceably, without needing continual recurrence to the State legislatures. I like the organization of the government into legislative, judiciary and executive. I like the power given the legislature to levy taxes, and for that reason solely, I approve of the greater House being chosen by the people directly. For though I think a House so chosen, will be very far inferior to the present Congress, will be very illy qualified to legislate for the Union, for foreign nations, etc., yet this evil does not weigh against the good, of preserving inviolate the fundamental principle, that the people are not to be taxed but by representatives chosen immediately by themselves. I am captivated by the compromise of the opposite claims of the great and little States, of the latter to equal, and the former to proportional influence. I am much pleased too, with the substitution of the method of voting by person, instead of that of voting by States; and I like the negative given to the Executive, conjointly with a third of either House; though I should have liked it better, had the judiciary been associated for that purpose, or invested separately with a similar power. There are other good things of less moment.

I will now tell you what I do not like. First, the omission of a bill of rights, providing clearly, and without the aid of sophism, for freedom of religion, freedom of the press, protection against standing armies, restriction of monopolies, the eternal and unremitting force for the habeas corpus laws, and trials by jury in all matters of fact triable by the laws of the land, and not by the laws of nations. To say, as Mr. Wilson does, that a bill of rights was not necessary, because all is reserved in the case of the general government which is not given, while in the particular ones, all is given which is not reserved, might do for the audience to which it was addressed; but it is surely a *gratis dictum,* the reverse of which might just as well be said; and it is opposed by strong inferences from the body of the instrument, as well as from the omission of the cause of our present Confederation, which had made the reservation in express terms. It was hard to conclude, because there has been a want of uniformity among the States as to the cases triable by jury, because some have been so incautious as to dispense with this mode of trial in certain cases, therefore, the more prudent States shall be reduced to the same level of calamity. It would have been much more just and wise to have concluded the other way, that as most of the States had preserved with jealousy this sacred palladium of liberty, those who had wandered, should be brought back to it and to have established general right rather than general wrong. For I consider all the ill as established, which may be established. I have a right to nothing, which another has a right to take away; and Congress will have a right to take away trials by jury in all civil cases. Let me add, that a bill of rights is what the people are entitled to against every government on earth, general or particular; and what no just government should refuse, or rest on inference.

. . . At all events, I hope you will not be discouraged from making other trials, if the present one should fail. We are never permitted to despair of the commonwealth. I have told you freely what I like, and what I dislike, merely as a matter of curiosity. . . . I own I am not a friend to a very energetic government. It is always oppressive. It places the governors indeed more at their ease, at the expense of the people. The late rebellion in Massachusetts [Shay's Rebellion] has given more alarm, than I think it should have done. Calculate that one rebellion in thirteen States in the course of eleven years, is but one for each State in a century and a half. No country should be so long without one. Nor will any degree of power in the hands of government, prevent insurrections. In England, where the hand of power is heavier than with us, there are seldom half a dozen years without an insurrection. In France, where it is still heavier . . . , and where there are always two or three in the course of the three years I have been here, in every one of which greater numbers were engaged than in Massachusetts, and a great deal more blood was spilt. In Turkey, where the sole nod of the despot is death, insurrections are the events of every day. . . .

And say, finally, whether peace is best preserved by giving

energy to the government, or information to the people. This last is the most certain, and the most legitimate engine of government. Educate and inform the whole mass of the people. Enable them to see that it is their interest to preserve peace and order, and they will preserve them. And it requires no very high degree of education to convince them of this. They are the only sure reliance for the preservation of our liberty. After all, it is my principle that the will of the majority should prevail. If they approve the proposed constitution in all its parts, I shall concur in it cheerfully, in hopes they will amend it, whenever they shall find it works wrong.

RATIFICATION OF THE CONSTITUTION:

There was little debate in the smaller states. Four of them —Delaware, New Jersey, Georgia and Connecticut— promptly ratified the Constitution. Elsewhere, however, the struggle continued to be intense and close.

In the end the supporters of the Constitution did carry the day, but the margin of victory was slim. Massachusetts ratified by 187 against 168. In Virginia 89 delegates voted Yes and 79, No. In New York the Constitution squeezed through by a mere 3 votes—30 to 27. But by June 21, 1788, when New Hampshire ratified (57 to 47), the Constitution already had the required nine states, and so it went into effect. In two states, North Carolina and Rhode Island, the opposition was so great that the Constitution was not ratified until the Federal Government was already set up. Rhode Island ratified on May 29, 1790, well over a year after the new government had been inaugurated.

BILL OF RIGHTS:

To allay the widespread public criticism and to obtain ratification, defenders of the Constitution promised a Bill of Rights to protect the citizens against the government. A series of amendments were thus introduced in the first Congress, the first ten of which came to be known as the Bill of Rights, containing strict and permanent guarantees against undue and illegal governmental encroachments upon the individual. The Bill of Rights went into effect by November, 1791. An integral part of the Constitution, the Bill of Rights may be considered as one of the noblest and most massive achievements of the American democracy.

RATIFICATION DATES AND VOTES:

State	*Ratification Date*	*Vote* YES	NO
Delaware	December 7, 1787	Unanimous	
Pennsylvania	December 12, 1787	46	23
New Jersey	December 18, 1787	Unanimous	
Georgia	January 2, 1788	Unanimous	
Connecticut	January 9, 1788	128	40
Massachusetts	February 6, 1788	187	168
Maryland	April 26, 1788	63	11
South Carolina	May 23, 1788	149	73
New Hampshire	June 21, 1788	57	47
Virginia	June 25, 1788	89	79
New York	July 26, 1788	30	27
North Carolina	November 21, 1789	195	77
Rhode Island	May 29, 1790	34	32

Chapter III

Delegates and Signers

Of the delegates elected to the Constitutional Convention, a few did not attend the sessions at all. Some others were not pleased with the final outcome. The result was that when the Constitution was completed, only thirty-nine delegates signed it.

The following are lists of delegates and signers:

LIST OF DELEGATES
(Alphabetical)

	Did he sign or not?
Baldwin, Abraham	Yes
Bassett, Richard	Yes
Bedford, Gunning, Jr.	Yes
Blair, John	Yes
Blount, William	Yes
Brearly, David	Yes
Broom, Jacob	Yes
Butler, Pierce	Yes
Carroll, Daniel	Yes
Clymer, George	Yes
Davie, William R.	No
Dayton, Jonathan	Yes
Dickinson, John	Yes
Ellsworth, Oliver	No
Few, William	Yes
Fitzsimmons,* Thomas	Yes
Franklin, Benjamin	Yes
Gerry, Elbridge	No
Gilman, Nicholas	Yes

* Also spelled Fitzsimons.

	Did he sign or not?
Gorham, Nathaniel	Yes
Hamilton, Alexander	Yes
Houston, William	No
Houston, William C.	No
Ingersoll, Jared	Yes
Jenifer, Daniel of St. Thomas	Yes
Johnson, William Samuel	Yes
King, Rufus	Yes
Langdon, John	Yes
Lansing, John	No
Livingston, William	Yes
McClurg, James	No
McHenry, James	Yes
Madison, James, Jr.	Yes
Martin, Alexander	No
Martin, Luther	No
Mason, George	No
Mercer, John Francis	No
Mifflin, Thomas	Yes
Morris, Gouverneur	Yes
Morris, Robert	Yes
Paterson, William	Yes
Pierce, William	No
Pinckney, Charles	Yes
Pinckney, Charles Cotesworth	Yes
Randolph, Edmund	No
Read, George	Yes
Rutledge, John	Yes
Sherman, Roger	Yes
Spaight, Richard Dobbs	Yes
Strong, Caleb	No
Washington, George	Yes
Williamson, Hugh	Yes
Wilson, James	Yes
Wythe, George	No
Yates, Robert	No

LIST OF DELEGATES
(by States)

The following were present at some time during the deliberations of the Convention:

1. *Connecticut:*

Oliver Ellsworth
William Samuel Johnson*
Roger Sherman*

2. *Delaware:*

Richard Bassett*
Gunning Bedford, Jr.*
Jacob Broom*
John Dickinson*
George Read*

3. *Georgia:*

Abraham Baldwin*
William Few*
William Houston
William Pierce

4. *Maryland:*

Daniel Carroll*
Daniel Jenifer*
James McHenry*
Luther Martin
John Francis Mercer

5. *Massachusetts:*

Elbridge Gerry
Nathaniel Gorham*
Rufus King*
Caleb Strong

6. *New Hampshire:*

Nicholas Gilman*
John Langdon*

7. *New Jersey:*

David Brearly*
Jonathan Dayton*
William Churchill Houston
William Livingston*
William Paterson*

8. *New York:*

Alexander Hamilton*
John Lansing
Robert Yates

9. *North Carolina:*

William Blount*
William R. Davie
Alexander Martin
Richard Dobbs Spaight*
Hugh Williamson*

* Those who signed the Constitution.

10. *Pennsylvania:*

George Clymer*
Thomas Fitzsimmons*
Benjamin Franklin*
Jared Ingersoll*

Thomas Mifflin
Gouverneur Morris*
Robert Morris*
James Wilson*

11. *Rhode Island*

None

12. *South Carolina:*
Pierce Butler*
Charles Pinckney*
Charles Cotesworth Pinckney*
John Rutledge*

13. *Virginia:*

John Blair*
James McClurg
James Madison, Jr.*
George Mason
Edmund Randolph
George Washington*
George Wythe

* Those who signed the Constitution.

SIGNERS
(Alphabetical)

Last Name	*Given Name*	*State*	*Occupation*	*Dates*
1. Baldwin	Abraham	Ga.	Lawyer	1754-1807
2. Bassett	Richard	Del.	Lawyer	1745-1815
3. Bedford	Gunning	Del.	Lawyer	1747-1812
4. Blair	John	Va.	Lawyer	1732-1800
5. Blount	William	N. C.	Politician	1744-1800
6. Brearly	David	N. J.	Lawyer	1745-1790
7. Broom	Jacob	Del.	Politician	1752-1810
8. Butler	Pierce	S. C.	Planter	1744-1822
9. Carroll	Daniel	Md.	Politician	1730-1796
10. Clymer	George	Pa.	Merchant	1739-1813
11. Dayton	Jonathan	N. J.	Politician	1760-1824
12. Dickinson	John	Del.	Lawyer	1732-1808
13. Few	William	Ga.	Soldier, Banker	1748-1828
14. Fitzsimmons	Thomas	Pa.	Businessman	1741-1811
15. Franklin	Benjamin	Pa.	Philosopher	1706-1790
16. Gilman	Nicholas	N. H.	Lawyer	1755-1814
17. Gorham	Nathaniel	Mass.	Merchant	1738-1796
18. Hamilton	Alexander	N. Y.	Lawyer	1757-1804
19. Ingersoll	Jared	Pa.	Lawyer	1749-1822
20. Jenifer	Daniel of St. Thomas	Md.	Politician	1723-1790
21. Johnson	William Samuel	Conn.	Lawyer	1727-1819
22. King	Rufus	Mass.	Lawyer	1755-1827
23. Langdon	John	N. H.	Merchant	1741-1819
24. Livingston	William	N. J.	Lawyer	1723-1790
25. McHenry	James	Md.	Physician	1753-1816
26. Madison	James	Va.	Lawyer	1751-1836
27. Mifflin	Thomas	Pa.	General	1744-1800
28. Morris	Gouverneur	Pa.	Lawyer	1752-1816
29. Morris	Robert	Pa.	Merchant	1734-1806
30. Paterson	William	N. J.	Lawyer	1745-1806
31. Pinckney	Charles	S. C.	Lawyer	1757-1824
32. Pinckney	Charles Cotesworth	S. C.	General	1746-1825
33. Read	George	Del.	Lawyer	1733-1798
34. Rutledge	John	S. C.	Lawyer	1739-1800
35. Sherman	Roger	Conn.	Lawyer	1721-1793
36. Spaight	Richard Dobbs	N. C.	Politician	1758-1802
37. Washington	George	Va.	Planter	1732-1799
38. Williamson	Hugh	N. C.	Physician	1735-1819
39. Wilson	James	Pa.	Lawyer	1742-1798

Chapter IV

Contemporary Pen Portraits of the Delegates

A number of the delegates to the Constitutional Convention were, or subsequently became, famous. At least two—Washington and Franklin—were world figures. Some—particularly Hamilton and Madison—became important American statesmen. Others continued to play great roles in their states or in the Congress. A few are not well known to posterity. The following portrait sketches by contemporaries are, therefore, of special interest. They throw a fresh light on the delegates, both on the historically known and the obscure ones.

A. Major Pierce's character sketches

The following sketches of the delegates were written by Major William Pierce, who represented Georgia at the convention. Major Pierce thus described himself:

Pierce, William (*c.* 1740-1789):

"My own character I shall not attempt to draw, but leave those who may choose to speculate on it, to consider it in any light that their fancy or imagination may depict. I am conscious of having discharged my duty as a Soldier through the course of the late revolution with honor and propriety; and my services in Congress and the Convention were bestowed with the best intention towards the interest of Georgia, and towards the general welfare of the Confederacy. I possess ambition, and it was that, and the flattering opinion which some of my Friends had of me, that gave me a seat in the wisest Council in the World, and furnished me with an opportunity of giving these short Sketches of the Characters who composed it."

Baldwin, Abraham (1754-1807):

"Mr. Baldwin is a Gentleman of superior abilities, and joins in a public debate with great art and eloquence. Having laid the foundation of a compleat classical education at Harvard College, he pursues every other study with ease. He is well acquainted with Books and Characters, and has an accommodating turn of mind, which enables him to gain the confidence of Men, and to understand them. He is a practising Attorney in Georgia, and has been twice a Member of Congress. Mr. Baldwin is about 38 years of age." (He was actually thirty-three years old at the Philadelphia Convention.)

Bassett, Richard (1745-1815):

"Mr. Bassett is a religious enthusiast, lately turned Methodist, and serves his Country because it is the will of the people that he should do so. He is a Man of plain sense, and has modesty enough to hold his Tongue. He is a Gentlemanly Man, and is in high estimation among the Methodists. Mr. Bassett is about 36 years old." (He was actually forty-two.)

Bedford, Gunning (1747-1812):

"Mr. Bedford was educated for the Bar, and in his profession, I am told, has merit. He is a bold and nervous Speaker, and has a very commanding and striking manner;—but he is warm and impetuous in his temper, and precipitate in his judgment. Mr. Bedford is about 32 years old [he was actually forty], and very corpulant."

Blair, John (1732-1800):

"Mr. Blair is one of the most respectable Men in Virginia, both on account of his Family as well as fortune. He is one of the Judges of the Supreme Court in Virginia, and acknowledged to have a very extensive knowledge of the Laws. Mr. Blair is, however, no Orator, but his good sense, and most excellent principles, compensate for other deficiencies. He is about 50 years of age." (He was actually fifty-five.)

Blount, William (1744-1800):

"Mr. Blount is a character strongly marked for integrity and honor. He has been twice a Member of Congress, and in that office discharged his duty with ability and faithfulness. He is no Speaker, nor does he possess any of those talents that make Men shine;—he is plain, honest, and sincere. Mr. Blount is about 36 years of age." (He was actually forty-three.)

Brearly, David (1745-1790):

"Mr. Brearly is a man of good, rather than of brilliant parts. He is a Judge of the Supreme Court of New Jersey and is very much in the esteem of the people. As an Orator he has little to boast of, but as a Man he has every virtue to recommend him. Mr. Brearly is about 40 years of age." (Actually he was forty-two.)

Broom, Jacob (1752-1810):

"Mr. Broom is a plain good Man, with some abilities, but nothing to render him conspicuous. He is silent in public, but chearful and conversable in private. He is about 35 years old."

Butler, Pierce (1744-1822):

"Mr. Butler is a character much respected for the many excellent virtues which he possesses. But as a politician or an Orator, he has no pretentions to either. He is a Gentleman of fortune, and takes rank among the first in South Carolina. He has been appointed to Congress, and is now a Member of the Legislature of South Carolina. Mr. Butler is about 30 years of age [he was forty-three]; an Irishman by birth."

Carroll, Daniel (1730-1796):

"Mr. Carroll is a Man of large fortune, and influence in his State. He possesses plain good sense, and is in the full confidence of his Countrymen. This Gentleman is about 57 years of age."

Clymer, George (1739-1813):

"Mr. Clymer is a Lawyer of some abilities;—he is a respectable Man, and much esteemed. Mr. Clymer is about 40 years old." (Actually he was forty-eight.)

Davie, William Richardson (1756-1820):

"Mr. Davey is a Lawyer of some eminence in his State. He is said to have a good classical education, and is a Gentleman of considerable literary talents. He was silent in the Convention, but his opinion was always respected. Mr. Davey is about 30 years of age."

Dayton, Jonathan (1760-1824):

"Capt. Dayton is a young Gentleman of talents, with an ambition to exert them. He possesses a good education and reading; he speaks well, and seems desirous of improving himself in Oratory. There is an impetuosity in his temper that is injurious to him; but there is an honest rectitude about him that makes him a valuable Member of Society, and secures to him the esteem of all good Men. He is about 30 years old [actually he was twenty-seven, and the youngest member of the convention], served with me as a Brother Aid to General Sullivan in the Western expedition of '79."

Dickinson, John (1732-1808):

"Mr. Dickinson has been famed through all America, for his Farmers Letters; he is a Scholar, and said to be a Man of very extensive information. When I saw him in the Convention I was induced to pay the greatest attention to him whenever he spoke. I had often heard that he was a great Orator, but I found him an indifferent Speaker. With an affected air of wisdom he labors to produce a trifle,—his language is irregular and incorrect,—his flourishes (for he sometimes attempts them), are like expiring flames, they just shew themselves and go out;—no traces of them are left on the mind to chear or animate it. He is, however, a good writer and will ever be considered one of the most important characters in the United States. He is about 55 years old, and was bred a Quaker."

Ellsworth, Oliver (1745-1807):

"Mr. Ellsworth is a Judge of the Supreme Court in Connecticut;—he is a Gentleman of a clear, deep, and copious understanding; eloquent, and connected in public debate; and always attentive to his duty. He is very happy in a reply, and choice in selecting such parts of his adversary's arguments as he finds make the strongest impressions,—in order to take off the force of them, so as to admit the power of his own. Mr. Ellsworth is about 37 years of age [actually he was forty-two], a Man much respected for his integrity, and venerated for his abilities."

Few, William (1748-1828):

"Mr. Few possesses a strong natural Genius, and from application has acquired some knowledge of legal matters;—he practices at the bar of Georgia, and speaks tolerably well in the Legislature. He has been twice a Member of Congress, and served in that capacity with fidelity to his State, and honor to himself. Mr. Few is about 35 years of age." (Actually he was thirty-nine.)

Fitzsimmons, Thomas (1741-1811):

"Mr. Fitzsimons is a Merchant of considerable talents, and speaks very well I am told, in the Legislature of Pennsylvania. He is about 40 years old." (Actually he was forty-six.)

Franklin, Benjamin (1706-1790):

"Dr. Franklin is well known to be the greatest philosopher of the present age;—all the operation of nature he seems to understand—the very heavens obey him, and the Clouds yield up their Lightning to be imprisoned in his rod. But what claim he has to the politician, posterity must determine. It is certain that he does not shine much in public Council, —he is no Speaker, nor does he seem to let politics engage his attention. He is, however, a most extraordinary Man, and tells a story in a style more engaging than anything I ever heard. Let his Biographer finish his character. He is 82 years old, and possesses an activity of mind equal to a youth of 25 years of age."

Gerry, Elbridge (1744-1814):

"Mr. Gerry's character is marked for integrity and perseverance. He is a hesitating and laborious speaker;—possesses a great degree of confidence and goes extensively into all subjects that he speaks on, without respect to elegance or flower of diction. He is connected and sometimes clear in his arguments, conceives well, and cherishes as his first virtue, a love for his Country. Mr. Gerry is very much of a Gentleman in his principles and manners;—he has been engaged in the mercantile line and is a Man of property. He is about 37 years of age." (Actually he was forty-three.)

Gilman, Nicholas (1755-1814):

"Mr. Gilman is modest, genteel, and sensible. There is nothing brilliant or striking in his character, but there is something respectable and worthy in the Man—about 30 years of age." (Actually he was thirty-two.)

Gorham, Nathaniel (1738-1796):

"Mr. Gorham is a Merchant in Boston, high in reputation, and much in the esteem of his Country-men. He is a Man of very good sense, but not much improved in his education. He is eloquent and easy in public debate, but has nothing fashionable or elegant in his style;—all he aims at is to convince, and where he fails it never is from his auditors not understanding him, for no Man is more perspicuous and full. He has been President of Congress, and three years a Member of that Body. Mr. Gorham is about 46 years of age [actually he was forty-nine], rather lusty, and has an agreeable and pleasing manner."

Hamilton, Alexander (1757-1804):

"Colo. Hamilton is deservedly celebrated for his talents. He is a practitioner of the Law, and reputed to be a finished Scholar. To a clear and strong judgment he unites the ornaments of fancy, and whilst he is able, convincing, and engaging in his eloquence the Heart and Head sympathize in approving him. Yet there is something too feeble in his voice to be equal to the strains of oratory;—it is my opinion that he is rather a convincing Speaker, than a blazing Orator. Colo. Hamilton requires time to think,—he enquires into every part of his subject with the searchings of philosophy, and when he comes forward he comes highly charged with interesting matter, there is no skimming over the surface of a subject with him, he must sink to the bottom to see what foundation it rests on.—His language is not always equal, sometimes didactic like Bolingbroke's and at others light and tripping like Stern's. His eloquence is not so defusive as to trifle with the senses, but he rambles just enough to strike and keep up the attention. He is about 33 years old [he was actually thirty], of small stature, and lean. His manners are tinctured with stiffness, and sometimes with a degree of vanity that is highly disagreeable."

Houston, William Churchill (*c.* 1746-1788):

"Mr. Houston is an Attorney at Law, and has been a Member of Congress for the State of Georgia. He is a Gentleman of Family, and was educated in England. As to his legal or political knowledge he has very little to boast of. Nature seems to have done more for his corporeal than mental powers. His Person is striking, but his mind very little improved with useful or elegant knowledge. He has none of the talents requisite for the Orator, but in public debate is confused and irregular. Mr. Houston is about 30 years of age [he was actually forty-one], of an amiable and sweet temper, and of good and honorable principles."

Ingersoll, Jared (1749-1822):

"Mr. Ingersol is a very able Attorney, and possesses a clear legal understanding. He is well educated in the Classic's, and is a Man of very extensive reading. Mr. Ingersol speaks well, and comprehends his subject fully. There is a modesty in his character that keeps him back. He is about 36 years old." (He was actually thirty-eight.)

Jenifer, Daniel of St. Thomas (1723-1790):

"Mr. Jenifer is a Gentleman of fortune in Maryland;—he is always in good humour, and never fails to make his company pleased with him. He sits silent in the Senate, and seems to be conscious that he is no politician. From his long continuance in single life, no doubt but he has made the vow of celibacy. He speaks warmly of the Ladies notwithstanding. Mr. Jenifer is about 55 years of Age [he was actually sixty-four], and once served as an Aid de Camp to Major Genl. Lee."

Johnson, William Samuel (1727-1819):

"Dr. Johnson is a character much celebrated for his legal knowledge; he is said to be one of the first classics in America, and certainly possesses a very strong and enlightened understanding.

"As an Orator in my opinion, there is nothing in him that warrants the high reputation which he has for public speaking. There is something in the tone of his voice not pleasing to the Ear,—but he is eloquent and clear,—always abounding with information and instruction. He was once employed as an Agent for the State of Connecticut to state her claims to certain landed territory before the British House of Commons; this Office he discharged with so much dignity, and made such an ingenious display of his powers, that he laid the foundation of a reputation which will probably last much longer than his own life. Dr. Johnson is about sixty years of age, possesses the manners of a Gentleman, and engages the Hearts of Men by the sweetness of his temper, and that affectionate style of address with which he accosts his acquaintance."

King, Rufus (1755-1827):

"Mr. King is a Man much distinguished for his eloquence and great parliamentary talents. He was educated in Massachusetts, and is said to have good classical as well as legal knowledge. He has served for three years in the Congress of the United States with great and deserved applause, and is at this time high in the confidence and approbation of his Country-men. This Gentleman is about thirty-three years of age, about five feet ten Inches high, well formed, an handsome face, with a strong expressive Eye, and a sweet high toned voice. In his public speaking there is something peculiarly strong and rich in his expression, clear and convincing in his arguments, rapid and irresistible at times in his eloquence but he is not always equal. His action is natural, swimming, and graceful, but there is a rudeness of manner sometimes accompanying it. But take him *tout en semble*, he may with propriety be ranked among the Luminaries of the present Age."

Langdon, John (1741-1819):

"Mr. Langdon is a Man of considerable fortune, possesses a liberal mind, and a good plain understanding—about 40 years old." (He was actually forty-six.)

Lansing, John (1754-1829):

"Mr. Lansing is a practising Attorney at Albany, and Mayor of that Corporation. He has a hesitation in his speech, that will prevent his being an Orator of any eminence;—his legal knowledge I am told is not extensive, nor his education a good one. He is however a Man of good sense, plain in his manners, and sincere in his friendships. He is about 32 years of age."

Livingston, William (1723-1790):

"Governor Livingston is confessedly a Man of the first rate talents, but he appears to me rather to indulge a sportiveness of wit, than a strength of thinking. He is however equal to anything, from the extensiveness of his education and genius. His writings teem with satyr and a neatness of style. But he is no Orator, and seems little acquainted with the guiles of policy. He is about 60 years old [actually he was sixty-four], and remarkably healthy."

Madison, James (1751-1836):

"Mr. Maddison is a character who has long been in public life; and what is very remarkable every Person seems to acknowledge his greatness. He blends together the profound politician, with the Scholar. In the management of every great question he evidently took the lead in the Convention, and tho' he cannot be called an Orator, he is a most agreeable, eloquent, and convincing Speaker. From a spirit of industry and application which he possesses in a most eminent degree, he always comes forward the best informed Man of any point in debate. The affairs of the United States, he perhaps, has the most correct knowledge of, of any Man in the Union. He has been twice a Member of Congress, and was always thought one of the ablest Members that ever sat in that Council. Mr. Maddison is about 37 years of age, a Gentleman of great modesty,—with a remarkable sweet temper. He is easy and unreserved among acquaintance, and has a most agreeable style of conversation."

Martin, Alexander (1740-1807):

"Mr. Martin was lately Governor of North Carolina, which office he filled with credit. He is a Man of sense, and undoubtedly is a good politician, but he is not formed to shine in public debate, being no Speaker. Mr. Martin was once a Colonel in the American Army, but proved unfit for the field. He is about 40 years of age." (Actually he was forty-seven.)

Martin, Luther (1748-1826):

"Mr. Martin was educated for the Bar, and is Attorney general for the State of Maryland. This Gentleman possesses a good deal of information, but he has a very bad delivery, and so extremely prolix, that he never speaks without tiring the patience of all who hear him. He is about 34 years of age." (Actually he was thirty-nine.)

Mason, George (1725–1792):

"Mr. Mason is a Gentleman of remarkable strong powers, and possesses a clear and copious understanding. He is able and convincing in debate, steady and firm in his principles, and undoubtedly one of the best politicians in America. Mr. Mason is about 60 years old [actually he was sixty-two], with a fine strong constitution."

McClurg, James (*c.* 1746-1823):

"Mr. McClurg is a learned physician, but having never appeared before in public life his character as a politician is not sufficiently known. He attempted once or twice to speak, but with no great success. It is certain that he has a foundation of learning, on which, if he pleases, he may erect a character of high renown. The Doctor is about 38 years of age [actually he was forty-one], a Gentleman of great respectability, and a fair and unblemished character."

McHenry, James (1753-1816):

"Mr. McHenry was bred a physician, but he afterwards

turned Soldier and acted as Aid to Genl. Washington and the Marquis de la Fayette. He is a Man of specious talents, with nothing of genious to improve them. As a politician there is nothing remarkable in him, nor has he any of the graces of the Orator. He is however, a very respectable young Gentleman, and deserves the honor which his Country has bestowed on him. Mr. McHenry is about 32 years of age." (Actually he was thirty-four.)

Mifflin, Thomas (1744-1800):

"General Mifflin is well known for the activity of his mind, and the brilliancy of his parts. He is well informed and a graceful Speaker. The General is about 40 years of age [actually he was forty-three], and a very handsome man."

Morris, Gouverneur (1752-1816):

"Mr. Governeur Morris is one of those Genius's in whom every species of talents combine to render him conspicuous and flourishing in public debate:—He winds through all the mazes of rhetoric, and throws around him such a glare that he charms, captivates, and leads away the senses of all who hear him. With an infinite stretch of fancy he brings to view things when he is engaged in deep argumentation, that render all the labor of reasoning easy and pleasing. But with all these powers he is fickle and inconstant,—never pursuing one train of thinking—nor ever regular. He has gone through a very extensive course of reading, and is acquainted with all the sciences. No Man has more wit,—nor can any one engage the attention more than Mr. Morris. He was bred to the Law, but I am told he disliked the profession, and turned merchant. He is engaged in some great mercantile matters with his namesake Mr. Robt. Morris. This Gentleman is about 38 years old [actually he was thirty-five], he has been unfortunate in losing one of his Legs, and getting all the flesh taken off his right arm by a scald, when a youth."

Morris, Robert (1734-1806):

"Robert Morris is a merchant of great eminence and wealth; an able Financier, and a worthy Patriot. He has an understanding equal to any public object, and possesses an energy of mind that few Men can boast of. Although he is not learned, yet he is as great as those who are. I am told that when he speaks in the Assembly of Pennsylvania, that he bears down all before him. What could have been his reason for not Speaking in the Convention I know not—but he never once spoke on any point. This Gentleman is about 50 years old." (Actually he was fifty-three.)

Paterson, William (1745-1806):

"Mr. Patterson is one of those kind of Men whose powers break in upon you, and create wonder and astonishment. He is a Man of great modesty, with looks that bespeak talents of no great extent—but he is a Classic, a Lawyer, and an Orator;—and of a disposition so favorable to his advancement that every one seemed ready to exalt him with their praises. He is very happy in the choice of time and manner of engaging in a debate, and never speaks but when he understands his subject well. This Gentleman is about 34 years of age [actually he was forty-two], of a very low stature."

Pinckney, Charles (1757-1824):

"Mr. Charles Pinckney is a young Gentleman of the most promising talents. He is, altho' only 24 ys of age [actually he was thirty, and the third youngest member of the Convention], in possession of a very great variety of knowledge. Government, Law, History and Phylosophy are his favorite studies, but he is intimately acquainted with every species of polite learning, and has a spirit of application and industry beyond most Men. He speaks with great neatness and perspicuity, and treats every subject as fully, without running into prolixity, as it requires. He has been a Member of Congress, and served in that Body with ability and eclat."

Pinckney, Charles Cotesworth (1746-1825):

"Mr. Chs Cotesworth Pinckney is a Gentleman of Family and fortune in his own State. He has received the advantage of a liberal education, and possesses a very extensive degree of legal knowledge. When warm in a debate he sometimes speaks well,—but he is generally considered an indifferent Orator. Mr. Pinckney was an Officer of high rank in the American army, and served with great reputation through the War. He is now about 40 years of age."

Randolph, Edmund (1753-1813):

"Mr. Randolph is Governor of Virginia,—a young Gentleman in whom unite all the accomplishments of the Scholar, and the States-man. He came forward with the postulata, or first principles, on which the Convention acted, and he supported them with a force of eloquence and reasoning that did him great honor. He has a most harmonious voice, a fine person and striking manner. Mr. Randolph is about 32 years of age." (Actually he was thirty-four.)

Read, George (1733-1798):

"Mr. Read is a Lawyer and a Judge:—his legal abilities are said to be very great, but his powers of Oratory are fatiguing and tiresome to the last degree;—his voice is feeble, and his articulation so bad that few can have patience to attend to him. He is a very good Man, and bears an amiable character with those who know him. Mr. Read is about 50 [he was actually fifty-four], of a low stature, and a weak constitution."

Rutledge, John (1739-1800):

"Mr. Rutledge is one of those characters who was highly mounted at the commencement of the late revolution;—his reputation in the first Congress gave him a distinguished rank among the American Worthies. He was bred to the Law, and now acts as one of the Chancellors of South Carolina. This Gentleman is much famed in his own State as an Orator, but in my opinion he is too rapid in his public speaking to be denominated an agreeable Orator. He is undoubtedly a man of abilities, and a Gentleman of distinction and fortune. Mr. Rutledge was once Governor of South Carolina. He is about 48 years of age."

Sherman, Roger (1721-1793):

"Mr. Sherman exhibits the oddest shaped character I ever remember to have met with. He is awkward, un-meaning, and unaccountably strange in his manner. But in his train of thinking there is something regular, deep and comprehensive; yet the oddity of his address, the vulgarisms that accompany his public speaking, and that strange New England cant which runs through his public as well as his private speaking make everything that is connected with him grotesque and laughable:—and yet he deserves infinite praise—no Man has a better Heart or a clearer Head. If he cannot embellish he can furnish thoughts that are wise and useful. He is an able politician, and extremely artful in accomplishing any particular object;—it is remarked that he seldom fails. I am told he sits on the Bench in Connecticut, and is very correct in the discharge of his Judicial functions. In the early part of his life he was a Shoe-maker;—but despising the lowness of his condition, he turned Almanack maker, and so progressed upwards to a Judge. He has been several years a Member of Congress, and discharged the duties of Office with honor and credit to himself, and advantage to the State he represented. He is about 60." (Actually he was sixty-six.)

Spaight, Richard Dobbs (1758-1802):

"Mr. Spaight is a worthy Man, of some abilities, and fortune. Without possessing a Genius to render him brilliant, he is able to discharge any public trust that his Country may repose in him. He is about 31 years of age." (Actually he was twenty-nine, and hence the second youngest member of the convention.)

Strong, Caleb (1745-1819):

"Mr. Strong is a lawyer of some eminence,—he has received a liberal education, and has good connections to recommend him. As a Speaker he is feeble, and without confidence. This Gentn. is about 35 years of age [actually he was forty-two], and greatly in the esteem of his Colleagues."

Washington, George (1732-1799):

"Genl. Washington is well known as the Commander in chief of the late American Army. Having conducted these states to independence and peace, he now appears to assist in framing a Government to make the People happy. Like Gustavus Vasa, he may be said to be the deliverer of his Country;—like Peter the Great he appears as the politician and the States-man; and like Cincinnatus he returned to his farm perfectly contented with being only a plain Citizen, after enjoying the highest honor of the Confederacy,—and now only seeks for the approbation of his Country-men by being virtuous and useful. The General was conducted to the Chair as President of the Convention by the unanimous voice of its Members. He is in the 52d year of his age." (Actually he was fifty-five.)

Williamson, Hugh (1735-1819):

"Mr. Williamson is a Gentleman of education and talents. He enters freely into public debate from his close attention to most subjects, but he is no Orator. There is a great degree of good humour and pleasantry in his character; and in his manners there is a strong trait of the Gentleman. He is about 48 years of age." (Actually he was fifty-two.)

Wilson, James (1742-1798):

"Mr. Wilson ranks among the foremost in legal and political knowledge. He has joined to a fine genius all that can set him off and show him to advantage. He is well acquainted with Man, and understands all the passions that influence him. Government seems to have been his peculiar Study, all the political institutions of the World he knows in detail, and can trace the causes and effects of every revolution from the earliest stages of the Greecian commonwealth down to the present time. No man is more clear, copious, and comprehensive than Mr. Wilson, yet he is no great Orator. He draws the attention not by the charm of his eloquence, but by the force of his reasoning. He is about 45 years old."

Wythe, George (1726-1806):

"Mr. Wythe is the famous Professor of Law at the University of William and Mary. He is confessedly one of the most learned legal Characters of the present age. From his close attention to the study of general learning he has acquired a compleat knowledge of the dead languages and all the sciences. He is remarked for his exemplary life, and universally esteemed for his good principles. No Man it is said understands the history of Government better than Mr. Wythe,—nor any one who understands the fluctuating conditions to which all societies are liable better than he does, yet from his too favorable opinion of Men, he is no great politician. He is a neat and pleasing Speaker, and a most correct and able Writer. Mr. Wythe is about 55 years of age." (Actually he was sixty-one.)

Yates, Robert (1724-1796):

"Mr. Yates is said to be an able Judge. He is a Man of great legal abilities, but not distinguished as an Orator. Some of his Enemies say he is an anti-federal Man, but I discovered no such disposition in him. He is about 45 years old [actually he was sixty-three], and enjoys a great share of health."

B. French character sketches *

The following sketches are from the report of the French Minister Otto to Foreign Minister Montmorin in Paris. They were written in 1788.

Baldwin, Abraham:

"Reasonable and well intentioned, but never had the occasion to distinguish himself. The Congress will enable him to do so by appointing him one of the Commissioners to settle its debts to the States."

Dayton, Jonathan:

"Little known, having no other merit than that of being the son of a good patriot and the benefactor of M. d'Anteroches, from which one may presume that he likes the French."

Dickinson, John:

"Author of the Letters of a Pennsylvania Farmer; very rich; had been anti-English at the beginning of the Revolution, without however favoring independence, having actually voted against it publicly. He is old, feeble and without influence."

Ellsworth, Oliver:

"Mr. Ellsworth, former member of Congress, is absolutely of the same outlook and disposition [as Benjamin Huntington, a friend of France]. The same may be said of Mr. [Roger] Sherman. In general, the men of that State

* Translated from the French by Saul K. Padover.

[Connecticut] have a national outlook which is rarely found elsewhere on the continent. They show a greater republican simplicity; they are well off without being opulent. The rural economy and domestic industry have developed quite far in Connecticut; the people there are happy."

Few, William:

"Without being a genius, he has more knowledge than his name and appearance would indicate. Although still young, he had been constantly employed during the war. His colleagues have a good opinion of him. He is very timid and awkward in society, unless one speaks to him about business."

Franklin, Benjamin:

"Dr. Franklin, the present President of the State [Pennsylvania], is too well known to need deserved praising. He feels, more than any other American, that in order to be a true patriot it is necessary to be a friend of France. Unfortunately, this philosopher, who has known how to brave the lightning of heaven and of the English Parliament, will not long continue to fight against the infirmities of age. We must regret that immortality belongs only to his name and writings."

Gerry, Elbridge:

"Mr. Elb. Gerry is a little man, very intriguing and full of small shrewdnesses, which have hitherto brought him sufficient success. Of all the members of the Congress, he has been active the longest. He has acquired a great knowledge of public affairs, which he uses to arouse esteem among his fellow-citizens. In 1782 he had delivered a pretty effective speech in the legislature at Boston against ratification of the Consular Convention. He pretends a great liking for Chevalier de La Luzerne, but one should be on guard against his fine claims. In general, we have very few friends among the powerful men of Massachusetts; our commerce does not interest them and our fisheries are in their way. . . . The people in general like the French, since they often saw our fleet and recall the services which we have rendered them."

Gilman, Nicholas:

"A pretentious young man; little loved by his colleagues; one calls him mockingly *The Congress*. Still, he has the advantage of having represented his State [New Hampshire] at the great Convention in Philadelphia and of having signed the new Constitution. . . ."

Hamilton, Alexander:

"Great orator; intrepid in public debate. Zealous and even extremist partisan of the new Constitution and a declared enemy of Gov. Clinton. . . . He is one of these rare men who has distinguished himself equally on the field of battle and at the bar. He owes everything to his talents. . . . He has a bit too much affectation and too little prudence. . . . He is too impetuous and owing to a desire to lead everything, he fails of his goal. His eloquence is often out of place in public debates, where precision and clarity are preferred to brilliant imagination. It is believed that Mr. H. is the author of the pamphlet entitled *The Federalist*. Here again he has failed of his goal. That work is of no use to the educated, and it is too learned and too long for the ignorant. Nevertheless, it has given him great fame, and has led to the giving of the name *Hamilton* to a small frigate which was carried through the streets of New York during the great Federal procession. . . . A stranger in this State, where he was educated through charity, Mr. Hamilton has found a means of carrying off the daughter of General Schuyler, a great landowner and very influential."

Langdon, John:

"One of the most interesting and amiable men in the United States; former governor of New Hampshire, and head of a powerful party, which is in opposition to General Sullivan. Mr. L. has made a great fortune in commerce; he is the Rob. Morris of his State, spending generously and attracting many citizens through his liberality. He was one of the principal members of the Philadelphia Convention, but he stayed there only a few days, and though his colleagues had offered him the presidency, he did not wish to remain there, because he had in mind the Governorship of New Hampshire and because his business did not permit him a long absence. He is sincerely attached to France and even in favor of our institutions and manners. In order to spread the taste for our furniture, he has imported some of the best from Paris. It is said that he is jealous of his wife, something quite rare in America. Many French officers have found to their chagrin that this jealousy was entirely unfounded."

Livingston, William:

"William Livingston, Esq., Governor [of New Jersey] since the beginning of the Revolution, very well informed, firm, patriotic, preferring the public welfare to popularity and having often endangered his position by opposing bad laws in the legislature. Although he does not cease to criticize the people, he is always re-elected, since even his enemies agree that he is one of the cleverest and most virtuous men on the continent."

Madison, James:

"Well-informed, wise, moderate, docile, studious; perhaps more profound than Mr. Hamilton, but less brilliant; intimate friend of Mr. Jefferson and sincerely attached to France. He was at the Congress very young and he appears to be particularly dedicated to public affairs. He could be some day Governor of his State, if his modesty would permit him to accept that place. Last time he refused to accept the presidency of the Congress. He is a man who should be studied a long time in order to form a just opinion of him."

Martin, Luther:

"A distinguished lawyer who has written much against the resolutions of the Philadelphia Convention, of which he was a member."

Mifflin, Thomas:

"Former General, president of the Congress, orator, etc. A declared and proven friend of France. Very popular and leading with astonishing facility that monster of a hundred heads called the people. A good lawyer. a good officer, a good patriot, and an agreeable society man. He does well everything he undertakes. . . ."

Morris, Gouverneur:

"Citizen of the State of New York, but always in contact with Rob. Morris and having represented Pennsylvania several times. Celebrated lawyer; one of the best organized heads on the continent, but without manners, and, if his enemies are to be believed, without principles; infinitely interesting in conversation, having made a special study of finances. He works constantly with Mr. Rob. Morris. He is more feared than admired, but few people esteem him."

Morris, Robert:

"Superintendent of Finances during the war, the most powerful merchant in his State. A good head above all, and experienced, but not studious. He has grown a bit cold towards France. . . . Still it will be easy to win him back through proper handling. This is a man of the greatest weight, to whose friendship we cannot be indifferent."

Randolph, Edmund:

"Present Governor [of Virginia], one of the most distinguished men in America by his talents and influence; nevertheless, he has lost a bit of his standing through his too-violent opposition to the ratification of the new Constitution. . . . We may consider him as being very indifferent to France."

Rutledge, John:

"Governor [of South Carolina] during the war, member of Congress and of the [Philadelphia] Convention, as well as of other great conferences. The most eloquent, but also the proudest and most imperious man in the United States. He uses his great influence and his knowledge as a lawyer for not paying his debts, which greatly exceed his fortune. His son is traveling in France for his education."

Williamson, Hugh:

"Physician and former professor of astronomy. Excessively bizarre, loving to hold forth, but speaking with spirit. It is difficult to know his character well; it is even possible that he does not have any; but his activity has given him much influence in Congress for some time."

Wilson, James:

"Distinguished jurist. It was he who was designated by Mr. Gerard to be the lawyer of the French nation, a place which has since been recognized as useless. A haughty man, an intrepid aristocrat, active, eloquent, profound, a dissembler, known by the name of *James the Caledonian* which his enemies have given him. His participation in public affairs has led to a disorganization of his fortune. Indifferently attached to France."

Chapter V

Some Comments on the Constitution

ABRAHAM LINCOLN'S VIEW OF THE CONSTITUTION:

Lincoln viewed the Constitution as a basic frame of government for freedom and union. He expressed his ideas in the following unusual "Fragment on the Constitution and the Union," written about 1860:

> All this is not the result of accident. It has a philosophical cause. Without the *Constitution* and the *Union,* we could not have attained the result; but even these, are not the primary cause of our great prosperity. There is something back of these, entwining itself more closely about the human heart. That something, is the principle of "Liberty to all"—the principle that clears the *path* for all—gives *hope* to all—and, by consequence, *enterprise,* and *industry* to all.
>
> The *expression* of that principle, in our Declaration of Independence, was most happy, and fortunate. *Without* this, as well as *with* it, we could have declared our independence of Great Britain; but without it, we could not, I think, have secured our free government, and consequent prosperity. No oppressed people will *fight,* and *endure,* as our fathers did, without the promise of something better, than a mere change of masters.
>
> The assertion of that *principle,* at *that time,* was *the* word, *"fitly spoken"* which has proved an "apple of gold" to us. The *Union,* and the *Constitution,* are the *picture* of *silver,* subsequently framed around it. The picture was made, not to *conceal,* or *destroy* the apple; but to *adorn,* and *preserve* it. The *picture* was made *for* the apple—*not* the apple for the picture.

WOODROW WILSON'S DESCRIPTION OF THE CONSTITUTION:

Long before he became President of the United States, Woodrow Wilson, one of the profoundest students of American history and politics, thus analyzed the importance of the Constitution in his book *Congressional Government* (1885):

> The Constitution is now, like Magna Carta and the Bill of Rights, only the sap-centre of a system of government vastly larger than the stock from which it has branched—a system some of whose forms have only very indistinct and rudimental beginnings in the simple substance of the Constitution, and which exercises many functions apparently quite foreign to the primitive properties contained in the fundamental law.
>
> The Constitution itself is not a complete system; it takes none but the first steps in organization. It does little more than lay a foundation of principles. It provides with all possible brevity for the establishment of a government having, in several distinct branches, executive, legislative, and judicial powers. It vests executive power in a single chief magistrate, for whose election and inauguration it makes carefully definite provision, and whose privileges and prerogatives it defines with succinct clearness; it grants specifically enumerated powers of legislation to a representative Congress, outlining the organization of the two houses of that body . . . ; and it establishes a Supreme Court with ample authority. . . . Here the Constitution's work of organization ends, and the fact that it attempts nothing more is its chief strength. For it to go beyond elementary provisions would be to lose elasticity and adaptability. The growth of the nation and the consequent development of the governmental system would snap asunder a constitution which could not adapt itself to the measure of the new conditions of an advancing society. If it could not stretch itself to the measure of the times, it must be thrown off and left behind, as a by-gone device; and there can, therefore, be no question that our Constitution has proved lasting because of its simplicity. It is a cornerstone, not a complete building; or, rather, to return to the old figure, it is a root, not a perfect vine.

LORD BRYCE'S COMMENT ON THE CONSTITUTION:

In his book *The American Commonwealth* (1888), Bryce, one of the keenest British observers of American life, wrote of the Constitution:

> The Constitution of 1789 deserves the veneration with which the Americans have been accustomed to regard it. It is true that many criticisms have been passed upon its arrangement, upon its omissions, upon the artificial character of some of the institutions it creates. . . . Yet, after all deductions, it ranks above every other written constitution for the intrinsic excellence of its scheme, its adaptation to the circumstances of the people, the simplicity, brevity, and precision of its language, its judi-

cious mixture of definiteness in principle with elasticity in details.

BRIEFER COMMENTS:

"Every word of [the Constitution] decides a question between power and liberty."—James Madison, 1792

"That precious depository of American happiness, the Constitution of the United States."—George Washington, 1794

"Our national constitution, the ark of our safety, and grand palladium of our happiness."—Thomas Jefferson, 1800

"The result of the collected wisdom of our country."—Thomas Jefferson, 1801

"Competent to render our fellow citizens the happiest and the securest on whom the sun has ever shone."—Thomas Jefferson, 1813

"The Constitution . . . is a charter of limited powers."—John Quincy Adams, 1825

"A sacred instrument."—Martin Van Buren, 1837

"Your Constitution is all sail and no anchor."—Thomas Babington Macaulay, 1857

"We are under a Constitution, but the Constitution is what the judges say it is."—Charles Evans Hughes, 1907

"The Constitution was not meant to hold the government back to the time of horses and wagons."—Woodrow Wilson, 1908

"It [the Constitution] is an experiment, as all life is an experiment."—Oliver Wendell Holmes, 1919

"Our Constitution is so simple and practical that it is possible always to meet extraordinary needs by changes in emphasis and arrangement without loss of essential form. That is why our constitutional system has proved itself the most superbly enduring political mechanism the modern world has produced."—Franklin D. Roosevelt, 1933

"The Constitution . . . is what living men and women think it is."—Charles A. Beard, 1936

Chapter VI

Text of the Constitution

A. THE CONSTITUTION OF THE UNITED STATES

We the People of the United States, in order to form a more perfect Union, establish Justice, ensure Domestic Tranquillity, provide for the common Defence, promote the general Welfare, and secure the Blessings of Liberty to ourselves and our Posterity, do ordain and establish this CONSTITUTION for the United States of America.

ARTICLE I.

Sec. 1. ALL legislative powers herein granted shall be vested in a Congress of the United States, which shall consist of a Senate and House of Representatives.

Sec. 2. The House of Representatives shall be composed of members chosen every second year by the people of the several states, and the electors in each state shall have the qualifications requisite for electors of the most numerous branch of the state legislature.

No person shall be a representative who shall not have attained to the age of 25 years, and been seven years a citizen of the United States, and who shall not, when elected, be an inhabitant of that state in which he shall be chosen.

Representatives and direct taxes shall be apportioned among the several states which may be included within this union, according to their respective numbers, which shall be determined by adding to the whole number of free persons,[1] including those bound to service for a term of years, and ex-

[1] "*which shall be determined . . . free persons*"—modified by the Fourteenth Amendment.

cluding Indians not taxed, three-fifths of all other persons.[2] The actual enumeration shall be made within three years after the first meeting of the Congress of the United States, and within every subsequent term of ten years, in such manner as they shall by law direct. The number of representatives shall not exceed one for every 30,000, but each state shall have at least one representative; and until such enumeration shall be made, the state of New-Hampshire shall be entitled to choose three, Massachusetts eight, Rhode-Island and Providence Plantations one, Connecticut five, New-York six, New-Jersey four, Pennsylvania eight, Delaware one, Maryland six, Virginia ten, North-Carolina five, South-Carolina five, and Georgia three.

When vacancies happen in the representation from any state, the executive authority thereof shall issue writs of election to fill such vacancies.

The House of Representatives shall choose their speaker and other officers; and shall have the sole power of impeachment.

Sec. 3. The Senate of the United States shall be composed of two senators from each state, chosen by the legislature thereof, for six years; [3] and each senator shall have one vote.

Immediately after they shall be assembled in consequence of the first election, they shall be divided as equally as may be into three classes. The seats of the senators of the first class shall be vacated at the expiration of the second year, of the second class at the expiration of the fourth year, and of the third class at the expiration of the sixth year, so that one-third may be chosen every second year; and if vacancies happen by resignation, or otherwise, during the recess of the legislature of any state, the executive thereof may make temporary appointments until the next meeting of the legislature, which shall then fill such vacancies.[4]

No person shall be a senator who shall not have attained to the age of 30 years, and been nine years a citizen of the United States, and who shall not, when elected, be an inhabitant of that state for which he shall be chosen.

The vice-president of the United States shall be president

[2] "*three-fifths . . . persons*"—superseded by the Fourteenth Amendment.

[3] "*The Senate . . . for six years*"—superseded by the Seventeenth Amendment.

[4] "*and if vacancies . . . such vacancies*"—modified by the Seventeenth Amendment.

of the Senate, but shall have no vote, unless they be equally divided.

The Senate shall choose their other officers, and also a president *pro tempore,* in the absence of the vice-president, or when he shall exercise the office of president of the United States.

The Senate shall have the sole power to try all impeachments. When sitting for that purpose, they shall be on oath or affirmation. When the president of the United States is tried, the chief justice shall preside: And no person shall be convicted without the concurrence of two-thirds of the members present.

Judgment in cases of impeachment shall not extend further than to removal from office, and disqualification to hold and enjoy any office of honour, trust or profit under the United States; but the party convicted shall nevertheless be liable and subject to indictment, trial, judgment and punishment, according to law.

Sec. 4. The times, places and manner of holding elections for senators and representatives, shall be prescribed in each state by the legislature thereof: But the Congress may at any time by law make or alter such regulations, except as to the places of choosing senators.

The Congress shall assemble at least once in every year, and such meeting shall be on the first Monday in December, unless they shall by law appoint a different day.[5]

Sec. 5. Each house shall be the judge of the elections, returns and qualifications of its own members, and a majority of each shall constitute a quorum to do business; but a smaller number may adjourn from day to day, and may be authorized to compel the attendance of absent members, in such manner, and under such penalties as each house may provide.

Each house may determine the rules of its proceedings, punish its members for disorderly behaviour, and, with the concurrence of two-thirds, expel a member.

Each house shall keep a journal of its proceedings, and from time to time publish the same, excepting such parts as may, in their judgment, require secrecy; and the yeas and nays of the members of either house on any question, shall, at the desire of one-fifth of those present, be entered on the journal.

[5] *"The Congress . . . a different day"*—superseded by the Twentieth Amendment.

Neither house, during the session of Congress, shall, without the consent of the other, adjourn for more than three days, nor to any other place than that in which the two houses shall be sitting.

Sec. 6. The senators and representatives shall receive a compensation for their services, to be ascertained by law, and paid out of the treasury of the United States. They shall in all cases, except treason, felony and breach of the peace, be privileged from arrest during their attendance at the session of their respective houses, and in going to and returning from the same; and for any speech or debate in either house, they shall not be questioned in any other place.

No senator or representative shall, during the time for which he was elected, be appointed to any civil office under the authority of the United States, which shall have been created, or the emoluments whereof shall have been increased during such time; and no person holding any office under the United States, shall be a member of either house during his continuance in office.

Sec. 7. All bills for raising revenue shall originate in the House of Representatives; but the Senate may propose or concur with amendments as on other bills.

Every bill which shall have passed the House of Representatives and the Senate, shall, before it become a law, be presented to the president of the United States; if he approve, he shall sign it, but if not, he shall return it, with his objections, to that house in which it shall have originated, who shall enter the objections at large on their journal, and proceed to reconsider it. If after such reconsideration, two-thirds of that house shall agree to pass the bill, it shall be sent, together with the objections, to the other house, by which it shall likewise be reconsidered, and if approved by two-thirds of that house, it shall become a law. But in all such cases the votes of both houses shall be determined by yeas and nays, and the names of the persons voting for and against the bill shall be entered on the journal of each house respectively. If any bill shall not be returned by the president within ten days, (Sundays excepted) after it shall have been presented to him, the same shall be a law, in like manner as if he had signed it, unless the Congress by their adjournment prevent its return, in which case it shall not be a law.

Every order, resolution, or vote to which the concurrence of the Senate and House of Representatives may be necessary, (except on a question of adjournment) shall be presented to the president of the United States; and before the same shall take effect, shall be approved by him, or, being disapproved by him, shall be re-passed by two-thirds of the Senate and House of Representatives, according to the rules and limitations prescribed in the case of a bill.

Sec. 8. The Congress shall have power to lay and collect taxes, duties, imposts and excises, to pay the debts and provide for the common defence and general welfare of the United States; but all duties, imposts and excises shall be uniform throughout the United States:

To borrow money on the credit of the United States:

To regulate commerce with foreign nations, and among the several states, and with the Indian tribes:

To establish an uniform rule of naturalization, and uniform laws on the subject of bankruptcies throughout the United States:

To coin money, regulate the value thereof, and of foreign coin, and fix the standard of weights and measures:

To provide for the punishment of counterfeiting the securities and current coin of the United States:

To establish post-offices and post-roads:

To promote the progress of science and useful arts, by securing for limited times to authors and inventors the exclusive right to their respective writings and discoveries:

To constitute tribunals inferior to the supreme court:

To define and punish piracies and felonies committed on the high seas, and offences against the law of nations:

To declare war, grant letters of marque and reprisal, and make rules concerning captures on land and water:

To raise and support armies, but no appropriation of money to that use shall be for a longer term than two years:

To provide and maintain a navy:

To make rules for the government and regulation of the land and naval forces:

To provide for calling forth the militia to execute the laws of the union, suppress insurrections and repel invasions:

To provide for organizing, arming and disciplining the militia, and for governing such part of them as may be employed in the service of the United States, reserving to the states respectively, the appointment of the officers, and the authority of training the militia according to the discipline prescribed by Congress:

To exercise exclusive legislation in all cases whatsoever, over such district (not exceeding ten miles square) as may, by cession of particular states, and the acceptance of Congress, become the seat of the government of the United

States, and to exercise like authority over all places purchased by the consent of the legislature of the state in which the same shall be, for the erection of forts, magazines, arsenals, dock-yards, and other needful buildings: And,

To make all laws which shall be necessary and proper for carrying into execution the foregoing powers, and all other powers vested by this constitution in the government of the United States, or in any department or officer thereof.

Sec. 9. The migration or importation of such persons as any of the states now existing shall think proper to admit, shall not be prohibited by the Congress prior to the year 1808, but a tax or duty may be imposed on such importations, not exceeding 10 dollars for each person.

The privilege of the writ of *habeas corpus* shall not be suspended, unless when in cases of rebellion or invasion the public safety may require it.

No bill of attainder or *ex post facto* law shall be passed.

No capitation, or other direct tax shall be laid unless in proportion to the *census* or enumeration herein before directed to be taken.[6]

No tax or duty shall be laid on articles exported from any state.

No preference shall be given by any regulation of commerce or revenue to the ports of one state or those of another: nor shall vessels bound to, or from one state, be obliged to enter, clear, or pay duties in another.

No money shall be drawn from the treasury but in consequence of appropriations made by law; and a regular statement and account of the receipts and expenditures of all public money shall be published from time to time.

No title of nobility shall be granted by the United States: And no person holding any office or profit or trust under them, shall, without the consent of the Congress, accept of any present, emolument, office, or title, of any kind whatever, from any king, prince or foreign state.

Sec. 10. No state shall enter into any treaty, alliance, or confederation; grant letters of marque and reprisal; coin money; emit bills of credit; make any thing but gold and silver coin a tender in payment of debts; pass any bill of attainder, *ex post facto* law, or law impairing the obligation of contracts, or grant any title of nobility.

No state shall, without the consent of the Congress, lay

[6] *"No capitation . . . to be taken"*—modified by the Sixteenth Amendment.

any imposts or duties on imports or exports, except what may be absolutely necessary for executing its inspection laws; and the net produce of all duties and imposts, laid by any state on imports or exports, shall be for the use of the treasury of the United States; and all such laws shall be subject to the revision and control of the Congress.

No state shall, without the consent of Congress, lay any duty of tonnage, keep troops, or ships of war in time of peace, enter into any agreement or compact with another state, or with a foreign power, or engage in a war, unless actually invaded, or in such imminent danger as will not admit of delay.

ARTICLE II.

Sec. 1. The executive power shall be vested in a president of the United States of America. He shall hold his office during the term of four years, and, together with the vice-president, chosen for the same term, be elected as follows:

Each state shall appoint, in such manner as the legislature thereof may direct, a number of electors, equal to the whole number of senators and representatives to which the state may be entitled in the Congress; but no senator or representative, or person holding an office of trust or profit under the United States, shall be appointed an elector.

The electors shall meet in their respective states, and vote by ballot for two persons, of whom one at least shall not be an inhabitant of the same state with themselves. And they shall make a list of all the persons voted for, and of the number of votes for each; which list they shall sign and certify, and transmit sealed to the seat of the government of the United States, directed to the president of the Senate. The president of the Senate shall, in the presence of the Senate and House of Representatives, open all the certificates and the votes shall then be counted. The person having the greatest number of votes shall be the president, if such number be a majority of the whole number of electors appointed; and if there be more than one who have such majority, and have an equal number of votes, then the House of Representatives shall immediately choose by ballot one of them for president; and if no person have a majority, then from the five highest on the list, the said House shall, in like manner, choose the president. But in choosing the president, the votes shall be taken by states, the representation from each state having one vote; a quorum for this purpose shall consist of a member or members from two-thirds of the states, and a majority of all the states shall be necessary to a choice. In every case, after the choice of the president, the person having the greatest number of votes of the electors shall be the vice-president. But if there should remain two or more who have equal votes, the Senate shall choose from them by ballot the vice-president.[7]

The Congress may determine the time of choosing the electors, and the day on which they shall give their votes; which day shall be the same throughout the United States.

No person except a natural born citizen, or a citizen of the United States, at the time of the adoption of this constitution, shall be eligible to the office of president; neither shall any person be eligible to that office, who shall not have attained to the age of 35 years, and been 14 years a resident within the United States.

In case of the removal of the president from office, or of his death, resignation, or inability to discharge the powers and duties of the said office, the same shall devolve on the vice-president, and the Congress may by law provide for the case of removal, death, resignation, or inability, both of the president and vice-president, declaring what officer shall then act as president, and such officer shall act accordingly, until the disability be removed, or a president shall be elected.

The president shall, at stated times, receive for his services, a compensation, which shall neither be increased nor diminished during the period for which he shall have been elected, and he shall not receive within that period any other emolument from the United States, or any of them.

Before he enter on the execution of his office, he shall take the following oath or affirmation:

"I do solemnly swear (or affirm) that I will faithfully execute the office of president of the United States, and will to the best of my ability, preserve, protect and defend the constitution of the United States."

Sec. 2. The president shall be commander in chief of the army and navy of the United States, and of the militia of the several states, when called into the actual service of the United States; he may require the opinion, in writing, of the principal officer in each of the executive departments, upon any subject relating to the duties of their respective offices, and he shall have power to grant reprieves and pardons for

[7] *"The electors shall meet . . . the vice-president"*—superseded by the Twelfth Amendment, which is modified by the Twentieth.

offences against the United States, except in cases of impeachment.

He shall have power, by and with the advice and consent of the Senate, to make treaties, provided two-thirds of the senators present concur; and he shall nominate, and by and with the advice and consent of the Senate, shall appoint ambassadors, other public ministers and consuls, judges of the supreme court, and all other officers of the United States, whose appointments are not herein otherwise provided for, and which shall be established by law. But the Congress may by law vest the appointment of such inferior officers, as they think proper in the president alone, in the courts of law, or in the heads of departments.

The president shall have power to fill up all vacancies that may happen during the recess of the Senate, by granting commissions, which shall expire at the end of their next session.

Sec. 3. He shall, from time to time, give to the Congress information of the state of the union, and recommend to their consideration, such measures as he shall judge necessary and expedient; he may, on extraordinary occasions, convene both houses, or either of them, and in case of disagreement between them, with respect to the time of adjournment, he may adjourn them to such time as he shall think proper; he shall receive ambassadors and other public ministers; he shall take care that the laws be faithfully executed, and shall commission all the officers of the United States.

Sec. 4. The president, vice-president, and all civil officers of the United States shall be removed from office on impeachment for, and conviction of, treason, bribery, or other high crimes and misdemeanors.

ARTICLE III.

Sec. 1. The judicial power of the United States, shall be vested in one supreme court, and in such inferior courts as the Congress may, from time to time, ordain and establish. The judges, both of the supreme and inferior courts, shall hold their offices during good behaviour, and shall, at stated times, receive for their services a compensation, which shall not be diminished during their continuance in office.

Sec. 2. The judicial power shall extend to all cases, in law and equity, arising under this constitution, the laws of the United States, and treaties made, or which shall be made under their authority; to all cases affecting ambassadors, other public ministers and consuls; to all cases of admiralty and maritime jurisdiction; to controversies to which the United States shall be a party: to controversies between two or more states, between a state and citizens of another state,[8] between citizens of different states, between citizens of the same state, claiming lands under grants of different states, and between a state, or the citizens thereof, and foreign states, citizens or subjects.

In all cases affecting ambassadors, other public ministers and consuls, and those in which a state shall be party, the supreme court shall have original jurisdiction. In all the other cases before-mentioned, the supreme court shall have appellate jurisdiction, both as to law and fact, with such exceptions, and under such regulations as the Congress shall make.

The trial of all crimes, except in cases of impeachment, shall be by jury; and such trial shall be held in the state where the said crimes shall have been committed; but when not committed within any state, the trial shall be at such place or places as the Congress may by law have directed.

Sec. 3. Treason against the United States shall consist only in levying war against them, or in adhering to their enemies, giving them aid and comfort. No person shall be convicted of treason unless on the testimony of two witnesses to the same overt act, or on confession in open court.

The Congress shall have power to declare the punishment of treason, but no attainder of treason shall work corruption of blood, or forfeiture, except during the life of the person attainted.

ARTICLE IV

Sec. 1. Full faith and credit shall be given in each state to the public acts, records and judicial proceedings of every other state. And the Congress may by general laws prescribe the manner in which such acts, records and proceedings shall be proved, and the effect thereof.

Sec. 2. The citizens of each state shall be entitled to all privileges and immunities of citizens in the several states.

A person charged in any state with treason, felony, or other crime, who shall flee from justice, and be found in another state, shall, on demand of the executive authority of the

[8] "*between a state . . . another state*"—limited by the Eleventh Amendment.

state from which he fled, be delivered up, to be removed to the state having jurisdiction of the crime.

No person held to service or labour in one state, under the laws thereof, escaping into another, shall, in consequence of any law or regulation therein, be discharged from such service or labour, but shall be delivered up on claim of the party to whom such service or labour may be due.[9]

Sec. 3. New states may be admitted by the Congress into this union; but no new state shall be formed or erected within the jurisdiction of any other state, nor any state be formed by the junction of two or more states, or parts of states, without the consent of the legislatures of the states concerned, as well as of the Congress.

The Congress shall have power to dispose of and make all needful rules and regulations respecting the territory or other property belonging to the United States; and nothing in this constitution shall be so construed as to prejudice any claims of the United States, or of any particular state.

Sec. 4. The United States shall guarantee to every state in this union, a republican form of government, and shall protect each of them against invasion; and on application of the legislature, or of the executive (when the legislature cannot be convened), against domestic violence.

ARTICLE V.

The Congress, whenever two-thirds of both houses shall deem it necessary, shall propose amendments to this constitution, or on the application of the legislatures of two-thirds of the several states, shall call a convention for proposing amendments, which, in either case, shall be valid to all intents and purposes, as part of this constitution, when ratified by the legislatures of three-fourths of the several states, or by conventions in three-fourths thereof, as the one or the other mode of ratification may be proposed by the Congress: Provided, that no amendment which may be made prior to the year 1808, shall in any manner affect the first and fourth clauses in the ninth section of the first article; and that no state, without its consent, shall be deprived of its equal suffrage in the Senate.

[9] *"No person . . . may be due"*—superseded by the Thirteenth Amendment in regard to slaves.

ARTICLE VI.

All debts contracted and engagements entered into, before the adoption of this constitution, shall be as valid against the United States under this constitution, as under the confederation.

This constitution, and the laws of the United States which shall be made in pursuance thereof; and all treaties made, or which shall be made, under the authority of the United States, shall be the supreme law of the land; and the judges in every state shall be bound thereby, any thing in the constitution or laws of any state to the contrary notwithstanding.

The senators and representatives before-mentioned, and the members of the several state legislatures, and all executive and judicial officers, both of the United States and of the several states, shall be bound by oath or affirmation, to support this constitution; but no religious test shall ever be required as a qualification to any office or public trust under the United States.

ARTICLE VII.

The ratification of the conventions of nine states, shall be sufficient for the establishment of this constitution between the states so ratifying the same.

DONE in convention, by the unanimous consent of the states present, the 17th day of September, in the year of our Lord 1787, and of the independence of the United States of America the 12th. In witness whereof we have hereunto subscribed our names.

GEORGE WASHINGTON, *President,*
And Deputy from Virginia.

New-Hampshire,	John Langdon, Nicholas Gilman.
Massachusetts,	Nathaniel Gorham, Rufus King.
Connecticut,	William Samuel Johnson, Roger Sherman.

New-York,	Alexander Hamilton.
New-Jersey,	William Livingston, David Brearly, William Paterson, Jonathan Dayton.
Pennsylvania,	Benjamin Franklin, Thomas Mifflin, Robert Morris, George Clymer, Thomas Fitzsimons, Jared Ingersoll, James Wilson, Gouverneur Morris.
Delaware,	George Read, Gunning Bedford, jun., John Dickinson, Richard Bassett, Jacob Broom.
Maryland,	James M'Henry, Daniel of St. Thomas Jenifer, Daniel Carroll.
Virginia,	John Blair, James Madison, jun.
North-Carolina,	William Blount, Richard Dobbs Spaight, Hugh Williamson.
South-Carolina,	John Rutledge, Charles Cotesworth Pinckney Charles Pinckney, Pierce Butler.
Georgia,	William Few, Abraham Baldwin.
Attest:	WILLIAM JACKSON, *Secretary.*

B. AMENDMENTS TO THE CONSTITUTION

ARTICLE I.

Congress shall make no law respecting an establishment of religion, or prohibiting the free exercise thereof; or abridging the freedom of speech or of the press; or the right of the people peaceably to assemble, and to petition the government for a redress of grievances.

ARTICLE II.

A well-regulated militia being necessary to the security of a free state, the right of the people to keep and bear arms shall not be infringed.

ARTICLE III.

No soldier shall, in time of peace, be quartered in any house without the consent of the owner, nor in time of war but in a manner to be prescribed by law.

ARTICLE IV.

The right of the people to be secure in their persons, houses, papers, and effects, against unreasonable searches and seizures, shall not be violated, and no warrants shall issue but upon probable cause, supported by oath or affirmation, and particularly describing the place to be searched, and the persons or things to be seized.

ARTICLE V.

No person shall be held to answer for a capital or other infamous crime unless on a presentment or indictment of a grand jury, except in cases arising in the land or naval forces, or in the militia, when in actual service, in time of war or public danger; nor shall any person be subject for the same offence to be twice put in jeopardy of life or limb; nor shall be compelled in any criminal case to be a witness against himself, nor be deprived of life, liberty, or property, without due process of law; nor shall private property be taken for public use without just compensation.

ARTICLE VI.

In all criminal prosecutions, the accused shall enjoy the right to a speedy and public trial, by an impartial jury of the state and district wherein the crime shall have been committed, which district shall have been previously ascertained by law, and to be informed of the nature and cause of the accusation; to be confronted with the witnesses against him; to have compulsory process for obtaining witnesses in his favor, and to have the assistance of counsel for his defence.

ARTICLE VII.

In suits at common law, where the value in controversy shall exceed twenty dollars, the right of trial by jury shall be preserved, and no fact tried by a jury shall be otherwise reexamined in any court of the United States than according to the rules of the common law.

ARTICLE VIII.

Excessive bail shall not be required, nor excessive fines imposed, nor cruel and unusual punishments inflicted.

ARTICLE IX.

The enumeration in the constitution of certain rights shall not be construed to deny or disparage others retained by the people.

ARTICLE X.

The powers not delegated to the United States by the constitution, nor prohibited by it to the states, are reserved to the states respectively, or to the people.

[The foregoing ten amendments were adopted at the first session of Congress, and were declared to be in force, December 15, 1791.]

ARTICLE XI.

The judicial power of the United States shall not be construed to extend to any suit in law or equity, commenced or prosecuted against one of the United States, by citizens of another state, or by citizens or subjects of any foreign state.

[*Declared in force, January 8, 1798.*]

ARTICLE XII.

The electors shall meet in their respective states, and vote by ballot for president and vice-president, one of whom at least shall not be an inhabitant of the same state with themselves; they shall name in their ballots the person voted for as president, and in distinct ballots the person voted for as vice-president; and they shall make distinct lists of all persons voted for as president, and of all persons voted for as vice-president, and of the number of votes for each, which lists they shall sign and certify, and transmit, sealed, to the seat of the government of the United States directed to the president of the Senate; the president of the Senate shall, in the presence of the Senate and House of Representatives, open all the certificates, and the votes shall then be counted; the person having the greatest number of votes for president shall be the president, if such number be a majority of the whole number of electors appointed; and if no person have such majority, then from the persons having the highest numbers not exceeding three, on the list of those voted for as president, the House of Representatives shall choose immediately, by ballot, the president. But in choosing the president, the votes shall be taken by states, the representation from each state having one vote; a quorum for this purpose shall consist of a member or members from two-thirds of the states, and a majority of all the states shall be necessary to a choice. And if the House of Representatives shall not choose a president, whenever the right of choice shall devolve upon them, before the fourth day of March next following, then the vice-president shall act as president, as in the case of the death or other constitutional disability of the president. The person having the greatest number of votes as vice-president shall be the vice-president, if such number be a majority of the whole number of electors appointed, and if no person have a majority, then from the two highest numbers on the list the Senate shall choose the vice-president; a quorum for the purpose shall consist of two-thirds of the whole number of senators, and a majority of the whole number shall be necessary to a choice. But no person constitutionally ineligible to the office of president shall be eligible to that of vice-president of the United States.

[*Declared in force, September 25, 1804.*]

ARTICLE XIII.

Sec. 1. Neither slavery nor involuntary servitude, except as a punishment for crime whereof the party shall have been duly convicted, shall exist within the United States, or any place subject to their jurisdiction.

Sec. 2. Congress shall have power to enforce this article by appropriate legislation.

[*Declared in force, December 18, 1865.*]

ARTICLE XIV.

Sec. 1. All persons born or naturalized in the United States, and subject to the jurisdiction thereof, are citizens of the United States and of the state wherein they reside. No state shall make or enforce any law which shall abridge the privileges or immunities of citizens of the United States; nor shall any state deprive any person of life, liberty, or property without due process of law; nor deny to any person within its jurisdiction the equal protection of the law.

Sec. 2. Representatives shall be apportioned among the several States according to their respective numbers, counting the whole number of persons in each state, excluding Indians not taxed. But when the right to vote at any election for the choice of electors for president and vice-president of the United States, representatives in Congress, the executive and judicial officers of a State, or the members of the legislature thereof, is denied to any of the male members of such state being of twenty-one years of age, and citizens of the United States, or in any way abridged, except for participation in rebellion or other crime, the basis of representation therein shall be reduced in the proportion which the number of such male citizens shall bear to the whole number of male citizens twenty-one years of age in such state.

Sec. 3. No person shall be a senator or representative in Congress, or elector of president and vice-president, or hold any office, civil or military, under the United States, or under any state, who, having previously taken an oath, as a member of Congress, or as an officer of the United States, or as a member of any state legislature, or as an executive or judicial officer of any state, to support the constitution of the United States, shall have engaged in insurrection or rebellion against the same, or given aid and comfort to the enemies thereof. But Congress may, by a vote of two-thirds of each House, remove such disability.

Sec. 4. The validity of the public debt of the United States, authorized by law, including debts incurred for payment of pensions and bounties for services in suppressing insurrection or rebellion, shall not be questioned. But neither the United States nor any state shall assume or pay any debt or obligation incurred in aid of insurrection or rebellion against the United States, or any claim for the loss or emancipation of any slave; but all such debts, obligations, and claims shall be held illegal and void.

Sec. 5. The Congress shall have power to enforce, by appropriate legislation, the provisions of this article.

[*Declared in force, July 28, 1868.*]

ARTICLE XV.

Sec. 1. The right of citizens of the United States to vote shall not be denied or abridged by the United States or by any state on account of race, color, or previous condition of servitude.

Sec. 2. The Congress shall have power to enforce this article by appropriate legislation.

[*Declared in force, March 30, 1870.*]

ARTICLE XVI.

The Congress shall have power to lay and collect taxes on incomes, from whatever source derived, without apportionment among the several States, and without regard to any census or enumeration.

[*Declared in force, February 25, 1913.*]

ARTICLE XVII.

The Senate of the United States shall be composed of two senators from each state, elected by the people thereof for six years; and each senator shall have one vote. The electors in each state shall have the qualifications requisite for electors of the most numerous branch of the state legislatures.

When vacancies happen in the representation of any state in the senate, the executive authority of such state shall issue writs of election to fill such vacancies; provided, that the legislature of any state may empower the executive thereof to make temporary appointments until the people fill the vacancies by election as the legislature may direct.

This amendment shall not be so construed as to affect the election or term of any senator chosen before it becomes valid as part of the Constitution.

[*Declared in force, May 31, 1913.*]

ARTICLE XVIII.

Sec. 1. After one year from the ratification of this article the manufacture, sale, or transportation of intoxicating liquors within, the importation thereof into, or exportation thereof from the United States and all territory subiect to the jurisdiction thereof, for beverage purposes is hereby prohibited.

Sec. 2. The Congress and the several states shall have concurrent power to enforce this article by appropriate legislation.

Sec. 3. This article shall be inoperative unless it shall have been ratified as an amendment to the Constitution by the legislatures of the several states, as provided in the Constitution, within seven years from the date of submission hereof to the states by the Congress.

[*Declared in force, January 29, 1919; repealed by Twenty-first Amendment.*]

ARTICLE XIX.

The right of citizens of the United States to vote shall not be denied or abridged by the United States or by any state on account of sex.

Congress shall have power to enforce this article by appropriate legislation.

[*Declared in force, August 26, 1920.*]

ARTICLE XX

Sec. 1. The terms of the President and Vice-President shall

end at noon on the 20th day of January, and the terms of senators and representatives at noon on the 3rd day of January, of the years in which such terms would have ended if this article had not been ratified; and the terms of their successors shall then begin.

Sec. 2. The Congress shall assemble at least once in every year, and such meeting shall begin at noon on the 3rd day of January, unless they shall by law appoint a different day.

Sec. 3. If, at the time fixed for the beginning of the term of President, the President elect shall have died, the Vice-President elect shall become President. If a President shall not have been chosen before the time fixed for the beginning of his term, or if the President elect shall have failed to qualify, then the Vice-President elect shall act as President until a President shall have qualified; and the Congress may by law provide for the case wherein neither a President elect nor a Vice-President elect shall have qualified, declaring who shall then act as President, or the manner in which one who is to act shall be selected, and such person shall act accordingly until a President or Vice-President shall have qualified.

Sec. 4. The Congress may by law provide for the case of the death of any of the persons from whom the House of Representatives may choose a President, wherever the right of choice shall have devolved upon them, and for the case of the death of any of the persons from whom the Senate may choose a Vice-President, whenever the right of choice shall have devolved upon them.

Sec. 5. Sections 1 and 2 shall take effect on the 15th day of October following the ratification of this article.

Sec. 6. This article shall be inoperative unless it shall have been ratified as an amendment to the Constitution by the legislatures of three-fourths of the several states within seven years from the date of its submission.

[*Declared in force, February 6, 1933.*]

ARTICLE XXI.

Sec. 1. The eighteenth article of amendment to the Constitution of the United States is hereby repealed.

Sec. 2. The transportation or importation into any state, territory, or possession of the United States, for delivery or use therein of intoxicating liquors, in violation of the laws thereof, is hereby prohibited.

Sec. 3. This article shall be inoperative unless it shall have been ratified as an amendment to the Constitution by conventions in the several states, as provided in the Constitution, within seven years from the date of the submission hereof to the states by the Congress.

[*Declared in force, December 5, 1933.*]

ARTICLE XXII.

No person shall be elected to the office of the President more than twice, and no person who has held the office of President, or acted as President, for more than two years of a term to which some other person was elected President shall be elected to the office of the President more than once. But this Article shall not apply to any person holding the office of the President when this Article was proposed by the Congress, and shall not prevent any person who may be holding the office of President, or acting as President, during the term within which this Article becomes operative from holding the office of President or acting as President during the remainder of such term.

[*Declared in force, February 26, 1951.*]

ARTICLE XXIII.

Sec. 1. The District constituting the seat of Government of the United States shall appoint in such manner as the Congress may direct:

A number of electors of President and Vice President equal to the whole number of Senators and Representatives in Congress to which the District would be entitled if it were a State, but in no event more than the least populous State; they shall be in addition to those appointed by the States, but they shall be considered for the purposes of the election of President and Vice President, to be electors appointed by a State; and they shall meet in the District and perform such duties as provided by the twelfth article of amendment.

Sec. 2. The Congress shall have power to enforce this article by appropriate legislation.

[*Declared in force, April 3, 1961.*]

ARTICLE XXIV.

Sec. 1. The right of citizens of the United States to vote in any primary or other election for President or Vice President, for electors for President or Vice President, or for Senator or

Representative in Congress, shall not be denied or abridged by the United States or any State by reason of failure to pay any poll tax or other tax.

Sec. 2. The Congress shall have the power to enforce this article by appropriate legislation.

[*Declared in force, January 23, 1964.*]

ARTICLE XXV.

Sec. 1. In case of the removal of the President from office or his death or resignation, the Vice President shall become President.

Sec. 2. Whenever there is a vacancy in the office of the Vice President, the President shall nominate a Vice President who shall take the office upon confirmation by a majority vote of both houses of Congress.

Sec. 3. Whenever the President transmits to the President pro tempore of the Senate and the Speaker of the House of Representatives his written declaration that he is unable to discharge the powers and duties of his office, and until he transmits to them a written declaration to the contrary, such powers and duties shall be discharged by the Vice President as Acting President.

Sec. 4. Whenever the Vice President and a majority of either the principal officers of the executive departments or of such other body as Congress may by law provide, transmit to the President pro tempore of the Senate and the Speaker of the House of Representatives their written declaration that the President is unable to discharge the powers and duties of his office, the Vice President shall immediately assume the powers and duties of the office as Acting President.

Thereafter, when the President transmits to the President pro tempore of the Senate and the Speaker of the House of Representatives his written declaration that no inability exists, he shall resume the powers and duties of the office unless the Vice President and a majority of either the principal officers of the executive department or of such other body as Congress may by law provide, transmit within four days to the President pro tempore of the Senate and the Speaker of the House of Representatives their written declaration that the President is unable to discharge the powers and duties of his office. Thereupon Congress shall decide the issue, assembling within 48 hours for that purpose if not in session. If the Congress, within 21 days after receipt of the latter written declaration, or, if Congress is not in session, within 21 days after

Congress is required to assemble, determines by two-thirds vote of both houses that the President is unable to discharge the powers and duties of his office, the Vice President shall continue to discharge the same as Acting President; otherwise, the President shall resume the powers and duties of his office.

[*Submitted for ratification by the State Legislatures, July 6, 1965.*]

Appendix

Chronological Table

1786	September 11. Conference at Annapolis recommended a Constitutional Convention
1787	February 21. Congress resolved in favor of a Constitutional Convention
	May 14. Convention met at Philadelphia
	September 17. Constitution completed and signed
	September 19. Constitution printed in Philadelphia newspapers
	December 7. Delaware ratified Constitution
	December 12. Pennsylvania ratified Constitution
	December 18. New Jersey ratified Constitution
1788	January 2. Georgia ratified Constitution
	January 4. Connecticut ratified Constitution
	February 6. Massachusetts ratified Constitution
	April 28. Maryland ratified Constitution
	May 23. South Carolina ratified Constitution
	June 21. New Hampshire ratified Constitution
	June 25. Virginia ratified Constitution

July 26. New York ratified Constitution

1789 March 4. Federal Government inaugurated in New York

April 1. First House of Representatives was organized

April 6. George Washington elected President

April 30. Washington inaugurated

September 25. First ten Amendments adopted by Congress

November 21. North Carolina ratified Constitution

1790 May 29. Rhode Island ratified Constitution

1791 December 15. First ten Amendments (Bill of Rights) declared to be in force

Part II

The United States Supreme Court

Introduction

Selected Supreme Court Decisions Expounding the Constitution

Included here are more than three dozen (some being combined cases) Supreme Court decisions. They were selected to show the range and complexities of the problems that arose unavoidably in a federal system based on a written *Constitution. Such a Constitution, containing general propositions stated with brevity, by its very nature requires interpretation as to meaning, application, and intent, particularly when legislative acts are challenged by some aggrieved party or person. When legal opinions conflict, some body must adjudicate and decide what is or is not "constitutional." This has been the role of the United States Supreme Court, notably since the days of Chief Justice John Marshall, who, in the pioneering decision of* Marbury v. Madison, *asserted: "It is, emphatically, the province and duty of the judicial department, to say what the law is."*

The panorama of judicial decisions, ranging in time from George Washington to Lyndon B. Johnson, offers a striking commentary on the soundness of the original Constitution and the flexibility of its Supreme Court expounders. The decisions also show that there is no "last word" in regard to the Constitution. Times change, new personalities take their seat on the Bench, fresh viewpoints are introduced. In consequence, Supreme Court opinions, which, by and large, reflect the current of "sensed or known" ideas of the time, undergo changes in both interpretation and emphasis. On occasion, the Court also reverses itself completely, upsetting previous decisions. Dramatic examples of such reversals, contained in this book, are Minersville . . . v. Gobitis *which was overthrown three years later by* West Virginia . . . v. Barnette, *and* Gideon v. Wainwright *which overturned* Betts v. Brady, *the latter in force for some twenty years.*

Each case presented in the following pages elucidates some important aspect of American life—economic, political, social—that called for interpretation or decision on the part of the highest court in the land. The topics included are:

TABLE OF CONTENTS

TABLE OF CONTENTS (Continued)

Chapter VII

The Federal System

"The Congress shall have power to . . . make all laws which shall be necessary and proper for carrying into execution the foregoing powers . . ."—Art. I, Sec. 8

"The judicial power of the United States, shall be vested in one Supreme Court . . ."—Art. III, Sec. 1

"The judicial power shall extend . . . to controversies between two or more states, between a state and citizens of another state . . ."—Art. III, Sec. 2

"This Constitution, and the laws of the United States . . . shall be the supreme law of the land . . ."—Art. VI

In this Chapter:

Chisholm v. Georgia (1793)
McCulloch v. Maryland (1819)
Cohens v. Virginia (1821)
Missouri v. Holland (1920)
Pennsylvania v. Nelson (1956)

The States are subject to federal jurisdiction under the Constitution.

1. *CHISHOLM v. GEORGIA* (1793)

The decision in this case, a milestone in the development

of American federalism, interpreted the Constitution in such a way as to give a citizen the right to sue a State. In effect, it denied a State's pretensions to sovereignty.

Background: *Chisholm and a group of other South Carolina citizens sued Georgia for property confiscated during the American Revolution. The crucial question was: Could a State be sued in a federal court, or was it sovereign? The Supreme Court, pursuant to Art. III, Sec. 2 of the Constitution, ruled, by a vote of four to one, that States were under federal jurisdiction and hence could be sued by a citizen.*

Georgia denied the legality of the decision, and threatened to punish any official who would attempt to execute the judgment of the Supreme Court.

The protest against the decision led to the enactment of the Eleventh Amendment (1798).

Some Related Cases:

(On Federal Supremacy):

Texas v. White (1869)
Lincoln County v. Luning (1890)
Hans v. Louisiana (1890)
Monaco v. Mississippi (1934)

JUSTICE WILSON:

This is a case of uncommon magnitude. One of the parties to it is a State; certainly respectable, claiming to be sovereign. The question to be determined is whether this State, so respectable, and whose claim soars so high, is amenable to the jurisdiction of the Supreme Court of the United States? This question, important in itself, will depend on others, more important still; and may, perhaps, be ultimately resolved into one, no less radical than this—"do the people of the United States form a nation?" . . .

To the Constitution of the United States the term sovereign is totally unknown. There is but one place where it could have been used with propriety. But, even in that place it would not, perhaps, have comported with the delicacy of those who ordained and established that Constitution. They might have announced themselves "sovereign" people of the United States: But serenely conscious of the fact, they avoided the ostentatious declaration. . . .

In one sense, the term sovereign has for its correlative, subject. In this sense, the term can receive no application; for it has no object in the Constitution of the United States. Under that Constitution there are citizens, but no subjects. "Citizens of the United States." "Citizens of another State." "Citizens of different States." "A State or citizen thereof." The term, subject, occurs indeed, once in the instrument; but to mark the contrast strongly, the epithet "foreign" is prefixed. In this sense, I presume the State of Georgia has no claim upon her own citizens: In this sense, I am certain, she can have no claim upon the citizens of another State. . . .

As a judge of this court, I know, and can decide upon the knowledge, that the citizens of Georgia, when they acted upon the large scale of the union, as a part of the "People of the United States," did not surrender the supreme or sovereign power to that State; but, as to the purposes of the union, retained it to themselves. As to the purposes of the union, therefore, Georgia is not a sovereign State. . . .

Under this view, the question is naturally subdivided into two others. 1. Could the Constitution of the United States vest a jurisdiction over the State of Georgia? 2. Has that Constitution vested such jurisdiction in this court? I have already remarked, that in the practice, and even in the science of politics, there has been frequently a strong current against the natural order of things; and an inconsiderate or an interested disposition to sacrifice the end to the means. This remark deserves a more particular illustration. Even in almost every nation, which has been denominated free, the State has assumed a supercilious pre-eminence above the people who have formed it: Hence the haughty notions of state independence, state sovereignty, and state supremacy. In despotic governments, the Government has usurped, in a similar manner, both upon the state and the people: Hence all arbitrary doctrines and pretensions concerning the supreme, absolute, and incontrollable power of government. In each, man is degraded from the prime rank, which he ought to hold in human affairs; In the latter, the state as well as the man is degraded. Of both degradations, striking instances occur in history, in politics, and in common life. . . .

In the United States, and in the several States which compose the union, we go not so far; but still we go one step farther than we ought to go in this unnatural and inverted order of things. The States, rather than the people, for whose sakes the States exist, are frequently the objects which attract and arrest our principal attention. This, I believe, has produced much of the confusion and perplexity, which have appeared in several proceedings and several publications on state politics, and on the politics too, of the United States. Sentiments and expressions of this inaccurate kind prevail in our common, even in our convivial, language. Is a toast asked? "The United States" instead of the "People of the United States," is the toast given. This is not politically correct. The toast is meant to present to view the first great object in the union: It presents only the second; It presents only the artificial person, instead of the natural persons, who spoke it into existence. A State I cheerfully admit, is the noblest work of man: But man himself, free and honest, is, I speak as to this world, the noblest work of God. . . .

With the strictest propriety, therefore, classical and political, our national scene opens with the most magnificent object which the nation could present. "The people of the United States" are the first personages introduced. Who were those people? They were the citizens of thirteen States, each of which had a separate constitution and government, and all of which were connected together by articles of confederation. To the purposes of public strength and felicity that confederacy was totally inadequate. A requisition on the several States terminated its legislative authority; Executive or judicial authority it had none. In order, therefore, to form a more perfect union, to establish justice, to insure domestic tranquility, to provide for common defence, and to secure the blessings of liberty, those people, among whom were the people of Georgia, ordained and established the present constitution. By that constitution, legislative power is vested, executive power is vested, judicial power is vested.

The question now opens fairly to our view, could the people of those States, among whom were those of Georgia, bind those States, and Georgia, among the others, by the legislative, executive, and judicial power so vested? If the principles on which I have founded myself are just and true, this question must, unavoidably, receive an affirmative answer. If those States were the work of those people, those people, and that I may apply the case closely, the people of Georgia, in particular, could alter, as they pleased, their former work; to any given degree, they could diminish as well as enlarge it. Any or all of the former state powers they could extinguish or transfer. The inference which necessarily results is, that the constitution ordained and established by those people; and, still closely to apply the case, in particular, by the people of Georgia, could vest jurisdiction or judicial power over those States, and over the State of Georgia in particular.

The next question under this head is—has the constitution done so? Did those people mean to exercise this, their undoubted power? These questions may be resolved, either by fair and conclusive deductions, or by direct and explicit declarations. In order, ultimately, to discover, whether the people of the United States intended to bind those States by the judicial power vested by the national Constitution, a previous inquiry will naturally be: Did those people intend to bind those states by the legislative power vested by that Constitution? The Articles of Confederation, it is well known, did not operate upon individual citizens, but operated only upon States. This defect was remedied by the national Constitution, which, as all allow, has an operation on individual citizens. But if an opinion, which some seem to entertain, be just; the defect remedied, on one side, was balanced by a defect introduced on the other: for they seem to think, that the present Constitution operates only on individual citizens, and not on States. This opinion, however, appears to be altogether unfounded. When certain laws of the States are declared to be "subject to the revision and control of the Congress"; it cannot, surely, be contended, that the legislative power of the national Government was meant to have no operation on the several States. The fact, uncontrovertibly established in one instance, proves the principle in all other instances, to which the facts will be found to apply. We may then infer, that the people of the United States intended to bind the several States, by the legislative power of the national Government.

In order to make the discovery, at which we ultimately aim, a second previous inquiry will naturally be—Did the people of the United States intend to bind the several States, by the executive power of the national Government? The affirmative answer to the former question directs, unavoidably, an affirmative answer to this. Ever since the time of Bracton, his maxim, I believe, has been deemed a good one—"*Supervacuum esset, leges condere, nisi esset qui leges tueretur.*" (It would be superfluous to make laws, unless those laws, when made, were to be enforced.) When the laws are plain, and the application of them is uncontroverted, they are enforced immediately by the executive authority of government. When the application of them is doubtful or intricate, the interposition of the judicial authority becomes necessary. The same principle, therefore, which directed us from the first to the second step, will direct us to the third and last step of our deduction. Fair and conclusive deduction, then, evinces that the people of the United States did vest this court with jurisdiction over the State of Georgia. The same truth may be deduced from the declared objects and the general texture of the Constitution of the United States. One of its declared objects is, to form a union more perfect than, before that time, had been formed. Before that time the Union possessed legislative, but unenforced legislative power over the States. Nothing could be more natural than to intend that this legislative power should be enforced by powers executive and judicial. Another declared object is "to establish justice." This points, in a particular manner, to the judicial authority. And when we view this object in conjunction with the declaration, "that no state shall pass a law impairing the obligation of contracts," we shall probably think that this object points, in a particular manner, to the jurisdiction of the court over the several States. What good purpose could this constitutional provision secure if a State might pass a law impairing the obligation of its own contracts, and be amenable, for such a violation of right, to no controlling judiciary power? We have seen, that on principles of general jurisprudence, a State, for the breach of a contract, may be liable for damages. A third declared object is, "to insure domestic tranquillity." This tranquillity is most likely to be disturbed by controversies between States. These consequences will be most peaceably and effectually decided by the establishment and by the exercise of a superintending judicial authority. By such exercise and establishment, the law of nations—the rule between contending States—will be enforced among the several States in the same manner as municipal law.

Whoever considers, in a combined and comprehensive view, the general texture of the Constitution, will be satisfied that the people of the United States intended to form themselves into a nation for national purposes. They instituted, for such purposes, a national Government complete in all its parts, with powers legislative, executive and judiciary; and in all those powers extending over the whole Nation. Is it congruous that, with regard to such purposes, any man or body of men, any person, natural or artificial, should be permitted to claim successfully an entire exemption from the jurisdiction of the national Government? Would not such claims, crowned with success, be repugnant to our very existence as a nation? When so many trains of deduction, coming from different quarters, converge and unite at last in the same point, we may safely conclude, as the legitimate result of this Constitution, that the State of Georgia is amenable to the jurisdiction of this court.

But, in my opinion, this doctrine rests not upon the legitimate result of fair and conclusive deduction from the Constitution; it is confirmed, beyond all doubt, by the direct and explicit declaration of the Constitution itself. "The judicial power of the United States shall extend to controversies between two states." Two States are supposed to have a controversy between them; this controversy is supposed to be brought before those vested with the judicial power of the United States; can the most consummate degree of professional ingenuity devise a mode by which this "controversy between two states" can be brought before a court of law, and yet neither of those States be a defendant? "The judicial power of the United States shall extend to controversies between a state and citizens of another state." Could the strictest legal language; could even that language which is peculiarly appropriated to an art, deemed by a great master to be one of the most honorable, laudable, and profitable things in our law; could this strict and appropriated language describe with more precise accuracy the cause now depending before the tribunal? Causes, and not parties to causes, are weighed by justice in her equal scales; on the former, solely, her attention is fixed; to the latter she is, as she is painted, blind. . . .

CHIEF JUSTICE JAY:

The question we are now to decide has been accurately

stated, viz.: Is a State suable by individual citizens of another State? . . .

The revolution, or rather the Declaration of Independence, found the people already united for general purposes, and at the same time, providing for their more domestic concerns, by state conventions, and other temporary arrangements. From the crown of Great Britain, the sovereignty of their country passed to the people of it; and it was then not an uncommon opinion, that the unappropriated lands, which belonged to that crown, passed, not to the people of the Colony or States within whose limits they were situated, but to the whole people; on whatever principles this opinion rested, it did not give way to the other, and thirteen sovereignties were considered as emerged from the principles of the revolution, combined with local convenience and considerations; the people nevertheless continued to consider themselves, in a national point of view, as one people; and they continued without interruption to manage their national concerns accordingly; afterwards, in the hurry of the war, and in the warmth of mutual confidence, they made a confederation of the States, the basis of a general Government. Experience disappointed the expectations they had formed from it; and then the people, in their collective and national capacity, established the present Constitution. It is remarkable that in establishing it, the people exercised their own rights, and their own proper sovereignty, and conscious of the plentitude of it, they declared with becoming dignity, "We the people of the United States," "do ordain and establish this Constitution." Here we see the people acting as sovereigns of the whole country; and in the language of sovereignty, establishing a Constitution by which it was their will, that the State Governments should be bound, and to which the state constitutions should be made to conform. Every state constitution is a compact made by and between the citizens of a state to govern themselves in a certain manner; and the Constitution of the United States is likewise a compact made by the people of the United States to govern themselves as to general objects, in a certain manner. By this great compact however, many prerogatives were transferred to the national Government, such as those of making war and peace, contracting alliances, coining money, &c. . . .

It may be asked, What is the precise sense and latitude in which the words "to establish justice," as here used, are to be understood? The answer to this question will result from the provisions made in the Constitution on this head. They are specified in the 2d section of the 3d article, where it is ordained, that the judicial power of the United States shall extend to . . . controversies between two or more States; because domestic tranquillity requires, that the contentions of States should be peaceably terminated by the common judicatory; and because, in a free country, justice ought not to depend on the will of either of the litigants . . .

It is politic, wise and good, that not only the controversies in which a State is plaintiff, but also those in which a State is defendant, should be settled; both cases, therefore, are within the reason of the remedy; and ought to be so adjudged, unless the obvious, plain and literal sense of the words forbid it. If we attend to the words, we find them to be express, positive, free from ambiguity, and without room for such implied expressions: "The judicial power of the United States shall extend to controversies between a state and citizens of another state." If the Constitution really meant to extend these powers only to those controversies in which a State might be plaintiff, to the exclusion of those in which citizens had demands against a State, it is inconceivable, that it should have attempted to convey that meaning in words, not only so incompetent, but also repugnant to it; if it meant to exclude a certain class of these controversies, why were they not expressly excepted; on the contrary, not even an intimation of such intention appears in any part of the Constitution. It cannot be pretended, that where citizens urge and insist upon demands against a State, which the State refuses to admit and comply with, that there is no controversy between them. If it is a controversy between them, then it clearly falls not only within the spirit, but the very words of the Constitution. What is it to the cause of justice, and how can it affect the definition of the word controversy, whether the demands which cause the dispute, are made by a State against citizens of another State, or by the latter against the former? When power is thus extended to a controversy, it necessarily, as to all judicial purposes, is also extended to those between whom it subsists. . . .

I perceive, and therefore candor urges me to mention, a circumstance, which seems to favor the opposite side of the question. It is this: the same section of the Constitution which extends the judicial power to controversies "between a state and the citizens of another state," does also extend that power to controversies to which the United States are a party. Now, it may be said, if the word party comprehends both plaintiff and defendant, it follows, that the United States may be sued by any citizen, between whom and them there may be a controversy. This appears to me to be fair reasoning; but the same principles of candor which urge me to mention this objection, also urge me to suggest an important difference between the two cases. It is this, in all cases of actions against States or individual citizens, the national courts are supported in all their legal and constitutional proceedings and judgments, by the arm of the executive power of the United States; but in cases of actions against the United States, there is no power which the courts can call to their aid. From this distinction, important conclusions are deducible, and they place the case of a State, and the case of the United States, in very different points of view. . . .

Justice Iredell dissented. . .

The supremacy of the Constitution over the States is beyond question.

2. *McCULLOCH v. MARYLAND* (1819)

This decision, one of Chief Justice Marshall's most notable ones, affirmed the supremacy of the Constitution as being inherent in its very nature. It is, therefore, an important step in the growth of federal power vis-a-vis the States.

Background: *In 1818 Maryland passed a law taxing the notes issued by banks not chartered by the States. The law was aimed at the Bank of the United States; McCulloch, the cashier of its Baltimore branch, refused to pay the $15,000 annual tax. Sued by the State, he lost the case in the Maryland Court of Appeals, and brought a writ of error against it to the United States Supreme Court. In this unanimous decision, the Supreme Court held that Maryland had no right to tax the Bank of the United States, and, consequently, the act of the state legislature was "unconstitutional and void."*

It is interesting to note that a century and a half later, a State court challenged this decision. On December 29, 1967, the New York State Court of Appeals ruled unanimously that the State could tax federally chartered banks—and that McCulloch v. Maryland *was obsolete. This, of course, is not the last word on the subject.*

Some Related Cases
(On Constitutional Supremacy):
United States v. Fisher (1805)
Martin v. Hunter's Lessee (1816)
Davis v. Elmira Savings Bank (1896)
Spokane County v. United States (1929)

CHIEF JUSTICE MARSHALL DELIVERED THE OPINION OF THE COURT:

In the case now to be determined, the defendant, a sovereign State, denies the obligation of a law enacted by the legislature of the Union; and the plaintiff, on his part, contests the validity of an Act which has been passed by the legislature of that State. The Constitution of our country, in its most interesting and vital parts, is to be considered; the conflicting powers of the Government of the Union and of its members, as marked in that Constitution, are to be discussed; and an opinion given, which may essentially influence the great operations of the Government. No tribunal can approach such a question without a deep sense of its importance, and of the awful responsibility involved in its decision. But it must be decided peacefully, or remain a source of hostile legislation, perhaps of hostility of a still more serious nature; and if it is to be so decided, by this tribunal alone can the decision be made. On the Supreme Court of the United States has the Constitution of our country devolved this important duty.

The first question made in the cause is, has Congress power to incorporate a bank? It has been truly said, that this can scarcely be considered as an open question, entirely unprejudiced by the former proceedings of the nation respecting it. The principle now contested was introduced at a very early period of our history, has been recognized by many successive legislatures, and has been acted upon by the judicial department, in cases of peculiar delicacy, as a law of undoubted obligation. . . .

The power now contested was exercised by the first Congress elected under the present Constitution. The bill for incorporating the Bank of the United States did not steal upon an unsuspecting legislature, and pass unobserved. Its principle was completely understood, and was opposed with equal zeal and ability. After being resisted, first in the fair and open field of debate, and afterwards in the executive cabinet, with as much persevering talent as any measure has ever experienced, and being supported by arguments which convinced minds as pure and as intelligent as this country can boast, it became a law. The original Act was permitted to expire; but a short experience of the embarrassments to which the refusal to revive it exposed the Government, convinced those who were most prejudiced against the measure of its necessity, and induced the passage of the present law. It would require no ordinary share of intrepidity to assert, that a measure adopted under these circumstances, was a bold and plain usurpation, to which the Constitution gave no countenance. These observations belong to the cause: but they are not made under the impression that, were the question entirely new, the law would be found irreconcilable with the Constitution.

In discussing this question, the counsel for the State of Maryland have deemed it of some importance, in the construction of the Constitution, to consider that instrument not as emanating from the people, but as the act of sovereign and independent States. The powers of the general Government, it has been said, are delegated by the States, who alone are truly sovereign; and must be exercised in subordination to the States, who alone possess supreme dominion. It would be difficult to sustain this proposition. The convention which framed the Constitution was, indeed, elected by the state legislatures. But the instrument, when it came from their hands, was a mere proposal, without obligation, or pretensions to it. It was reported to the then existing Congress of the United States, with a request that it might "be submitted to a convention of delegates, chosen in each state by the people thereof, under the recommendation of its legislature, for their assent and ratification." This mode of proceeding was adopted; and by the convention, by Congress, and by the state legislatures, the instrument was submitted to the *people*. They acted upon it, in the only manner in which they can act safely, effectively, and wisely, on such a subject, by assembling in convention. It is true, they assembled in their several States; and where else should they have assembled? No political dreamer was ever wild enough to think of breaking down the lines which separate the States, and of compounding the American people into one common mass. Of consequence, when they act, they act in their States. But the measures they adopt do not, on that account, cease to be the measures of the people themselves, or become the measures of the State Governments.

From these conventions the Constitution derives its whole authority. The Government proceeds directly from the people; is "ordained and established" in the name of the people; and is declared to be ordained, "in order to form a more perfect union, establish justice, insure domestic tranquillity, and secure the blessings of liberty, to themselves and to their posterity." The assent of the States, in their sovereign capacity, is implied in calling a convention, and thus submitting that instrument to the people. But the people were at perfect liberty to accept or reject it; and their act was final. It required not the affirmance, and could not be negatived, by the State Governments. The Constitution, when thus adopted, was of complete obligation, and bound the State sovereignties. . . .

It has been said that the people had already surrendered all their powers to the State sovereignties, and had nothing more to give. But, surely, the question whether they may resume and modify the powers granted to government, does not remain to be settled in this country. Much more might the legitimacy of the general Government be doubted, had it been created by the States. The powers delegated to the State sovereignties were to be exercised by themselves, not by a distinct and independent sovereignty, created by themselves. To the formation of a league, such as was the confederation, the State sovereignties were certainly competent. But when, "in order to form a more perfect union," it was deemed necessary to change this alliance into an effective government, possessing great and sovereign powers, and acting directly on the people, the necessity of referring it to the people, and of deriving its powers directly from them, was felt and acknowledged by all.

The Government of the Union, then (whatever may be the influence of this fact on the case), is emphatically and truly a government of the people. In form and in substance it emanates from them, its powers are granted by them, and are to be exercised directly on them, and for their benefit.

This Government is acknowledged by all to be one of enumerated powers. The principle, that it can exercise only the powers granted to it, would seem too apparent, to have required to be enforced by all those arguments, which its enlightened friends, while it was depending before the people, found it necessary to urge; that principle is now universally admitted. But the question respecting the extent of the powers actually granted, is perpetually arising, and will probably continue to arise, as long as our system shall exist. In discussing these questions, the conflicting powers of the general and State Governments must be brought into view, and the supremacy of their respective laws, when they are in opposition, must be settled.

If any one proposition could command the universal assent of mankind, we might expect that it would be this—that the Government of the Union, though limited in its powers, is supreme within its sphere of action. This would seem to result, necessarily, from its nature. It is the Government of all; its powers are delegated by all; it represents all, and acts for all. Though any one State may be willing to control its operations, no State is willing to allow others to control them. The nation, on those subjects on which it can act, must necessarily bind its component parts. But this question is not left to mere reason: the people have, in express terms, decided it, by saying, "this Constitution, and the laws of the United States, which shall be made in pursuance thereof," "shall be the supreme law of the land," and by requiring that the members of the state legislatures, and the officers of the executive and judicial departments of the States, shall take the oath of fidelity to it. The Government of the United States, then, though limited in its powers, is supreme; and its laws, when made in pursuance of the Constitution, form the supreme law of the land, "anything in the constitution or laws of any state, to the contrary notwithstanding."

Among the enumerated powers, we do not find that of establishing a bank or creating a corporation. But there is no phrase in the instrument which, like the articles of confederation, excludes incidental or implied powers; and which requires that everything granted shall be expressly and minutely described. Even the 10th Amendment, which was framed for the purpose of quieting the excessive jealousies which had been excited, omits the word "expressly," and declares only that the powers "not delegated to the United States, nor prohibited to the States, are reserved to the states or to the people"; thus leaving the question, whether the particular power which may become the subject of contest, has been delegated to the one government, or prohibited to the other, to depend on a fair construction of the whole instrument. The mén who drew and adopted this Amendment had experienced the embarrassments resulting from the insertion of this word in the articles of confederation, and probably omitted it, to avoid those embarrassments. A constitution, to contain an accurate detail of all the subdivisions of which its great powers will admit, and of all the means by which they may be carried into execution, would partake of the prolixity of a legal code, and could scarcely be embraced by the human mind. It would, probably, never be understood by the public. Its nature, therefore, requires, that only its great outlines should be marked, its important objects designated, and the minor ingredients which compose those objects, be deduced from the nature of the objects themselves. That this idea was entertained by the framers of the American Constitution, is not only to be inferred from the nature of the instrument, but from the language. Why else were some of the limitations, found in the 9th section of the 1st article, introduced? It is also, in some degree, warranted, by their having omitted to use any restrictive term which might prevent its receiving a fair and just interpretation. In considering this question, then, we must never forget, that it is a *constitution* we are expounding.

Although, among the enumerated powers of government, we do not find the word "bank," or "incorporation," we find the great powers, to lay and collect taxes; to borrow money; to regulate commerce; to declare and conduct war; and to raise and support armies and navies. The sword and the purse, all the external relations, and no inconsiderable portion of the industry of the nation, are intrusted to its government. It can never be pretended, that these vast powers draw after them others of inferior importance, merely because they are inferior. Such an idea can never be advanced. But it may with great reason be contended, that a government, intrusted with such ample powers, on the due execution of which the happiness and prosperity of the Nation so vitally depends, must also be intrusted with ample means for their execution. The power being given, it is the interest of the Nation to facilitate its execution. It can never be their interest, and cannot be presumed to have been their intention, to clog and embarrass its execution, by withholding the most appropriate means. Throughout this vast republic, from the St. Croix to the Gulf of Mexico, from the Atlantic to the Pacific, revenue is to be collected and expended, armies are to be marched and supported. The exigencies of the Nation may require, that the treasure raised in the north should be transported to the south, that raised in the east, conveyed to the west, or that this order should be reversed. Is that construction of the Constitution to be preferred, which would render these operations difficult, hazardous, and expensive? Can we adopt that construction (unless the words imperiously require it), which would impute to the framers of that instrument, when granting these powers for the public good, the intention of impending their exercise by withholding a choice of means? If, indeed, such be the mandate of the Constitution, we have only to obey; but that instrument does not profess to enumerate the means by which the powers it confers may be executed; nor does it prohibit the creation of a corporation, if the existence of such a being be essential to the beneficial exercise of those powers. It is, then, the subject of fair inquiry, how far such means may be employed.

It is not denied, that the powers given to the Government imply the ordinary means of execution. That, for example, of raising revenue, and applying it to national purposes, is admitted to imply the power of conveying money from place to place, as the exigencies of the nation may require, and of employing the usual means of conveyance. But it is denied, that the Government has its choice of means, or, that it may employ the most convenient means, if, to employ them, it be necessary to erect a corporation. On what foundation does this argument rest? On this alone: the power of creating a corporation, is one appertaining to sovereignty, and is not expressly conferred on Congress. This is true. But all legislative powers appertain to sovereignty. The original power of giving the law on any subject whatever, is a sovereign power; and if the Government of the Union is restrained from creating a corporation, as a means for performing its functions, on the single reason that the creation of a corporation is an act of sovereignty; if the sufficiency of this reason be acknowledged, there would be some difficulty in sustaining the authority of Congress to pass other laws for the accomplishment of the same objects. The Government which has a right to do an act, and has imposed on it, the duty of performing that act, must, according to the dictates of reason, be allowed to select the means; and those who contend that it may not select any appropriate means, that one particular mode of effecting the object is expected, take upon themselves the burden of establishing that exception. . . .

. . . The power of creating a corporation, though appertaining to sovereignty, is not, like the power of making war, or levying taxes, or of regulating commerce, a great substantive and independent power, which cannot be implied as incidental to other powers, or used as a means of executing them. It is never the end for which other powers are exercised, but a means by which other objects are accomplished. No contributions are made to charity, for the sake of an incorporation, but a corporation is created to administer the charity; no seminary of learning is instituted, in order to be incorporated, but the corporate character is conferred to subserve the purposes of education. No city was ever built, with the sole object of being incorporated, but is incorporated as affording the best means of being well governed. The power of creating a corporation is never used for its own sake, but for the purpose of effecting something else. No sufficient reason is, therefore, perceived, why it may not pass as incidental to those powers which are expressly given, if it be a direct mode of executing them.

But the Constitution of the United States has not left the right of Congress to employ the necessary means, for the execution of the powers conferred on the Government, to general reasoning. To its enumeration of powers is added, that of making "all laws which shall be necessary and proper, for carrying into execution the foregoing powers, and all other powers vested by this Constitution, in the government of the United States, or in any department thereof." The counsel for the State of Maryland have urged various arguments, to prove that this clause, though, in terms, a grant of power, is not so in effect; but is really restrictive of the general right, which might otherwise be implied, of selecting means for executing the enumerated powers. In support of this proposition, they have found it necessary to contend, that this clause was inserted for the purpose of conferring on Congress the power of making laws. That, without it, doubts might be entertained whether Congress could exercise its powers in the form of legislation.

But could this be the object for which it was inserted? . . . Could it be necessary to say, that a legislature should exercise legislative powers, in the shape of legislation? After allowing each house to prescribe its own course of proceeding, after describing the manner in which a bill should become a law, would it have entered into the mind of a single member of the convention, that an express power to make laws was necessary to enable the legislature to make them? That a legislature, endowed with legislative powers, can legislate, is a proposition too self-evident to have been questioned.

But the argument on which most reliance is placed, is drawn from the peculiar language of this clause. Congress is not empowered by it to make all laws, which may have relation to the powers conferred on the Government, but only such as may be "necessary and proper" for carrying them into execution. The word "necessary" is considered as controlling the whole sentence, and as limiting the right to pass laws for the execution of the granted powers, to such as are indispensable, and without which the power would be nugatory. That it excludes the choice of means, and leaves to Congress, in each case, that only which is most direct and simple.

Is it true, that this is the sense in which the word "necessary" is always used? Does it always import an absolute physical necessity, so strong, that one thing, to which another may be termed necessary, cannot exist without that other? We think it does not. If reference be had to its use, in the common affairs of the world, or in approved authors, we find that it frequently imports no more than that one thing is convenient, or useful, or essential to another. To employ the means necessary to an end, is generally understood as employing any means calculated to produce the end, and not as being confined to those single means, without which the end would be entirely unattainable. Such is the character of human language, that no word conveys to the mind, in all situations, one single definite idea; and nothing is more common than to use words in a figurative sense. Almost all compositions contain words, which, taken in their rigorous sense, would convey a meaning different from that which is obviously intended. It is essential to just construction, that many words which import something excessive, should be understood in a more mitigated sense—in that sense which common usage justifies. The word "necessary" is of this description. It has not a fixed character, peculiar to itself. It admits of all degrees of comparison; and is often connected with words, which increase or diminish the impression the mind receives of the urgency it imports. A thing may be necessary, very necessary, absolutely or indispensably necessary. To no mind would the same idea be conveyed by these several phrases. This comment on the word is well illustrated by the passage cited at the bar, from the 10th section of the 1st article of the Constitution. It is, we think, impossible to compare the sentence which prohibits a State from laying "imposts, or duties on imports or exports, except what may be *absolutely* necessary for executing its inspection laws," with that which authorizes Congress "to make all laws which shall be necessary and proper for carrying into execution" the powers of the general Government, without feeling a conviction, that the convention understood itself to change materially the meaning of the word "necessary" by prefixing the word "absolutely." This word, then, like others, is used in various senses; and, in its construction, the subject, the context, the intention of the person using them, are all to be taken into view.

Let this be done in the case under consideration. The subject is the execution of those great powers on which the welfare of a nation essentially depends. It must have been the intention of those who gave these powers, to insure, as far as human prudence could insure, their beneficial execution. This could not be done, by confining the choice of means to such narrow limits as not to leave it in the power of Congress to adopt any which might be appropriate, and which were conducive to the end. This provision is made in a constitution, intended to endure for ages to come, and consequently, to be adapted to the various *crises* of human affairs. To have prescribed the means by which government should, in all future time, execute its powers, would have been to change, entirely, the character of the instrument, and give it the properties of a legal code. It would have been an unwise attempt to provide, by immutable rules, for exigencies which, if foreseen at all, must have been seen dimly, and which can be best provided for as they occur. To have declared, that the best means shall not be used, but those alone, without which the power given would be nugatory, would have been to deprive the legislature of the capacity to avail itself of experience, to exercise its reason, and to accommodate its legislation to circumstances. If we apply this principle of construction to any of the powers of the Government, we shall find it so pernicious in its operation that we shall be compelled to discard it. . . .

The baneful influence of this narrow construction on all the operations of the Government, and the absolute impracticability of maintaining it, without rendering the Government incompetent to its great objects, might be illustrated by numerous examples drawn from the Constitution, and from our laws. The good sense of the public has pronounced, without hesitation, that the power of punishment appertains to sovereignty, and may be exercised, whenever the sovereign has a right to act, as incidental to his constitutional powers. It is a means for carrying into execution all sovereign powers, and may be used, although not indispensably necessary. It is a right incidental to the power, and conducive to its beneficial exercise.

If this limited construction of the word "necessary" must be abandoned, in order to punish, whence is derived the rule which would reinstate it, when the Government would carry its powers into execution, by means not vindictive in their nature? If the word "necessary" means "needful," "requisite," "essential," "conducive to," in order to let in the power of punishment for the infraction of law; why is it not equally comprehensive, when required to authorize the use of means which facilitate the execution of the powers of government, without the infliction of punishment?

In ascertaining the sense in which the word "necessary" is used in this clause of the Constitution, we may derive some aid from that with which it is associated. Congress shall have power "to make all laws which shall be necessary and proper to carry into execution" the powers of the Government. If the word "necessary" was used in that strict and rigorous sense for which the counsel for the State of Maryland contend, it would be an extraordinary departure from the usual course of the human mind, as exhibited in composition, to add a word, the only possible effect of which is, to qualify that strict and rigorous meaning; to present to the mind the idea of some choice of means of legislation, not strained and compressed within the narrow limits for which gentlemen contend.

But the argument which most conclusively demonstrates the error of the construction contended for by the counsel for the State of Maryland, is founded on the intention of the convention, as manifested in the whole clause. To waste time and argument in proving that, without it, Congress might carry its powers into execution, would be not much less idle than to hold a lighted taper to the sun. As little can it be required to prove, that in the absence of this clause, Congress would have some choice of means. That it might employ those which, in its judgment, would most advantageously effect the object to be accomplished. That any means adapted to the end, any means which tended directly to the execution of the constitutional powers of the Government, were in themselves constitutional. This clause, as construed by the State of Maryland, would abridge, and almost annihilate, this useful and necessary right of the legislature to select its means. That this could not be intended is, we should think, had it not been already controverted, too apparent for controversy.

We think so for the following reasons: 1st. The clause is placed among the powers of Congress, not among the limitations on those powers. 2d. Its terms purport to enlarge, not to diminish the powers vested in the Government. It purports to be an additional power, not a restriction on those already granted. No reason has been, or can be assigned, for thus concealing an intention to narrow the discretion of the national legislature, under words which purport to enlarge it. The Framers of the Constitution wished its adoption, and well knew that it would be endangered by its strength, not by its weakness. Had they been capable of using language which would convey to the eye one idea, and, after deep reflection, impress on the mind, another, they would rather have disguised the grant of power, than its limitation. If then, their intention had been, by this clause, to restrain the free use of means which might otherwise have been implied, that intention would have been inserted in another place, and would have been expressed in terms resembling these. "In carrying into execution the foregoing powers and all others," &c., "no laws shall be passed but such as are necessary and proper." Had the intention been to make this clause restrictive, it would unquestionably have been so in form as well as in effect.

The result of the most careful and attentive consideration bestowed upon this clause is, that if it does not enlarge, it cannot be construed to restrain the powers of Congress, or to impair the right of the legislature to exercise its best judgment in the selection of measures, to carry into execution the constitutional powers of the Government. If no other motive for its insertion can be suggested, a sufficient one is found in the desire to remove all doubts respecting the right to legislate on that vast mass of incidental powers which must be involved in the Constitution, if that instrument be not a splendid bauble.

We admit, as all must admit, that the powers of the Government are limited, and that its limits are not to be transcended. But we think the sound construction of the Constitution must allow to the national legislature that discretion, with respect to the means by which the powers it confers are to be carried into execution, which will enable that body to perform the high duties assigned to it, in the manner most beneficial to the people. Let the end be legitimate, let it be within the scope of the Constitution, and all means which are appropriate, which are plainly adapted to that end, which are not prohibited, but consistent with the letter and spirit of the Constitution, are constitutional. . . .

It being the opinion of the Court, that the Act incorporating the bank is constitutional; and that the power of establishing a branch in the State of Maryland might be properly exercised by the bank itself, we proceed to inquire—

Whether the State of Maryland may, without violating the Constitution, tax that branch? That the power of taxation is one of vital importance; that it is retained by the States; that it is not abridged by the grant of a similar power to the Government of the Union; that it is to be concurrently exercised by the two governments are truths which have never been denied. But such is the paramount character of the Constitution, that its capacity to withdraw any subject from the action of even this power, is admitted. The States are expressly forbidden to lay any duties on imports or exports, except what may be absolutely necessary for executing their inspection laws. If the obligation of this prohibition must be conceded—if it may restrain a State from exercising of its taxing power on imports and exports the same paramount character would seem to restrain, as it certainly may restrain, a State from such other exercise of this power, as is in its nature incompatible with, and repugnant to, the constitutional laws of the Union. A law, absolutely repugnant to another, as entirely repeals that other as if express terms of repeal were used.

On this ground, the counsel for the bank place its claim to be exempted from the power of a State to tax its operations. There is no express provision for the case, but the claim has been sustained on a principle which so entirely pervades the Constitution, is so intermixed with the materials which compose it, so interwoven with its web, so blended with its texture, as to be incapable of being separated from it, without rending it into shreds. This great principle is, that the Constitution and the laws made in pursuance thereof are supreme; that they control the Constitution and laws of the respective States, and cannot be controlled by them. From this, which may be almost termed an axiom, other propositions are deduced as corollaries, on the truth or error of which, and on their application to this case, the cause has been supposed to depend. These are, 1st. That a power to create implies a power to preserve: 2d. That a power to destroy, if wielded by a different hand, is hostile to, and incompatible with, these powers to create and preserve: 3d. That where this repugnancy exists, that authority which is supreme must control, not yield to that over which it is supreme. . . .

The power of Congress to create, and of course, to continue, the bank, was the subject of the preceding part of this opinion; and is no longer to be considered as questionable. That the power of taxing it by the States may be exercised so as to destroy it, is too obvious to be denied. But taxation is said to be an absolute power, which acknowledges no other limits than those expressly prescribed in the Constitution, and like sovereign power of every other description, is trusted to the discretion of those who use it. But the very terms of this argument admit, that the sovereignty of the State, in the article of taxation itself, is subordinate to, and may be controlled by, the Constitution of the United States. How far it has been controlled by that instrument must be a question of construction. In making this construction, no principle not declared, can be admissible, which would defeat the legitimate operations of a supreme government. It is of the very essence of supremacy, to remove all obstacles to its action within its own sphere, and so to modify every power vested in subordinate governments, as to exempt its own operations from their own influence. This effect need not be stated in terms. It is so involved in the declaration of supremacy, so necessarily implied in it, that the expression of it could not make it more certain. We must, therefore, keep it in view, while construing the Constitution. . . .

The sovereignty of a State extends to everything which exists by its own authority, or is introduced by its permission; but does it extend to those means which are employed by Congress to carry into execution—powers conferred on that body by the people of the United States? We think it demonstrable that it does not. Those powers are not given by the people of a single State. They are given by the people of the United States, to a government whose laws, made in pursuance of the Constitution, are declared to be supreme. Consequently, the people of a single State cannot confer a sovereignty which will extend over them.

If we measure the power of taxation residing in a State, by the extent of sovereignty which the people of a single State possess, and can confer on its government, we have an intelligible standard, applicable to every case to which the power may be applied. We have a principle which leaves the power of taxing the people and property of a State unimpaired; which leaves to a State the command of all its resources, and which places beyond its reach, all those powers which are conferred by the people of the United States on the Government of the Union, and all those means which are given for the purpose of carrying those powers into execution. We have a principle which is safe for the States, and safe for the Union. We are relieved, as we ought to be; from clashing sovereignty; from interfering powers; from a repugnancy between a right in one government to pull down, what there is an acknowledged right in another to build up; from the incompatibility of a right in one government to destroy, what there is a right in another to preserve. We are not driven to the perplexing inquiry, so unfit for the judicial department, what degree of taxation is the legitimate use, and what degree may amount to the abuse of the power. The attempt to use it on the means employed by the Government of the Union, in pursuance of the Constitution, is itself an abuse, because it is the usurpation of a power, which the people of a single State cannot give. We find, then, on just theory, a total failure of this original right to tax the means employed by the Government of the Union, for the execution of its powers. The right never existed, and the question whether it has been surrendered, cannot arise.

But, waiving this theory for the present, let us resume the inquiry, whether this power can be exercised by the respective States, consistently with a fair construction of the Constitution? That the power to tax involves the power to destroy; that the power to destroy may defeat and render useless the power to create; that there is a plain repugnance in conferring on one government a power to control the constitutional measures of another, which other, with respect to those very measures, is declared to be supreme over that which exerts the control, are propositions not to be denied. But all inconsistencies are to be reconciled by the magic of the word *confidence*. Taxation, it is said, does not necessarily and unavoidably destroy. To carry it to the excess of destruction, would be an abuse, to presume which, would banish that confidence which is essential to all government. But is this a case of confidence? Would the people of any one State trust those of another with a power to control the most significant operations of their State Government? We know they would not. Why, then, should we suppose, that the people of any one State should be willing to trust those of another with a power to control the operations of a government to which they have confided their most important and most valuable interests? In the legislature of the Union alone, are all represented. The legislature of the Union alone, therefore, can be trusted by the people with the power of controlling measures which concern all, in the confidence that it will not be abused. This, then, is not a case of confidence, and we must consider it as it really is.

If we apply the principle for which the State of Maryland contends, to the Constitution generally, we shall find it capable of changing totally the character of that instrument. We shall find it capable of arresting all the measures of the Government, and of prostrating it at the foot of the States. The American people have declared their Constitution and the laws made in pursuance thereof, to be supreme; but this principle would transfer the supremacy, in fact, to the States. If the States may tax one instrument, employed by the Government in the execution of its powers, they may tax any and every other instrument. They may tax the mail; they may tax the mint; they may tax patent rights; they may tax the papers of the custom-house; they may tax judicial process; they may tax all the means employed by the Government, to an excess which would defeat all the ends of government. This was not intended by the American people. They did not design to make their Government dependent on the States. . . .

. . . If the controlling power of the States be established; if their supremacy as to taxation be acknowledged; what is to restrain their exercising this control in any shape they may please to give it? Their sovereignty is not confined to taxation; that is not the only mode in which it might be displayed. The question is, in truth, a question of supremacy; and if the right of the States to tax the means employed by the general Government be conceded, the declaration that the Constitution, and the laws made in pursuance thereof, shall be the supreme law of the land, is empty and unmeaning declamation. . . .

It has also been insisted, that, as the power of taxation in the general and State Governments is acknowledged to be concurrent, every argument which would sustain the right of the general Government to tax banks chartered by the States, will equally sustain the right of the States to tax banks chartered by the general Government. But the two cases are not on the same reason. The people of all the States have created the general Government, and have conferred upon it the general power of taxation. The people of all the States, and the States themselves, are represented in Congress, and, by their representatives, exercise this power. When they tax the chartered institutions of the States, they tax their constituents; and these taxes must be uniform. But when a State taxes the operations of the Government of the United States, it acts upon institutions created, not by their own constituents, but by people over whom they claim no control. It acts upon the measures of a government created by others as well as themselves, for the benefit of others in common with themselves. The difference is that which always exists, and always must exist, between the action of the whole on a part, and the action of a part on the whole—between the laws of a government declared to be supreme, and those of a government which, when in opposition to those laws, is not supreme.

But if the full application of this argument could be admitted, it might bring into question the right of Congress to tax the state banks, and could not prove the right of the States to tax the Bank of the United States.

The Court has bestowed on this subject its most deliberate consideration. The result is a conviction that the States have no power, by taxation or otherwise, to retard, impede, burden, or in any manner control, the operations of the constitutional laws enacted by Congress to carry into execution the powers vested in the general Government. This is, we think, the unavoidable consequence of that supremacy which the Constitution has declared. We are unanimously of opinion, that the law passed by the legislature of Maryland, imposing a tax on the Bank of the United States, is unconstitutional and void.

This opinion does not deprive the States of any resources which they originally possessed. It does not extend to a tax paid by the real property of the bank in common with the other real property within the State, nor to a tax imposed on the interest which the citizens of Maryland may hold in this institution, in common with other property of the same description throughout the State. But this is a tax on the operations of the bank, and is, consequently, a tax on the operation of an instrument employed by the Government of the Union to carry its powers into execution. Such a tax must be unconstitutional.

The jurisdiction of the Supreme Court has supremacy over the States.

3. *COHENS v. VIRGINIA* (1821)

This case is, in essence, a further elaboration of Chief Justice Marshall's basic position that the Constitution is the supreme law of the land.

Background: *P. J. and M. J. Cohen were convicted in Virginia for selling lottery tickets in violation of a State statute. They brought a writ of error to the Supreme Court under Sec. 25 of the Judiciary Act of 1789. Virginia's defense was that it was exempt from such suits under the Eleventh Amendment. In this decision, Justice Marshall upheld Virginia on the merits of the case, but reaffirmed at great length the theory that under the Constitution the Supreme Court has jurisdiction over the States in "all the cases described" (under Art. III, Sec. 2).*

Some Related Cases
(On Judicial Supremacy):
Osborn v. Bank of the United States (1821)
In re Pacific Railway Commission (1887)
Smith v. Adams (1889)
Muskrat v. United States (1911)

MR. CHIEF JUSTICE MARSHALL DELIVERED THE OPINION OF THE COURT:

This is a writ of error to a judgment rendered in the Court of Hustings for the borough of Norfolk, on an information for selling lottery tickets, contrary to an Act of the legislature of Virginia. In the State court, the defendant claimed the protection of an Act of Congress. A case was agreed between the parties, which states the Act of Assembly on which the prosecution was founded, and the Act of Congress on which the defendant relied, and concludes in these words: "If upon this case the Court shall be of opinion that the Acts of Congress before mentioned were valid, and, on the true construction of those acts, the lottery tickets sold by the defendants as aforesaid, might lawfully be sold within the State of Virginia, notwithstanding the Act or statute of the general assembly of Virginia prohibiting such sale, then judgment to be entered for the defendants: And if the court should be of opinion that the statute or Act of the general assembly of the State of Virginia, prohibiting such sale, is valid, notwithstanding the said Acts of Congress, then judgment to be entered that the defendants are guilty, and that the commonwealth recover against them one hundred dollars and cost."

Judgment was rendered against the defendants; and the court in which it was rendered being the highest court of the State in which the cause was cognizable, the record has been brought into this court by a writ of error.

The defendant in error moves to dismiss this writ, for want of jurisdiction.

In support of this motion, three points have been made, and argued with the ability which the importance of the question merits. These points are—

1st. That a State is a defendant.

2nd. That no writ of error lies from this court to a state court.

[Point 3 has been omitted.]

The questions presented to the court by the two first points made at the bar are of great magnitude, and may truly be said vitally to affect the Union. They exclude the inquiry whether the Constitution and laws of the United States have been violated by the judgment which the plaintiffs in error seek to review; and maintain that, admitting such violation, it is not in the power of the Government to apply a corrective. They maintain that the Nation does not possess a department capable of restraining, peaceably, and by authority of law, any attempts which may be made, by a part, against the legitimate powers of the whole; and that the Government is reduced to the alternative of submitting to such attempts, or of resisting them by force. They maintain that the Constitution of the United States has provided no tribunal for the final construction of itself, or of the laws or treaties of the Nation; but that this power may be exercised in the last resort by the courts of every State of the Union. That the Constitution, laws and treaties may receive as many constructions as there are States; and that this is not a mischief, or, if a mischief is irremediable. . . .

1st. The first question to be considered is, whether the jurisdiction of this court is excluded by the character of the parties, one of them being a State, and the other a citizen of that State?

The 2d section of the third article of the Constitution defines the extent of the judicial power of the United States. Jurisdiction is given to the courts of the Union in two classes of cases. In the first, their jurisdiction depends on the character of the cause, whoever may be the parties. This class comprehends "all cases in law and equity arising under this Constitution, the laws of the United States, and treaties made, or which shall be made, under their authority." This clause extends the jurisdiction of the Court to all the cases described, without making in its terms any exception whatever, and without any regard to the condition of the party. If there be any exception, it is to be implied against the express words of the article.

In the second class, the jurisdiction depends entirely on the character of the parties. In this are comprehended "controversies between two or more states, between a state and citizens of another state," "and between a state and foreign states, citizens, or subjects." If these be the parties, it is entirely unimportant what may be the subject of controversy. Be it what it may, these parties have a constitutional right to come into the courts of the Union. . . .

If . . . a case arising under the Constitution, or a law, must be one in which a party comes into court to demand something conferred on him by the Constitution or a law, we think the construction too narrow. A case in law or equity consists of the right of the one party, as well as of the other, and may truly be said to arise under the Constitution or a law of the United States, whenever its correct decision depends on the construction of either. . . .

The jurisdiction of the Court, then, being extended by the letter of the Constitution to all cases arising under it, or under the laws of the United States, it follows that those who would withdraw any case of this description from that jurisdiction, must sustain the exemption they claim, on the spirit and true meaning of the Constitution, which spirit and true meaning must be so apparent as to overrule the words which its framers have employed. The counsel for the defendant in error have undertaken to do this; and have laid down the general proposition, that a sovereign independent State is not suable, except by its own consent.

This general proposition will not be controverted. But its consent is not requisite in each particular case. It may be given in a general law. And if a State has surrendered any portion of its sovereignty, the question whether a liability to suit be a part of this portion, depends on the instrument by which the surrender is made. If upon a just construction of that instrument, it shall appear that the State has submitted to be sued, then it has parted with this sovereign right of judging in every case on the justice of its own pretensions, and has intrusted that power to a tribunal in whose impartiality it confides.

The American States, as well as the American people, have believed a close and firm Union to be essential to their liberty and to their happiness. They have been taught by experience, that this Union cannot exist without a government for the whole; and they have been taught by the same experience that this government would be a mere shadow, that must disappoint all their hopes, unless invested with large portions of that sovereignty which belongs to independent States. Under the influence of this opinion, and thus instructed by experience, the American people in the conventions of their respective States, adopted the present Constitution.

If it could be doubted whether, from its nature, it were not supreme in all cases where it is empowered to act, that doubt would be removed by the declaration that "this constitution, and the laws of the United States which shall be made in pursuance thereof and all treaties made, or which shall be made, under the authority of the United States, shall be the supreme law of the land; and the judges in every state shall be bound thereby, anything in the constitution or laws of any state to the contrary notwithstanding."

This is the authoritative language of the American people; and, if gentlemen please, of the American States. It marks with lines too strong to be mistaken, the characteristic distinction between the Government of the Union and those of the States. The general Government, though limited as to its objects, is supreme with respect to those objects. This principle is a part of the Constitution; and if there be any who deny its necessity, none can deny its authority.

To this supreme Government ample powers are confided; and if it were possible to doubt the great purposes for which they were so confided, the people of the United States have declared that they are given "in order to form a more perfect union, establish justice, insure domestic tranquillity, provide for the common defense, promote the general welfare, and secure the blessings of liberty to themselves and their posterity."

With the ample powers confided to this supreme Government, for these interesting purposes, are connected many express and important limitations on the sovereignty of the States, which are made for the same purposes. The powers of the Union on the great subjects of war, peace, and commerce, and on many others, are in themselves limitations of the sovereignty of the States; but in addition to these, the sovereignty of the States is surrendered in many instances where the surrender can only operate to the benefit of the people, and where, perhaps, no other power is conferred on Congress than a conservative power to maintain the principles established in the Constitution. The maintenance of these principles in their purity is certainly among the great duties of the Government. One of the instruments by which this duty may be peaceably performed is the judicial department. It is authorized to decide all cases, of every description, arising under the Constitution or laws of the United States. From this general grant of jurisdiction, no exception is made of those cases in which a State may be a party. When we consider the situation of the Government of the Union and of a State, in relation to each other; the nature of our Constitution; the subordination of the State Governments to that Constitution; the great purpose for which jurisdiction over all cases arising under the Constitution and laws of the United States, is confided to the judicial department; are we at liberty to insert in this general grant, an exception of those cases in which a State may be a party? Will the spirit of the Constitution justify this attempt to control its words? We think it will not. We think a case arising under the Constitution or laws of the United States, is cognizable in the courts of the Union, whoever may be the parties to that case. . . .

One of the express objects, then, for which the judicial department was established, is the decision of controversies between States, and between a State and individuals. The mere circumstance, that a State is a party, gives jurisdiction to the Court. How, then, can it be contended, that the very same instrument, in the very same section, should be so construed, as that this same circumstance should withdraw a case from the jurisdiction of the Court, where the Constitution or laws of the United States are supposed to have been violated? The Constitution gave to every person having a claim upon a State, a right to submit his case to the Court of the Nation. However unimportant his claim might be, however little the community might be interested in its decision, the framers of our Constitution thought it necessary for the purpose of justice, to provide a tribunal as superior to influence as possible, in which that claim might be decided. . . .

The mischievous consequences of the construction contended for on the part of Virginia, are also entitled to great consideration. It would prostrate, it has been said, the Government and its laws at the feet of every State in the Union. And would not this be its effect? What power of the Government could be executed by its own means, in any State disposed to resist its execution by a course of legislation? The laws must be executed by individuals acting within the several States. If these individuals may be exposed to penalties, and if the courts of the Union cannot correct the judgments by which these penalties may be enforced, the course of the Government may be, at any time, arrested by the will of one of its members. Each member will possess a *veto* on the will of the whole. . . .

These collisions may take place in times of no extraordinary commotion. But a constitution is framed for ages to come, and is designed to approach immortality as nearly as human institutions can approach it. Its course cannot always be tranquil. It is exposed to storms and tempests, and its framers must be unwise statesmen indeed, if they have not provided it, as far as its nature will permit, with the means of self-preservation from the perils it may be destined to encounter. No government ought to be so defective in its organization, as not to contain within itself the means of securing the execution of its own laws against other dangers than those which occur every day. Courts of justice are the means most usually employed; and it is reasonable to expect that a government should repose on its own courts, rather than on others. There is certainly nothing in the circumstances under which our Constitution was formed; nothing in the history of the times, which would justify the opinion that the confidence reposed in the States was so implicit as to leave in them and their tribunals the power of resisting or defeating, in the form of law, the legitimate measures of the Union. . . .

. . . If jurisdiction depended entirely on the character of the parties, and was not given where the parties have not an original right to come into court, that part of the 2d section of the 3d article, which extends the judicial power to all cases arising under the Constitution and laws of the United States, would be surplusage. It is to give jurisdiction where the character of the parties would not give it, that this very important part of the clause was inserted. It may be true, that the partiality of the state tribunals, in ordinary controversies between a State and its citizens, was not apprehended, and therefore the judicial power of the Union was not extended to such cases; but this was not the sole nor the greatest object for which this department was created. A more important, a much more interesting object, was the preservation of the Constitution and laws of the United States, so far as they can be preserved by judicial authority; and therefore the jurisdiction of the courts of the Union was expressly extended to all cases arising under that Constitution and those laws. If the Constitution or laws may be violated by proceedings instituted by a State against its own citizens, and if that violation may be such as essentially to affect the Constitution and the laws, such as to arrest the progress of the government in its constitutional course, why should these cases be excepted from that provision which expressly extends the judicial power of the Union to *all* cases arising under the Constitution and laws? . . .

It is most true, that this court will not take jurisdiction if it should not: but it is equally true, that it must take jurisdiction, if it should. The judiciary cannot, as the legislature may, avoid a measure, because it approaches the confines of the Constitution. We cannot pass it by, because it is doubtful. With whatever doubts, with whatever difficulties, a case may be attended, we must decide it, if it be brought before us. We have no more right to decline the exercise of jurisdiction which is given, than to usurp that which is not given. The one or the other would be treason to the Constitution. Questions may occur, which we would gladly avoid; but we cannot avoid them. All we can do is, to exercise our best judgment, and conscientiously to perform our duty. In doing this, on the present occasion, we find this tribunal invested with appellate jurisdiction in all cases arising under the Constitution and laws of the United States. We find no exception to this grant, and we cannot insert one. . . .

This leads to a consideration of the 11th amendment. It is in these words: "The judicial power of the United States shall not be construed to extend to any suit in law or equity commenced or prosecuted against one of the United States, by citizens of another state, or by citizens or subjects of any foreign state." It is a part of our history, that, at the adoption of the Constitution, all the States were greatly indebted; and the apprehension that these debts might be prosecuted in the federal courts, formed a very serious objection to that instrument. Suits were instituted; and the court maintained its jurisdiction. The alarm was general; and, to quiet the apprehensions that were so extensively entertained, this amendment was proposed in Congress, and adopted by the State legislatures. That its motive was not to maintain the sovereignty of a State from the degradation supposed to attend a compulsory appearance before the tribunal of the nation, may be inferred from the terms of the amendment. It does not comprehend controversies between two or more States, or between a State and a foreign state. The jurisdiction of the court still extends to these cases: and in these a State may still be sued. We must ascribe the amendment, then, to some other cause than the dignity of a State. There is no difficulty in finding this cause. Those who were inhibited from commencing a suit against a State, or from prosecuting one which might be commenced before the adoption of the amendment, were persons who might probably be its creditors. There was not much reason to fear that foreign or sister states would be creditors to any considerable amount, and there was reason to retain the jurisdiction of the Court in those cases, because it might be essential to the preservation of peace. The amendment, therefore, extended to suits commenced or prosecuted by individuals, but not to those brought by States. . . .

A general interest might well be felt in leaving to a State the full power of consulting its convenience in the adjustment of its debts, or of other claims upon it; but no interest could be felt in so changing the relations between the whole and its parts, as to strip the Government of the means of protecting, by the instrumentality of its courts, the Constitution and laws from active violation. . . .

Under the Judiciary Act, the effect of a writ of error is simply to bring the record into court, and submit the judgment of the inferior tribunal to re-examination. It does not in any manner act upon the parties; it acts only on the record. It removes the record into the supervising tribunal. Where, then, a State obtains a judgment against an individual, and the court rendering such judgment overrules a defense set up under the Constitution or laws of the United States, the transfer of this record into the Supreme Court for the sole purpose of inquiring whether the judgment violates the Constitution of the United States, can, with no propriety, we think, be denominated a suit commenced or prosecuted against the State whose judgment is so far re-examined. Nothing is demanded from the State. No claim against it or any description is asserted or prosecuted. The party is not to be restored to the possession of anything. Essentially, it is an appeal on a single point; and the defendant who appeals from a judgment rendered against him, is never said to commence or prosecute a suit against the plaintiff who has obtained the judgment. . . .

It is, then, the opinion of the Court, that the defendant who removes a judgment rendered against him by a state court into this court, for the purpose of re-examining the question, whether that judgment be in violation of the Constitution or laws of the United States, does not commence or prosecute a suit against the state. . . .

2d. The second objection to the jurisdiction of the Court is, that its appellate power cannot be exercised, in any case, over the judgment of a state court.

This objection is sustained chiefly by arguments drawn from the supposed total separation of the judiciary of a State from that of the Union, and their entire independence of each other. The argument considers the federal judiciary as completely foreign to that of a State; and as being no more connected with it, in any respect whatever, than the court of a foreign state. If this hypothesis be just, the argument founded on it is equally so; but if the hypothesis be not supported by the Constitution, the argument fails with it.

This hypothesis is not founded on any words in the Constitution, which might seem to countenance it, but on the unreasonableness of giving a contrary construction to words which seem to require it; and on the incompatibility of the application of the appellate jurisdiction to the judgments of state courts, with that constitutional relation which subsists between the Government of the Union and the governments of those States which compose it.

Let this unreasonableness, this total incompatibility, be examined.

That the United States form, for many, and for most important purposes, a single nation, has not yet been denied. In war, we are one people. In making peace, we are one people. In all commercial regulations, we are one and the same people. In many other respects, the American people are one; and the Government which is alone capable of controlling and managing their interests in all these respects, is the Government of the Union. It is their government, and in that character, they have no other. America has chosen to be, in many respects, and to many purposes, a nation; and for all these purposes, her government is complete; to all these objects it is competent. The people have declared, that in the exercise of all powers given for these objects, it is supreme. It can, then, in effecting these objects, legitimately control all individuals or governments within the American territory. The constitution and laws of a State, so far as they are repugnant to the Constitution and laws of the United States, are absolutely void. These States are constituent parts of the United States; they are members of one great empire—for some purposes sovereign, for some purposes subordinate.

In a government so constituted, is it unreasonable, that the judicial power should be competent to give efficacy to the constitutional laws of the legislature? That department can decide on the validity of the constitution or law of a State, if it be repugnant to the Constitution or to a law of the United States. Is it unreasonable, that it should also be empowered to decide on the judgment of a state tribunal enforcing such unconstitutional law? Is it so very unreasonable, as to furnish a justification for controlling the words of the Constitution?

We think it is not. We think that in a government acknowledgedly supreme, with respect to objects of vital interest to the nation, there is nothing inconsistent with sound reason, nothing incompatible with the nature of government, in making all its departments supreme, so far as respects those objects, and so far as is necessary to their attainment. The exercise of the appellate power over those judgments of the state tribunals which may contravene the Constitution or laws of the United States, is, we believe, essential to the attainment of those objects.

The propriety of entrusting the construction of the Constitution, and laws made in pursuance thereof, to the judiciary of the Union has not, we believe, as yet, been drawn into question. It seems to be a corollary from this political axiom, that the federal courts should either possess exclusive jurisdiction in such cases, or a power to revise the judgment rendered in them, by the state tribunals. If the federal and state courts have concurrent jurisdiction in all cases arising under the Constitution, laws, and treaties of the United States; and if a case of this description brought in a state court cannot be removed before judgment, nor revised after judgment, then the construction of the Constitution, laws, and treaties of the United States is not confided particularly to their judicial department, but is confided equally to that department and to the state courts, however they may be constituted. "Thirteen independent courts," says a very celebrated statesman (and we have now more than twenty such courts), "of final jurisdiction over the same causes, arising upon the same laws, is a hydra in government, from which nothing but contradiction and confusion can proceed."

Dismissing the unpleasant suggestion, that any motives which may not be fairly avowed, or which ought not to exist, can ever influence a State or its courts, the necessity of uniformity, as well as correctness in expounding the Constitution and laws of the United States, would itself suggest the propriety of vesting in some single tribunal the power of deciding, in the last resort, all cases in which they are involved.

We are not restrained, then, by the political relations between the general and State Governments, from construing the words of the Constitution, defining the judicial power, in their true sense. We are not bound to construe them more restrictively than they naturally import.

They give to the Supreme Court appellate jurisdiction in all cases arising under the Constitution, laws, and treaties of the United States. The words are broad enough to comprehend all cases of this description, in whatever court they may be decided. . . .

The Framers of the Constitution would naturally examine the state of things existing at the time; and their work sufficiently attests that they did so. All acknowledge that they were convened for the purpose of strengthening the confederation by enlarging the powers of the Government, and by giving efficacy to those which it before possessed, but could not exercise. They inform us themselves, in the instrument they presented to the American public, that one of its objects was to form a more perfect union. . . .

This opinion has been already drawn out to too great a length to admit of entering into a particular consideration of the various forms in which the counsel who made this point has, with much ingenuity, presented his argument to the Court. The argument, in all its forms, is essentially the same. It is founded, not on the words of the Constitution, but on its spirit —a spirit extracted, not from the words of the instrument, but from his view of the nature of our Union, and of the great fundamental principle on which the fabric stands. To this argument, in all its forms, the same answer may be given. Let the nature and objects of our Union be considered; let the great fundamental principles, on which the fabric stands, be examined; and we think, the result must be, that there is nothing so extravagantly absurd, in giving to the court of the nation the power of revising the decisions of local tribunals, on questions which affect the nation, as to require that words which import this power should be restricted by a forced construction. . . .

Judgment affirmed.

[On the merits of the case, the Court held that the federal statute authorizing a lottery in the District of Columbia had no effect outside the limits of the District, and therefore upheld the conviction under the Virginia statute.]

The treaty-making power of Congress has supremacy over the States.

4. *MISSOURI v. HOLLAND* (1920)

In this decision the powers of the national Government, if written into a treaty, take supremacy over the States and are almost limitless.

Background: *The case involved the constitutionality of the Migratory Bird Treaty Act (July 3, 1918), which, pursuant to a treaty between the United States and Great Britain, undertook to regulate and protect bird migration between Can-*

ada and the United States. The State of Missouri sought to prevent a federal game warden from enforcing the act, and upon losing the case in the District Court, appealed to the Supreme Court. Speaking for the majority (seven to two) of the Court, Justice Holmes held that Congress had wide powers under the treaty-making provision of the Constitution.

Some Related Cases
(On the Treaty-Making Power):
Geofroy v. Riggs (1890)
In re Ross (1891)
Neely v. Henkel (1901)
Nielsen v. Johnson (1929)

MR. JUSTICE HOLMES DELIVERED THE OPINION OF THE COURT:

. . . The question raised is the general one whether the treaty and statute are void as an interference with the rights reserved to the States.

To answer this question it is not enough to refer to the Tenth Amendment, reserving the powers not delegated to the United States, because by Article II, Section 2, the power to make treaties is delegated expressly, and by Article VI treaties made under the authority of the United States, along with the Constitution and laws of the United States made in pursuance thereof, are declared the supreme law of the land. If the treaty is valid there can be no dispute about the validity of the statute under Article I, Section 8, as a necessary and proper means to execute the powers of the Government. The language of the Constitution as to the supremacy of treaties being general, the question before us is narrowed to an inquiry into the ground upon which the present supposed exception is placed.

It is said that a treaty cannot be valid if it infringes the Constitution, that there are limits, therefore, to the treaty-making power, and that one such limit is that what an Act of Congress could not do unaided, in derogation of the powers reserved to the States, a treaty cannot do. An earlier Act of Congress that attempted by itself and not in pursuance of a treaty to regulate the killing of migratory birds within the States had been held bad in the District Court. *United States v. Shauver,* 214 Fed. Rep. 154. *United States v. McCullagh,* 221 Fed. Rep. 288. Those decisions were supported by arguments that migratory birds were owned by the States in their sovereign capacity for the benefit of their people, and that under cases like *Geer v. Connecticut,* 161 U.S. 519, this control was one that Congress had no power to displace. The same argument is supposed to apply now with equal force.

Whether the two cases cited were decided rightly or not they cannot be accepted as a test of the treaty power. Acts of Congress are the supreme law of the land only when made in pursuance of the Constitution, while treaties are declared to be so when made under the authority of the United States. It is open to question whether the authority of the United States means more than the formal acts prescribed to make the convention. We do not mean to imply that there are no qualifications to the treaty-making power; but they must be ascertained in a different way. It is obvious that there may be matters of the sharpest exigency for the national well-being that an Act of Congress could not deal with but that a treaty followed by such an Act could, and it is not lightly to be assumed that, in matters requiring national action, "a power which must belong to and somewhere reside in every civilized government" is not to be found. *Andrews v. Andrews,* 188 U.S. 14, 33. What was said in that case with regard to the powers of the States applies with equal force to the powers of the nation in cases where the States individually are incompetent to act. We are not yet discussing the particular case before us but only are considering the validity of the test proposed. With regard to that we may add that when we are dealing with words that also are a constituent act, like the Constitution of the United States we must realize that they have called into life a being the development of which could not have been foreseen completely by the most gifted of its begetters. It was enough for them to realize or to hope that they had created an organism; it has taken a century and has cost their successors much sweat and blood to prove that they created a nation. The case before us must be considered in the light of our whole experience and not merely in that of what was said a hundred years ago. The treaty in question does not contravene any prohibitory words to be found in the Constitution. The only question is whether it is forbidden by some invisible radiation from the general terms of the Tenth Amendment. We must consider what this country has become in deciding what the Amendment has reserved.

The State as we have intimated founds its claim of exclusive authority upon an assertion of title to migratory birds, an assertion that is embodied in statute. No doubt it is true that as between a State and its inhabitants the State may regulate the killing and sale of such birds, but it does not follow that its authority is exclusive of paramount powers. To put the claim of the State upon title is to lean upon a slender reed. Wild birds are not in the possession of anyone; and possession is the beginning of ownership. The whole foundation of the State's rights is the presence within their jurisdiction of birds that yesterday had not arrived, tomorrow may be in another State and in a week a thousand miles away. If we are to be accurate we cannot put the case of the State upon higher ground than that the treaty deals with creatures that for the moment are within the State borders, that it must be carried out by officers of the United States within the same territory, and that but for the treaty the State would be free to regulate this subject itself. . . .

Here a national interest of very nearly the first magnitude is involved. It can be protected only by national action in concert with that of another power. The subject-matter is only transitorily within the State and has no permanent habitat therein. But for the treaty and the statute there soon might be no birds for any powers to deal with. We see nothing in the Constitution that compels the Government to sit by while a food supply is cut off and the protectors of our forests and our crops are destroyed. It is not sufficient to rely upon the States. The reliance is vain, and were it otherwise, the question is whether the United States is forbidden to act. We are of opinion that the treaty and statute must be upheld. *Carey v. South Dakota*, 250 U.S. 118.

Decree affirmed.

Mr. Justice Van Devanter and Mr. Justice Pitney dissent.

Congress is paramount in the field of sedition regulation.

5. *PENNSYLVANIA v. NELSON* (1956)

The Supreme Court here affirmed the supremacy of the national Government in regulating sedition acts.

Background: *Nelson, a member of the Communist Party, was convicted under a Pennsylvania sedition law. The Pennsylvania Supreme Court reversed the conviction on the ground that sedition against the United States was a federal, and not a state matter and was controlled by the Smith Act of 1940. Pennsylvania appealed to the United States Supreme Court, and the latter, by a vote of six to three (Justices Reed, Burton, and Minton dissenting), upheld that state's Supreme Court ruling.*

Some Related Cases
(On Sedition):

Dennis v. United States (1951) (see p 276)
Yates v. United States (1957)
Barenblatt v. United States (1959)
Scales v. United States (1959)
Gojack v. United States (1966)

MR. JUSTICE WARREN DELIVERED THE OPINION OF THE COURT:

The precise holding of the [Pennsylvania] court, and all that is before us for review, is that the Smith Act of 1940, as amended in 1948, which prohibits the knowing advocacy of the overthrow of the Government of the United States by force and violence, supersedes the enforceability of the Pennsylvania Sedition Act which proscribes the same conduct. . . .

It should be said at the outset that the decision in this case does not affect the right of States to enforce their sedition laws at times when the Federal Government has not occupied the field and is not protecting the entire country from seditious conduct. The distinction between the two situations was clearly recognized by the court below. Nor does it limit the jurisdiction of the States where the Constitution and Congress have specifically given them concurrent jurisdiction, as was done under the Eighteenth Amendment and the Volstead Act. . . . Neither does it limit the right of the State to protect itself at any time against sabotage or attempted violence of all kinds. Nor does it prevent the State from prosecuting where the same act constitutes both a federal offense and a state offense under the police power. . . .

Where, as in the instant case, Congress has not stated specifically whether a federal statute has occupied a field in which the States are otherwise free to legislate, different criteria have furnished touchstones for decision. Thus,

"This Court, in considering the validity of state laws in the light of . . . federal laws touching the same subject, has made use of the following expressions: conflicting; contrary to; occupying the field; repugnance; difference; irreconcilability; inconsistency; violation; curtailment; and interference. But none of these expressions provides an infallible constitutional test or an exclusive constitutional yardstick. In the final analysis, there can be no one crystal clear, distinctly marked formula." *Hines v. Davidowitz,* 312 U.S. 52.

[In a footnote, Chief Justice Warren dismisses a point treated as crucial near the end of Justice Reed's dissenting opinion, namely, that Congress specifically showed its intention not to supersede state criminal statutes by any provision of Title 18 USC, where the Smith Act appears. The Chief Justice points out that Section 3231 provides for the original jurisdiction of the district courts, followed immediately by the provision cited by Justice Reed. "Nothing in this Title shall be held to take away or impair the jurisdiction of the courts of the several States under the laws thereof." The Chief Justice concludes that "the office of the second sentence is merely to limit the effect of the jurisdictional grant of the first sentence. There was no intention to resolve particular supersession questions by the Section."]

. . . In this case, we think that each of several tests of supersession is met.

First. "The scheme of federal regulation is so pervasive as to make reasonable the inference that Congress left no room for the States to supplement it.

". . . Looking to all of [the federal Acts] in the aggregate, the conclusion is inescapable that Congress has intended to occupy the field of sedition. Taken as a whole, they evince a congressional plan which makes it reasonable to determine that no room has been left for the States to supplement it. Therefore, a state sedition statute is superseded regardless of whether it purports to supplement the federal law. . . ."

Second, the federal statutes "touch a field in which the federal interest is so dominant that the federal system [must] be assumed to preclude enforcement of state laws on the same subject." . . .

Third, enforcement of state sedition acts presents a serious danger of conflict with the administration of the federal program. Since 1939, in order to avoid a hampering of uniform enforcement of its program by sporadic local prosecutions, the Federal Government has urged local authorities not to intervene in such matters, but to turn over to the federal authorities immediately and unevaluated all information concerning subversive activities.

Since we find that Congress has occupied the field to the exclusion of parallel state legislation, that the dominant interest of the Federal Government precludes state intervention, and that the administration of state Acts would conflict with the operation of the federal plan, we are convinced that the decision of the Supreme Court of Pennsylvania is unassailable.

We are not unmindful of the risk of compounding punishments which would be created by finding concurrent state power. In our view of the case, we do not reach the question whether the double or multiple punishment for the same overt acts directed against the United States has constitutional sanction. Without compelling indication to the contrary, we will not assume that Congress intended to permit the possibility of double punishment. . . .

The judgment of the Supreme Court of Pennsylvania is

Affirmed.

Chapter VIII

Judicial Review and the Constitution

"The judicial power of the United States, shall be vested in one Supreme Court . . ."—Art. III, Sec. 1

"The judicial power shall extend to all cases, in law and equity, arising under the Constitution . . ."—Art. III, Sec. 2

In this Chapter:
Marbury v. Madison (1803)
Dred Scott v. Sandford (1857)
Baker v. Carr (1962)

The Supreme Court has the power to void legislation repugnant to the Constitution.

6. *MARBURY v. MADISON* (1803)

The importance of this case lies in the fact that it was the first one in which the Supreme Court ruled that a law of Congress was void. This established a precedent which has been followed ever since.

Background: *On the eve of his retirement from the Presidency, John Adams appointed William Marbury justice of the peace. The new President, Thomas Jefferson, ordered his Secretary of State, James Madison, not to deliver the commission to Marbury. The latter then sued for a writ of mandamus requiring Madison to give him his commission. In his decision, Chief Justice Marshall made two points. One was that the President had no right to deny Marbury his commis-*

sion; the second was that the Judiciary Act of 1789, which gave the Supreme Court the power to issue writs of mandamus, was contrary to the Constitution. Thus the Supreme Court took upon itself the historic power of declaring Acts of Congress unconstitutional and, therefore, void.

Some Related Cases
(On Judicial Review):

Van Horne's Lessee v. Dorrance (1795)
Ware v. Hylton (1797)
Adkins v. Children's Hospital (1923)
United States v. Butler (1936)

MR. CHIEF JUSTICE MARSHALL:

The question whether an Act repugnant to the Constitution can become the law of the land, is a question deeply interesting to the United States; but, happily, not of an intricacy proportioned to its interest. It seems only necessary to recognize certain principles, supposed to have been long and well established, to decide it.

That the people have an original right to establish, for their future government, such principles as, in their opinion, shall most conduce to their own happiness, is the basis on which the whole American fabric has been erected. The exercise of this original right is a very great exertion; nor can it nor ought it to be frequently repeated. The principles, therefore, so established, are deemed fundamental. And as the authority from which they proceed is supreme, and can seldom act, they are designed to be permanent. This original and supreme will organizes the government, and assigns to different departments their respective powers. It may either stop here, or establish certain limits not to be transcended by those departments.

The Government of the United States is of the latter description. The powers of the legislature are defined and limited; and that those limits may not be mistaken, or forgotten, the Constitution is written. To what purpose are powers limited, and to what purpose is that limitation committed to writing, if these limits may, at any time, be passed by those intended to be restrained? The distinction between a government with limited and unlimited powers is abolished, if those limits do not confine the persons on whom they are imposed, and if acts prohibited and acts allowed are of equal obligation. It is a proposition too plain to be contested, that the Constitution controls any legislative Act repugnant to it; or, that the legislature may alter the Constitution by an ordinary Act.

Between these alternatives there is no middle ground. The Constitution is either a superior paramount law, unchangeable by ordinary means, or it is on a level with ordinary legislative Acts, and, like other Acts, is alterable when the legislature shall please to alter it. If the former part of the alternative be true, then a legislative Act contrary to the Constitution is not law; if the latter part be true, then written constitutions are absurd attempts, on the part of the people, to limit a power in its own nature illimitable.

Certainly all those who have framed written constitutions contemplate them as forming the fundamental and paramount law of the nation, and, consequently, the theory of every such government must be, that an Act of the Legislature, repugnant to the Constitution, is void. This theory is essentially attached to a written constitution, and is consequently to be considered, by this court, as one of the fundamental principles of our society. It is not, therefore, to be lost sight of in the further consideration of this subject.

If an Act of the Legislature, repugnant to the Constitution, is void, does it, notwithstanding its validity, bind the courts, and oblige them to give it effect? Or, in other words, though it be not law, does it constitute a rule as operative as if it was a law? This would be to overthrow in fact what was established in theory; and would seem, at first, an absurdity too gross to be insisted on. It shall, however, receive a more attentive consideration.

It is emphatically the province and duty of the judicial department to say what the law is. Those who apply the rule to particular cases, must of necessity expound and interpret that rule. If two laws conflict with each other, the courts must decide on the operation of each. So if a law be in opposition to the Constitution; if both the law and the Constitution apply to a particular case, so that the Court must either decide that case conformably to the law, disregarding the Constitution, or conformably to the Constitution, disregarding the law, the court must determine which of these conflicting rules governs the case. This is of the very essence of judicial duty. If, then, the courts are to regard the Constitution, and the Constitution is superior to any ordinary Act of the Legislature, the Constitution, and not such ordinary Act, must govern the case to which they both apply.

Those, then, who controvert the principle that the Constitution is to be considered, in court, as a paramount law, are reduced to the necessity of maintaining that courts must close their eyes on the Constitution, and see only the law. This doctrine would subvert the very foundation of all written constitutions. It would declare that an Act, which, according to the principles and theory of our government, is entirely void, is yet, in practice, completely obligatory. It would declare that if the legislature shall do what is expressly forbidden, such Act, notwithstanding the express prohibition, is in reality effectual. It would be giving to the Legislature a practical and real omnipotence, with the same breath which professes to restrict their powers within narrow limits. It is prescribing limits, and declaring that those limits may be passed at pleasure.

That it thus reduces to nothing what we have deemed the greatest improvement on political institutions, a written constitution, would of itself be sufficient, in America, where written constitutions have been viewed with so much reverence, for rejecting the construction. But the peculiar expressions of the Constitution of the United States furnish additional arguments in favor of its rejection. The judicial power of the United States is extended to all cases arising under the Constitution. Could it be the intention of those who gave this power, to say that in using it the Constitution should not be looked into? That a case arising under the Constitution should be decided without examining the instrument under which it arises? This is too extravagant to be maintained. In some cases, then, the Constitution must be looked into by the judges. And if they can open it at all, what part of it are they forbidden to read or to obey?

There are many other parts of the Constitution which serve to illustrate this subject. It is declared that "no tax or duty shall be laid on articles exported from any State." Suppose a duty on the export of cotton, of tobacco, or of flour; and a suit instituted to recover it. Ought judgment to be rendered in such a case? Ought the judges to close their eyes on the Constitution, and only see the law? The Constitution declares "that no bill of attainder or *ex post facto* law shall be passed." If, however, such a bill should be passed, and a person should be prosecuted under it, must the court condemn to death those victims whom the Constitution endeavors to preserve? "No person," says the Constitution, "shall be convicted of treason unless on the testimony of two witnesses to the same overt act, or on confession in open court." Here the language of the Constitution is addressed especially to the courts. It prescribes, directly for them, a rule of evidence not to be departed from. If the legislature should change that rule, and declare one witness, or a confession out of court, sufficient for conviction, must the constitutional principle yield to the legislative Act?

From these, and many other selections which might be made, it is apparent that the framers of the Constitution contemplated that instrument as a rule for the government of the courts, as well as of the legislature. Why otherwise does it direct the judges to take an oath to support it? This oath certainly applies in an especial manner to their conduct in their official character. How immoral to impose it on them, if they were to be used as the instruments, and the knowing instruments, for violating what they swear to support! The oath of office, too, imposed by the legislature, is completely demonstrative of the legislative opinion on this subject. It is in these words: "I do solemnly swear that I will administer justice without respect to persons, and do equal right to the poor and to the rich; and that I will faithfully and impartially discharge all the duties incumbent on me as . . . , according to the best of my abilities and understanding, agreeably to the Constitution and laws of the United States." Why does a judge swear to discharge his duties agreeably to the Constitution of the United States, if that Constitution forms no rules for his government—if it is closed upon him, and cannot be inspected by him? If such be the real state of things, this is worse than solemn mockery. To prescribe, or to take this oath, becomes equally a crime.

It is also not entirely unworthy of observation, that in declaring what shall be the supreme law of the land, the Constitution itself is first mentioned; and not the laws of the United States generally, but those only which shall be made in pursuance of the Constitution, have that rank. Thus, the particular phraseology of the Constitution of the United States confirms and strengthens the principle, supposed to be essential to all written constitutions, that a law repugnant to the Constitution, is void; and that courts, as well as other departments, are bound by that instrument.

The rule must be discharged.

[Mandamus denied.]

The Court's power to define citizenship.

7. *DRED SCOTT v. SANDFORD* (1857)

This is one of the most famous as well as history-making decisions of the United States Supreme Court. Its significance is actually more historic than constitutional, in the sense that it helped to crystallize and sharpen the split in public opinion which ultimately led to the Civil War. In this decision, written by Chief Justice Taney, the Court, by a vote of seven to two, denied that a Negro was a citizen even though he happened to live in a free State. The Court also declared the Missouri Compromise (1820) unconstitutional.

Background: *In 1834, Dred Scott, a slave, was taken by his master from the slave State of Missouri to the free State of Illinois and then to the Wisconsin Territory, where slavery was forbidden by the Missouri Compromise. Scott was later brought back to Missouri and in 1846 he sued for his freedom on the ground that he had lived in free States. The case went to the Supreme Court, which ruled that Scott was not a citizen either of Missouri or of the United States, and hence he could not sue in federal courts.*

Some Related Cases
(On Citizenship):

United States v. Gordon (1861)
United States v. Wong Kim Ark (1898)
Arver v. United States (1918)
Lam Mow v. Nagle (1928)

MR. CHIEF JUSTICE TANEY DELIVERED THE OPINION OF THE COURT:

There are two leading questions presented by the record:

1. Had the Circuit Court of the United States jurisdiction to hear and determine the case between these parties? And,

2. If it had jurisdiction, is the judgment it has given erroneous or not?

The plaintiff in error, who was also the plaintiff in the court below, was, with his wife and children, held as slaves by the defendant, in the State of Missouri, and he brought this action in the Circuit Court of the United States for that district, to assert the title of himself and his family to freedom.

The declaration is . . . that he and the defendant are citizens of different States; that is, that he is a citizen of Missouri, and the defendant a citizen of New York.

The defendant pleaded in abatement to the jurisdiction of the court, that the plaintiff was not a citizen of the State of Missouri, as alleged in his declaration, being a Negro of African descent whose ancestors were of pure African blood, and who were brought into this country and sold as slaves.

To this plea the plantiff demurred, and the defendant joined in demurrer. . . .

Before we speak of the pleas in bar, it will be proper to dispose of the questions which have arisen on the plea in abatement.

That plea denies the right of the plaintiff to sue in a court of the United States, for the reasons therein stated.

If the question raised by it is legally before us, and the court should be of opinion that the facts stated in it disqualify the plaintiff from becoming a citizen, in the sense in which that word is used in the Constitution of the United States, then the judgment of the Circuit Court is erroneous, and must be reversed. . . .

The question to be decided is, whether the facts stated in the plea are sufficient to show that the plaintiff is not entitled to sue as a citizen in a court of the United States.

This is certainly a very serious question, and one that now for the first time has been brought for decision before this court. But it is brought here by those who have a right to bring it, and it is our duty to meet it and decide it.

The question is simply this: Can a Negro, whose ancestors were imported into this country, and sold as slaves, become a member of the political community formed and brought into existence by the Constitution of the United States, and as such become entitled to all the rights, and privileges, and immunities, guarantied by that instrument to the citizen? One of which rights is the privilege of suing in a court of the United States in the cases specified in the Constitution.

It will be observed, that the plea applied to that class of persons only whose ancestors were Negroes of the African race, and imported into this country, and sold and held as slaves. The only matter in issue before the court, therefore, is, whether the descendants of such slaves, when they shall be emancipated, or who are born of parents who had become free before their birth, are citizens of a State, in the sense in which the word citizen is used in the Constitution of the United States. And this being the only matter in dispute on the pleadings, the court must be understood as speaking in this opinion of that class only, that is of persons who are the descendants of Africans who were imported into this country and sold as slaves. . . .

We proceed to examine the case as presented by the pleadings.

The words "people of the United States" and "citizens" are synonymous terms, and mean the same thing. They both describe the political body who, according to our republican institutions, form the sovereignty, and who hold the power and conduct the government through their representatives. They are what we familiarly call the "sovereign people," and every citizen is one of this people, and a constituent member of this sovereignty. The question before us is, whether the class of persons described in the plea in abatement compose a portion of this people, and are constituent members of this sovereignty? We think they are not, and that they are not included, and were not intended to be included under the word "citizens" in the Constitution, and can, therefore, claim none of the rights and privileges which that instrument provides for and secures to citizens of the United States. On the contrary, they were at that time considered as a subordinate and inferior class of beings, who had been subjugated by the dominant race, and whether emancipated or not, yet remained subject to their authority, and had no rights or privileges but such as those who held the power and the government might choose to grant them. . . .

In discussing this question, we must not confound the rights of citizenship which a State may confer within its own limits, and the rights of citizenship as a member of the Union. It does not by any means follow because he has all the rights and privileges of a citizen of a State, that he must be a citizen of the United States. He may have all of the rights and privileges of the citizen of a State, and yet not be entitled to the rights and privileges of a citizen in any other State. For, previous to the adoption of the Constitution of the United States, every State had the undoubted right to confer on whomsoever it pleased the character of a citizen, and to endow him with all its rights. But this character, of course, was confined to the boundaries of the State, and gave him no rights or privileges in other States beyond those secured to him by the laws of nations and the comity of States. Nor have the several States surrendered the power of conferring these rights and privileges by adopting the Constitution of the United States. Each State may still confer them upon an alien, or any one it thinks proper, or upon any class or description of persons; yet he would not be a citizen in the sense in which that word is used in the Constitution of the United States, nor entitled to sue as such in one of its courts, nor to the privileges and immunities of a citizen in the other States. The rights which he would acquire would be restricted to the State which gave them. . . .

It is very clear, therefore, that no State can, by any Act or law of its own, passed since the adoption of the Constitution, introduce a new member into the political community created by the Constitution of the United States. It cannot make him a member of this community by making him a member of its own. And for the same reason it cannot introduce any person, or description of persons, who were not intended to be embraced in this new political family, which the Constitution brought into existence, but were intended to be excluded from it.

The question then arises, whether the provisions of the Constitution, in relation to the personal rights and privileges to which the citizen of a State should be entitled, embraced the Negro African race, at that time in this country, or who might afterwards be imported, who had then or should afterwards be made free in any State; and to put it in the power of a single State to make him a citizen of the United States, and endue him with the full rights of citizenship in every other State without their consent. Does the Constitution of the United States act upon him whenever he shall be made free under the laws of a State, and raised there to the rank of a citizen, and immediately clothe him with all the privileges of a citizen in every other State, and in its own courts?

The Court thinks the affirmative of these propositions cannot be maintained. And if it cannot, the plaintiff in error could not be a citizen of the State of Missouri, within the meaning of the Constitution of the United States, and, consequently, was not entitled to sue in its courts.

It is true, every person, and every class and description of persons, who were at the time of the adoption of the Constitution recognized as citizens in the several States, became also citizens of this new political body; but none other; it was formed by them, and for them and their posterity, but for no one else. And the personal rights and privileges guarantied to citizens of this new sovereignty were intended to embrace those only who were then members of the several state communities, or who should afterwards, by birthright or otherwise, become members, according to the provisions of the Constitution and the principles on which it was founded.

It becomes necessary, therefore, to determine who were citizens of the several States when the Constitution was adopted. And in order to do this, we must recur to the governments and institutions of the thirteen Colonies, when they separated from Great Britain and formed new sovereignties. . . . We must inquire who, at that time, were recognized as the people or citizens of a State. . . .

In the opinion of the Court, the legislation and histories of the times, and the language used in the Declaration of Independence, show, that neither the class of persons who had been imported as slaves, nor their descendants, whether they had become free or not, were then acknowledged as a part of the people, nor intended to be included in the general words used in that memorable instrument.

It is difficult at this day to realize the state of public opinion in relation to that unfortunate race, which prevailed in the civilized and enlightened portions of the world at the time of the Declaration of Independence, and when the Constitution of the United States was framed and adopted. . . .

They had for more than a century before been regarded as beings of an inferior order; and altogether unfit to associate with the white race, either in social or political relations; and so far inferior that they had no rights which the white man was bound to respect; and that the Negro might justly and lawfully be reduced to slavery for his benefit. . . . This opinion was at that time fixed and universal in the civilized portion of the white race. It was regarded as an axiom in morals as well as in politics, which no one thought of disputing, or supposed to be open to dispute; and men in every grade and position in society daily and habitually acted upon it in their private pursuits, as well as in matters of public concern, without doubting for a moment the correctness of this opinion. . . .

The legislation of the different Colonies furnishes positive and undisputable proof of this fact. . . .

The language of the Declaration of Independence is equally conclusive. . . .

This state of public opinion had undergone no change when the Constitution was adopted, as is equally evident from its provisions and language. . . .

But there are two clauses in the Constitution which point directly and specifically to the Negro race as a separate class of persons, and show clearly that they were not regarded as a portion of the people or citizens of the Government then formed.

One of these clauses reserves to each of the thirteen States the right to import slaves until the year 1808, if he thinks it proper. And the importation which it thus sanctions was unquestionably of persons of the race of which we are speaking, as the traffic in slaves in the United States had always been confined to them. And by the other provision the States pledge themselves to each other to maintain the right of property of the master, by delivering up to him any slave who may have escaped from his service, and be found within their respective territories. . . . And these two provisions show, conclusively, that neither the description of persons therein referred to, nor their descendants, were embraced in any of the other provisions of the Constitution; for certainly these two clauses were not intended to confer on them or their posterity the blessings of liberty, or any of the personal rights so carefully provided for the citizens . . .

Indeed, when we look to the condition of this race in the several States at the time, it is impossible to believe that these rights and privileges were intended to be extended to them. . . .

The legislation of the States therefore shows, in a manner not to be mistaken, the inferior and subject condition of that race at the time the Constitution was adopted, and long afterwards, throughout the thirteen States by which that instrument was framed; and it is hardly consistent with the respect due to these States, to suppose that they regarded at that time, as fellow-citizens and members of the sovereignty, a class of beings whom they had thus stigmatized; . . . More especially, it cannot be believed that the large slave-holding States regarded them as included in the word "citizens," or would have consented to a constitution which might compel them to receive them in that character from another State. For if they were so received, and entitled to the privileges and immunities of citizens, it would exempt them from the operation of the special laws and from the police regulations which they considered to be necessary for their own safety. . . . And all of this would be done in the face of the subject race of the same color, both free and slaves, inevitably producing discontent and insubordination among them, and endangering the peace and safety of the State.

But it is said that a person may be a citizen, and entitled to that character, although he does not possess all the rights which may belong to other citizens; as, for example, the right to vote, or to hold particular offices; and that yet, when he goes into another State, he is entitled to be recognized there as a citizen although the State may measure his rights by the rights which it allows to persons of a like character or class, resident in the State, and refuse to him the full rights of citizenship.

This argument overlooks the language of the provision in the Constitution of which we are speaking.

Undoubtedly, a person may be a citizen, that is, a member of the community who form sovereignty, although he exercises no share of the political power, and is incapacitated from holding particular offices. . . .

So, too, a person may be entitled to vote by the law of the State, who is not a citizen even of the State iself. And in some of the States of the Union foreigners not naturalized are allowed to vote. And the State may give the right to free Negroes and mulattoes, but that does not make them citizens of the State, and still less of the United States. And the provision in the Constitution giving privileges and immunities in other States, does not apply to them.

Neither does it apply to a person who, being the citizen of a State, migrates to another State. For then he becomes subject to the laws of the State in which he lives, and he is no longer a citizen of the State from which he removed. And the State in which he resides may then, unquestionably, determine his *status* or condition, and place him among the class of persons who are not recognized as citizens, but belong to an inferior and subject race; and may deny him the privileges and immunities enjoyed by its citizens. . . .

. . . But if he ranks as a citizen of the State to which he belongs, within the meaning of the Constitution of the United States, then, whenever he goes into another State, the Constitution clothes him, as to the rights of person, with all the privileges and immunities which belong to citizens of the State. And if persons of the African race are citizens of a State, and of the United States, they would be entitled to all of these privileges and immunities in every State, and the State could not restrict them; for they would hold these privileges and immunities, under the paramount authority of the Federal Government, and its courts would be bound to maintain and enforce them, the Constitution and laws of the State to the contrary notwithstanding. . . .

And upon a full and careful consideration of the subject, the Court is of opinion that, upon the facts stated in the plea in abatement, Dred Scott was not a citizen of Missouri within the meaning of the Constitution of the United States, and not entitled as such to sue in its courts; and, consequently, that the Circuit Court had no jurisdiction of the case, and that the judgment on the plea in abatement is erroneous. . . .

We proceed, therefore, to inquire whether the facts relied on by the plaintiff entitled him to his freedom. . . .

In considering this part of the controversy, two questions arise: 1st. Was he, together with his family, free in Missouri by reason of the stay in the territory of the United States hereinbefore mentioned? And 2nd. If they were not, is Scott himself free by reason of his removal to Rock Island, in the State of Illinois, as stated in the above admissions?

We proceed to examine the first question.

The Act of Congress, upon which the plaintiff relies, declares that slavery and involuntary servitude, except as a punishment for crime, shall be forever prohibited in all that part of the territory ceded by France, under the name of Louisiana, which lies north of thirty-six degrees thirty minutes north latitude, and not included within the limits of Missouri. And the difficulty which meets us at the threshold of this part of the inquiry is, whether Congress was authorized to pass this law under any of the powers granted to it by the Constitution; for if the authority is not given by that instrument, it is the duty of this court to declare it void and inoperative, and incapable of conferring freedom upon any one who is held as a slave under the laws of any one of the States.

The counsel for the plaintiff has laid much stress upon that article in the Constitution which confers on Congress the power "to dispose of and make all needful rules and regulations respecting the territory or other property belonging to the United States"; but, in the judgment of the court, that provision has no bearing on the present controversy, and the power there given, whatever it may be, is confined, and was intended to be confined, to the territory which at that time belonged to, or was claimed by, the United States, and was within their boundaries as settled by the treaty with Great Britain, and can have no influence upon a territory afterwards acquired from a foreign Government. It was a special provision for a known and particular territory, and to meet a present emergency, and nothing more. . . .

If this clause is construed to extend to territory acquired by the present Government from a foreign nation, outside of the limits of any charter from the British Government to a colony, it would be difficult to say, why it was deemed necessary to give the Government the power to sell any vacant lands belonging to the sovereignty which might be found within it; and if this was necessary, why the grant of this power should precede the power to legislate over it and establish a Government there; and still more difficult to say, why it was deemed necessary so specially and particularly to grant the power to make needful rules and regulations in relation to any personal or movable property it might acquire there. For the words, *other property* necessarily, by every known rule of interpretation, must mean property of a different description from territory or land. And the difficulty would perhaps be insurmountable in endeavouring to account for the last member of the sentence, which provides that "nothing in this Constitution shall be so construed as to prejudice any claims of the United States or any particular State," or to say how any particular State could have claims in or to a territory ceded by a foreign Government, or to account for associating this provision with the preceding provisions of the clause, with which it would appear to have no connection. . . .

But the power of Congress over the person or property of a citizen can never be a mere discretionary power under our Constitution and form of Government. The powers of the Government and the rights and privileges of the citizen are regulated and plainly defined by the Constitution itself. And when the Territory becomes a part of the United States, the Federal Government enters into possession in the character impressed upon it by those who created it. It enters upon it with its powers over the citizen strictly defined, and limited by the Constitution, from which it derives its own existence, and by virtue of which alone it continues to exist and act as a Government and sovereignty. It has no power of any kind beyond it; and it cannot, when it enters a Territory of the United States, put off its character, and assume discretionary or despotic powers which the Constitution has denied to it. It cannot create for itself a new character separated from the citizens of the United States, and the duties it owes them under the provisions of the Constitution. The Territory being a part of the United States, the Government and the citizen both enter it under the authority of the Constitution, with their respective rights defined and marked out; and the Federal Government can exercise no power over his person or property, beyond what that instrument confers, nor lawfully deny any right which it has reserved. . . .

The rights of private property have been guarded with equal care. Thus the rights of property are united with the rights of person, and placed on the same ground by the fifth amendment to the Constitution. . . . An Act of Congress which deprives a person of the United States of his liberty or property merely because he came himself or brought his property into a particular Territory of the United States, and who had committed no offense against the laws, could hardly be dignified with the name of due process of law. . . .

And this prohibition is not confined to the States, but the words are general, and extend to the whole territory over which the Constitution gives it power to legislate, including those portions of it remaining under territorial government, as well as that covered by States. It is a total absence of power everywhere within the dominion of the United States, and places the citizens of a territory, so far as these rights are concerned, on the same footing with citizens of the States, and guards them as firmly and plainly against any inroads which the general government might attempt, under the plea of implied or incidental powers. And if Congress itself cannot do this—if it is beyond the powers conferred on the Federal Government—it will be admitted, we presume, that it could not authorize a Territorial Government to exercise them. It could confer no power on any local government, established by its authority, to violate the provisions of the Constitution.

It seems, however, to be supposed that there is a difference between property in a slave and other property, and that different rules may be applied to it in expounding the Constitution of the United States. And the laws and usages of nations, and the writings of eminent jurists upon the relation of master and slave and their mutual rights and duties, and the powers which governments may exercise over it, have been dwelt upon in the argument.

But . . . if the Constitution recognizes the right of property of the master in a slave, and makes no distinction between that description of property and other property owned by a citizen, no tribunal, acting under the authority of the United States, whether it be legislative, executive or judicial, has a right to draw such a distinction, or deny to it the benefit of the provisions and guarantees which have been provided for the protection of private property against the encroachment of the Government.

Now . . . the right of property in a slave is distinctly and expressly affirmed in the Constitution. The right to traffic in it, like an ordinary article of merchandise and property, was guarantied to the citizens of the United States, in every State that might desire it, for twenty years. And the Government in express terms is pledged to protect it in all future time, if the slave escapes from his owner. . . . And no word can be found in the Constitution which gives Congress a greater power over slave property, or which entitles property of that kind to less protection than property of any other description. The only power conferred is the power coupled with the duty of guarding and protecting the owner in his rights.

Upon these considerations, it is the opinion of the court that the Act of Congress which prohibited a citizen from holding and owning property of this kind in the Territory of the United States north of the line therein mentioned, is not warranted by the Constitution, and is therefore void; and that neither Dred Scott himself, nor any of his family, were made free by being carried into this Territory; even if they had been carried there by the owner, with the intention of becoming a permanent resident. . . .

Upon the whole, therefore, it is the judgment of this court, that it appears by the record before us that the plaintiff in error is not a citizen of Missouri, in the sense in which that word is used in the Constitution; and that the Circuit Court of the United States, for that reason, had no jurisdiction in the case, and could give no judgment in it

Its judgment for the defendant must, consequently be reversed, and a mandate issued directing the suit to be dismissed for want of jurisdiction.

[Mr. Justice McLean and Mr. Justice Curtis dissented.]

State electoral malapportionment is a denial of the Equal Protection clause of the Fourteenth Amendment.

8. *BAKER v. CARR* (1962)

This is a memorable case, far-reaching in its implications. Here, for the first time, the Supreme Court entered the area of State reapportionment, hitherto shunned as a "political" and "nonjusticiable" question.

Background: *The facts of the case are stated in the first three paragraphs of the decision.*

The Court ruled, by a vote of six to two (Justices Frankfurter and Harlan dissenting, and Justice Whittaker not participating), that the subject of apportionment was constitutionally "justiciable" and that electoral malapportionment was a violation of the Equal Protection guarantee of the Fourteenth Amendment. In effect, this historic decision compels the States to redraw their electoral districts according to population.

Some Related Cases
(On Apportionment):

Wood v. Broom (1932)
Smiley v. Holm (1932)
Colegrove v. Green (1946)
MacDougall v. Green (1948)
South v. Peters (1950)
Reynolds v. Sims (1964)
WMCA v. Lomenzo (1964)

JUSTICE BRENNAN DELIVERED THE OPINION OF THE COURT:

Between 1901 and 1961, Tennessee has experienced substantial growth and redistribution of her population. In 1901 the population was 2,020,616, of whom 487,380 were eligible to vote. The 1960 Federal Census reports the State's population at 3,567,089, of whom 2,092,891 are eligible to vote. The relative standings of the counties in terms of qualified voters have changed significantly. It is primarily the continued application of the 1901 Apportionment Act to this shifted and enlarged voting population which gives rise to the present controversy.

Indeed, the complaint alleges that the 1901 statute, even as of the time of its passage, "made no apportionment of Representatives and Senators in accordance with the constitutional formula . . . , but instead arbitrarily and capriciously apportioned representatives in the Senate and House without reference . . . to any logical or reasonable formula whatever." It is further alleged that "because of the population changes since 1900, and the failure of the legislature to reapportion itself since 1901," the 1901 statute became "unconstitutional and obsolete." Appellants also argue that, because of the composition of the legislature effected by the 1901 apportionment Act, redress in the form of a state constitutional amendment to change the entire mechanism for reapportioning, or any other change short of that, is difficult or impossible. . . .

Because we deal with this case on appeal from an order of dismissal granted on appellees' motions, precise identification of the issues presently confronting us demands clear exposition of the grounds upon which the District Court rested in dismissing the case. . . .

The District Court was uncertain whether our cases withholding federal judicial relief rested upon a lack of federal jurisdiction or upon the inappropriateness of the subject matter for judicial consideration—what we have designated "nonjusticiability." The distinction between the two grounds is significant. In the instance of nonjusticiability, consideration of the cause is not wholly and immediately foreclosed; rather, the Court's inquiry necessarily proceeds to the point of deciding whether the duty asserted can be judicially identified and its breach judicially determined, and whether protection for the right asserted can be judicially molded. In the instance of lack of jurisdiction the cause either does not "arise under" the Federal Constitution, laws or treaties (or fall within one of the other enumerated categories of Art. 3, Sec. 2), or is not a "case or controversy" within the meaning of that section; or the cause is not one described by any jurisdictional statute. Our conclusion . . . that this cause presents no nonjusticiable "political question" settles the only possible doubt that it is a case or controversy. Under the present heading of "Jurisdiction of the Subject Matter" we hold only that the matter set forth in the complaint does arise under the Constitution. . . .

The complaint alleges that the 1901 statute effects an apportionment that deprives the appellants of the equal protection of the laws in violation of the Fourteenth Amendment. Dismissal of the complaint upon the ground of lack of jurisdiction of the subject matter would, therefore, be justified only if that claim were "so attenuated and unsubstantial as to be absolutely devoid of merit," . . . Since the District Court obviously and correctly did not deem the asserted federal constitutional claim unsubstantial and frivolous, it should not have dismissed the complaint for want of jurisdiction of the subject matter. . . .

We hold that the appellants do have standing to maintain this suit. Our decisions plainly support this conclusion. Many of the cases have assumed rather than articulated the premise in deciding the merits of similar claims. And *Colegrove v. Green*, . . . squarely held that voters who allege facts showing disadvantage to themselves as individuals have standing to sue. [A footnote points out that the concurring opinion of Justice Rutledge and Justice Black's dissenting opinion held there was standing, and expressed doubt whether Justice Frankfurter's opinion . . . intimated lack of it.]

. . . The mere fact that the suit seeks protection of a political right does not mean it presents a political question. Such an objection "is little more than a play upon words." . . . Rather, it is argued that apportionment cases, whatever the actual wording of the complaint, can involve no federal constitutional right except one resting on the guaranty of a republican form of government, and that complaints based on that clause have been held to present political questions which are nonjusticiable.

We hold that the claim pleaded here neither rests upon nor implicates the Guaranty clause and that its justiciability is therefore not foreclosed by our decisions of cases involving that clause. The District Court misinterpreted *Colegrove v. Green* and other decisions of this Court on which it relied. Appellants' claim that they are being denied equal protection is justiciable, and if "discrimination is sufficiently shown, the right to relief under the equal protection clause is not diminished by the fact that the discrimination relates to political rights." . . . To show why we reject the argument based on the Guaranty clause, we must examine the authorities under it. But because there appears to be some uncertainty as to why those cases did present political questions, and specifically as to whether this apportionment case is like those cases, we deem it necessary first to consider the contours of the "political question" doctrine. . . .

It is apparent that several formulations which vary slightly according to the settings in which the questions arise may describe a political question, although each has one or more elements which identifies it as essentially a function of the separation of powers. Prominent on the surface of any case held to involve a political question is found a textually demonstrable constitutional commitment of the issue to a coordinate political department; or a lack of judicially discoverable and manageable standards for resolving it; or the impossibility of deciding without an initial policy determination of a kind clearly for nonjudicial discretion; or the impossibility of a court's undertaking independent resolution without expressing lack of the respect due coordinate branches of government; or an unusual need for unquestioning adherence to a political decision already made; or the potentiality of embarrassment from multifarious pronouncements by various departments on one question.

Unless one of these formulations is inextricable from the case at bar, there should be no dismissal for nonjusticiability on the ground of a political question's presence. The doctrine of which we treat is one of "political questions," not one of "political cases." The courts cannot reject as "no lawsuit" a bona fide controversy as to whether some action denominated "political" exceeds constitutional authority. . . .

Several factors were thought by the Court in Luther [*Luther v. Borden*] to make the question there "political": the commitment to the other branches of the decision as to which is the lawful state government; the unambiguous action by the President, in recognizing the charter government as the lawful authority; the need for finality in the executive's decision; and the lack of criteria by which a court could determine which form of government was republican.

But the only significance that Luther could have for our immediate purposes is in its holding that the Guaranty clause is not a repository of judicially manageable standards which a court could utilize independently in order to identify a State's lawful government. The Court has since refused to resort to the Guaranty clause—which alone has been invoked for the purpose—as the source of a constitutional standard for invalidating state action. . . .

We come, finally, to the ultimate inquiry whether our precedents as to what constitutes a nonjusticiable "political question" bring the case before us under the umbrella of that doctrine. A natural beginning is to note whether any of the common characteristics which we have been able to identify and label descriptively are present. We find none: The question here is the consistency of state action with the Federal Constitution. We have no question decided, or to be decided, by a political branch of Government coequal with this Court. Nor do we risk embarrassment of our Government abroad, or grave disturbance at home if we take issue with Tennessee as to the constitutionality of her action here challenged. Nor need the appellants, in order to succeed in this action, ask the Court to enter upon policy determinations for which judicially manageable standards are lacking. Judicial standards under the Equal Protection clause are well developed and familiar, and it has been open to courts since the enactment of the Fourteenth Amendment to determine, if on the particular facts they must, that a discrimination reflects no policy, but simply arbitrary and capricious action.

This case does, in one sense, involve the allocation of political power within a State, and the appellants might conceivably have added a claim under the Guaranty clause. Of course, as we have seen, any reliance on that clause would be futile. But because any reliance on the Guaranty clause could not have succeeded it does not follow that appellants may not be heard on the equal protection claim which in fact they tender. True, it must be clear that the Fourteenth Amendment claim is not so enmeshed with those political question elements which render Guaranty clause claims nonjusticiable as actually to present a political question itself. But we have found that not to be the case here. . . .

We conclude then that the nonjusticiability of claims resting on the Guaranty clause which arises from their embodiment of questions that were thought "political," can have no bearing upon the justiciability of the equal protection claim presented in this case. Finally, we emphasize that it is the involvement in Guaranty clause claims of the elements thought to define "political questions," and no other feature, which could render them nonjusticiable. Specifically, we have said that such claims are not held nonjusticiable because they touch matters of state governmental organization. . . .

Article I, Sections 2, 4, and 5 and Amendment 14, Section 2 relate only to congressional elections and obviously do not govern apportionment of state legislatures. However, our decisions in favor of justiciability even in light of those provisions plainly afford no support for the District Court's conclusion that the subject matter of this controversy presents a political question. Indeed, the refusal to award relief in *Colegrove* resulted only from the controlling view of a want of equity. . . .

We conclude that the complaint's allegations of a denial of equal protection present a justiciable constitutional cause of action upon which appellants are entitled to a trial and a decision. The right asserted is within the reach of judicial protection under the Fourteenth Amendment. . . .

[Mr. Justice Whittaker did not participate.]

MR. JUSTICE FRANKFURTER DISSENTING, JOINED BY MR. JUSTICE HARLAN:

The Court today reverses a uniform course of decision established by a dozen cases, including one by which the very claim now sustained was unanimously rejected only five years ago. The impressive body of rulings thus cast aside reflected the equally uniform course of our political history regarding the relationship between population and legislative representation—a wholly different matter from denial of the franchise to individuals because of race, color, religion or sex. Such a massive repudiation of the experience of our whole past in asserting destructively novel judicial power demands a detailed analysis of the role of this court in our constitutional scheme. Disregard of inherent limits in the effective exercise of the Court's "judicial power" not only presages the futility of judicial intervention in the essentially political conflict of forces by which the relation between population and representation has time out of mind been and now is determined. It may well impair the Court's position as the ultimate organ of "the supreme law of the land" in that vast range of legal problems, often strongly entangled in popular feeling, on which this Court must pronounce. The Court's authority—possessed neither of the purse nor the sword —ultimately rests on sustained public confidence in its moral sanction. Such feeling must be nourished by the Court's complete detachment, in fact and in appearance, from political entanglements and by abstention from injecting itself into the clash of political forces in political settlements. . . .

For this court to direct the District Court to enforce a claim to which the Court has over the years consistently found itself required to deny legal enforcement and at the same time to find it necessary to withhold any guidance to the lower court how to enforce this turnabout, new legal claim, manifests an odd—indeed an esoteric—conception of judicial propriety. . . .

Even assuming the indispensable intellectual disinterestedness on the part of judges in such matters, they do not have accepted legal standards of criteria or even reliable analogies to draw upon for making judicial judgments. To charge courts with the task of accommodating the incommensurable factors of policy that underlie these mathematical puzzles is to attribute, however flatteringly, omnicompetence to judges. . . .

We were soothingly told at the bar of this court that we need not worry about the kind of remedy a court could effectively fashion once the abstract constitutional right to have courts pass on a state-wide system of electoral districting is recognized as a matter of judicial rhetoric, because legislatures would heed the Court's admonition. This is not only an euphoric hope. It implies a sorry confession of judicial impotence in place of a frank acknowledgment that there is not under our Constitution a judicial remedy for every political mischief, for every undesirable exercise of legislative power. The Framers carefully and with deliberate forethought refused so to enthrone the judiciary. In this situation, as in others of like nature, appeal for relief does not belong here. Appeal must be to an informed, civically militant electorate. In a democratic society like ours, relief must come through an aroused popular conscience that sears the conscience of the people's representatives. In any event there is nothing judicially more unseemly nor more self-defeating than for this court to make interrorem pronouncements, to indulge in merely empty rhetoric, sounding a word of promise to the ear, sure to be disappointing to the hope. . . .

At first blush, this charge of discrimination based on legislative underrepresentation is given the appearance of a more private, less impersonal claim, than the assertion that the frame of government is askew. Appellants appear as representatives of a class that is prejudiced as a class, in contradistinction to the polity in its entirety. However, the discrimination relied on is the deprivation of what appellants conceive to be their proportionate share of political influence. This, of course, is the practical effect of any allocation of power within the institutions of government. Hardly any distribution of political authority that could be assailed as rendering government nonrepublican would fail similarly to operate to the prejudice of some groups, and to the advantage of others, within the body politic. . . .

What, then, is this question of legislative apportionment? Appellants invoke the right to vote and to have their votes counted. But they are permitted to vote and their votes are counted. They go to the polls, they cast their ballots, they send their representatives to the state councils. Their complaint is simply that the representatives are not sufficiently numerous or powerful—in short, that Tennessee has adopted a basis of representation with which they are dissatisfied. Talk of "debasement" or "dilution" is circular talk. One cannot speak of "debasement" or "dilution" of the value of a vote until there is first defined a standard of reference as to what a vote should be worth. What is actually asked of the Court in this case is to choose among competing bases of representation—ultimately, really, among competing theories of political philosophy—in order to establish an appropriate frame of government for the State of Tennessee and thereby for all the States of the Union. . . .

. . . What Tennessee illustrates is an old and still widespread method of representation—representation by local geographical division, only in part respective of population—in preference to others, others, forsooth, more appealing. Appellants contest this choice and seek to make this court the arbiter of the disagreement. They would make the Equal Protection clause the charter of adjudication, asserting that the equality which it guarantees comports, if not the assurance of equal weight to every voter's vote, at least the basic conception that representation ought to be proportionate to population, a standard by reference to which the reasonableness of apportionment plans may be judged.

To find such a political conception legally enforceable in the broad and unspecific guarantee of equal protection is to rewrite the Constitution. . . .

DISSENTING OPINION OF MR. JUSTICE HARLAN, JOINED BY MR. JUSTICE FRANKFURTER:

In the last analysis, what lies at the core of this controversy is a difference of opinion as to the function of representative government. It is surely beyond argument that those who have the responsibility for devising a system of representation may permissibly consider that factors other than bare numbers should be taken into account. The existence of the United States Senate is proof enough of that. To consider that we may ignore the Tennessee Legislature's judgment in this instance because that body was the product of an asymmetrical electoral apportionment would in effect be to assume the very conclusion here disputed. Hence we must accept the present form of the

Tennessee Legislature as the embodiment of the State's choice, or, more realistically, its compromise, between competing political philosophies. The federal courts have not been empowered by the Equal Protection clause to judge whether this resolution of the State's internal political conflict is desirable or undesirable, wise or unwise. . . .

From a reading of the majority and concurring opinions one will not find it difficult to catch the premises that underlie this decision. The fact that the appellants have been unable to obtain political redress of their asserted grievances appears to be regarded as a matter which should lead the Court to stretch to find some basis for judicial intervention. While the Equal Protection clause is invoked, the opinion for the Court notably eschews explaining how, consonant with past decisions, the undisputed facts in this case can be considered to show a violation of that constitutional provision. . . .

In conclusion, it is appropriate to say that one need not agree, as a citizen, with what Tennessee has done or failed to do, in order to deprecate, as a judge, what the majority is doing today. Those observers of the Court who see it primarily as the last refuge for the correction of all inequality or injustice, no matter what its nature or source, will no doubt applaud this decision and its break with the past. Those who consider that continuing national respect for the Court's authority depends in large measure upon its wise exercise of self-restraint and discipline in constitutional adjudication, will view the decision with deep concern.

I would affirm.

MR. JUSTICE CLARK, CONCURRING:

One emerging from the rash of opinions with their accompanying clashing of views may well find himself suffering a mental blindness. The Court holds that the appellants have alleged a cause of action. However, it refuses to award relief here—although the facts are undisputed—and fails to give the District Court any guidance whatever. One dissenting opinion, bursting with words that go through so much and conclude with so little, condemns the majority action as "a massive repudiation of the experience of our whole past." Another describes the complaint as merely asserting conclusory allegations that Tennessee's apportionment is "incorrect," "arbitrary," "obsolete," and "unconstitutional." I believe it can be shown that this case is distinguishable from earlier cases dealing with the distribution of political power by a State, that a patent violation of the Equal Protection clause of the United States Constitution has been shown, and that an appropriate remedy may be formulated. . . .

It is true that the apportionment policy incorporated in Tennessee's constitution, i.e., state-wide numerical equality of representation with certain minor qualifications, is a rational one. On a county-by-county comparison a districting plan based thereon naturally will have disparities in representation due to the qualifications. But this to my mind does not raise constitutional problems, for the over-all policy is reasonable. However, the root of the trouble is not in Tennessee's constitution, for admittedly its policy has not been followed. The discrimination lies in the action of Tennessee's Assembly in allocating legislative seats to counties or districts created by it. Try as one may, Tennessee's apportionment just cannot be made to fit the pattern cut by its constitution. This was the finding of the District Court. The policy of the Constitution referred to by the dissenters, therefore, is of no relevance here. We must examine what the Assembly has done. The frequency and magnitude of the inequalities in the present districting admit of no policy whatever. . . .

Although I find the Tennessee apportionment statute offends the Equal Protection clause, I would not consider intervention by this court into so delicate a field if there were any other relief available to the people of Tennessee. But the majority of the people of Tennessee have no "practical opportunities for exerting their political weight at the polls" to correct the existing "invidious discrimination." Tennessee has no initiative and referendum. I have searched diligently for other "practical opportunities" present under the law. I find none other than through the federal courts. The majority of the voters have been caught up in a legislative strait jacket. Tennessee has an "informed, civically militant electorate" and "an aroused popular conscience," but it does not sear "the conscience of the people's representatives." . . . It is said that there is recourse in Congress and perhaps that may be, but from a practical standpoint this is without substance. To date Congress has never undertaken such a task in any State. We therefore must conclude that the people of Tennessee are stymied and without judicial intervention will be saddled with the present discrimination in the affairs of their state government. . . .

As John Rutledge (later Chief Justice) said 175 years ago in the course of the Constitutional Convention, a chief function of the Court is to secure the national rights. Its decision today supports the proposition for which our forebears fought and many died, namely that "to be fully conformable to the principle of right, the form of government must be representative." That is the keystone upon which our government was founded and lacking which no republic can survive. It is well for this court to practice self-restraint and discipline in constitutional adjudication, but never in its history have those principles received sanction where the national rights of so many have been so clearly infringed for so long a time. National respect for the courts is more enhanced through the forthright enforcement of those rights rather than by rendering them nugatory through the interposition of subterfuges. In my view the ultimate decision today is in the greatest tradition of this court.

Chapter IX

Powers of the President

"He [the President] shall have power, by and with the advice and consent of the Senate, to make treaties, provided two-thirds of the senators present concur; and he shall nominate, and by and with the advice and consent of the Senate, shall appoint ambassadors, other public ministers and consuls, judges of the supreme court, and all other officers of the United States . . ."—Art. II, Sec. 2

". . . he shall take care that the laws be faithfully executed . . ."—Art. II, Sec. 3

In this Chapter:

Myers v. United States (1926)
United States v. Curtiss-Wright Export Corp. (1936)
Youngstown Co. v. Sawyer (1952)

The President has the power to remove executive officials.

9. *MYERS v. UNITED STATES* (1926)

This is the first case in which the Supreme Court took up the question of whether the President had the power to remove executive officials of the Federal Government. The problem had come up after the Civil War, in connection with President Andrew Johnson, who was impeached largely for challenging the validity of the Tenure of Office Act of March 2, 1867, but it did not reach the Supreme Court. It was not until 1926, after two years of indecision, that the Court ruled, by a vote of six to three, that the Congress could not limit the President's power of removal.

Background: *In 1920 President Woodrow Wilson removed Frank S. Myers, a Portland (Oregon) postmaster, who had been appointed by him with the "advice and consent of the Senate." Myers appealed to the Supreme Court on the ground that his removal was a violation of the law of 1876, which required that postmasters could be removed only with "the advice and consent of the Senate." In its decision, written by ex-President and Chief Justice Taft, the Court upheld President Wilson and thus established the constitutionality of presidential removal power without the need to consult the Senate.*

Some Related Cases

(On the Removal Power):

United States v. Perkins (1886)
Parsons v. United States (1897)
Shurtleff v. United States (1903)
Humphrey's Executor v. United States (1935)
Morgan v. TVA (1939)
Wiener v. United States (1958)

MR. CHIEF JUSTICE TAFT DELIVERED THE OPINION OF THE COURT:

This case presents the question whether under the Constitution the President has the exclusive power of removing executive officers of the United States whom he has appointed by and with the advice and consent of the Senate. . . .

By the 6th section of the Act of Congress of July 12, 1876 . . . under which Myers was appointed with the advice and consent of the Senate as a first-class postmaster, it is provided that:

"Postmasters of the first, second, and third classes shall be appointed and may be removed by the President by and with the advice and consent of the Senate, and shall hold their offices for four years unless sooner removed or suspended according to law."

The Senate did not consent to the President's removal of Myers during his term. If this statute in its requirement that his term should be four years unless sooner removed by the President by and with the consent of the Senate is valid, the appellant, Myers' administratrix, is entitled to recover his unpaid salary for his full term and the judgment of the Court of Claims must be reversed. The Government maintains that the requirement is invalid, for the reason that under Article II of the Constitution the President's power of removal of executive officers appointed by him with the advice and consent of the Senate is full and complete without consent of the Senate. . . .

The question where the power of removal of executive officers appointed by the President by and with the advice and consent of the Senate was vested, was presented early in the first session of the First Congress. There is no express provision respecting removals in the Constitution, except as Section 4 of Article II . . . provides for removal from office by impeachment. The subject was not discussed in the Constitutional Convention. . . .

The vesting of the executive power in the President was essentially a grant of the power to execute the laws. But the President alone and unaided could not execute the laws. He must execute them by the assistance of subordinates. This view has since been repeatedly affirmed by this court. . . . As he is charged specifically to take care that they be faithfully executed, the reasonable implication, even in the absence of express words, was that as part of his executive power he should select those who were to act for him under his direction in the execution of the laws. The further implication must be, in the absence of any express limitation respecting removals, that as his selection of administrative officers is essential to the execution of the laws by him, so must be his power of removing those for whom he cannot continue to be responsible. . . . It was urged that the natural meaning of the term "executive power" granted the President included the appointment and removal of executive subordinates. If such appointments and removals were not an exercise of the executive power, what were they? They certainly were not the exercise of legislative or judicial power in government as usually understood. . . .

It was pointed out in this great debate [of 1789] that the power of removal, though equally essential to the executive power, is different in its nature from that of appointment. . . . A veto by the Senate—a part of the legislative branch of the Government—upon removals is a much greater limitation upon the executive branch, and a much more serious blending of the legislative with the executive, than a rejection of a proposed appointment. It is not to be implied. The rejection of a nominee of the President for a particular office does not greatly embarrass him in the conscientious discharge of his high duties in the selection of those who are to aid him, because the President usually has an ample field from which to select for office, according to his preference, competent and capable men. The Senate has full power to reject newly proposed appointees whenever the President shall remove the incumbents. Such a check enables the Senate to prevent the filling of offices with bad or incompetent men, or with those against whom there is tenable objection.

The power to prevent the removal of an officer who has

served under the President is different from the authority to consent to or reject his appointment. When a nomination is made, it may be presumed that the Senate is, or may become, as well advised as to the fitness of the nominee as the President, but in the nature of things the defects in ability or intelligence or loyalty in the administration of the laws of one who has served as an officer under the President are facts as to which the President, or his trusted subordinates, must be better informed than the Senate, and the power to remove him may therefore be regarded as confined for very sound and practical reasons, to the governmental authority which has administrative control. The power of removal is incident to the power of appointment, not to the power of advising and consenting to appointment, and when the grant of the executive power is enforced by the express mandate to take care that the laws be faithfully executed, it emphasizes the necessity for including within the executive power as conferred the exclusive power of removal. . . .

A reference of the whole power of removal to general legislation by Congress is quite out of keeping with the plan of government devised by the Framers of the Constitution. It could never have been intended to leave to Congress unlimited discretion to vary fundamentally the operation of the great independent executive branch of government and thus most seriously to weaken it. It would be a delegation by the convention to Congress of the function of defining the primary boundaries of another of the three great divisions of government. The inclusion of removals of executive officers in the executive power vested in the President by Article II according to its usual definition, and the implication of his power of removal of such officers from the provision of Section 2 expressly recognizing in him the power of their appointment, are a much more natural and appropriate source of the removing power.

It is reasonable to suppose also that had it been intended to give to Congress power to regulate or control removals in the manner suggested, it would have been included among the specifically enumerated legislative powers in Article I, or in the specified limitations on the executive power in Article II. The difference between the grant of legislative power under Article I to Congress which is limited to powers therein enumerated, and the more general grant of the executive power to the President under Article II is significant. The fact that the executive power is given in general terms strengthened by specific terms where emphasis is appropriate, and limited by direct expressions where limitation is needed, and that no express limit is placed on the power of removal by the executive is a convincing indication that none was intended. . . .

We come now to consider an argument advanced and strongly pressed on behalf of the complainant, that this case concerns only the removal of a postmaster; that a postmaster is an inferior officer; that such an office was not included within the legislative decision of 1789, which related only to superior officers to be appointed by the President by and with the advice and consent of the Senate. . . .

The power to remove inferior executive officers, like that to remove superior executive officers, is an incident of the power to appoint them, and is in its nature an executive power. The authority of Congress given by the excepting clause to vest the appointment of such inferior officers in the heads of departments carries with it authority incidentally to invest the heads of departments with power to remove. It has been the practice of Congress to do so and this court has recognized that power. The Court also has recognized in the *Perkins* case that Congress, in committing the appointment of such inferior officers to the heads of departments, may prescribe incidental regulations controlling and restricting the latter in the exercise of the power of removal. But the Court never has held, nor reasonably could hold, although it is argued to the contrary on behalf of the appellant, that the excepting clause enables Congress to draw to itself, or to either branch of it, the power to remove or the right to participate in the exercise of that power. To do this would be to go beyond the words and implications of that clause and to infringe the constitutional principle of the separation of governmental powers.

Assuming then the power of Congress to regulate removals as incidental to the exercise of its constitutional power to vest appointments of inferior officers in the heads of departments, certainly so long as Congress does not exercise that power, the power of removal must remain where the Constitution places it, with the President, as part of the executive power, in accordance with the legislative decision of 1789 which we have been considering. . . .

For the reasons given, we must therefore hold that the provision of the law of 1876 by which the unrestricted power of removal of first-class postmasters is denied to the President is in violation of the Constitution and invalid. This leads to an affirmance of the judgment of the Court of Claims. . . .

Judgment affirmed.

In the conduct of foreign policy the President has "broad discretion."

10. *UNITED STATES v. CURTISS-WRIGHT EXPORT CORPORATION* (1936)

This is an extremely important decision as regards presidential power in foreign affairs. After analyzing the Presi-

dent's functions in international relations, the Court concludes by interpreting the Constitution in such a way as to grant him "broad discretion" in conducting America's foreign policy.

Background: *In 1934 the Curtiss-Wright Export Corporation sold to Bolivia, then engaged in war in the Chaco, fifteen machine guns. This was a violation of the Joint Resolution of Congress and the President's Proclamation of May 28, 1934, prohibiting the sale of arms and munitions to nations at war. Indicted, the Curtiss-Wright Corporation demurred on the ground that such a delegation of power to the President was not valid. The District Court upheld the demurrer, and the United States appealed to the Supreme Court, which reversed the lower court and sustained the President.*

Some Related Cases

(On Presidential Power in Foreign Policy and War):

Holmes v. Jennison (1840)
Hampton & Co. v. United States (1928)
Panama Refining Co. v. Ryan (1935)
United States v. Belmont (1937)
United States v. Pink (1942)
Mitchell v. United States (1967)
Mora v. United States (1967)

MR. JUSTICE SUTHERLAND DELIVERED THE OPINION OF THE COURT:

First. It is contended that by the Joint Resolution, the going into effect and continued operation of the resolution was conditioned (a) upon the President's judgment as to its beneficial effect upon the re-establishment of peace between the countries engaged in armed conflict in the Chaco; (b) upon the making of a proclamation, which was left to his unfettered discretion, thus constituting an attempted substitution of the President's will for that of Congress; (c) upon the making of a proclamation putting an end to the operation of the resolution, which again was left to the President's unfettered discretion; and (d) further, that the extent of its operation in particular cases was subject to limitation and exception by the President, controlled by no standard. In each of these particulars, appellees urged that Congress abdicated its essential functions and delegated them to the Executive.

Whether, if the Joint Resolution had related solely to internal affairs it would be open to the challenge that it constituted an unlawful delegation of legislative power to the Executive, we find it unnecessary to determine. The whole aim of the resolution is to affect a situation entirely external to the United States, and falling within the category of foreign affairs. The determination which we are called to make, therefore, is whether the Joint Resolution, as applied to that situation, is vulnerable to attack under the rule that forbids a delegation of the law-making power. In other words, assuming (but not deciding) that the challenged delegation, if it were confined to internal affairs, would be invalid, may it nevertheless be sustained on the ground that its exclusive aim is to afford a remedy for a hurtful condition within foreign territory?

It will contribute to the elucidation of the question if we first consider the differences between the powers of the Federal Government in respect of foreign or external affairs and those in respect of domestic or internal affairs. That there are differences between them, and that these differences are fundamental, may not be doubted.

The two classes of powers are different, both in respect of their origin and their nature. The broad statement that the Federal Government can exercise no powers except those specifically enumerated in the Constitution, and such implied powers as are necessary and proper to carry into effect the enumerated powers, is categorically true only in respect of our internal affairs. In that field, the primary purpose of the Constitution was to carve from the general mass of legislative powers *then possessed by the States* such portions as it was thought desirable to vest in the Federal Government, leaving those not included in the enumeration still in the States. *Carter v. Carter Coal Co.* 298 U.S. 238, 294. That this doctrine applies only to powers which the States had, is self evident. And since the States severally never possessed international powers, such powers could not have been carved from the mass of state powers but obviously were transmitted to the United States from some other source. During the colonial period, those powers were possessed exclusively by and were entirely under control of the Crown. By the Declaration of Independence, "the Representatives of the United States of America" declared the United (not the several) Colonies to be free and independent States, and as such to have "full Power to levy War, conclude Peace, contract Alliances, establish Commerce and do all other Acts and Things which Independent States may of right do."

As a result of the separation from Great Britain by the colonies acting as a unit, the powers of external sovereignty passed from the Crown not to the colonies severally, but to the colonies in their collective and corporate capacity as the United States of America. Even before the Declaration, the colonies were a unit in foreign affairs, acting through a common agency —namely the Continental Congress, composed of delegates from the thirteen colonies. That agency exercised the powers of war and peace, raised an army, created a navy, and finally adopted the Declaration of Independence. Rulers come and go; governments end and forms of government change; but sovereignty survives. A political society cannot endure without a supreme will somewhere. Sovereignty is never held in suspense. When, therefore, the external sovereignty of Great Britain in respect of the colonies ceased, it immediately passed to the Union. *See Penhallow v. Doane,* 3 Dall. 54, 80–81. That fact was given practical application almost at once. The treaty of peace, made on September 23, 1783, was concluded between his Britannic Majesty and the "United States of America." . . .

The Union existed before the Constitution, which was ordained and established among other things to form "a more perfect Union." Prior to that event, it is clear that the Union, declared by the Articles of Confederation to be "perpetual," was the sole possessor of external sovereignty and in the Union it remained without change save in so far as the Constitution in express terms qualified its exercise. The Framers' Convention was called and exerted its powers upon the irrefutable postulate that though the states were several their people in respect to foreign affairs were one. . . .

It results that the investment of the Federal Government with the powers of external sovereignty did not depend upon the affirmative grants of the Constitution. The powers to declare and wage war, to conclude peace, to make treaties, to maintain diplomatic relations with other sovereignties, if they had never been mentioned in the Constitution, would have vested in the Federal Government as necessary concomitants of nationality. Neither the Constitution nor the laws passed in pursuance of it have any force in foreign territory unless in respect of our own citizens; and operations of the nation in such territory must be governed by treaties, international understandings and compacts, and the principles of international law. As a member of the family of nations, the right and power of the United States in that field are equal to the right and power of the other members of the international family. Otherwise, the United States is not completely sovereign. The power to acquire territory by discovery and occupation, the power to expel undesirable aliens, the power to make such international agreements as do not constitute treaties in the constitutional sense; none of which is expressly affirmed by the Constitution, nevertheless exist as inherently inseparable from the conception of nationality. This the Court recognized, and in each of the cases cited found the warrant for its conclusions not in the provisions of the Constitution, but in the law of nations. . . .

Not only, as we have shown, is the federal power over external affairs in origin and essential character different from that over internal affairs, but participation in the exercise of the power is significantly limited. In this vast external realm, with its important, complicated, delicate and manifold problems, the

President alone has the power to speak or listen as a representative of the nation. He *makes* treaties with the advice and consent of the Senate; but he alone negotiates. Into the field of negotiation the Senate cannot intrude; and Congress itself is powerless to invade it. . . .

It is important to bear in mind that we are here dealing not alone with an authority vested in the President by an exertion of legislative power, but with such an authority plus the very delicate, plenary and exclusive power of the President as the sole organ of the Federal Government in the field of international relations—a power which does not require as a basis for its exercise an Act of Congress, but which, of course, like every other governmental power, must be exercised in subordination to the applicable provisions of the Constitution. It is quite apparent that if, in the maintenance of our international relations, embarrassment—perhaps serious embarrassment—is to be avoided and success for our aims achieved, congressional legislation which is to be made effective through negotiation and inquiry within the international field must often accord to the President a degree of discretion and freedom from statutory restriction which would not be admissible were domestic affairs alone involved. Moreover he, not Congress, has the better opportunity of knowing the conditions which prevail in foreign countries, and especially is this true in time of war. He has his confidential sources of information. He has his agents in the form of diplomatic, consular and other officials. Secrecy in respect of information gathered by them may be highly necessary, and the premature disclosure of it productive of harmful results. Indeed, so clearly is this true that the first President refused to accede to a request to lay before the House of Representatives the instructions, correspondence and documents relating to the negotiation of the Jay Treaty. . . .

In the light of the foregoing observations, it is evident that this court should not be in haste to apply a general rule which will have the effect of condemning legislation like that under review as constituting an unlawful delegation of legislative power. The principles which justify such legislation find overwhelming support in the unbroken legislative practice which has prevailed almost from the inception of the national government to the present day. . . .

The result of holding that the joint resolution here under attack is void and unenforceable as constituting an unlawful delegation of legislative power would be to stamp this multitude of comparable acts and resolutions as likewise invalid. And while this court may not, and should not, hesitate to declare Acts of Congress, however many times repeated, to be unconstitutional if beyond all rational doubt it finds them to be so, an impressive array of legislation such as we have just set forth, enacted by nearly every Congress from the beginning of our national existence to the present day, must be given unusual weight in the process of reaching a correct determination of the problem. A legislative practice such as we have here, evidenced not by only occasional instances, but marked by the movement of a steady stream for a century and a half of time, goes a long way in the direction of proving the presence of unassailable ground for the constitutionality of the practice, to be found in the origin and history of the power involved, or in its nature, or in both combined. . . .

Both upon principle and in accordance with precedent, we conclude there is sufficient warrant for the broad discretion vested in the President to determine whether the enforcement of the statute will have a beneficial effect upon the re-establishment of peace in the affected countries; whether he shall make proclamation to bring the resolution into operation; whether and when the resolution shall cease to operate and to make proclamation accordingly; and to prescribe limitations and exceptions to which the enforcement of the resolution shall be subject. . . .

The judgment of the court below must be reversed and the cause remanded for further proceedings in accordance with the foregoing opinion.

Reversed.

Mr. Justice McReynolds does not agree. He is of opinion that the court below reached the right conclusion and its judgment ought to be affirmed.

Mr. Justice Stone took no part in the consideration of decision of this case.

The President may not seize property without congressional authorization.

11. *YOUNGSTOWN SHEET AND TUBE COMPANY* et al. *v. SAWYER* (1952)

The significance of this decision is that it attempts to put some restraints on presidential power, which had been expanding steadily for at least two decades. Specifically, the case dealt with the crucial problem of whether the President had a constitutional right to seize American property under the guise of war necessity.

Background: *The facts of the case are stated in the second paragraph of the decision. After President Truman ordered his Secretary of Commerce, Charles Sawyer, to seize the steel companies, in order to continue production needed for the*

Korean War, Youngstown Sheet & Tube Company, joined by other steel companies, appealed to the Supreme Court. Acting with rare swiftness (the arguments were heard on May 12, 1952, and the decision handed down on June 2), the Court, by a vote of six to three, ruled that the President had no statutory authority for his action: "There is no statute that expressly authorizes the President to take possession of property as he did here."

In his dissent, Chief Justice Vinson, joined by Justices Reed and Minton, defended the President's seizure order as being within his power and duty as Commander-in-Chief. According to the dissenting opinion, national emergencies call for prompt executive action, "with or without explicit statutory authorization."

Some Related Cases
(On Presidential Economic Power):

Little v. Barreme (1804)
Kendall v. United States (1838)
Mississippi v. Johnson (1867)
United States v. Lee (1882)
Philadelphia Co. v. Stimson (1912)
United States v. Pewee Coal Co. (1951)

MR. JUSTICE BLACK DELIVERED THE OPINION OF THE COURT:

We are asked to decide whether the President was acting within his constitutional power when he issued an order directing the Secretary of Commerce to take possession of and operate most of the Nation's steel mills. The mill owners argue that the President's order amounts to lawmaking, a legislative function which the Constitution has expressly confided to the Congress and not to the President. The Government's position is that the order was made on findings of the President that his action was necessary to avert a national catastrophe which would inevitably result from a stoppage of steel production, and that in meeting this grave emergency the President was acting within the aggregate of his constitutional powers as the Nation's Chief Executive and the Commander-in-Chief of the Armed Forces of the United States. The issue emerges here from the following series of events:

In the latter part of 1951, a dispute arose between the steel companies and their employees over terms and conditions that should be included in new collective bargaining agreements. Long-continued conferences failed to resolve the dispute. On

December 18, 1951, the employees' representative, United Steelworkers of America, C.I.O., gave notice of an intention to strike when the existing bargaining agreements expired on December 31. Thereupon the Federal Mediation and Conciliation Service intervened in an effort to get labor and management to agree. This failing, the President on December 22, 1951, referred the dispute to the Federal Wage Stabilization Board to investigate and make recommendations for fair and equitable terms of settlement. This Board's report resulted in no settlement. On April 4, 1952, the Union gave notice of a nation-wide strike called to begin at 12:01 A.M. April 9. The indispensability of steel as a component of substantially all weapons and other war materials led the President to believe that the proposed work stoppage would immediately jeopardize our national defense and that governmental seizure of the steel mills was necessary in order to assure the continued availability of steel. Reciting these considerations for his action, the President, a few hours before the strike was to begin, issued Executive Order 10340. . . . The order directed the Secretary of Commerce to take possession of most of the steel mills and keep them running. . . .

The President's power, if any, to issue the order must stem either from an act of Congress or from the Constitution itself. There is no statute that expressly authorizes the President to take possession of property as he did here. Nor is there any Act of Congress to which our attention has been directed from which such a power can fairly be implied. Indeed, we do not understand the Government to rely on statutory authorization for this seizure. . . .

Moreover, the use of the seizure technique to solve labor disputes in order to prevent work stoppages was not only unauthorized by any congressional enactment; prior to this controversy, Congress had refused to adopt that method of settling labor disputes. When the Taft-Hartley Act was under consideration in 1947, Congress rejected an amendment which would have authorized such governmental seizures in cases of emergency. . . .

It is clear that if the President had authority to issue the order he did, it must be found in some provision of the Constitution. And it is not claimed that express constitutional language grants this power to the President. The contention is that presidential power should be implied from the aggregate of his powers under the Constitution. Particular reliance is placed on provisions in Article II which say that "the executive Power shall be vested in a president . . ."; that "he shall take care that the laws be faithfully executed"; and that he "shall be commander-in-chief of the army and navy of the United States."

The order cannot properly be sustained as an exercise of the President's military power as Commander-in-Chief of the Armed Forces. The Government attempts to do so by citing a number of cases upholding broad powers in military commanders engaged in day-to-day fighting in a theater of war. Such cases need not concern us here. Even though "theater of war" be an expanding concept, we cannot with faithfulness to our constitutional system hold that the Commander-in-Chief of the Armed Forces has the ultimate power as such to take possession of private property in order to keep labor disputes from stopping production. This is a job for the Nation's lawmakers, not for its military authorities.

Nor can the seizure order be sustained because of the several constitutional provisions that grant executive power to the President. In the framework of our Constitution, the President's power to see that the laws are faithfully executed refutes the idea that he is to be a lawmaker. The Constitution limits his functions in the lawmaking process to the recommending of laws he thinks wise and the vetoing of laws he thinks bad. And the Constitution is neither silent nor equivocal about who shall make laws which the President is to execute. The first section of the first article says that "All legislative powers herein granted shall be vested in a Congress of the United States . . ." After granting many powers to the Congress, Article I goes on to provide that Congress may "make all laws which shall be necessary and proper for carrying into execution the foregoing powers and all other powers vested by this Constitution in the Government of the United States, or in any department or officer thereof." . . .

It is said that other Presidents without congressional authority have taken possession of private business enterprises in order to settle labor disputes. But even if this be true, Congress has not thereby lost its exclusive constitutional authority to make laws necessary and proper to carry out the powers vested by the Constitution "in the Government of the United States, or any department or officer thereof."

The Founders of this Nation entrusted the lawmaking power to the Congress alone in both good and bad times. It would do no good to recall the historical events, the fears of power and the hopes for freedom that lay behind their choice. Such a review would but confirm our holding that this seizure order cannot stand.

The judgment of the District Court is

Affirmed.

Mr. Justice Frankfurter, concurring:

In adopting the provisions which it did, by the Labor Management Relations Act of 1947, for dealing with a "national emergency" arising out of a breakdown in peaceful industrial relations, Congress was very familiar with Government seizure as a protective measure. On a balance of considerations Congress chose not to lodge this power in the President. . . .

Nothing can be plainer than that Congress made a conscious choice of policy in a field full of perplexity and peculiarly within legislative responsibility for choice. In formulating legislation for dealing with industrial conflicts, Congress could not more clearly and emphatically have withheld authority than it did in 1947. . . .

. . . But it is now claimed that the President has seizure power by virtue of the Defense Production Act of 1950 and its amendments. And the claim is based on the occurrence of new events—Korea and the need for stabilization, etc.—although it was well known that seizure power was withheld by the Act of 1947, and although the President, whose specific requests for other authority were in the main granted by Congress, never suggested that in view of the new events he needed the power of seizure which Congress in its judgment had decided to withhold from him. . . .

A scheme of government like ours no doubt at times feels the lack of power to act with complete, all-embracing, swiftly moving authority. No doubt a government with distributed authority, subject to be challenged in the courts of law, at least long enough to consider and adjudicate the challenge, labors under restrictions from which other governments are free. It has not been our tradition to envy such governments. In any event our government was designed to have such restrictions. The price was deemed not too high in view of the safeguards which these restrictions afford. . . .

MR. JUSTICE DOUGLAS, CONCURRING:

If we sanctioned the present exercise of power by the President, we would be expanding Article 2 of the Constitution and rewriting it to suit the political conveniences of the present emergency. Article 2 which vests the "executive Power" in the President defines that power with particularity. Article 2, Section 2 makes the Chief Executive the Commander-in-Chief of the Army and Navy. But our history and tradition rebel at the thought that the grant of military power carries with it authority over civilian affairs. Article 2, Section 3 provides that the President shall "from time to time give to the Congress information of the state of the Union, and recommend to their consideration such measures as he shall judge necessary and expedient." The power to recommend legislation, granted to the President, serves only to emphasize that it is his function to recommend and that it is the function of the Congress to legislate. Article 2, Section 3 also provides that the President "shall take care that the laws be faithfully executed." But as Mr. Justice Black and Mr. Justice Frankfurter point out the power to execute the laws starts and ends with the laws Congress has enacted. . . .

[MR. JUSTICE JACKSON, concurred in the judgment and opinion of the Court.]

MR. JUSTICE BURTON, CONCURRING:

The controlling fact here is that Congress, within its constitutionally delegated power, has prescribed for the President specific procedures, exclusive of seizure, for his use in meeting the present type of emergency. Congress has reserved to itself the right to determine where and when to authorize the seizure of property in meeting such an emergency. Under these circumstances, the President's order of April 8 invaded the jurisdiction of Congress. It violated the essence of the principle of the separation of governmental powers. Accordingly, the injunction against its effectiveness should be sustained. . . .

MR. JUSTICE CLARK, CONCURRING IN THE JUDGMENT OF THE COURT:

The limits of presidential power are obscure. However, Article II, no less than Article I, is part of "a constitution intended to endure for ages to come, and, consequently, to be adapted to the various crises of human affairs." Some of our Presidents, such as Lincoln, "felt that measures otherwise unconstitutional might become lawful by becoming indispensable to the preservation of the Constitution through the preservation of the nation."

Others, such as Theodore Roosevelt, thought the President to be capable, as a "steward" of the people, of exerting all power save that which is specifically prohibited by the Constitution or the Congress. In my view—taught me not only by the decision of Chief Justice Marshall in *Little v. Barreme*, but also by a score of other pronouncements of distinguished members of this bench—the Constitution does grant to the President extensive authority in times of grave and imperative national emergency. In fact, to my thinking, such a grant may well be necessary to the very existence of the Constitution itself. As Lincoln aptly said, "[is] it possible to lose the Nation and yet preserve the Constitution?" In describing this authority I care not whether one calls it "residual," "inherent," "moral," "implied," "aggregate," "emergency," or otherwise. I am of the conviction that those who have had the gratifying experience of being the President's lawyer have used one or more of these adjectives only with the utmost of sincerity and the highest of purpose.

I conclude that where Congress has laid down specific procedures to deal with the type of crisis confronting the President, he must follow those procedures in meeting the crisis; but that in the absence of such action by Congress, the President's independent power to act depends upon the gravity of the situation confronting the nation. I cannot sustain the seizure in question because here, as in *Little v. Barreme*, Congress had prescribed methods to be followed by the President in meeting the emergency at hand. . . .

. . . The hard fact remains that neither the Defense Production Act nor Taft-Hartley authorized the seizure challenged here, and the Government made no effort to comply with the procedures established by the Selective Service Act of 1948, a statute which expressly authorizes seizures when producers fail to supply necessary defense materiel. . . .

MR. CHIEF JUSTICE VINSON, WITH WHOM MR. JUSTICE REED AND MR. JUSTICE MINTON JOIN, DISSENTING:

In passing upon the question of presidential powers in this case, we must first consider the context in which those powers were exercised.

Those who suggest that this is a case involving extraordinary powers should be mindful that these are extraordinary times. A world not yet recovered from the devastation of World War II has been forced to face the threat of another and more terrifying global conflict. . . .

The steel mills were seized for a public use. The power of eminent domain, invoked in this case, is an essential attribute of sovereignty and has long been recognized as a power of the Federal Government. . . .

Admitting that the Government could seize the mills, plaintiffs claim that the implied power of eminent domain can be exercised only under an Act of Congress; under no circumstances, they say, can that power be exercised by the President unless he can point to an express provision in enabling legislation. This was the view adopted by the District Judge when he granted the preliminary injunction. Without an answer, without hearing evidence, he determined the issue on the basis of his "fixed conclusion . . . that defendant's acts are illegal" because the President's only course in the face of an emergency is to present the matter to Congress and await the final passage of legislation which will enable the Government to cope with threatened disaster.

Under this view, the President is left powerless at the very moment when the need for action may be most pressing and when no one, other than he, is immediately capable of action. Under this view, he is left powerless because a power not expressly given to Congress is nevertheless found to rest exclusively with Congress. . . .

In passing upon the grave constitutional question presented in this case, we must never forget, as Chief Justice Marshall admonished, that the Constitution is "intended to endure for ages to come, and, consequently, to be adapted to the various *crises* of human affairs," and that "its means are adequate to its ends." Cases do arise presenting questions which could not have been foreseen by the Framers. In such cases, the Constitution has been treated as a living document adaptable to new situations. But we are not called upon today to expand the Constitution to meet a new situation. For, in this case, we need only look to history and time-honored principles of constitutional law—principles that have been applied consistently by all branches of the Government throughout our history. It is those who assert the invalidity of the Executive Order who seek to amend the Constitution in this case. . . .

A review of executive action demonstrates that our Presidents have on many occasions exhibited the leadership contemplated by the Framers when they made the President Commander-in-Chief, and imposed upon him the trust to "take care that the laws be faithfully executed." With or without explicit statutory authorization, Presidents have at such times dealt with national emergencies by acting promptly and resolutely to enforce legislative programs, at least to save those programs until Congress could act. Congress and the courts have responded to such executive initiative with consistent approval. . . .

[The Chief Justice then surveys executive actions from Washington to Truman dealing with various national emergencies.]

This is but a cursory summary of executive leadership. But it amply demonstrates that Presidents have taken prompt action to enforce the laws and protect the country whether or not Congress happened to provide in advance for the particular method of execution. At the minimum, the executive actions reviewed herein sustain the action of the President in this case. And many of the cited examples of presidential practice go far beyond the extent of power necessary to sustain the President's order to seize the steel mills. The fact that temporary executive siezures of industrial plants to meet an emergency have not been directly tested in this court furnishes not the slightest suggestion that such actions have been illegal. Rather, the fact that Congress and the courts have consistently recognized and given their support to such executive action indicates that such a power of seizure has been accepted throughout our history. . . .

As the District Judge stated, this is no time for "timorous" judicial action. But neither is this a time for timorous executive action. Faced with the duty of executing the defense programs which Congress had enacted and the disastrous effects that any stoppage in steel production would have on those programs, the President acted to preserve those programs by seizing the steel mills. There is no question that the possession was other than temporary in character and subject to congressional direction—either approving, disapproving or regulating the manner in which the mills were to be administered and returned to the owners. The President immediately informed Congress of his action and clearly stated his intention to abide by the legislative will. No basis for claims of arbitrary action, unlimited powers or dictatorial usurpation of congressional power appears from the facts of this case. On the contrary, judicial, legislative and executive precedents throughout our history demonstrate that in this case the President acted in full conformity with his duties under the Constitution. Accordingly, we would reverse the order of the District Court.

Chapter X

Contract Clause

"No state shall . . . pass any . . . *ex post facto* law, or law impairing the obligation of contracts . . ." —Art. I, Sec. 10

In this Chapter:
Calder v. Bull (1798)
Dartmouth College v. Woodward (1819)

The prohibition of *ex post facto* laws applies only to criminal, and not civil, laws.

12. *CALDER v. BULL* (1798)

This is the first decision in which the Supreme Court defined the meaning of ex post facto *laws. It also spelled out the extent of the power of republican legislatures within the framework of natural law.*

Background: *The Connecticut legislature passed a law granting a citizen named Bull and his wife the right to a new hearing after the period of his appeal against a probate court decision had expired. Another claimant, Calder, after losing his appeal in the highest Connecticut court, took his case to the United States Supreme Court on the ground that the act of the Connecticut legislature was retrospective, that is, an* ex post facto *law, and as such, forbidden by Art. I, Sec. 10 of the Constitution. The Supreme Court, in this decision, upheld the Connecticut court, explaining that this was a civil case and that the* ex post facto *prohibition is applicable only to criminal law.*

Some Related Cases
(On *Ex Post Facto* Laws):

Ex Parte Garland (1867)
Burgess v. Salmon (1878)
Holden v. Minnesota (1890)
Bankers Trust v. Blodgett (1923)
Lindsey v. Washington (1937)

JUSTICE CHASE:

The counsel for the plaintiffs in error contend, that the . . . law of the legislature of Connecticut, granting a new hearing, in the above case, is an *ex post facto* law, prohibited by the Constitution of the United States; that any law of the Federal Government, or of any of the State Governments, contrary to the Constitution of the United States, is void; and that this court possesses the power to declare such law void.

It appears to me a self-evident proposition, that the several state legislatures retain all the powers of legislation, delegated to them by the state constitutions; which are not expressly taken away by the Constitution of the United States. The establishing of courts of justice, the appointment of judges, and the making of regulations for the administration of justice within each State, according to its laws, on all subjects not intrusted to the Federal Government, appears to me to be the peculiar and exclusive province and duty of the state legislatures. All the powers delegated by the people of the United States to the Federal Government are defined, and no *constructive* powers can be exercised by it, and all the powers that remain in the State Governments are indefinite. . . . The sole inquiry is, whether this resolution or law of Connecticut . . . is an *ex post facto* law, within the prohibition of the Federal Constitution?

Whether the legislature of any of the States can revise and correct by law, a decision of any of its courts of justice, although not prohibited by the constitution of the State, is a question of very great importance, and not necessary now to be determined; because the resolution or law in question does not go so far. I cannot subscribe to the omnipotence of a state legislature, or that it is absolute and without control; although its authority should not be expressly restrained by the Constitution, or fundamental law of the State. The people of the United States erected their constitutions or forms of government, to establish justice, to promote the general welfare, to secure the blessings of liberty; and to protect their persons and property from violence. The purposes for which men enter into society will determine the nature and terms of the social compact; and as they are the foundation of the legislative power, they will decide what are the proper objects of it. The nature and ends of legislative power will limit the exercise of it. This fundamental principle flows from the very nature of our free republican governments, that no man should be compelled to do what the laws do not require, nor to refrain from acts which the laws permit. There are acts which the federal or state legislature cannot do, without exceeding their authority. There are certain vital principles in our free republican governments which will determine and overrule an apparent and flagrant abuse of legislative power; as to authorize manifest injustice by positive law; or to take away that security for personal liberty, or private property, for the protection whereof the Government was established. An Act of the legislature (for I cannot call it a law), contrary to the great first principles of the social compact, cannot be considered a rightful exercise of legislative authority. The obligation of a law in governments established on express compact, and on republican principles, must be determined by the nature of the power on which it is founded.

A few instances will suffice to explain what I mean. A law that punished a citizen for an innocent action, or, in other words, for an act which, when done, was in violation of no existing law; a law that destroys, or impairs, the lawful private contracts of citizens; a law that makes a man a judge in his own cause; or a law that takes property from A, and gives it to B. It is against all reason and justice for a people to intrust a legislature with such powers; and, therefore, it cannot be presumed that they have done it. The genius, the nature, and the spirit of our State Governments amount to a prohibition of such acts of legislation; and the general principles of law and reason forbid them. The legislature may enjoin, permit, forbid and punish; they may declare new crimes, and establish rules of conduct for all its citizens in future cases; they may command what is right, and prohibit what is wrong; but they cannot change innocence into guilt, or punish innocence as a crime; or violate the right of an antecedent lawful private contract, or the right of private property. To maintain that our federal or state legislature possesses such powers, if they had not been expressly restrained, would, in my opinion, be a political heresy altogether inadmissible in our free republican governments. . . .

The Constitution of the United States, Article I, Section 9, prohibits the legislature of the United States from passing any *ex post facto* law; and in Section 10 lays several restrictions on the authority of the legislatures of the several States; and among them, "that no state shall pass any *ex post facto* law." . . .

I will state what laws I consider *ex post facto* laws, within the words and the intent of the prohibition. 1st. Every law that makes an action done before the passing of the law, and which was innocent when done, criminal; and punishes such action. 2d. Every law that aggravates a crime, or makes it greater than it was, when committed. 3d. Every law that changes the punishment, and inflicts a greater punishment, than the law annexed to the crime, when committed. 4th. Every law that alters the legal rules of evidence, and receives less, or different testimony, than the law required at the time of the commission of the offense, in order to convict the offender. All these, and similar laws, are manifestly unjust and oppressive. In my opinion, the true distinction is between *ex post facto* laws, and restrospective laws. Every *ex post facto* law must necessarily be retrospective: but every retrospective law is not an *ex post facto* law; the former only are prohibited. Every law that takes away or impairs rights vested, agreeably to existing laws, is retrospective, and is generally unjust, and may be oppressive; and it is a good general rule, that a law should have no retrospect; but there are cases in which laws may justly, and for the benefit of the community, and also of individuals, relate to a time antecedent to their commencement; as statutes of oblivion or of pardon. They are certainly retrospective, and literally both concerning and after the facts committed. But I do not consider any law *ex post facto,* within the prohibition, that mollifies the rigor of the criminal law; but only those that create or aggravate the crime; or increase the punishment, or change the rules of evidence, for the purpose of conviction. Every law that is to have an operation before the making thereof, as to commence at an antecedent time; or to save time from the statute of limitations; or to excuse acts which were unlawful, and before committed, and the like, is retrospective. But such laws may be proper or necessary, as the case may be. There is a great and apparent difference between making an unlawful act lawful; and the making an innocent action criminal, and punishing it as a crime. The expressions "*ex post facto* laws" are technical, they had been in use long before the Revolution, and had acquired an appropriate meaning by legislators, lawyers and authors. The celebrated and judicious Sir William Blackstone, in his Commentaries, considers an *ex post facto* law precisely in the same light I have done. His opinion is confirmed by his successor, Mr. Wooddeson; and by the author of *The Federalist,* who I esteem superior to both, for his extensive and accurate knowledge of the true principles of government. . . . If the term *ex post facto* law is to be construed to include and to prohibit the enacting any law after the fact, it will greatly restrict the power of the federal and state legislatures; and the consequences of such a construction may not be foreseen. . . .

It is not to be presumed that the federal or state legislatures will pass laws to deprive citizens of rights vested in them by existing laws; unless for the benefit of the whole community; and on making full satisfaction. The restraint against making any *ex post facto* laws was not considered, by the Framers of the Constitution, as extending to prohibit the depriving a citizen even of a vested right to property; or the provision, "that private property should not be taken for public use, without just compensation," was unnecessary.

It seems to me that the right of property, in its origin, could only arise from compact express or implied, and I think it the better opinion, that the right, as well as the mode or manner of acquiring property, and of alienating or transferring, inheriting or transmitting it, is conferred by society, is regulated by civil institution, and is always subject to the rules prescribed by positive law. When I say that a right is vested in a citizen. I mean, that he has the power to do certain actions, or to possess certain things, according to the law of the land. . . .

I am of opinion that the decree of the supreme court of errors of Connecticut be affirmed, with costs.

JUSTICE PATERSON:

I had an ardent desire to have extended the provision in the Constitution to retrospective laws in general. There is neither policy nor safety in such laws; and therefore, I have always had a strong aversion against them. It may, in general, be truly observed of retrospective laws of every description, that they neither accord with sound legislation, nor the fundamental principles of the social compact. But on full consideration, I am convinced, that *ex post facto* laws must be limited in the manner already expressed; they must be taken in their technical, which is also their common and general, acceptation, and are not to be understood in their literal sense.

JUSTICE IREDELL:

If . . . a government, composed of legislative, executive and judicial departments, were established, by a constitution which imposed no limits on the legislative power, the consequence would inevitably be, that whatever the legislative power chose to enact, would be lawfully enacted, and the judicial power could never interpose to pronounce it void. It is true, that some speculative jurists have held, that a legislative Act against natural justice must, in itself, be void; but I cannot think that, under such a government any court of justice would possess a power to declare it so. Sir William Blackstone, having put the strong case of an Act of Parliament, which authorizes a man to try his own cause, explicitly adds, that even in that case, "there is no court that has power to defeat the intent of the legislature, when couched in such evident and express words, as leave no doubt whether it was the intent of the legislature, or no."

In order, therefore, to guard against so great an evil, it has been the policy of all the American States, which have, individually, framed their state constitutions, since the Revolution, and of the people of the United States, when they framed the Federal Constitution, to define with precision the objects of the legislative power, and to restrain its exercise within marked and settled boundaries. If any Act of Congress, or of the legislature of a State, violates those constitutional provisions, it is unquestionably void; though, I admit, that as the authority to declare it void is of a delicate and lawful nature, the Court will never resort to that authority, but in a clear and urgent case. If, on the other hand, the legislature of the Union, or the legislature of any member of the Union, shall pass a law, within the general scope of their constitutional power, the Court cannot pronounce it to be void, merely because it is, in their judgment, contrary to the principles of natural justice. The ideas of natural justice are regulated by no fixed standard: the ablest and the purest men have differed upon the subject; and all that the Court could properly say, in such an event, would be, that the legislature (possessed of an equal right of opinion) had passed an Act which, in the opinion of the judges, was inconsistent with the abstract principles of natural justice. There are then but two lights, in which the subject can be viewed: 1st. If the legislature pursue the authority delegated to them, their Acts are valid. 2d. If they transgress the boundaries of that authority, their Acts are invalid. In the former case, they exercise the discretion vested in them by the people, to whom alone they are responsible for the faithful discharge of their trust: but in the latter case, they violate a fundamental law, which must be our guide, whenever we are called upon, as judges, to determine the validity of a legislative Act.

Still, however, in the present instance, the Act or resolution of the legislature of Connecticut, cannot be regarded as an *ex post facto* law; for the true construction of the prohibition extends to criminal, not to civil issues. . . .

The policy, the reason and humanity of the prohibition, do not . . . extend to civil cases, to cases that merely affect the private property of citizens. Some of the most necessary and important Acts of legislation are, on the contrary, founded upon the principle, that private rights must yield to public exigencies. Highways are run through private grounds; fortifications, lighthouses, and other public edifices, are necessarily sometimes built upon the soil owned by individuals. In such, and similar cases, if the owners should refuse voluntarily to accommodate the public, they must be constrained, so far as the public necessities require; and justice is done, by allowing them a reasonable equivalent. Without the possession of this power, the operations of government would often be obstructed, and society itself would be endangered. It is not sufficient to urge, that the power may be abused, for such is the nature of all power—such is the tendency of every human institution: and, it might as fairly be said, that the power of taxation, which is only circumscribed by the discretion of the body in which it is vested, ought not to be granted, because the legislature, disregarding its true objects, might, for visionary and useless projects, impose a tax to the amount of nineteen shillings in the pound. We must be content to limit power, where we can, and where we cannot, consistently with its use, we must be content to repose a salutary confidence. It is our consolation, that there never existed a government, in ancient or modern times, more free from danger in this respect, than the governments of America. . . .

Judgment affirmed.

Charters, being contracts, are protected against interference by legislatures.

13. *DARTMOUTH COLLEGE v. WOODWARD* (1819)

This case is important because it was one of the earliest in which the United States Supreme Court interpreted the Constitution to apply to a corporation charter which it considered a contract. This meant that henceforth charters, being contracts, could not be impaired by any legislative enactment. The decision, written by Chief Justice Marshall, had an influence on American economic and business history in the sense that it encouraged and protected corporate business against legislation.

Background: *In 1769 King George III granted a charter establishing Dartmouth College in that year. In 1816 the State of New Hampshire changed the royal charter and, under the new one, set up another board of trustees. The old board protested that this was unconstitutional because it violated the previous charter which was, it argued, a contract. The Supreme Court, in this historic case, agreed with the old board.*

Some Related Cases
(On Obligation of Contracts):
- *Fletcher v. Peck* (1810)
- *Sturges v. Crowninshield* (1819)
- *Providence Bank v. Billings* (1830)
- *Charles River Bridge Co. v. Warren Bridge Co.* (1837)
- *Paul v. Virginia* (1869)
- *New Orleans v. New Orleans Waterworks Co.* (1891)
- *Atlantic Coast Line R. Co. v. Goldsboro* (1914)
- *Pennsylvania Hospital v. Philadelphia* (1917)
- *Perry v. United States* (1935)
- *Asbury Hospital v. Cass County* (1945)
- *Connecticut Mutual Life Insurance Co. v. Moore* (1948)

THE OPINION OF THE COURT WAS DELIVERED BY CHIEF JUSTICE MARSHALL:

It can require no argument to prove, that the circumstances of this case constitute a contract. An application is made to the crown for a charter to incorporate a religious and literary institution. In the application, it is stated, that large contributions have been made for the object, which will be conferred on the corporation, as soon as it shall be created. The charter is granted, and on its faith the property is conveyed. Surely, in this transaction every ingredient of a complete and legitimate contract is to be found. The points for consideration are, 1. Is this contract protected by the Constitution of the United States? 2. Is it impaired by the Acts under which the defendant holds? . . .

The parties in this case differ less on general principles, less on the true construction of the Constitution in the abstract, than on the application of those principles to this case, and on the true construction of the charter of 1769. This is the point on which the cause essentially depends. If the act of incorporation be a grant of political power, if it creates a civil institution, to be employed in the administration of the government, or if the funds of the college be public property, or if the State of New Hampshire, as a government, be alone interested in its transactions, the subject is one in which the legislature of the State may act according to its judgment, unrestrained by any limitation of its power imposed by the Constitution of the United States.

But if this be a private eleemosynary institution, endowed with a capacity to take property, for objects unconnected with government, whose funds are bestowed by individuals, on the faith of the charter; if the donors have stipulated for the future disposition and management of those funds, in the manner prescribed by themselves; there may be more difficulty in the case, although neither the persons who have made these stipulations, nor those for whose benefit they were made, should be parties to the cause. Those who are no longer interested in the property, may yet retain such an interest in the preservation of their own arrangements, as to have a right to insist, that those arrangements shall be held sacred. Or, if they have themselves disappeared, it becomes a subject of serious and anxious inquiry, whether those whom they have legally empowered to represent them forever, may not assert all the rights which they possessed, while in being; whether, if they be without personal representatives, who may feel injured by a violation of the compact, the trustees be not so completely their representatives, in the eye of the law, as to stand in their place, not only as respects the government of the college, but also as respects the maintenance of the college charter. It becomes then the duty of the court, most seriously to examine this charter, and to ascertain its true character. . . .

A corporation is an artificial being, invisible, intangible, and existing only in contemplation of law. Being the mere creature of law, it possesses only those properties which the charter of its creation confers upon it, either expressly or as incidental to its very existence. These are such as are supposed best calculated to effect the object for which it was created. Among the most important are immortality, and, if the expression may be allowed, individuality; properties by which a perpetual succession of many persons are considered as the same, and may act as a single individual. . . . It is no more a State instrument than a natural person exercising the same powers would be. If, then, a natural person, employed by individuals in the education of youth, or for the government of a seminary in which youth is educated, would not become a public officer, or be considered as a member of the civil government, how is it that this artificial being, created by law for the purpose of being employed by the same individuals for the same purposes, should become a part of the civil government of the country? Is it because its existence, its capacities, its powers, are given by law? Because the government has given it the power to take and to hold property in a particular form and for particular purposes, has the Government a consequent right substantially to change that form, or to vary the purposes to which the property is to be applied? This principle has never been asserted or recognized, and is supported by no authority. Can it derive aid from reason?

The objects for which a corporation is created are universally such as the Government wishes to promote. . . . The benefit to the public is considered as an ample compensation for the faculty it confers, and the corporation is created. If the advantages to the public constitute a full compensation for the faculty it gives, there can be no reason for exacting a further compensation, by claiming a right to exercise over this artificial being a power which changes its nature, and touches the fund for the security and application of which it was created. There can be no reason for implying in a charter, given for a valuable consideration, a power which is not only not expressed, but is in direct contradiction to its express stipulations.

From the fact, then, that a charter of incorporation has been granted, nothing can be inferred which changes the character of the institution, or transfers to the Government any new power over it. The character of civil institutions does not grow out of their incorporation, but out of the manner in which they are formed, and the objects for which they are created. The right to change them is not founded on their being incorporated, but on their being the instruments of Government, created for its purpose. The same institutions, created for the same objects, though not incorporated, would be public institutions, and, of course, be controllable by the legislature. The incorporating act neither gives nor prevents this control. Neither, in reason, can the incorporating act change the character of a private eleemosynary institution. . . .

From this review of the charter, it appears that Dartmouth College is an eleemosynary institution, incorporated for the purpose of perpetuating the application of the bounty of the donors to the specified objects of that bounty; that its trustees or governors were originally named by the founder, and invested with the power of perpetuating themselves; that they are not public officers, nor is it a civil institution participating in the administration of government; but a charity school, or a seminary of education, incorporated for the preservation of its property, and the perpetual application of that property to the objects of its creation.

Yet a question remains to be considered of more real difficulty, on which more doubt has been entertained than on all that have been discussed. The founders of the college, at least those whose contributions were in money, have parted with the property bestowed upon it, and their representatives have no interest in that property. The donors of land are equally without interest so long as the corporation shall exist. Could they be found, they are unaffected by any alteration in its constitution, and probably regardless of its form or even of its existence. The students are fluctuating, and no individual among our youth has a vested interest in the institution which can be asserted in a court of justice. Neither the founders of the college, nor the youth for whose benefit it was founded, complain of the alteration made in its charter, or think themselves injured by it. The trustees alone complain, and the trustees have no beneficial interest to be protected. Can this be such a contract as the Constitution intended to withdraw from the power of state legislation? Contracts, the parties to which have a vested beneficial interest, and those only, it has been said, are the objects about which the Constitution is solicitous, and to which its protection is extended.

The Court has bestowed on this argument the most deliberate consideration, and the result will be stated. Dr. Wheelock, acting for himself and for those who, at his solicitation, had made contributions to his school, applied for this charter, as the instrument which should enable him and them to perpetuate their beneficent intention. It was granted. An artificial, immortal being was created by the crown, capable of receiving and distributing forever, according to the will of the donors, the donations which should be made to it. On this being, the contributions which had been collected were immediately bestowed. These gifts were made, not indeed to make a profit for the donors or their posterity, but for something, in their opinion, of inestimable value; for something which they deemed a full equivalent for the money with which it was purchased. The consideration for which they stipulated, is the perpetual application of the fund to its object, in the mode prescribed by themselves. Their descendants may take no interest in the preservation of this consideration. But in this respect their descendants are not their representatives. They are represented by the corporation. The corporation is the assignee of their rights, stands in their place, and distributes their bounty, as they would themselves have distributed it had they been immortal. So with respect to the students who are to derive learning from this source. The corporation is a trustee for them also. Their potential rights, which, taken distributively, are imperceptible, amount collectively to a most important interest. These are, in the aggregate, to be exercised, asserted, and protected by the corporation. They were as completely out of the donors, at the instant of their being vested in the corporation, and as incapable of being asserted by the students, as at present. . . .

This is plainly a contract to which the donors, the trustees, and the crown (to whose rights and obligations New Hampshire succeeds) were the original parties. It is a contract made on a valuable consideration. It is a contract for the security and disposition of property. It is a contract on the faith of which real and personal estate has been conveyed to the corporation. It is then a contract within the letter of the Constitution, and within its spirit also, unless the fact that the property is invested by the donors in trustees, for the promotion of religion and education, for the benefit of persons who are perpetually changing, though the objects remain the same, shall create a particular exception, taking this case out of the prohibition contained in the Constitution. . . .

It is more than possible that the preservation of rights of this description was not particularly in the view of the Framers of the Constitution, when the clause under consideration was introduced into that instrument. It is probable that interferences of more frequent recurrence, to which the temptation was stronger, and of which the mischief was more extensive, constituted the great motive for imposing this restriction on the state legislatures. But although a particular and a rare case may not, in itself, be of sufficient magnitude to induce a rule, yet it must be governed by the rule, when established, unless some plain and strong reason for excluding it can be given. It is not enough to say, that this particular case was not in the mind of the Convention when the article was framed, nor of the American people when it was adopted. It is necessary to go further, and to say that, had this particular case been suggested, the language would have been so varied as to exclude it, or it would have been made a special exception. The case being within the words of the rule, must be within its operation likewise, unless there be something in the literal construction so obviously absurd or mischievous, or repugnant to the general spirit of the instrument, as to justify those who expound the Constitution in making it an exception.

On what safe and intelligible ground can this exception stand? There is no expression in the Constitution, no sentiment delivered by its contemporaneous expounders, which would justify us in making it. In the absence of all authority of this kind, is there, in the nature and reason of the case itself, that which would sustain a construction of the Constitution not warranted by its words? Are contracts of this description of a character to excite so little interest that we must exclude them from the provisions of the Constitution, as being unworthy of the attention of those who framed the instrument? Or does public policy so imperiously demand their remaining exposed to legislative alteration as to compel us, or rather permit us to say, that these words, which were introduced to give stability to contracts, and which in their plain import comprehend this contract, must yet be so construed as to exclude it? . . .

If the insignificance of the object does not require that we should exclude contracts respecting it from the protection of the Constitution, neither, as we conceive, is the policy of leaving them subject to legislative alteration so apparent, as to require a forced construction of that instrument, in order to effect it. These eleemosynary institutions do not fill the place, which would otherwise be occupied by government, but that which would otherwise remain vacant. They are complete acquisitions to literature. They are donations to education; donations, which any government must be disposed rather to encourage than to discountenance. It requires no very critical examination of the human mind, to enable us to determine, that one great inducement to these gifts is the conviction felt by the giver, that the disposition he makes of them is immutable. It is probable, that no man was, and that no man ever will be, the founder of a college, believing at the time, that an act of incorporation constitutes no security for the institution; believing, that it is immediately to be deemed a public institution, whose funds are to be governed and applied, not by the will of the donor, but by the will of the legislature. All such gifts are made in the pleasing, perhaps delusive hope, that the charity will flow forever in the channel which the givers have marked out for it. If every man finds in his own bosom strong evidence of the universality of this sentiment, there can be but little reason to imagine, that the Framers of our Constitution were strangers to it, and that, feeling the necessity and policy of giving permanence and security to contracts, of withdrawing them from the influence of legislative bodies, whose fluctuating policy, and repeated interferences, produced the most perplexing and injurious embarrassments, they still deemed it necessary to leave these contracts subject to those interferences. The motives for such an exception must be very powerful, to justify the construction which makes it. . . .

2. We next proceed to the inquiry, whether its obligation has

been impaired by those acts of the legislature of New Hampshire, to which the special verdict refers? . . .

It has been already stated, that the Act "to amend the charter, and enlarge and improve the corporation of Dartmouth College," increases the number of trustees to twenty-one, gives the appointment of the additional members to the executive of the State, and creates a board of overseers, to consist of twenty-five persons, of whom twenty-one are also appointed by the executive of New Hampshire, who have power to inspect and control the most important acts of the trustees.

On the effect of this law [of 1816], two opinions cannot be entertained. Between acting directly, and acting through the agency of trustees and overseers, no essential difference is perceived. The whole power of governing the college is transferred from trustees appointed according to the will of the founder, expressed in the charter, to the executive of New Hampshire. The management and application of the funds of this eleemosynary institution, which are placed by the donors in the hands of trustees named in the charter, and empowered to perpetuate themselves, are placed by this Act under the control of the government of the State. The will of the State is substituted for the will of the donors, in every essential operation of the college. This is not an immaterial change. The founders of the college contracted not merely for the perpetual application of the funds which they gave to the object for which those funds were given; they contracted, also, to secure that application by the constitution of the corporation. They contracted for a system which should, as far as human foresight can provide, retain forever the government of the literary institution they had formed, in the hands of persons approved by themselves. This system is totally changed. The charter of 1769 exists no longer. It is reorganized; and reorganized in such a manner as to convert a literary institution, moulded according to the will of its founders, and placed under the control of private literary men, into a machine entirely subservient to the will of government. This may be for the advantage of this college in particular, and may be for the advantage of literature in general: but it is not according to the will of the donors, and is subversive of that contract on the faith of which their property was given. . . .

It results from this opinion, that the Acts of the legislature of New Hampshire, which are stated in the special verdict found in this cause, are repugnant to the Constitution of the United States; and that the judgment on this special verdict ought to have been for the plaintiffs. The judgment of the State Court must, therefore, be reversed.

[Justices Washington and Story delivered separate opinions with the same holding. Justice Duvall dissented.]

. . . it is considered, ordered and adjudged by this court, now here, that the aforesaid judgment of the said Superior Court of judicature of the State of New Hampshire be, and the same hereby is, reversed and annulled. . . .

Chapter XI

Commerce Power

"The Congress shall have power to . . . regulate commerce with foreign nations, and among the several states . . ."—Art. I, Sec. 8

In this Chapter:
Gibbons v. Ogden (1824)
National Labor Relations Board v. Jones & Laughlin Steel Corp. (1937)
Wickard v. Filburn (1942)

Commerce is more than mere "traffic"; it involves a whole range of interconnected activities protected by the Constitution.

14. *GIBBONS v. OGDEN* (1824)

In this decision, Chief Justice Marshall, following his general philosophy of strengthening the central authority, interpreted the famous "Commerce clause" of the Constitution in such a way as to enable the Federal Government to regulate and encourage commerce with the widest possible leeway.

Background: *Robert Livingston and Robert Fulton had been given exclusive right by the State of New York to navigate steamboats in the waters of the State. Aaron Ogden, who acquired this right, sued a competitor named Gibbons in order to prevent him from operating boats on the Hudson River. Ogden lost.*

Some Related Cases
(On the Commerce Clause):
Brown v. Maryland (1827)
Thurlow v. Massachusetts (1847)
Brown v. Houston (1885)
Parker v. Brown (1943)
Southern Pacific v. Arizona (1945)
Hood v. DuMond (1949)

CHIEF JUSTICE MARSHALL DELIVERED THE OPINION OF THE COURT:

As preliminary to the very able discussions of the Constitution, which we have heard from the bar, and as having some influence on its construction, reference has been made to the political situation of these States, anterior to its formation. It has been said, that they were sovereign, were completely independent, and were connected with each other only by a league. This is true. But when these allied sovereigns converted their league into a government, when they converted their congress of ambassadors, deputed to deliberate on their common concerns, and to recommend measures of general utility, into a legislature, empowered to enact laws on the most interesting subjects, the whole character in which the States appear, underwent a change, the extent of which must be determined by a fair consideration of the instrument by which that change was effected.

This instrument contains an enumeration of powers expressly granted by the people to their government. It has been said, that these powers ought to be construed strictly. But why ought they to be so construed? Is there one sentence in the Constitution which gives countenance to this rule? In the last of the enumerated powers, that which grants, expressly, the means for carrying all others into execution, Congress is authorized "to make all laws which shall be necessary and proper" for the purpose. But this limitation on the means which may be used, is not extended to the powers which are conferred; nor is there one sentence in the Constitution, which has been pointed out by the gentlemen of the bar, or which we have been able to discern, that prescribes this rule. We do not, therefore, think ourselves justified in adopting it. What do gentlemen mean, by a strict construction? If they contend only against that enlarged construction, which would extend words beyond their natural and obvious import, we might question the application of the term, but should not controvert the principle. If they contend for that narrow construction which, in support of some theory not to be found in the Constitution, would deny to the Government those powers which the words of the grant, as usually understood, import, and which are consistent with the general views and objects of the instrument—for that narrow construction, which would cripple the Government, and render it unequal to the objects for which it is declared to be instituted, and to which the powers given, as fairly understood, render it competent—then we cannot perceive the propriety of this strict construction, nor adopt it as the rule by which the Constitution is to be expounded. As men whose intentions require no concealment, generally employ the words which most directly and aptly express the ideas they intend to convey, the enlightened patriots who framed our Constitution, and the people who adopted it, must be understood to have employed words in their natural sense, and to have intended what they have said. If, from the imperfection of human language, there should be serious doubts respecting the extent of any given power, it is a well-settled rule, that the objects for which it was given, especially, when those objects are expressed in the instrument itself, should have great influence in the construction. . . . We know of no rule for construing the extent of such powers, other than is given by the language of the instrument which confers them, taken in connection with the purposes for which they were conferred.

The words are: "Congress shall have power to regulate commerce with foreign nations, and among the several states, and with the Indian tribes." The subject to be regulated is commerce; and our Constitution being, as was aptly said at the bar, one of enumeration, and not of definition, to ascertain the extent of the power, it becomes necessary to settle the meaning of the word. The counsel for the appellee would limit it to traffic, to buying and selling, or the interchange of commodities, and do not admit that it comprehends navigation. This would restrict a general term, applicable to many objects, to one of its significations. Commerce, undoubtedly, is traffic, but it is something more—it is intercourse. It describes the commercial intercourse between nations, and parts of nations, in all its branches, and is regulated by prescribing rules for carrying on that intercourse. The mind can scarcely conceive a system for regulating commerce between nations which shall exclude all laws concerning navigation, which shall be silent on the admission of the vessels of the one nation into the ports of the other, and be confined to prescribing rules for the conduct of individuals, in the actual employment of buying and selling or of barter. If commerce does not include navigation, the Government of the Union has no direct power over that subject, and can make no law prescribing what shall constitute American vessels, or requiring that they shall be navigated by American seamen. Yet this power has been exercised from the commencement of the Government, has been exercised with the consent of all, and has been understood by all to be a commercial regulation. All America understands, and has uniformly understood, the word "commerce," to comprehend navigation. It was so understood, and must have been so understood, when the Constitution was framed. The power over commerce, including navigation, was one of the primary objects for which the people of America adopted their government, and must have been contemplated in forming it. The convention must have used the word in that sense, because all have understood it in that sense; and the attempt to restrict it comes too late. If the opinion that "commerce," as the word is used in the Constitution, comprehends navigation also, requires any additional confirmation, that additional confirmation is, we think, furnished by the words of the instrument itself. It is a rule of construction, acknowledged by all, that the exceptions from a power mark its extent; for it would be absurd, as well as useless, to except from a granted power, that which was not granted—that which the words of the grant could not comprehend. If, then, there are in the Constitution plain exceptions from the power over navigation, plain inhibitions to the exercise of that power in a particular way, it is a proof that those who made these exceptions, and prescribed these inhibitions, understood the power to which they applied as being granted. The 9th section of the last article declares, that "no preference shall be given, by any regulation of commerce or revenue, to the ports of one state over those of another." This clause cannot be understood as applicable to those laws only which are passed for the purposes of revenue, because it is expressly applied to commercial regulations; and the most obvious preference which can be given to one port over another, in regulating commerce, relates to navigation. But the subsequent part of the sentence is still more explicit. It is, "nor shall vessels bound to or from one state, be obliged to enter, clear or pay duties in another." These words have a direct reference to navigation. . . .

The word used in the Constitution, then, comprehends, and has been always understood to comprehend, navigation within its meaning; and a power to regulate navigation, is as expressly granted, as if that term has been added to the word "commerce." To what commerce does this power extend? The Constitution informs us, to commerce "with foreign nations, and among the several states, and with the Indian tribes." It has, we believe, been universally admitted, that these words comprehend every species of commercial intercourse between the United States and foreign nations. No sort of trade can be carried on between this country and any other, to which this power does not extend. It has been truly said, that commerce, as the word is used in the Constitution, is a unit, every part of which is indicated by the term.

If this be the admitted meaning of the word, in its application to foreign nations, it must carry the same meaning throughout the sentence, and remain a unit, unless there be some plain intelligible cause which alters it. The subject to which the power is next applied, is to commerce, "among the several states." The word "among" means intermingled with A thing which is among others, is intermingled with them. Commerce among the States, cannot stop at the external boundary line of each State, but may be introduced into the interior. It is not intended to say, that these words comprehend that commerce, which is completely internal, which is carried on between man and man in a State, or between different parts of the same State, and which does not extend to or affect other States. Such a power would be inconvenient, and is certainly unnecessary. Comprehensive as the word "among" is, it may very properly be restricted to that commerce which concerns more States than one. The phrase is not one which would probably have been selected to indicate the completely interior traffic of a State, because it is not an apt phrase for that purpose; and the enumeration of the particular classes of commerce to which the power was to be extended, would not have been made, had the intention been to extend the power to every description. The enumeration presupposes something not enumerated; and that something, if we regard the language or the subject of the sentence, must be the exclusively internal commerce of a State. The genius and character of the whole Government seem to be, that its action is to be applied to all the external concerns of the Nation, and to those internal concerns which affect the States generally; but not to those which are completely within a particular State, which do not affect other States, and with which it is not necessary to interfere, for the purpose of executing some of the general powers of the Government. The completely internal commerce of a State, then, may be considered as reserved for the State itself.

But, in regulating commerce with foreign nations, the power of Congress does not stop at the jurisdictional lines of the several States. It would be a very useless power, if it could not pass those lines. The commerce of the United States with foreign nations is that of the whole United States; every district has a right to participate in it. The deep streams which penetrate our country in every direction pass through the interior of almost every State in the Union, and furnish the means of exercising this right. If Congress has the power to regulate it, that power must be exercised whenever the subject exists. If it exists within the States, if a foreign voyage may commence or terminate at a port within a State, then the power of Congress may be exercised within a State.

This principle is, if possible, still more clear, when applied to commerce "among the several states." They either join each other, in which case they are separated by a mathematical line, or they are remote from each other, in which case other States lie between them. What is commerce "among" them; and how is it to be conducted? Can a trading expedition between two adjoining States, commence and terminate outside of each? And if the trading intercourse be between two States remote from each other, must it not commence in one, terminate in the other, and probably pass through a third? Commerce among the States must, of necessity, be commerce with the States. In the regulation of trade with the Indian tribes, the action of the law, especially, when the Constitution was made, was chiefly within a State. The power of Congress, then, whatever it may be, must be exercised within the territorial jurisdiction of the several States. The sense of the Nation on this subject is unequivocally manifested by the provisions made in the laws for transporting goods, by land, between Baltimore and Providence, between New York and Philadelphia, and between Philadelphia and Baltimore.

We are now arrived at the inquiry—what is this power? It is the power to regulate; that is, to prescribe the rule by which commerce is to be governed. This power, like all others vested in Congress, is complete in itself, may be exercised to its utmost extent, and acknowledges no limitations, other than are prescribed in the Constitution. These are expressed in plain terms, and do not affect the questions which arise in this case, or which have been discussed at the bar. If, as has always been understood, the sovereignty of Congress, though limited to specified objects, is plenary as to those objects, the power over commerce with foreign nations, and among the several States, is vested in Congress as absolutely as it would be in a single government, having in its constitution the same restrictions on the exercise of the power as are found in the Constitution of the United States. The wisdom and the discretion of Congress, their identity with the people, and the influence which their constituents possess at elections, are, in this, as in many other instances, as that, for example, of declaring war, the sole restraints on which they have relied, to secure them from its abuse. They are the restraints on which the people must often rely solely, in all representative governments. . . .

But it has been urged, with great earnestness, that although the power of Congress to regulate commerce with foreign nations, and among the several States, be co-extensive with the subject itself, and have no other limits than are prescribed in the Constitution, yet the States may severally exercise the same power within their respective jurisdictions. In support of this argument, it is said that they possessed it as an inseparable attribute of sovereignty before the formation of the Constitution, and still retain it, except so far as they have surrendered it by that instrument; that this principle results from the nature of the Government, and is secured by the Tenth Amendment; that an affirmative grant of power is not exclusive, unless in its own nature it be such that the continued exercise of it by the former possessor is inconsistent with the grant, and that this is not of that description. The appellant, conceding these postulates, except the last, contends that full power to regulate a particular subject implies the whole power, and leaves no residuum; that a grant of the whole is incompatible with the existence of a right in another to any part of it. Both parties have appealed to the Constitution, to legislative Acts, and judicial decisions; and have drawn arguments from all these sources to support and illustrate the propositions they respectively maintain.

The grant of the power to lay and collect taxes is, like the power to regulate commerce, made in general terms, and has never been understood to interfere with the exercise of the same power by the States; and hence has been drawn an argument which has been applied to the question under consideration. But the two grants are not, it is conceived, similar in their terms or their nature. Although many of the powers formerly exercised by the States are transferred to the Government of the Union, yet the State Governments remain, and constitute a most important part of our system. The power of taxation is indispensable to their existence, and is a power which, in its own nature, is capable of residing in, and being exercised by, different authorities at the same time. We are accustomed to see it placed, for different purposes, in different hands. Taxation is the simple operation of taking small portions from a perpetually accumulating mass, susceptible of almost infinite division; and a power in one to take what is necessary for certain purposes, is not in its nature incompatible with a power in another to take what is necessary for other purposes. Congress is authorized to lay and collect taxes, etc., to pay the debts, and provide for the common defense and general welfare of the United States. This does not interfere with the power of the States to tax for the support of their own governments; nor is the exercise of that power by the States an exercise of any portion of the power that is granted to the United States. In imposing taxes for state purposes, they are not doing what Congress is empowered to do. Congress is not empowered to tax for those purposes which are within the exclusive province of the States. When, then, each government exercises the power of taxation, neither is exercising the power of the other. But when a State proceeds to regulate commerce with foreign nations, or among the several States, it is exercising the very power that is granted to Congress, and is doing the very thing which Congress is authorized to do. There is no analogy, then, between the power of taxation and the power of regulating commerce.

In discussing the question whether this power is still in the States, in the case under consideration, we may dismiss from it the inquiry, whether it is surrendered by the mere grant to Congress, or is retained until Congress shall exercise the power. We may dismiss that inquiry because it has been exercised, and the regulations which Congress deemed it proper to make are now in full operation. The sole question is, can a State regulate commerce with foreign nations and among the States while Congress is regulating it? . . .

The idea that the same measure might, according to circumstances, be arranged with different classes of power, was no novelty to the Framers of our Constitution. Those illustrious statesmen and patriots had been, many of them, deeply engaged in the discussion which preceded the war of our revolution, and all of them were well read in those discussions. The right to regulate commerce, even by the imposition of duties, was not controverted; but the right to impose a duty for the purpose of revenue, produced a war as important, perhaps, in its consequences to the human race, as any the world has ever witnessed.

These restrictions [those in Art. I, Sec. 10, barring States from laying duties on imports or exports] . . . are on the taxing power, not on that to regulate commerce, and presuppose the existence of that which they restrain, not of that which they do not purport to restrain.

But the inspection laws are said to be regulations of commerce, and are certainly recognized in the Constitution as being passed in the exercise of a power remaining with the States.

That inspection laws may have a remote and considerable influence on commerce, will not be denied; but that a power to regulate commerce is the source from which the right to pass them is derived, cannot be admitted. The object of inspection laws, is to improve the quality of articles produced by the labor of a country; to fit them for exportation; or, it may be, for domestic use. They act upon the subject, before it becomes an article of foreign commerce, or of commerce among the States, and prepare it for that purpose. They form a portion of that immense mass of legislation, which embraces everything within the territory of a State, not surrendered to a general government; all of which can be most advantageously exercised by the States themselves. Inspection laws, can be most advantageously exercised by quarantine laws, health laws of every description, as well as laws for regulating the internal commerce of a State, and those which respect turnpike roads, ferries, etc., are component parts of this mass.

No direct general power over these objects is granted to Congress, and, consequently, they remain subject to state legislation. If the legislative power of the Union can reach them, it must be for national purposes; it must be, where the power is expressly given for a special purpose, or is clearly incidental to some power which is expressly given. It is obvious, that the Government of the Union, in the exercise of its express powers, that, for example, of regulating commerce with foreign nations and among the States, may use means that may also be employed by a State, in the exercise of its acknowledged powers; that, for example, of regulating commerce within the State. If Congress license vessels to sail from one port to another, in the same States, the act is supposed to be, necessarily, incidental to the power expressly granted to Congress, and implies no claim of a direct power to regulate the purely internal commerce of a State, or to act directly on its system of police. So, if a State, in passing laws on subjects acknowledged to be within its control, and with a view to those subjects, shall adopt a measure of the same character with one which Congress may adopt, it does not derive its authority from the particular power which has been granted, but from some other which remains with the State. All experience shows that the same measures, or measures scarcely distinguishable from each other, may flow from distinct powers; but this does not prove that the powers themselves are identical. Although the means used in their execution may sometimes approach each other so nearly as to be confounded, there are other situations in which they are sufficiently distinct to establish their individuality.

In our complex system, presenting the rare and difficult scheme of one general Government whose action extends over the whole, but which possesses only certain enumerated powers; and of numerous State Governments, which retain and exercise all powers not delegated to the Union, contests respecting power must arise. Were it even otherwise, the measures taken by the respective governments to execute their acknowledged powers would often be of the same description, and might sometimes interfere. This, however, does not prove that the one is exercising, or has a right to exercise, the powers of the other. . . .

It has been said that the Act of August 7, 1789, acknowledges a concurrent power in the States to regulate the conduct of pilots, and hence is inferred an admission of their concurrent right with Congress to regulate commerce with foreign nations, and amongst the States. But this inference is not, we think, justified by the fact. Although Congress cannot enable a State to legislate, Congress may adopt the provisions of a State on any subject. When the Government of the Union was brought into existence, it found a system for the regulation of its pilots in full force in every State. The Act which has been mentioned, adopts this system, and gives it the same validity as if its provisions had been specially made by Congress. But the Act, it may be said, is prospective also, and the adoption of laws to be made in future, presupposes the right in the maker to legislate on the subject. The Act unquestionably manifests an intention to leave this subject entirely to the States, until Congress should think proper to interpose; but the very enactment of such a law indicates an opinion that it was necessary; that the existing system would not be applicable to the new state of things, unless expressly applied to it by Congress. . . . The acknowledged power of a State to regulate its police, its domestic trade, and to govern its own citizens, may enable it to legislate on this subject to a considerable extent; and the adoption of its system by Congress, and the application of it to the whole subject of commerce, does not seem to the Court to imply a right in the States so to apply it of their own authority . . . the adoption of the state system being temporary, being only "until further legislative provision shall be made by Congress," shows, conclusively, an opinion, that Congress could control the whole subject, and might adopt the system of the States, or provide one of its own. . . .

Since, however, in exercising the power of regulating their own purely internal affairs, whether of trading or police, the States may sometimes enact laws, the validity of which depends on their [not] interfering with, and being contrary to, an Act of Congress passed in pursuance of the Constitution, the Court will enter upon the inquiry whether the laws of New York, as expounded by the highest tribunal of that State, have, in their application to this case, come into collision with an Act of Congress, and deprived a citizen of a right to which that Act entitles him. Should this collision exist, it will be immaterial whether those laws were passed in virtue of a concurrent power "to regulate commerce with foreign nations and among the several states," or, in virtue of a power to regulate their domestic trade and police. In one case and the other, the acts of New York must yield to the law of Congress, and the decision sustaining the privilege they confer, against a right given by a law of the Union, must be erroneous. This opinion has been frequently expressed in this court, and is founded, as well on the nature of the Government, as on the words of the Constitution. In argument, however, it has been contended, that if a law passed by a State, in the exercise of its acknowledged sovereignty, comes into conflict with a law passed by Congress in pursuance of the Constitution, they affect the subject, and each other, like equal opposing powers. But the Framers of our Constitution foresaw this state of things, and provided for it, by declaring the supremacy not only of itself, but of the laws made in pursuance of it.

The nullity of any Act, inconsistent with the Constitution, is produced by the declaration, that the Constitution is the supreme law. The appropriate application of that part of the clause which confers the same supremacy on laws and treaties, is to such Acts of the state legislatures as do not transcend their powers, but though enacted in the execution of acknowledged state powers, interfere with, or are contrary to, the laws of Congress, made in pursuance of the Constitution, or some treaty made under the authority of the United States. In every such case, the Act of Congress, or the treaty, is supreme; and the law of the State, though enacted in the exercise of powers not controverted, must yield to it. . . .

JUSTICE JOHNSON:

The history of the times will . . . sustain the opinion, that the grant of power over commerce, if intended to be commensurate with the evils existing, and the purpose of remedying those evils, could be only commensurate with the power of the States over the subject. . . .

The "power to regulate commerce," here meant to be granted, was that power to regulate commerce which previously existed in the States. But what was that power? The States were, unquestionably, supreme; and each possessed that power over commerce, which is acknowledged to reside in every sovereign State. The definition and limits of that power are to be sought among the features of international law; and, as it was not only admitted, but insisted on by both parties, in argument, that, "unaffected by a state of war, by treaties, or by municipal regulations, all commerce among independent states was legitimate," there is no necessity to appeal to the oracles of the *jus commune* for the correctness of that doctrine. The law of nations, regarding man as a social animal, pronounces all commerce legitimate, in a state of peace, until prohibited by positive law. The power of a sovereign State over commerce, therefore, amounts to nothing more than a power to limit and restrain it at pleasure. And since the power to prescribe the limits to its freedom, necessarily implies the power to determine what shall remain unrestrained, it follows, that the power must be exclusive; it can reside but in one potentate; and hence, the grant of this power carries with it the whole subject, leaving nothing for the State to act upon. . . .

. . . Power to regulate foreign commerce, is given in the same words, and in the same breath, as it were, with that over the commerce of the States and with the Indian tribes. But the power to regulate foreign commerce is necessarily exclusive. The States are unknown to foreign nations; their sovereignty exists only with relation to each other and the general Government. Whatever regulations foreign commerce should be subjected to in the ports of the Union, the general Government would be held responsible for them; and all other regulations, but those which Congress had imposed, would be regarded by foreign nations as trespasses and violations of national faith and comity.

But the language which grants the power as to one description of commerce, grants it as to all; and, in fact, if ever the exercise of a right, or acquiescence in a construction, could be inferred from contemporaneous and continued assent, it is that of the exclusive effect of this grant.

A right over the subject has never been pretended to, in any instance, except as incidental to exercise of some other unquestionable power. . . .

When speaking of the power of Congress over navigation, I do not regard it as a power incidental to that of regulating commerce; I consider it as the thing itself; inseparable from it as vital motion is from vital existence.

Commerce, in its simplest signification, means an exchange of goods; but in the advancement of society, labor, transportation, intelligence, care, and various mediums of exchange, become commodities, and enter into commerce; the subject, the vehicle, the agent, and their various operations, become the objects of commercial regulation. Shipbuilding, the carrying trade, and propagation of seamen, are such vital agents of commercial prosperity, that the nation which could not legislate over these subjects, would not possess power to regulate commerce. . . .

It is impossible, with the views which I entertain of the principle on which the commercial privileges of the people of the United States, among themselves, rests [sic], to concur in the view which this court takes of the effect of the coasting license in this cause. I do not regard it as the foundation of the right set up in behalf of the appellant. If there was any one object riding over every other in the adoption of the Constitution, it was to keep the commercial intercourse among the States free from all invidious and partial restraints. And I cannot overcome the conviction, that if the licensing act was repealed tomorrow, the rights of the appellant to a reversal of the decision complained of, would be as strong as it is under this license. . . .

. . . This court doth further direct, order and decree, that the bill of the said Aaron Ogden be dismissed, and the same is hereby dismissed accordingly.

Since the "stream of commerce" cuts across state lines, Congress has power to regulate its interrelated activities, including labor.

15. *NATIONAL LABOR RELATIONS BOARD* [*NLRB*] *v. JONES & LAUGHLIN STEEL CORP.* (1937)

This is a milestone decision in the field of labor. For the first time, the Supreme Court held that national labor regulation was constitutional.

Background: *In 1935 Congress passed the National Labor Relations Act to protect labor's right to organize, and to encourage collective bargaining. The National Labor Relations Board, set up under the Act, had the power to order business enterprises to stop "unfair labor practices." When the Jones & Laughlin Steel Corporation refused to comply with the Board's order, the case finally went to the Supreme Court. The Court, by a vote of five to four, upheld the constitutionality of the National Labor Relations Act (and hence the power of its Board to issue orders needed for compliance with it) on the ground that the ramifications of commerce—including labor—were nationwide and could no longer be left to regulation by the States, as had been the case until then.*

Some Related Cases
(On Labor Relations):

Nash v. United States (1913)
Hammer v. Dagenhart (1918)
Truax v. Corrigan (1921)
Carter v. Carter Coal Co. (1936)
United States v. Darby (1941)
American Federation of Labor v. American Sash Co. (1949)
Giboney v. Empire Storage Co. (1949)

MR. CHIEF JUSTICE HUGHES DELIVERED THE OPINION OF THE COURT:

The scope of the Act.—The Act is challenged in its entirety as an attempt to regulate all industry, thus invading the reserved powers of the States over their local concerns. It is asserted that the references in the Act to interstate and foreign commerce are colorable at best; that the Act is not a true regulation of such commerce or of matters which directly affect it but on the contrary has the fundamental object of placing under the compulsory supervision of the Federal Government all industrial labor relations within the Nation. The argument seeks support in the broad words of the preamble (section one) and in the sweep of the provisions of the Act, and it is further insisted that its legislative history shows an essential universal purpose in the light of which its scope cannot be limited by either construction or by the application of the separability clause.

If this conception of terms, intent and consequent inseparability were sound, the Act would necessarily fall by reason of the limitation upon the federal power which inheres in the constitutional grant, as well as because of the explicit reservation of the Tenth Amendment. *Schechter Corp. v. United States.* . . . The authority of the Federal Government may not be pushed to such an extreme as to destroy the distinction, which the commerce clause itself establishes, between commerce "among the several states" and the internal concerns of a State. That distinction between what is national and what is local in the activities of commerce is vital to the maintenance of our federal system.

But we are not at liberty to deny effect to specific provisions, which Congress has constitutional power to enact, by superimposing upon them inferences from general legislative declarations of an ambiguous character, even if found in the same statute. The cardinal principle of statutory construction is to save and not to destroy. We have repeatedly held that as between two possible interpretations of a statute, by one of which it would be unconstitutional and by the other valid, our plain duty is to adopt that which will save the Act. . . .

We think it clear that the National Labor Relations Act may be construed so as to operate within the sphere of constitutional authority. The jurisdiction conferred upon the Board, and invoked in this instance, is found in Section 10 (a), which provides:

"Section 10(a). The Board is empowered, as hereinafter provided, to prevent any person from engaging in any unfair labor practice (listed in Section 8) affecting commerce."

The critical words of this provision, prescribing the limits of the Board's authority in dealing with the labor practices, are "affecting commerce." . . .

There can be no question that the commerce thus contemplated by the Act (aside from that within a Territory or the District of Columbia) is interstate and foreign commerce in the constitutional sense. The Act also defines the term "affecting commerce" (Section 2 (6)):

"The term 'affecting commerce' means in commerce, or burdening or obstructing commerce or the free flow of commerce, or having led or tending to lead to a labor dispute burdening or obstructing commerce or the free flow of commerce."

This definition is one of exclusion as well as inclusion. The grant of authority to the Board does not purport to extend to the relationship between all industrial employees and employers. Its terms do not impose collective bargaining upon all industry regardless of effects upon interstate or foreign commerce. It purports to reach only what may be deemed to burden or obstruct that commerce and, thus qualified, it must be construed as contemplating the exercise of control within constitutional bounds. It is a familiar principle that Acts which directly burden or obstruct interstate or foreign commerce, or its free flow, are within the reach of the congressional power. Acts having that effect are not rendered immune because they grow out of labor disputes. . . . Whether or not particular action does affect commerce in such a close and intimate fashion as to be subject to federal control, and hence to lie within the authority conferred upon the Board, is left by the statute to be determined as individual cases arise. . . .

The application of the Act to employees engaged in production.—The principle involved.—Respondent says that whatever may be said of employees engaged in interstate commerce, the industrial relations and activities in the manufacturing department of respondent's enterprise are not subject to federal regulation. The argument rests upon the proposition that manufacturing in itself is not commerce. . . .

. . . Reference is made to our decision sustaining the Packers and Stockyards Act. *Stafford v. Wallace*. . . . The Court found that the stockyards were but a "throat" through which the current of commerce flowed and the transactions which there occurred could not be separated from that movement. Hence the sales at the stockyards were not regarded as merely local transactions, for while they created "a local change of title" they did not "stop the flow," but merely changed the private interests in the subject of the current. Distinguishing the cases which upheld the power of the State to impose a nondiscriminatory tax upon property which the owner intended to transport to another State, but which was not in actual transit and was held within the State subject to the disposition of the owner, the Court remarked: "The question, it should be observed, is not with respect to the extent of the power of Congress to regulate interstate commerce, but whether a particular exercise of state power in view of its nature and operation must be deemed to be in conflict with this paramount authority." . . .

Respondent contends that the instant case presents material distinctions. Respondent says that the Aliquippa plant is extensive in size and represents a large investment in buildings, machinery and equipment. The raw materials which are brought to the plant are delayed for long periods and, after being subjected to manufacturing processes "are changed substantially as to character, utility and value." . . .

We do not find it necessary to determine whether these features of defendant's business dispose of the asserted analogy to the "stream of commerce" cases. The instances in which that metaphor has been used are but particular, and not exclusive, illustrations of the protective power which the Government invokes in support of the present Act. The congressional authority to protect interstate commerce from burdens and obstructions is not limited to transactions which can be deemed to be an essential part of a "flow" of interstate or foreign commerce. Burdens and obstructions may be due to injurious action springing from other sources. The fundamental principle is that the power to regulate commerce is the power to enact "all appropriate legislation" for "its protection and advancement" (*The Daniel Ball,* 10 Wall. 557, 564); to adopt measures "to promote its growth and insure its safety" (*Mobile County v. Kimball,* 102 U.S. 691, 696, 697); "to foster, protect, control and restrain." *Second Employers' Liability Cases* [*Mondou v. New York, N. H. & H. R.R. Co.,* 223 U.S. 47]. See *Texas & N. O. R. Co. v. Railway Clerks,* 281 U.S. 548. That power is plenary and may be exerted to protect interstate commerce "no matter what the source of the dangers which threaten it." *Second Employers' Liability Cases,* . . . *Schechter Corporation v. United States.* Although activities may be intrastate in character when separately considered, if they have such a close and substantial relation to interstate commerce that their control is essential or appropriate to protect that commerce from burdens and obstructions, Congress cannot be denied the power to exercise that control. *Schechter Corporation v. United States.* Undoubtedly the scope of this power must be considered in the light of our dual system of government and may not be extended so as to embrace effects upon interstate commerce so indirect and remote that to embrace them, in view of our complex society, would effectually obliterate the distinction between what is national and what is local and create a completely centralized government. *Id.* The question is necessarily one of degree. As the Court said in *Chicago Board of Trade v. Olsen,* 262 U.S. 37, repeating what had been said in *Stafford v. Wallace; supra:* "Whatever amounts to more or less constant practice, and threatens to obstruct or unduly to burden the freedom of interstate commerce is within the regulatory power of Congress under the commerce clause and it is primarily for Congress to consider and decide the fact of the danger and meet it."

That intrastate activities, by reason of close and intimate relation to interstate commerce, may fall within federal control is demonstrated in the case of carriers who are engaged in both interstate and intrastate transportation. There federal control has been found essential to secure the freedom of interstate traffic from interference or unjust discrimination and to promote the efficiency of the interstate service. . . .

The close and intimate effect which brings the subject within the reach of federal power may be due to activities in relation to productive industry although the industry when separately viewed is local. This has been abundantly illustrated in the application of the federal Anti-Trust Act. In the *Standard Oil* and *American Tobacco* cases, 221 U.S. 1, 106, that statute was applied to combinations of employers engaged in productive industry. Counsel for the offending corporations strongly urged that the Sherman Act had no application because the acts complained of were not acts of interstate or foreign commerce, nor direct and immediate in their effect on interstate or foreign commerce, but primarily affected manufacturing and not commerce. . . .

It is thus apparent that the fact that the employees here concerned were engaged in production is not determinative. The question remains as to the effect upon interstate commerce of the labor practice involved. In the Schechter case, we found that the effect there was so remote as to be beyond the federal power. To find "immediacy or directness" there was to find it "almost everywhere," a result inconsistent with the maintenance of our federal system. In the *Carter* case, the Court was of the opinion that the provisions of the statute relating to production were invalid upon several grounds,—that there was improper delegation of legislative power, and that the requirements not only went beyond any sustainable measure of protection of interstate commerce but were also inconsistent with due process. These cases are not controlling here.

Effects of the unfair labor practice in respondent's enterprise. —Giving full weight to respondent's contention with respect to a break in the complete continuity of the "stream of commerce" by reason of respondent's manufacturing operations, the fact remains that the stoppage of those operations by industrial strife would have a most serious effect upon interstate commerce. In view of respondent's far-flung activities, it is idle to say that the effect would be indirect or remote. It is obvious that it would be immediate and might be catastrophic. We are asked to shut our eyes to the plainest facts of our national life and to deal with the question of direct and indirect effects in an intellectual vacuum. Because there may be but indirect and remote effects upon interstate commerce in connection with a host of local enterprises throughout the country, it does not follow that other industrial activities do not have such a close and intimate relation to interstate commerce as to make the presence of industrial strife a matter of the most urgent national concern. When industries organize themselves on a national scale, making their relation to interstate commerce the dominant factor in their activities, how can it be maintained that their industrial labor relations constitute a forbidden field into which Congress may not enter when it is necessary to protect interstate commerce from the paralyzing consequences of industrial war? We have often said that interstate commerce itself is a practical conception. It is equally true that interferences with that commerce must be appraised by a judgment that does not ignore actual experience. . . .

Our conclusion is that the order of the Board was within its competency and that the Act is valid as here applied. The judgment of the Circuit Court of Appeals is reversed and the cause is remanded for further proceedings in conformity with this opinion.

Reversed.

MR. JUSTICE MCREYNOLDS DELIVERED THE FOLLOWING DISSENTING OPINION:

Mr. Justice Van Devanter, Mr. Justice Sutherland, Mr. Justice Butler and I are unable to agree with the decisions just announced. . . .

The Court as we think departs from well-established principles followed in *A. L. A. Schechter Poultry Corp. v. United States* . . . and *Carter v. Carter Coal Co.* . . . Every consideration brought forward to uphold the Act before us was applicable to support the Acts held unconstitutional in causes decided within two years. And the lower courts rightly deemed them controlling.

By its terms the Labor Act extends to employers—large and small—unless excluded by definition, and declares that if one of these interferes with, restrains, or coerces any employee regarding his labor affiliations, etc., this shall be regarded as unfair labor practice. . . .

The three respondents happen to be manufacturing concerns—one large, two relatively small. The Act is now applied to each upon grounds common to all. Obviously what is determined as to these concerns may gravely affect a multitude of employers who engage in a great variety of private enterprises—mercantile, manufacturing, publishing, stockraising, mining, etc. It puts into the hands of a Board control over purely local industry beyond anything heretofore deemed permissible.

The argument in support of the Board affirms: "Thus the validity of any specific application of the preventive measures of this Act depends upon whether industrial strife resulting from the practices in the particular enterprise under consideration would be of the character which federal power could control if it occurred. If strife in that enterprise could be controlled, certainly it could be prevented."

Manifestly that view of congressional power would extend it into almost every field of human industry. . . .

Any effect on interstate commerce by the discharge of employees shown here, would be indirect and remote in the highest degree, as consideration of the facts will show. In No. 419 [*National Labor Relations Board v. Jones & Laughlin Steel Corp.*] ten men out of ten thousand were discharged; in the other cases only a few. The immediate effect in the factory may be to create discontent among all those employed and a strike may follow, which, in turn, may result in reducing production, which ultimately may reduce the volume of goods moving in interstate commerce. By this chain of indirect and progressively remote events we finally reach the evil with which it is said the legislation under consideration undertakes to deal. A more remote and indirect interference with interstate commerce or a more definite invasion of the powers reserved to the States is difficult, if not impossible, to imagine.

The Constitution still recognizes the existence of States with indestructible powers; the Tenth Amendment was supposed to put them beyond controversy.

The Congressional power of economic regulation extends even to production for home consumption.

16. *WICKARD v. FILBURN* (1942)

Does the Commerce clause under the Constitution include

the power to regulate all interstate economic activities, including agricultural production for home use on the farm? The answer, in this decision, is Yes.

Background: *Under the Agricultural Adjustment Act (AAA) of 1938, the Secretary of Agriculture was empowered to proclaim an annual wheat allocation acreage per farmer. Filburn, a wheat farmer, produced wheat in excess of his quota, and his refusal to pay the resulting penalty (on the ground, among others, that he used the excess for home consumption) was upheld by the District Court. Secretary of Agriculture Claude R. Wickard appealed to the Supreme Court, which ruled in his favor. The Supreme Court held that the congressional power to regulate was inclusive, even if it involved personal disadvantages. "It is of the essence of regulation," the Court stated, "that it lays a restraining hand on the self-interest of the regulated. . . ."*

Some Related Cases

(On Economic Regulation):

United States v. Butler (1936)
United States v. Rock Royal Cooperative (1939)
United States v. Wrightwood Dairy Co. (1942)
Mandeville Island Farms v. American C.S. Co. (1948)

MR. JUSTICE JACKSON DELIVERED THE OPINION OF THE COURT:

It is urged that under the Commerce clause of the Constitution, Article I, Section 8, clause 3, Congress does not possess the power it has in this instance sought to exercise. The question would merit little consideration since our decision in *United States v. Darby* . . . sustaining the federal power to regulate production of goods for commerce except for the fact that this Act extends federal regulation to production not intended in any part for commerce but wholly for consumption on the farm. The Act includes a definition of "market" and its derivatives so that as related to wheat in addition to its conventional meaning it also means to dispose of "by feeding (in any form) to poultry or livestock which, or the products of which, are sold, bartered, or exchanged, or to be so disposed of." Hence, marketing quotas not only embrace all that may be sold without penalty but also what may be consumed on the premises. Wheat produced on excess acreage is designated as "available for marketing" as so defined and the penalty is imposed thereon. Penalties do not depend upon whether any part of the wheat either within or without the quota is sold or intended to be sold. The sum of this is that the Federal Government fixes a quota including all that the farmer may harvest for sale or for his own farm needs, and declares that wheat produced on excess acreage may neither be disposed of nor used except upon payment of the penalty or except it is stored as required by the Act or delivered to the Secretary of Agriculture.

Appellee says that this is a regulation of production and consumption of wheat. Such activities are, he urges, beyond the reach of congressional power under the Commerce clause, since they are local in character, and their effects upon interstate commerce are at most "indirect." In answer the Government argues that the statute regulates neither production nor consumption, but only marketing; and, in the alternative, that if the Act does go beyond the regulation of marketing it is sustainable as a "necessary and proper" implementation of the power of Congress over interstate commerce.

The Government's concern lest the Act be held to be a regulation of production or consumption rather than of marketing is attributable to a few dicta and decisions of this court which might be understood to lay it down that activities such as "production," "manufacturing," and "mining" are strictly "local" and, except in special circumstances which are not present here, cannot be regulated under the commerce power because their effects upon interstate commerce are, as matter of law, only "indirect." Even today, when this power has been held to have great latitude, there is no decision of this court that such activities may be regulated where no part of the product is intended for interstate commerce or intermingled with the subjects thereof. We believe that a review of the course of decision under the Commerce clause will make plain, however, that questions of the power of Congress are not to be decided by reference to any formula which would give controlling force to nomenclature such as "production" and "indirect" and foreclose consideration of the actual effects of the activity in question upon interstate commerce. . . .

The Court's recognition of the relevance of the economic effects in the application of the Commerce clause . . . has made the mechanical application of legal formulas no longer feasible. Once an economic measure of the reach of the power granted to Congress in the Commerce clause is accepted, questions of federal power cannot be decided simply by finding the activity in question to be "production" nor can consideration of its economic effects be foreclosed by calling them "indirect." The present Chief Justice has said in summary of the present state of the law: "The commerce power is not confined in its exercise to the regulation of commerce among the states. It extends to those activities intrastate which so affect interstate commerce, or the exertion of the power of Congress over it, as to make regulation of them appropriate means to the attainment of a legitimate end, the effective execution of the granted power to regulate interstate commerce. . . . The power of Congress over interstate commerce is plenary and complete in itself, may be exercised to its utmost extent, and acknowledges no limitations other than are prescribed in the Constitution. . . . It follows that no form of state activity can constitutionally thwart the regulatory power granted by the Commerce clause to Congress. Hence the reach of that power extends to those intrastate activities which in a substantial way interfere with or obstruct the exercise of the granted power." *United States v. Wrightwood Dairy Co.*, 315 U.S. 110, 119.

Whether the subject of the regulation in question was "production," "consumption," or "marketing" is, therefore, not material for purposes of deciding the question of federal power before us. That an activity is of local character may help in a doubtful case to determine whether Congress intended to reach it. The same consideration might help in determining whether in the absence of congressional action it would be permissible for the State to exert its power on the subject matter, even though in so doing it to some degree affected interstate commerce. But even if appellant's activity be local and though it may not be regarded as commerce, it may still, whatever its nature, be reached by Congress if it exerts a substantial economic effect on interstate commerce and this irrespective of whether such effect is what might at some earlier time have been defined as "direct" or "indirect." . . .

The effect of consumption of home-grown wheat on interstate commerce is due to the fact that it constitutes the most variable factor in the disappearance of the wheat crop. Consumption on the farm where grown appears to vary in an amount greater than 20 per cent of average production. The total amount of wheat consumed as food varies but relatively little, and use as seed is relatively constant. . . .

It is well established by decisions of this court that the power to regulate commerce includes the power to regulate the prices at which commodities in that commerce are dealt in and practices affecting such prices. One of the primary purposes of the Act in question was to increase the market price of wheat and to that end to limit the volume thereof that could affect the market. It can hardly be denied that a factor of such volume and variability as home-consumed wheat would have a substantial influence on price and market conditions. This may arise because being in marketable condition such home-grown wheat overhangs the market and if induced by rising prices tends to flow into the market and check price increases. But if we assume that it is never marketed, it supplies a need of the man who grew it which would otherwise be reflected by purchases in the open market. Home-grown wheat in this sense competes with wheat in commerce. The stimulation of commerce is a use of the regulatory function quite as definitely as prohibitions or restrictions thereon. This record leaves us in no doubt that Congress may properly have considered that wheat consumed on the farm where grown if wholly outside the scheme of regulation would have a substantial effect in defeating and obstructing its purpose to stimulate trade therein at increased prices.

It is said, however, that this Act, forcing some farmers into the market to buy what they could provide for themselves, is an unfair promotion of the markets and prices of specializing wheat growers. It is of the essence of regulation that it lays a restraining hand on the self-interest of the regulated and that advantages from the regulation commonly fall to others. The conflicts of economic interest between the regulated and those who advantage by it are wisely left under our system to resolution by the Congress under its more flexible and responsible legislative process. Such conflicts rarely lend themselves to judicial determination. And with the wisdom, workability, or fairness, of the plan of regulation we have nothing to do. . . .

Reversed.

Chapter XII

Taxing Power

"The Congress shall have power to lay and collect taxes, duties, imposts and excises . . ."—Art. I, Sec. 8

"No capitation, or other direct tax shall be laid unless in proportion to the census or enumeration herein before directed to be taken." *—Art. I, Sec. 9

In this Chapter:
Hylton v. United States (1796)
United States v. Kahriger (1952)

The definition of a direct tax:

17. *HYLTON v. UNITED STATES* (1796)

Since the Constitution did not specify what a direct tax was, definition had to be left to judicial interpretation. This is the first case in which the Supreme Court undertook to define a direct tax.

Background: *In 1794 Congress passed a law levying a tax of $16 on each carriage. Hylton, claiming ownership of 125 carriages, appealed to the Supreme Court that this was a direct tax, which (under Article I, Section 9) can be levied only in proportion to the Census—something the Act of 1794 did not do. The Court, therefore, had to decide what a direct tax was. It concluded that there were only two direct taxes: "capitation or poll tax . . . and a tax on land." This definition was to remain in force for about a century; it was changed in the case of* Pollock v. Farmers' Loan & Trust Co. *in 1895.*

* This was modified by the Sixteenth Amendment (1913).

Some Related Cases
(On Taxation):

Knowlton v. Moore (1900)
McCray v. United States (1904)
Billings v. United States (1914)
New York Trust Co. v. Eisner (1921)

JUSTICE CHASE:

By the case stated, only one question is submitted to the opinion of this court—whether the law of Congress of the 5th of June 1794, entitled, "An act to lay duties upon carriages for the conveyance of persons," is unconstitutional and void?

The principles laid down, to prove the above law void, are these: that a tax on carriages is a direct tax, and, therefore, by the Constitution, must be laid according to the census, directed by the Constitution to be taken, to ascertain the number of representatives from each State. And that the tax in question on carriages is not laid by that rule of apportionment, but by the rule of uniformity, prescribed by the Constitution in the case of duties, imposts and excises; and a tax on carriages is not within either of those descriptions. . . .

It appears to me, that a tax on carriages cannot be laid by the rule of apportionment, without very great inequality and injustice. For example: suppose, two States, equal in census, to pay $80,000 each, by a tax on carriages, of eight dollars on every carriage: and in one State, there are 100 carriages, and in the other 1000. The owners of carriages in one State, would pay ten times the tax of owners in the other. A. in one State would pay for his carriage eight dollars, but B. in the other State, would pay for his carriage, eighty dollars. . . .

I think, an annual tax on carriages for the conveyance of persons, may be considered as within the power granted to Congress to lay duties. The term *duty,* is the most comprehensive, next to the general term *tax;* and practically, in Great Britain (whence we take our general ideas of taxes, duties, imposts, excises, customs, &c.), embraces taxes on stamps, tolls for passage, &c., and is not confined to taxes on importation only. It seems to me, that a tax on expense is an indirect tax; and I think an annual tax on a carriage for conveyance of persons, is of that kind; because a carriage is a consumable commodity; and such annual tax on it, is on the expense of the owner.

I am inclined to think, but of this I do not give a judicial opinion, that the direct taxes contemplated by the Constitution, are only two, to wit, a capitation or poll tax, simply, without regard to property, profession or any other circumstance; and a tax on land. I doubt, whether a tax, by a general assessment of personal property, within the United States, is included within the term direct tax. . . .

JUSTICE PATERSON:

. . . Whether direct taxes, in the sense of the Constitution, comprehend any other tax than a capitation tax, and tax on land, is a questionable point. If Congress, for instance, should tax, in the aggregate or mass, things that generally pervade all the States in the Union, then, perhaps the rule of apportionment would be the most proper, especially, if an assessment was to intervene. This appears by the practice of some of the States, to have been considered as a direct tax. Whether it be so, under the Constitution of the United States, is a matter of some difficulty; but as it is not before the Court, it would be improper to give any decisive opinion upon it. I never entertained a doubt that the principal, I will not say, the only, objects, that the Framers of the Constitution contemplated, as falling within the rule of apportionment, were a capitation tax and a tax on land. Local considerations, and the particular circumstances, and relative situation of the States, naturally lead to this view of the subject. The provision was made in favor of the southern States; they possessed a large number of slaves; they had extensive tracts of territory, thinly settled, and not very productive. A majority of the States had but few slaves, and several of them a limited territory, well settled, and in a high state of cultivation. The southern States, if no provision had been introduced in the Constitution, would have been wholly at the mercy of the other States. Congress in such case, might tax slaves, at discretion or arbitrarily, and land in every part of the Union, after the same rate or measure: so much a head in the first instance, and so much an acre, in the second. To guard them against imposition, in these particulars, was the reason of introducing the clause in the Constitution, which directs that representatives and direct taxes shall be apportioned among the States, according to their respective numbers. . . .

JUSTICE IREDELL:

As all direct taxes must be apportioned, it is evident, that the Constitution contemplated none as direct, but such as could be apportioned. If this cannot be apportioned, it is, therefore, not a direct tax in the sense of the Constitution.

That this tax cannot be apportioned, is evident. Suppose, ten dollars contemplated as a tax on each chariot, or post chaise, in the United States, and the number of both in all the United States be computed at 105, the number of representatives in Congress.

This would produce in the whole $1,050.00
The share of Virginia being 19/105 parts, would be .. 190.00
The share of Connecticut being 7/105 parts, would be .. 70.00
Then suppose Virginia had 50 carriages, Connecticut 2,
The share of Virginia being $190, this must, of course, be collected from the owners of carriages, and there would, therefore, be collected from each carriage.... 3.80
The share of Connecticut being $70, each carriage would pay 35.00

If any State had no carriages, there could be no apportionment at all. This mode is too manifestly absurd to be supported, and has not even been attempted in debate. . . .

Let the judgment of the Circuit Court be affirmed.

[Justices Wilson and Cushing did not deliver opinions.]

Government has a right to tax gambling.

18. *UNITED STATES v. KAHRIGER* (1952)

Can Congress use its taxing power to impose a tax on the gambling business, which might be generally an illegal occupation? In this decision, the Court ruled that it can.

Background: *In 1951 Congress levied a 10 per cent tax on persons engaged in the betting business. Kahriger challenged the tax as invalid, first because this type of taxing involved regulation reserved to the States, and secondly because it was a violation of the Fifth Amendment guarantee against self-incrimination. The Court, by a vote of six to three, decided, first, that the power of Congress to tax was so extensive that there were few "constitutional restraints" upon it; and, secondly, that the mere registration of the gambling business, as required by the 1951 law, was not a violation of the Fifth Amendment.*

Some Related Cases
(On the Tax Power):

United States v. Constantine (1935)
Sonzinsky v. United States (1937)
Sunshine Anthracite Co. v. Adkins (1940)
Helvering v. Lerner Stores Corp. (1941)
United States v. Sanchez (1950)
Marchetti v. United States (1968)
Grosso v. United States (1968)

MR. JUSTICE REED DELIVERED THE OPINION OF THE COURT:

It is conceded that a federal excise tax does not cease to be valid merely because it discourages or deters the activities taxed. Nor is the tax invalid because the revenue obtained is negligible. Appellee, however, argues that the sole purpose of the statute is to penalize only illegal gambling in the States through the guise of a tax measure. As with the . . . excise taxes which we have held to be valid, the instant tax has a regulatory effect. But regardless of its regulatory effect, the wagering tax produces revenue. As such it surpasses both the narcotics and firearms taxes which we have found valid.

It is axiomatic that the power of Congress to tax is extensive and sometimes falls with crushing effect on businesses deemed unessential or inimical to the public welfare, or where, as in dealings with narcotics, the collection of the tax also is difficult. As is well known, the constitutional restraints on taxing are few. . . . The remedy for excessive taxation is in the hands of Congress, not the courts. . . . It is hard to understand why the power to tax should raise more doubts because of indirect effects than other federal powers.

Penalty provisions in tax statutes added for breach of a regulation concerning activities in themselves subject only to state regulation have caused this court to declare the enactments invalid. Unless there are provisions extraneous to any tax need, courts are without authority to limit the exercise of the taxing power. All the provisions of this excise are adapted to the collection of a valid tax.

Nor do we find the registration requirements of the wagering tax offensive. All that is required is the filing of names, addresses, and places of business. This is quite general in tax returns. Such data are directly and intimately related to the collection of the tax and are "obviously supportable as in aid of a revenue purpose." . . .

Since appellee failed to register for the wagering tax, it is difficult to see how he can now claim the privilege even assuming that the disclosure of violations of law is called for. . . .

Assuming that respondent can raise the self-incrimination issue, that privilege has relation only to past acts, not to future acts that may or may not be committed. . . . If respondent wishes to take wagers subject to excise taxes, . . . he must pay an occupational tax and register. Under the registration provisions of the wagering tax, appellee is not compelled to confess to acts already committed, he is merely informed by the statute that in order to engage in the business of wagering in the future he must fulfill certain conditions. . . .

MR. JUSTICE JACKSON, CONCURRING:

Here is a purported tax law which requires no reports and lays no tax except on specified gamblers whose calling in most States is illegal. It requires this group to step forward and identify themselves, not because they like others have income, but because of its source. This is difficult to regard as a rational or good-faith revenue measure, despite the deference that is due Congress. On the contrary, it seems to be a plan to tax out of existence the professional gambler whom it has been found impossible to prosecute out of existence. . . .

It will be a sad day for the revenues if the goodwill of the people toward their taxing system is frittered away in efforts to accomplish by taxation moral reforms that cannot be accomplished by direct legislation. But the evil that can come from this statute will probably soon make itself manifest to Congress. The evil of a judicial decision impairing the legitimate taxing power by extreme constitutional interpretations might not be transient. Even though this statute approaches the fair limits of constitutionality, I join the decision of the Court. . . .

MR. JUSTICE BLACK, WITH WHOM MR. JUSTICE DOUGLAS CONCURS, DISSENTING:

The Court . . . here sustains an Act which requires a man to register and confess that he is engaged in the business of gambling. . . . I would hold that this Act violates the Fifth Amendment. . . .

MR. JUSTICE FRANKFURTER, DISSENTING:

When oblique use is made of the taxing power as to matters which substantively are not within the powers delegated to Congress, the Court cannot shut its eyes to what is obviously, because designedly, an attempt to control conduct which the Constitution left to the responsibility of the States, merely because Congress wrapped the legislation in the verbal cellophane of a revenue measure. . . . To allow what otherwise is excluded from congressional authority to be brought within it by casting legislation in the form of a revenue measure could, as so significantly expounded in the Child Labor Tax Case . . . offer an easy way for the legislative imagination to control "any one of the great numbers of subjects of public interest, jurisdiction of which the States have never parted with . . ." I say "significantly" because Mr. Justice Holmes and two of the Justices who had joined his dissent in *Hammer v. Dagenhart,* McKenna and Brandeis, JJ., agreed with the opinion in the Child Labor Tax Case. . . .

The context of the circumstances which brought forth this enactment . . . emphatically supports what was revealed on the floor of Congress, namely, that what was formally a means of raising revenue for the Federal Government was essentially an effort to check if not to stamp out professional gambling. . . .

The motive of congressional legislation is not for our scrutiny, provided only that the ulterior purpose is not expressed in ways which negate what the revenue words on their face express and, which do not seek enforcement of the formal revenue purpose through means that offend those standards of decency in our civilization against which due process is a barrier.

Chapter XIII

Due Process

"No person shall . . . be deprived of life, liberty, or property, without due process of law . . ."—Art. V (Fifth Amendment)

". . . nor shall any state deprive any person of life, liberty, or property without due process of law . . ."—Art. XIV (Fourteenth Amendment), Sec. 1

In this Chapter:
Slaughterhouse Cases (1873)
West Coast Hotel Co. v. Parrish (1937)

The Equal Protection clause of the Fourteenth Amendment, aimed solely against anti-Negro discriminatory laws, is not applicable to the power of the States to legislate freely in other areas.

19. *SLAUGHTERHOUSE CASES* (1873)

The significance of this decision lies in the fact that it is the first judicial interpretation of the Fourteenth Amendment. The Court interpreted it in the narrowest possible way. By a five to four vote, it ruled that the Fourteenth Amendment was designed exclusively to grant Negroes federal protection against discriminatory state laws, but was not applicable in regard to the "privileges and immunities" of other citizens. In other words, regardless of the Fourteenth Amendment, the States retained the power to regulate all other civil rights, including property relationships and the rights of contract.

This decision, basically in force until the first third of the twentieth century, ignored the intent and substance of the Fourteenth Amendment—namely, the safeguarding of Due Process. It set a precedent for subsequent decisions, which, up to about the era of the New Deal, in matters of social legislation tended to stress property rights more than equality and State rights in preference to federal power.

Background: *In 1869 the legislature of Louisiana granted a twenty-five-year monopoly to a slaughterhouse company to conduct its business in the city of New Orleans. Various butchers sought an injunction against the monopoly on the ground that it deprived them of the "privileges and immunities" that the Fourteenth Amendment guaranteed to all citizens. Losing in the Supreme Court of Louisiana, the butchers appealed to the United States Supreme Court, where they lost the case. It is interesting to note that four dissenting Justices upheld their claim. Justice Field, joined by Chief Justice Chase and Justice Swayne, stated that the Louisiana monopoly "entirely rejected and trampled" on the Fourteenth Amendment. Justice Bradley, the fourth dissenter, wrote that the monopoly was "an infringement of personal liberty."*

Some Related Cases

(On Freedom of Contract):

Crandall v. Nevada (1868)
Munn v. Illinois (Granger Cases) (1877)
Santa Clara County v. Southern Pacific R.R. Co. (1886)
Mugler v. Kansas (1887)
Spies v. Illinois (1887)
O'Neil v. Vermont (1892)
Allgeyer v. Louisiana (1897)
Maxwell v. Dow (1900)
Patterson v. Colorado (1907)
Twining v. New Jersey (1908)
Coppage v. Kansas (1915)

MR. JUSTICE MILLER DELIVERED THE OPINION OF THE COURT:

This statute is denounced not only as creating a monopoly and conferring odious and exclusive privileges upon a small number of persons at the expense of the great body of the community of New Orleans, but it is asserted that it deprives a large and meritorious class of citizens—the whole of the butchers of the city—of the right to exercise their trade, the business to which they have been trained and on which they depend for the support of themselves and their families; and that the unrestricted exercise of the business of butchering is necessary to the daily subsistence of the population of the city. . . .

It is not, and cannot be successfully controverted, that it is both the right and the duty of the legislative body—the supreme power of the State or municipality—to prescribe and determine the localities where the business of slaughtering for a great city may be conducted. To do this effectively it is indispensable that all persons who slaughter animals for food shall do it in those places *and nowhere else.*

The statute under consideration defines these localities and forbids slaughtering in any other. It does not, as has been asserted, prevent the butcher from doing his own slaughtering. On the contrary, the Slaughterhouse Company is required, under a heavy penalty, to permit any person who wishes to do so, to slaughter in their houses; and they are bound to make ample provision for the convenience of all slaughtering for the entire city. The butcher then is still permitted to slaughter, to prepare, and to sell his own meats; but he is required to slaughter at a specified place and to pay reasonable compensation for the use of the accommodations furnished him at that place.

The wisdom of the monopoly granted by the legislature may be open to question, but it is difficult to see a justification for the assertion that the butchers are deprived of the right to labor in their occupation, or the people of their daily service in preparing food, or how this statute, with the duties and guards imposed upon the company, can be said to destroy the business of the butcher, or seriously interfere with its pursuit.

The power here exercised by the legislature of Louisiana is, in its essential nature, one which has been, up to the present period in the constitutional history of this country, always conceded to belong to the States, however it may *now* be questioned in some of its details. . . .

Unless, therefore, it can be maintained that the exclusive privilege granted by this charter to the corporation is beyond the power of the legislature of Louisiana, there can be no just exception to the validity of the statute. And in this respect we are not able to see that these privileges are especially odious or objectionable. The duty imposed as a consideration for the privilege is well defined, and its enforcement well guarded. The prices or charges to be made by the company are limited by the statute, and we are not advised that they are on the whole exorbitant or unjust.

The proposition is, therefore, reduced to these terms: Can any exclusive privileges be granted to any of its citizens, or to a corporation, by the legislature of a State? . . .

The plaintiffs in error accepting this issue, allege that the statute is a violation of the Constitution of the United States in these several particulars:

That it creates an involuntary servitude forbidden by the Thirteenth Article of Amendment;

That it abridges the privileges and immunities of citizens of the United States;

That it denies to the plaintiffs the equal protection of the laws; and,

That it deprives them of their property without due process of law; contrary to the provisions of the first section of the Fourteenth Article of Amendment.

This court is thus called upon for the first time to give construction to these articles.

. . . On the most casual examination of the language of these Amendments [the 13th, 14th and 15th], no one can fail to be impressed with the one pervading purpose found in them all, lying at the foundation of each, and without which none of them would have been even suggested; we mean the freedom of the slave race, the security and firm establishment of that freedom, and the protection of the newly-made freeman and citizen from the oppressions of those who had formerly exercised unlimited dominion over him. It is true that only the Fifteenth Amendment, in terms, mentions the Negro by speaking of his color and his slavery. But it is just as true that each of the other articles was addressed to the grievances of that race, and designed to remedy them as the Fifteenth.

We do not say that no one else but the Negro can share in this protection. Both the language and spirit of these articles are to have their fair and just weight in any question of construction. Undoubtedly while Negro slavery alone was in the mind of the Congress which proposed the Thirteenth Article, it forbids any other kind of slavery, now or hereafter. If Mexican peonage or the Chinese cooly labor system shall develop slavery of the Mexican or Chinese race within our territory, this Amendment may safely be trusted to make it void. And so if other rights are assailed by the States which properly and necessarily fall within the protection of these articles, that protection will apply, though the party interested may not be of African descent. But what we do say, and what we wish to be understood is, that in any fair and just construction of any section or phrase of these Amendments, it is necessary to look to the purpose which we have said was the pervading spirit of them all, the evil which they were designed to remedy, and the process of continued addition to the Constitution, until that purpose was supposed to be accomplished, as far as constitutional law can accomplish it. . . .

The next observation is more important in view of the arguments of counsel in the present case. It is, that the distinction between citizenship of the United States and citizenship of a State is clearly recognized and established. Not only may a man be a citizen of the United States without being a citizen of a State, but an important element is necessary to convert the former into the latter. He must reside within the State to make him a citizen of it, but it is only necessary that he should be born or naturalized in the United States to be a citizen of the Union.

It is quite clear, then, that there is a citizenship of the United States, and a citizenship of a State, which are distinct from each other, and which depend upon different characteristics or circumstances in the individual.

We think this distinction and its explicit recognition in this Amendment of great weight in this argument, because the next paragraph of this same section, which is the one mainly relied on by the plaintiffs in error, speaks only of privileges and immunities of citizens of the United States, and does not speak of those of citizens of the several States. The argument, however, in favor of the plaintiffs rests wholly on the assumption that the citizenship is the same, and the privileges and immunities guaranteed by the clause are the same.

The language is, "No state shall make or enforce any law which shall abridge the privileges or immunities of citizens of *the United States.*" It is a little remarkable, if this clause was intended as a protection to the citizen of a State against the legislative power of his own State, that the word citizen of the State should be left out when it is so carefully used, and used in contradistinction to citizens of the United States, in the very sentence which precedes it. It is too clear for argument that the change in phraseology was adopted understandingly and with a purpose.

Of the privileges and immunities of the citizen of the United States, and of the privileges and immunities of the citizen of the State, and what they respectively are, we will presently consider; but we wish to state here that it is only the former which are placed by this clause under the protection of the Federal Constitution, and that the latter, whatever they may be, are not intended to have any additional protection by this paragraph of the amendment.

If, then, there is a difference between the privileges and immunities belonging to a citizen of the United States as such, and those belonging to the citizen of the State as such the latter must rest for their security and protection where they have heretofore rested; for they are not embraced by this paragraph of the amendment. . . .

Fortunately we are not without judicial construction of this clause of the Constitution. The first and the leading case on the subject is that of *Corfield v. Coryell,* 6 Fed. Cas. 3230, decided by Mr. Justice Washington in the Circuit Court for the District of Pennsylvania in 1823.

"The inquiry," he says, "is, what are the privileges and immunities of citizens of the several States? We feel no hesitation in confining these expressions to those privileges and immunities which are fundamental; which belong of right to the citizens of all free governments, and which have at all times been enjoyed by citizens of the several States which compose this Union, from the time of their becoming free, independent, and sovereign. What these fundamental principles are, it would be more tedious than difficult to enumerate. They may all, however, be comprehended under the following general heads: protection by the government, with the right to acquire and possess property of every kind, and to pursue and obtain happiness and safety, subject, nevertheless, to such restraints as the government may prescribe for the general good of the whole." . . .

It would be the vainest show of learning to attempt to prove by citations of authority, that up to the adoption of the recent Amendments, no claim or pretense was set up that those rights depended on the Federal Government for their existence or protection, beyond the very few express limitations which the Federal Constitution imposed upon the States—such, for instance, as the prohibition against *ex post facto* laws, bills of attainder, and laws impairing the obligation of contracts. But with the exception of these and a few other restrictions, the entire domain of the privileges and immunities of citizens of the States, as above defined, lay within the constititional and legislative power of the States, and without that of the Federal Government. Was it the purpose of the Fourteenth Amendment, by the simple declaration that no State should make or enforce any law which shall abridge the privileges and immunities of *citizens of the United States,* to transfer the security and protection of all the civil rights which we have mentioned, from the States to the Federal Government? And where it is declared that Congress shall have the power to enforce that article, was it intended to bring within the power of Congress the entire domain of civil rights heretofore belonging exclusively to the States?

All this and more must follow, if the proposition of the plaintiffs in error be sound. For not only are these rights subject to the control of Congress whenever in its discretion any of them are supposed to be abridged by state legislation, but that body may also pass laws in advance, limiting and restricting the exercise of legislative power by the States, in their most ordinary and usual functions, as in its judgment it may think proper on all such subjects. And still further, such a construction followed by the reversal of the judgments of the Supreme Court of Louisiana in these cases, would constitute this court a perpetual censor upon all legislation of the States, on the civil rights of their own citizens, with authority to nullify such as it did not approve as consistent with those rights, as they existed at the time of the adoption of this Amendment. The argument we admit is not always the most conclusive which is drawn from the consequences urged against the adoption of a particular construction of an instrument. But when, as in the case before us, these consequences are so serious, so far-reaching and pervading, so great a departure from the structure and spirit of our institutions; when the effect is to fetter and degrade the State Governments by subjecting them to the control of Congress, in the exercise of powers heretofore universally conceded to them of the most ordinary and fundamental character; when in fact it radically changes the whole theory of the relations of the State and Federal Governments to each other and of both these governments to the people; the argument has a force that is irresistible, in the absence of language which expresses such a purpose too clearly to admit of doubt.

We are convinced that no such results were intended by the Congress which proposed these Amendments, nor by the legislatures of the States which ratified them.

Having shown that the privileges and immunities relied on in the argument are those which belong to citizens of the States as such, and that they are left to the State Governments for security and protection, and not by this article placed under the special care of the Federal Government, we may hold ourselves excused from defining the privileges and immunities of citizens of the United States which no State can abridge, until some case involving those privileges may make it necessary to do so.

But lest it be said that no such privileges and immunities are to be found if those we have been considering are excluded, we venture to suggest some which owe their existence to the Federal Government, its national character, its Constitution, or its laws.

One of these is well described in the case of *Crandall v. Nevada,* 6 Wall. 35. It is said to be the right of the citizens of this great country, protected by implied guaranties of its Constitution, "to come to the seat of government to assert any claim he may have upon that government, to transact any business he may have with it, to seek its protection, to share its offices, to engage in administering its functions. He has the right of free access to its seaports, through which all operations of foreign commerce are conducted, to the sub-treasuries, land offices, and courts of justice in the several States." And quoting from the language of Chief Justice Taney in another case, it is said "that for all the great purposes for which the Federal Government was established, we are one people, with one common country, we are all citizens of the United States"; and it is, as such citizens, that their rights are supported in this court in *Crandall v. Nevada.* . . .

The argument has not been much pressed in these cases that the defendant's charter deprives the plaintiffs of their property without due process of law, or that it denies to them the equal protection of the law. The first of these paragraphs has been in the Constitution since the adoption of the Fifth Amendment, as a restraint upon the federal power. It is also to be found in some form of expression in the constitutions of nearly all the States, as a restraint upon the power of the States. This law, then, has practically been the same as it now is during the existence of the Government, except so far as the present Amendment may place the restraining power over the States in this matter in the hands of the Federal Government.

We are not without judicial interpretation, therefore, both state and national, of the meaning of this clause. And it is sufficient to say that under no construction of that provision that we have ever seen, or any that we deem admissible, can the restraint imposed by the State of Louisiana upon the exercise of their trade by the butchers of New Orleans be held to be a deprivation of property within the meaning of that provision.

"Nor shall any state deny to any person within its jurisdiction the equal protection of the laws."

In the light of the history of these Amendments, and the pervading purpose of them, which we have already discussed, it is not difficult to give a meaning to this clause. The existence of laws in the States where the newly emancipated Negroes resided, which discriminated with gross injustice and hardship against them as a class, was the evil to be remedied by this clause, and by it such laws are forbidden.

If, however, the States did not conform their laws to its requirements, then by the fifth section of the Article of Amendment Congress was authorized to enforce it by suitable legislation. We doubt very much whether any action of a State not directed by way of discrimination against the Negroes as a class, or on account of their race, will ever be held to come within the purview of this provision. It is so clearly a provision for that race and that emergency, that a strong case would be necessary for its application to any other. But as it is a State that is to be dealt with, and not alone the validity of its laws, we may safely leave that matter until Congress shall have exercised its power, or some case of state oppression, by denial of equal justice in its courts, shall have claimed a decision at our hands. We find no such case in the one before us, and do not deem it necessary to go over the argument again, as it may have relation to this particular clause of the Amendment. . . .

The judgments of the Supreme Court of Louisiana in these cases are

Affirmed.

MR. JUSTICE FIELD, DISSENTING:

The question presented is . . . one of the gravest importance, not merely to the parties here, but to the whole country. It is nothing less than the question whether the recent Amendments to the Federal Constitution protect the citizens of the United States against the deprivation of their common rights by state legislation. In my judgment the Fourteenth Amendment does afford such protection, and was so intended by the Congress which framed and the States which adopted it.

The Amendment does not attempt to confer any new privileges or immunities upon citizens, or to enumerate or define those already existing. It assumes that there are such privileges and immunities which belong of right to citizens as such, and ordains that they shall not be abridged by state legislation. If this inhibition has no reference to privileges and immunities of this character, but only refers, as held by the majority of the Court in their opinion, to such privileges and immunities as were before its adoption specially designated in the Constitution or necessarily implied as belonging to citizens of the United States, it was a vain and idle enactment, which accomplished nothing, and most unnecessarily excited Congress and the people on its passage. With privileges and immunities thus designated or implied no State could ever have interfered by its laws, and no new constitutional provision was required to inhibit such interference. The supremacy of the Constitution and the laws of the United States always controlled any state legislation of that character. But if the Amendment refers to the natural and inalienable rights which belong to all citizens, the inhibition has a profound significance and consequence.

What, then, are the privileges and immunities which are secured against abridgment by state legislation? . . .

The terms, privileges and immunities, are not new in the Amendment; they were in the Constitution before the Amendment was adopted. They are found in the second section of the fourth article, which declares that "the citizens of each state shall be entitled to all privileges and immunities of citizens in the several states," and they have been the subject of frequent consideration in judicial decisions. In *Corfield v. Coryell,* Mr. Justice Washington said he had "no hesitation in confining these expressions to those privileges and immunities which were, in their nature, fundamental; which belong of right to citizens of all free governments, and which have at all times been enjoyed by the citizens of the several States which compose the Union, from the time of their becoming free, independent, and sovereign"; and, in considering what those fundamental privileges were, he said that perhaps it would be more tedious than difficult to enumerate them, but that they might be "all comprehended under the following general heads: protection by the government; the enjoyment of life and liberty, with the right to acquire and possess property of every kind, and to pursue and obtain happiness and safety, subject, nevertheless, to such restraints as the government may justly prescribe for the general good of the whole." This appears to me to be a sound construction of the clause in question. The privileges and immunities designated are those *which of right belong to the citizens of all free governments.* Clearly among these must be placed the right to pursue a lawful employment in a lawful manner, without other restraint than such as equally affects all persons. In the discussions in Congress upon the passage of the Civil Rights Act repeated reference was made to this language of Mr. Justice Washington. It was cited by Senator Trumbull with the observation that it enumerated the very rights belonging to a citizen of the United States set forth in the first section of the Act, and with the statement that all persons born in the United

States, being declared by the Act citizens of the United States, would thenceforth be entitled to the rights of citizens, and that these were the great fundamental rights set forth in the Act; and that they were set forth "as appertaining to every freeman." . . .

This equality of right, with exemption from all disparaging and partial enactments, in the lawful pursuits of life, throughout the whole country, is the distinguishing privilege of citizens of the United States. To them, everywhere, all pursuits, all professions, all avocations are open without other restrictions than such as are imposed equally upon all others of the same age, sex, and condition. The State may prescribe such regulations for every pursuit and calling of life as will promote the public health, secure the good order and advance the general prosperity of society, but when once prescribed, the pursuit or calling must be free to be followed by every citizen who is within the conditions designated, and will conform to the regulations. This is the fundamental idea upon which our institutions rest, and unless adhered to in the legislation of the country our Government will be a republic only in name. The Fourteenth Amendment, in my judgment, makes it essential to the validity of the legislation of every State that this equality of right should be respected. How widely this equality has been departed from, how entirely rejected and trampled upon by the act of Louisiana, I have already shown. And it is to me a matter of profound regret that its validity is recognized by a majority of this court, for by it the right of free labor, one of the most sacred and imprescriptible rights of man, is violated. . . .

I am authorized by the Chief Justice [Chase], Mr. Justice Swayne, and Mr. Justice Bradley, to state that they concur with me in this dissenting opinion.

MR. JUSTICE BRADLEY, ALSO DISSENTING:

The right of a State to regulate the conduct of its citizens is undoubtedly a very broad and extensive one, and not to be lightly restricted. But there are certain fundamental rights which this right of regulation cannot infringe. It may prescribe the manner of their exercise, but it cannot subvert the rights themselves. . . .

The granting of monopolies, or exclusive privileges to individuals or corporations, is an invasion of the right of another to choose a lawful calling, and an infringement of personal liberty. It was so felt by the English nation as far back as the reigns of Elizabeth and James. A fierce struggle for the suppression of such monopolies, and for abolishing the prerogative of creating them, was made and was successful. . . . And ever since that struggle no English-speaking people have ever endured such an odious badge of tyranny. . . .

Lastly: Can the federal courts administer relief to citizens of the United States whose privileges and immunities have been abridged by a State? Of this I entertain no doubt. Prior to the Fourteenth Amendment this could not be done, except in a few instances, for the want of the requisite authority. . . .

Admitting, therefore, that formerly the States were not prohibited from infringing any fundamental privileges and immunities of citizens of the United States, except in a few specified cases, that cannot be said now, since the adoption of the Fourteenth Amendment. In my judgment, it was the intention of the people of this country in adopting that Amendment to provide national security against violation by the States of the fundamental rights of the citizen. . . .

In my opinion the judgment of the Supreme Court of Louisiana ought to be reversed.

[Mr. Justice Swayne also delivered a dissenting opinion.]

Minimum wage regulations by state legislatures or Congress are constitutional.

20. *WEST COAST HOTEL CO. v. PARRISH* (1937)

This is the first case in which the Supreme Court ruled that minimum wage regulations were not a violation of the Constitution. Specifically, the Court overturned a former decision, Adkins v. Children's Hospital *(1923), which had ruled that the setting of minimum wages for women and minors (as provided by an Act of Congress of September 19, 1918) violated the Due Process clause of the Fourteenth Amendment. The Adkins decision had served as an effective block against wage legislation until 1937.*

Background: *A Washington State law fixing minimum wages for women and minor workers was challenged by the West Coast Hotel Company on the ground that it was unconstitutional. The company cited the Adkins decision, as well as the similar one of* Morehead v. New York ex rel. Tipaldo *(1936), in support of its case. Losing in the Supreme Court of the State of Washington, the company carried its appeal to the United States Supreme Court. The latter, by a vote of five to four, validated the Washington State law and, in effect, made possible the enactment of further labor and other social legislation.*

Some Related Cases
(On Wages and Hours):
Lochner v. New York (1905)
Muller v. Oregon (1908)
Baltimore & Ohio R.R. v. Interstate Commerce Commission (1911)
Bunting v. Oregon (1917)
Stettler v. O'Hara (1917)
Wolff Packing Co. v. Industrial Court (1923)
Day-Brite Lighting, Inc. v. Missouri (1952)

MR. CHIEF JUSTICE HUGHES DELIVERED THE OPINION OF THE COURT:

This case presents the question of the constitutional validity of the minimum wage law of the State of Washington. . . .

The appellant relies upon the decision of this court in *Adkins v. Children's Hospital* . . . which held invalid the District of Columbia Minimum Wage Act which was attacked under the Due Process clause of the Fifth Amendment. On the argument at bar, counsel for the appellees attempted to distinguish the Adkins case upon the ground that the appellee was employed in a hotel and that the business of an inn-keeper was affected with a public interest. That effort at distinction is obviously futile, as it appears that in one of the cases ruled by the Adkins opinion the employee was a woman employed as an elevator operator in a hotel. *Adkins v. Lyons,* 261 U.S. 525, at p. 542.

The recent case of *Morehead v. New York* ex. rel. *Tipaldo,* 298 U.S. 587, came here on certiorari to the New York court which had held the New York Minimum Wage Act for women to be invalid. A minority of this court thought that the New York statute was distinguishable in a material feature from that involved in the Adkins case, and that for that and other reasons the New York statute should be sustained. But the Court of Appeals of New York had said that it found no material difference between the two statutes and this court held that the "meaning of the statute" as fixed by the decision of the state court "must be accepted here as if the meaning had been specifically expressed in the enactment." . . . That view led to the affirmance by this court of the judgment in the Morehead case, as the Court considered that the only question before it was whether the Adkins case was distinguishable and that reconsideration of that decision had not been sought. . . .

We think that the question which was not deemed to be open in the Morehead case is open and is necessarily presented here. The Supreme Court of Washington has upheld the minimum wage statute of that State. It has decided that the statute is a reasonable exercise of the police power of the State. In reaching that conclusion, the state court has invoked principles long established by this court in the application of the Fourteenth Amendment. The state court has refused to regard the decision in the Adkins case as determinative and has pointed to our decisions both before and since that case as justifying its position. We are of the opinion that this ruling of the state court demands on our part a re-examination of the Adkins case. The importance of the question, in which many States having similar laws are concerned, the close division by which the decision in the Adkins case was reached, and the economic conditions which have supervened, and in the light of which the reasonableness of the exercise of the protective power of the State must be considered, make it not only appropriate, but we think imperative, that in deciding the present case the subject should receive fresh consideration. . . .

The principle which must control our decision is not in doubt. The constitutional provision invoked is the Due Process clause of the Fourteenth Amendment governing the States, as the Due Process clause invoked in the Adkins case governed Congress. In each case the violation alleged by those attacking minimum wage regulation for women is deprivation of freedom of contract. What is this freedom? The Constitution does not speak of freedom of contract. It speaks of liberty and prohibits the deprivation of liberty without the due process of law. In prohibiting that deprivation the Constitution does not recognize an absolute and uncontrollable liberty. Liberty in each of its phases has its history and connotation. But the liberty safeguarded is liberty in a social organization which requires the protection of law against the evils which menace the health, safety, morals and welfare of the people. Liberty under the Constitution is thus necessarily subject to the restraints of due process, and regulation which is reasonable in relation to its subject and is adopted in the interests of the community is due process. . . .

The minimum wage to be paid under the Washington statute is fixed after full consideration by representatives of employers, employees and the public. It may be assumed that the minimum wage is fixed in consideration of the services that are performed in the particular occupations under normal conditions. Provision is made for special licenses at less wages in the case of women who are incapable of full service. The statement of Mr. Justice Holmes in the Adkins case is pertinent: "This statute does not compel anybody to pay anything. It simply forbids employment at rates below those fixed as the minimum requirement of health and right living. It is safe to assume that women will not be employed at even the lowest wages allowed unless they earn them, or unless the employer's business can sustain the burden. In short the law in its character and operation is like hundreds of so-called police laws that have been upheld." And Chief Justice Taft forcibly pointed out the consideration which is basic in a statute of this character: "Legislatures which adopt a requirement of maximum hours or minimum wages may be presumed to believe that when sweating employers are prevented from paying unduly low wages by positive law they will continue their business, abating that part of their profits, which were wrung from the necessities of their employees, and will concede the better terms required by the law, and that while in individual cases, hardship may result, the restriction will enure to the benefit of the general class of employees in whose interest the law is passed and so to that of the community at large."...

We think that the views thus expressed are sound and that the decision in the Adkins case was a departure from the true application of the principles governing the regulation by the State of the relation of employer and employed. . . .

. . . The legislature of the State was clearly entitled to consider the situation of women in employment, the fact that they are in the class receiving the least pay, that their bargaining power is relatively weak, and that they are the ready victims of those who would take advantage of their necessitous circumstances. The legislature was entitled to adopt measures to reduce the evils of the "sweating system," the exploiting of workers at wages so low as to be insufficient to meet the bare cost of living thus making their very helplessness the occasion of a most injurious competition. The legislature had the right to consider that its minimum wage requirements would be an important aid in carrying out its policy of protection. The adoption of similar requirements by many States evidences a deep-seated conviction both as to the presence of the evil and as to the means adapted to check it. Legislative response to that conviction cannot be regarded as arbitrary or capricious and that is all we have to decide. Even if the wisdom of the policy be regarded as debatable and its effects uncertain, still the legislature is entitled to its judgment. . . .

. . . We may take judicial notice of the unparalleled demands for relief which arose during the recent period of depression and still continue to an alarming extent despite the degree of economic recovery which has been achieved. It is unnecessary to cite official statistics to establish what is of common knowledge through the length and breadth of the land. While in the instant case no factual brief has been presented, there is no reason to doubt that the State of Washington has encountered the same social problem that is present elsewhere. The community is not bound to provide what is in effect a subsidy for unconscionable employers. The community may direct its law-making power to correct the abuse which springs from their selfish disregard of the public interest. . . .

Our conclusion is that the case of *Adkins v. Children's Hospital* should be, and it is, overruled. The judgment of the Supreme Court of the State of Washington is

Affirmed.

Chapter XIV

Equal Protection

"The citizens of each state shall be entitled to all privileges and immunities of citizens in the several states."—Art. IV, Sec. 2

"No state shall make or enforce any law which shall abridge the privileges or immunities of citizens of the United States . . ."—Art. XIV (Fourteenth Amendment), Sec. 1

"The right of citizens of the United States to vote shall not be denied or abridged by the United States or by any state on account of race, color, or previous condition of servitude."—Art. XV (Fifteenth Amendment), Sec. 1

In this Chapter:

Civil Rights Cases (1883)
Brown v. Board of Education (First Case: 1954)
Bolling v. Sharpe (1954)
Brown v. Board of Education (Second Case: 1955)
Cooper v. Aaron (1958)

Congress cannot protect social rights.

21. *CIVIL RIGHTS CASES* (1883)

This decision is important in that it illustrates the difficulty and complexity involved in the prolonged struggle for Negro rights. To appreciate it properly, it should be measured against such recent cases as Brown v. Board of Education *and* Cooper v. Aaron. *In the* Civil Rights Cases, *by a vote of eight to one, the Court, denying that the Federal Government had jurisdiction over social questions, in effect refused to grant protection to Negroes who sought equality in such matters as public accommodations.*

Background: *On March 11, 1875, Congress, determined to implement the Thirteenth and Fourteenth Amendments, passed the Civil Rights Act. The Act made it a crime for one person to deprive another of the "full and equal enjoyment of the accommodations, advantages, facilities, and privileges of inns, public conveyances on land or water, theatres, and other places of public amusement," regardless of color or previous conditions of servitude. Five Negroes, each having been separately denied some accommodation on account of color, appealed to the Supreme Court. The Court ruled that the Fourteenth Amendment involved protection of civil rights from invasion by state action rather than by individuals. The Civil Rights Act, extending to action by individuals in social (rather than political) matters, did not come under the purview of the Fourteenth Amendment and was, therefore, invalid. This decision ended, to all intents and purposes, all federal efforts to protect Negroes against discrimination until our own day.*

Some Related Cases

(On Negroes' Civil Rights):

Hall v. De Cuir (1878)
United States v. Harris (1883)
Yick Wo v. Hopkins (1886)
Louisiana N.O. & T.R.R. Co. v. Mississippi (1890)
Hodges v. United States (1906)
Cooper v. Aaron (1958) (see p. 252)

MR. JUSTICE BRADLEY DELIVERED THE OPINION OF THE COURT:

It is obvious that the primary and important question in all the cases is the constitutionality of the law: for if the law is unconstitutional none of the prosecutions can stand. . . .

The essence of the law is, not to declare broadly that all persons shall be entitled to the full and equal enjoyment of the accommodations, advantages, facilities, and privileges of inns, public conveyances, and theaters; but that such enjoyment shall not be subject to any conditions applicable only to citizens of a particular race or color, or who had been in a previous condition of servitude. . . .

Has Congress constitutional power to make such a law? Of

course, no one will contend that the power to pass it was contained in the Constitution before the adoption of the last three Amendments. The power is sought, first, in the Fourteenth Amendment, and the views and arguments of distinguished Senators, advanced while the law was under consideration, claiming authority to pass it by virtue of that Amendment, are the principal arguments adduced in favor of the power. We have carefully considered those arguments, as was due to the eminent ability of those who put them forward, and have felt, in all its force, the weight of authority which always invests a law that Congress deems itself competent to pass. But the responsibility of an independent judgment is now thrown upon this court; and we are bound to exercise it according to the best lights we have.

The first section of the Fourteenth Amendment (which is the one relied on), after declaring who shall be citizens of the United States, and of the several States, is prohibitory in its character, and prohibitory upon the States. It declares that:

"No state shall make or enforce any law which shall abridge the privileges or immunities of citizens of the United States; nor shall any state deprive any person of life, liberty, or property without due process of law; nor deny to any person within its jurisdiction the equal protection of the laws."

It is state action of a particular character that is prohibited. Individual invasion of individual rights is not the subject-matter of the Amendment. It has a deeper and broader scope. It nullifies and makes void all state legislation, and state action of every kind, which impairs the privileges and immunities of citizens of the United States, or which injures them in life, liberty or property without due process of law, or which denies to any of them the equal protection of the laws. It not only does this, but, in order that the national will, thus declared, may not be a mere *brutum fulmen,* the last section of the Amendment invests Congress with power to enforce it by appropriate legislation. To enforce what? To enforce the prohibition. To adopt appropriate legislation for correcting the effects of such prohibited state laws and state Acts, and thus to render them effectually null, void, and innocuous. This is the legislative power conferred upon Congress, and this is the whole of it. It does not invest Congress with power to legislate upon subjects which are within the domain of state legislation; but to provide modes of relief against state legislation, or state action, of the kind referred to. It does not authorize Congress to create a code of municipal law for the regulation of private rights; but to provide modes of redress against the operation of state laws, and the action of state officers executive or judicial, when these are subversive of the fundamental rights specified in the Amendment. Positive rights and privileges are undoubtedly secured by the Fourteenth Amendment; but they are secured by way of prohibition against state laws and state proceedings affecting those rights and privileges, and by power given to Congress to legislate for the purpose of carrying such prohibition into effect: and such legislation must necessarily be predicated upon such supposed state laws or state proceedings, and be directed to the correction of their operation and effect. . . .

. . . Until some state law has been passed, or some state action through its officers or agents has been taken, adverse to the rights of citizens sought to be protected by the Fourteenth Amendment, no legislation of the United States under said Amendment nor any proceeding under such legislation, can be called into activity: for the prohibitions of the Amendment are against state laws and acts done under state authority. Of course, legislation may, and should be, provided in advance to meet the exigency when it arises; but it should be adapted to the mischief and wrong which the Amendment was intended to provide against; and that is, state laws, or state action of some kind, adverse to the rights of the citizen secured by the Amendment. Such legislation cannot properly cover the whole domain of rights appertaining to life, liberty and property, defining them and providing for their vindication. That would be to establish a code of municipal law regulative of all private rights between man and man in society. It would be to make Congress take the place of the state legislatures and to supersede them. It is absurd to affirm that, because the rights of life, liberty and property (which include all civil rights that men have), are by the Amendment sought to be protected against invasion on the part of the State without due process of law, Congress may therefore provide due process of law for their vindication in every case; and that, because the denial by a State to any persons, of the equal protection of the laws, is prohibited by the Amendment, therefore Congress may establish laws for their equal protection. In fine, the legislation which Congress is authorized to adopt in this behalf is not general legislation upon the rights of the citizen, but corrective legislation, that is, such as may be necessary and proper for counteracting such laws as the States may adopt or enforce, and which, by the Amendment, they are prohibited from making or enforcing, or such acts and proceedings as the States may commit or take, and which, by the Amendment, they are prohibited from committing or taking. It is not necessary for us to state, if we could, what legislation would be proper for Congress to adopt. It is sufficient for us to examine whether the law in question is of that character.

An inspection of the law shows that it makes no reference whatever to any supposed or apprehended violation of the Fourteenth Amendment on the part of the States. It is not predicated on any such view. It proceeds *ex directo* to declare that certain acts committed by individuals shall be deemed offenses, and shall be prosecuted and punished by proceedings in the courts of the United States. It does not profess to be corrective of any constitutional wrong committed by the States; it does not make its operation to depend upon any such wrong committed. It applies equally to cases arising in States which have the justest laws respecting the personal rights of citizens, and whose authorities are ever ready to enforce such laws, as to those which arise in States that may have violated the prohibition of the Amendment. In other words, it steps into the domain of local jurisprudence, and lays down rules for the conduct of individuals in society toward each other, and imposes sanctions for the enforcement of those rules, without referring in any manner to any supposed action of the State or its authorities.

If this legislation is appropriate for enforcing the prohibitions of the Amendment, it is difficult to see where it is to stop. Why may not Congress with equal show of authority enact a code of laws for the enforcement and vindication of all rights of life, liberty, and property? If it is supposable that the States may deprive persons of life, liberty, and property without due process of law (and the Amendment itself does not suppose this), why should not Congress proceed at once to prescribe due process of law for the protection of every one of these fundamental rights, in every possible case, as well as to prescribe equal privileges in inns, public conveyances, and theatres? The truth is, that the implication of a power to legislate in this manner is based upon the assumption that if the States are forbidden to legislate or act in a particular way on a particular subject, and power is conferred upon Congress to enforce the prohibition, this gives Congress power to legislate generally upon that subject, and not merely power to provide modes of redress against such state legislation or action. The assumption is certainly unsound. It is repugnant to the Tenth Amendment of the Constitution, which declares that powers not delegated to the United States by the Constitution, nor prohibited by it to the States, are reserved to the States respectively or to the people. . . .

In this connection it is proper to state that civil rights, such as are guaranteed by the Constitution against state aggression, cannot be impaired by the wrongful acts of individuals, unsupported by state authority in the shape of laws, customs, or judicial or executive proceedings. The wrongful act of an individual, unsupported by any such authority, is simply a private wrong, or a crime of that individual; an invasion of the rights of the injured party, it is true, whether they affect his person, his property, or his reputation; but if not sanctioned in some way by the State, or not done under state authority, his rights remain in full force, and may presumably be vindicated by resort to the laws of the State for redress. An individual cannot deprive a man of his right to vote, to hold property, to buy and sell, to sue in the courts, or to be a witness or a juror; he may, by force or fraud, interfere with the enjoyment of the right in a particular case; he may commit an assault against the person, or commit murder, or use ruffian violence at the polls, or slander the good name of a fellow-citizen; but, unless protected in these wrongful acts by some shield of state law or state authority, he cannot destroy or injure the right; he will only render himself amenable to satisfaction or punishment; and amenable therefor to the laws of the State where the wrongful acts are committed. Hence, in all those cases where the Constitution seeks to protect the rights of the citizen against discriminative and unjust laws of the State by prohibiting such laws, it is not individual offenses, but abrogation and denial of rights, which it denounces, and for which it clothes the Congress with power to provide a remedy. This abrogation and denial of rights, for which the States alone were or could be responsible, was the great seminal and fundamental wrong which was intended to be remedied. And the remedy to be provided must necessarily be predicated upon that wrong. It must assume that in the cases provided for, the evil or wrong actually committed rests upon some state law or state authority for its excuse and perpetration. . . .

We have discussed the question presented by the law on the assumption that a right to enjoy equal accommodation and privileges in all inns, public conveyances, and places of public amusement, is one of the essential rights of the citizen which no State can abridge or interfere with. Whether it is such a right, or not, is a different question which, in the view we have taken of the validity of the law on the ground already stated, it is not necessary to examine. . . .

But the power of Congress to adopt direct and primary, as distinguished from corrective legislation, on the subject in hand, is sought, in the second place, from the Thirteenth Amendment, which abolishes slavery. This Amendment declares "that neither slavery, nor involuntary servitude, except as a punishment for crime, whereof the party shall have been duly convicted, shall exist within the United States, or any place subject to their jurisdiction"; and it gives Congress power to enforce the Amendment by appropriate legislation. . . .

When a man has emerged from slavery, and by the aid of beneficent legislation has shaken off the inseparable concomitants of that state, there must be some stage in the progress of his elevation when he takes the rank of a mere citizen, and ceases to be the special favorite of the laws, and when his rights as a citizen, or a man, are to be protected in the ordinary modes by which other men's rights are protected. There were thousands of free colored people in this country before the abolition of slavery, enjoying all the essential rights of life, liberty and property the same as white citizens; yet no one, at that time, thought that it was any invasion of his personal status as a freeman because he was not admitted to all the privileges enjoyed by white citizens, or because he was subjected to discriminations in the enjoyment of accommodations in inns, public conveyances and places of amusement. Mere discriminations on account of race or color were not regarded as badges of slavery. If, since that time, the enjoyment of equal rights in all these respects has become established by constitutional enactment, it is not by force of the Thirteenth Amendment (which merely abolishes slavery), but by force of the Fourteenth and Fifteenth Amendments. . . .

MR. JUSTICE HARLAN, DISSENTING:

There seems to be no substantial difference between my brethren and myself as to the purpose of Congress; for, they say that the essence of the law is, not to declare broadly that all persons shall be entitled to the full and equal enjoyment of the accommodations, advantages, facilities, and privileges of inns, public conveyances, and theatres; but that such enjoyment shall not be subject to conditions applicable only to citizens of a particular race or color, or who had been in a previous condition of servitude. The effect of the statute, the Court says, is, that colored citizens, whether formerly slaves or not, and citizens of other races, shall have the same accommodations and privileges in all inns, public conveyances, and places of amusement as are enjoyed by white persons; and vice versa.

The Court adjudges, I think erroneously, that Congress is without power, under either the Thirteenth or Fourteenth Amendment, to establish such regulations, and that the first and second sections of the statute are, in all their parts, unconstitutional and void. . . .

Congress has not, in these matters, entered the domain of state control and supervision. It does not, as I have said, assume to prescribe the general conditions and limitations under which inns, public conveyances, and places of public amusement, shall be conducted or managed. It simply declares, in effect, that since the nation has established universal freedom in this country, for all time, there shall be no discrimination, based merely upon race or color, in respect of the accommodations and advantages of public conveyances, inns, and places of public amusement.

I am of the opinion that such discrimination practiced by corporations and individuals in the exercise of their public or quasi-public functions is a badge of servitude, the imposition of which Congress may prevent under its power, by appropriate legislation, to enforce the Thirteenth Amendment; and, consequently, without reference to its enlarged power under the Fourteenth Amendment, the Act of March 1, 1875, is not, in my judgment, repugnant to the Constitution. . . . The assumption that this Amendment [the Fourteenth] consists wholly of prohibitions upon state laws and state proceedings in hostility to its language. The first clause of the first section—"All persons born or naturalized in the United States, and subject to the jurisdiction thereof, are citizens of the United States, and of the state wherein they reside"—is of a distinctly affirmative character. In its application to the colored race, previously liberated, it created and granted, as well citizenship of the United States, as citizenship of the State in which they respectively resided. It introduced all of that race, whose ancestors had been imported and sold as slaves, at once, into the political community known as the "People of the United States." They became, instantly, citizens of the United States, and of their respective States. Further, they were brought, by this supreme act of the nation, within the direct operation of that provision of the Constitution which declares that "the citizens of each state shall be entitled to all privileges and immunities of citizens in the several states." Article 4, Section 2.

The citizenship thus acquired by that race, in virtue of an affirmative grant from the Nation, may be protected, not alone by the judicial branch of the Government, but by congressional legislation of a primary direct character; this, because the power of Congress is not restricted to the enforcement of prohibitions upon state laws or state action. It is, in terms distinct and positive, to enforce "the *provisions* of *this article*" of amendment; not simply those of a prohibitive character, but the provisions—*all* of the provisions—affirmative and prohibitive, of the Amendment. It is, therefore, a grave misconception to suppose that the fifth section of the Amendment has reference exclusively to express prohibitions upon state laws or state action. If any right was created by that Amendment, the grant of power, through appropriate legislation, to enforce its provisions, authorizes Congress, by means of legislation, operating throughout the entire Union, to guard, secure, and protect that right. . . .

It is said that any interpretation of the Fourteenth Amendment different from that adopted by the majority of the Court, would imply that Congress had authority to enact a municipal code for all the States, covering every matter affecting the life, liberty, and property of the citizens of the several States. Not so. Prior to the adoption of that Amendment the constitutions of the several States, without perhaps an exception, secured all *persons* against deprivation of life, liberty, or property, otherwise than by the due process of law, and, in some form, recognized the right of all *persons* to the equal protection of the laws. Those rights, therefore, existed before that Amendment was proposed or adopted, and were not created by it. If, by reason of that fact, it be assumed that protection in these rights of persons still rests primarily with the States, and that Congress may not interfere except to enforce, by means of corrective legislation, the prohibitions upon state laws or state proceedings inconsistent with those rights, it does not at all follow, that privileges which have been granted *by the Nation,* may not be protected by primary legislation upon the part of Congress. The personal rights and immunities recognized in the prohibitive clauses of the Amendment were, prior to its adoption, under the protection, primarily, of the States, while rights, created by or derived from the United States, have always been, and, in the nature of things, should always be, primarily, under the protection of the general Government. Exemption from race discrimination in respect of the civil rights which are fundamental in *citizenship* in a republican government, is, as we have seen, a new right, created by the Nation, with express power in Congress, by legislation, to enforce the constitutional provision from which it is derived. If, in some sense, such race discrimination is, within the letter of the last clause of the first section, a denial of that equal protection of the laws which is secured against state denial to all persons, whether citizens or not, it cannot be possible that a mere prohibition upon such state denial, or a prohibition upon state laws abridging the privileges and immunities of citizens of the United States, takes from the nation the power which it has uniformly exercised of protecting, by direct primary legislation, those privileges and immunities which existed under the Constitution before the adoption of the Fourteenth Amendment, or have been created by that Amendment in behalf of those thereby made *citizens* of their respective States. . . .

But the Court says that Congress did not, in the Act of 1866, assume, under the authority given by the Thirteenth Amendment, to adjust what may be called the social rights of men and races in the community. I agree that government has nothing to do with social, as distinguished from technically legal, rights of individuals. No government ever has brought, or ever can bring, its people into social intercourse against their wishes. Whether one person will permit or maintain social relations with another is a matter with which government has no concern. I agree that if one citizen chooses not to hold social intercourse with another, he is not and cannot be made amenable to the law for his conduct in that regard; for even upon grounds of race, no legal right of a citizen is violated by the refusal of others to maintain merely social relations with him. What I affirm is that no State, nor the officers of any State, nor any corporation or individual wielding power under state authority for the public benefit or the public convenience, can, consistently either with the freedom established by the fundamental law, or with that equality of civil rights which now belongs to every citizen, discriminate against freemen or citizens, in those rights, because of their race, or because they once labored under the disabilities of slavery imposed upon them as a race. The rights which Congress, by the Act of 1875, endeavored to secure and protect are legal, not social rights. The right, for instance, of a colored citizen to use the accommodations of a public highway, upon the same terms as are permitted to white citizens, is no more a social right than his right, under the law, to use the public streets of a city or a town, or a turnpike road, or a public market, or a post office, or his right to sit in a public building with others, of whatever race, for the purpose of hearing the political questions of the day discussed. Scarcely a day passes without our seeing in this courtroom citizens of the white and black races sitting side by side, watching the progress of our business. It would never occur to anyone that the presence of a colored citizen in a courthouse, or courtroom, was an invasion of the social rights of white persons who may frequent such places. And yet, such a suggestion would be quite as sound in law—I say it with all respect—as is the suggestion that the claim of a colored citizen to use, upon the same terms as are permitted to white citizens, the accommodation of public inns, or places of public amusement, established under the license of the law, is an invasion of the social rights of the white race. . . .

Segregation in schools on the basis of race is a denial of equal rights and a violation of the Constitution.

22a. *BROWN v. BOARD OF EDUCATION OF TOPEKA.* (First Case: 1954)

22b. *BOLLING v. SHARPE (District of Columbia:* 1954)

22c. *BROWN v. BOARD OF EDUCATION OF TOPEKA* (Second Case: 1955)

These are epochal decisions of the United States Supreme Court. Racial segregation in employment, housing, recreation, education and other fields had long been widely practiced in the United States, despite the Fourteenth Amendment. The famous judicial doctrine of "separate but equal," in Plessy v. Ferguson (1896), *actually provided more separation than equality. Furthermore, the concept of separation was in itself a violation of the idea of equality as provided in the Constitution. Over the years, particularly between the 1930's and early 1950's, the Supreme Court moved gradually to strike down various state provisions in the realm of higher education that did not meet the "equal" requirements of* Plessy v. Ferguson. *In* Brown v. Board of Education, *which dealt specifically with elementary education, the Court took the final, logical step. In a unanimous decision, it outlawed segregation altogether. The consequences of the decision, stimulating the*

Negro drive for full equality in all fields, have been nothing short of revolutionary.

Background: *The facts of the case and the reasons behind it are given by Chief Justice Warren in the first dozen or so paragraphs of the decision.*

Brown v. Board of Education. *First Case, contains an analysis of the situation and a condemnation, based to a large extent on sociological literature, of the evils of segregation.* Brown v. Board of Education, *Second Case, provides guidance for the lower courts in enforcing the decision in the affected States, of which there were altogether seventeen, as well as the District of Columbia* (Bolling v. Sharpe) *and four States where public school segregation was permitted as a local option.*

Some Related Cases
(On Segregation):

Cummings v. County Board of Education (1899)
Buchanan v. Warley (1917)
Gong Lum v. Rice (1927)
Missouri v. Canada (1938)
Shelley v. Kraemer (1948)
Sipuel v. Oklahoma (1948)
Fisher v. Hurst (1948)
Sweatt v. Painter (1950)
McLaurin v. Oklahoma State Regents (1950)
McKissick v. Carmichael (1951)

22a. *BROWN V. BOARD OF EDUCATION* (First Case: 1954)

MR. CHIEF JUSTICE WARREN DELIVERED THE OPINION OF THE COURT:

These cases come to us from the States of Kansas, South Carolina, Virginia, and Delaware. They are premised on different facts and different local conditions, but a common legal question justifies their consideration together in this consolidated opinion.

In each of the cases, minors of the Negro race, through their legal representatives, seek the aid of the courts in obtaining admission to the public schools of their community on a nonsegregated basis. In each instance, they had been denied admission to schools attended by white children under laws requiring or permitting segregation according to race.

This segregation was alleged to deprive the plaintiffs of the equal protection of the laws under the Fourteenth Amendment. In each of the cases other than the Delaware case, a three-judge Federal District Court denied relief to the plaintiffs on the so-called "separate but equal" doctrine announced by this court in *Plessy v. Ferguson* [1896]. . . .

Under that doctrine, equality of treatment is accorded when the races are provided substantially equal facilities, even though these facilities be separate. In the Delaware case, the Supreme Court of Delaware adhered to that doctrine, but ordered that the plaintiffs be admitted to the white schools because of their superiority to the Negro schools.

The plaintiffs contend that segregated public schools are not "equal" and cannot be made "equal," and that, hence, they are deprived of the equal protection of the laws. Because of the obvious importance of the question presented, the Court took jurisdiction. Argument was heard in the 1952 term, and reargument was heard this term on certain questions propounded by the Court.

Reargument was largely devoted to the circumstances surrounding the adoption of the Fourteenth Amendment in 1868. It covered, exhaustively, consideration of the Amendment in Congress, ratification by the States, then existing practices in racial segregation, and the views of proponents and opponents of the Amendment.

This discussion and our own investigation convince us that, although these sources cast some light, it is not enough to resolve the problem with which we are faced.

At best, they are inconclusive. The most avid proponents of the postwar Amendments undoubtedly intended them to remove all legal distinctions among "all persons born or naturalized in the United States."

Their opponents, just as certainly, were antagonistic to both the letter and the spirit of the Amendments and wished them to have the most limited effect. What others in Congress and the state legislature had in mind cannot be determined with any degree of certainty.

An additional reason for the illusive nature of the Amendment's history, with respect to segregated schools, is the status of public education at that time. In the South, the movement toward free common schools, supported by general taxation, had not yet taken hold. Education of white children was largely in the hands of private groups. Education of Negroes was almost nonexistent, and practically all of the race was illiterate. In fact, any education of Negroes was forbidden by law in some States.

Today, in contrast, many Negroes have achieved outstanding success in the arts and sciences as well as in the business and professional world. It is true that public school education at the time of the Amendment had advanced further in the North, but the effect of the Amendment on Northern States was generally ignored in the congressional debates.

Even in the North, the conditions of public education did not approximate those existing today. The curriculum was usually rudimentary; ungraded schools were common in rural areas; the school term was but three months a year in many States; and compulsory school attendance was virtually unknown.

As a consequence, it is not surprising that there should be so little in the history of the Fourteenth Amendment relating to its intended effect on public education.

In the first cases in this court construing the Fourteenth Amendment, decided shortly after its adoption, the Court interpreted it as proscribing all State-imposed discriminations against the Negro race.

The doctrine of "separate but equal" did not make its appearance in this court until 1896 in the case of *Plessy v. Ferguson* . . . involving not education but transportation. . . .

American courts have since labored with the doctrine for over half a century. In this court, there have been six cases* involving the "separate but equal" doctrine in the field of public education. . . .

In none of these cases was it necessary to reexamine the doctrine to grant relief to the Negro plaintiff. And in *Sweatt v. Painter* [1950] . . . the Court expressly reserved decision on the question whether *Plessy v. Ferguson* should be held inapplicable to public education.

In the instant cases, that question is directly presented. Here, unlike *Sweatt v. Painter,* there are findings below that the Negro and white schools involved have been equalized, or are being equalized, with respect to buildings, curricula, qualifications and salaries of teachers, and other "tangible" factors.

Our decision, therefore, cannot turn on merely a comparison of these tangible factors in the Negro and white schools involved in each of the cases. We must look instead to the effect of segregation itself on public education.

In approaching this problem, we cannot turn the clock back to 1868, when the Amendment was adopted, or even to 1896, when *Plessy v. Ferguson* was written. We must consider public education in the light of its full development and its present place in American life throughout the nation. Only in this way can it be determined if segregation in public schools deprives these plaintiffs of the equal protection of the laws.

Today, education is perhaps the most important function of State and local governments. Compulsory school attendance laws and the great expenditures for education both demonstrate

* *Cummings v. County Board of Education; Gong Lum v. Rice; Missouri* ex rel. *Gaines v. Canada; Sipuel v. Oklahoma; Sweatt v. Painter; McLaurin v. Oklahoma State Regents.*

our recognition of the importance of education to our democratic society. It is required in the performance of our most basic public responsibilities, even service in the armed forces. It is the very foundation of good citizenship.

Today, it is a principal instrument in awakening the child to cultural values, in preparing him for later professional training, and in helping him to adjust normally to his environment.

In these days, it is doubtful that any child may reasonably be expected to succeed in life if he is denied the opportunity of an education. Such an opportunity, where the State has undertaken to prove it, is a right which must be made available to all on equal terms.

We come then to the question presented: Does segregation of children in public schools solely on the basis of race, even though the physical facilities and other "tangible" factors may be equal, deprive the children of the minority group of equal education opportunities? We believe that it does.

In *Sweatt v. Painter* . . . in finding that a segregated law school for Negroes could not provide them equal educational opportunities, this court relied in large part on "those qualities which are incapable of objective measurement but which make for greatness in a law school."

In *McLaurin v. Oklahoma State Regents* [1950] . . . the Court, in requiring that a Negro admitted to a white graduate school be treated like all other students, again resorted to intangible considerations: ". . . his ability to study, engage in discussions and exchange views with other students, and, in general, to learn his profession."

Such considerations apply with added force to children in grade and high schools. To separate them from others of similar age and qualifications solely because of their race generates a feeling of inferiority as to their status in the community that may affect their hearts and minds in a way unlikely ever to be undone.

The effect of this separation on their educational opportunities was well stated by a finding in the Kansas case by a court which nevertheless felt compelled to rule against the Negro plaintiffs:

> Segregation of white and colored children in public schools has a detrimental effect upon the colored children. The impact is greater when it has the sanction of the law; for the policy of separating the races is usually interpreted as denoting the inferiority of the Negro group.
>
> A sense of inferiority affects the motivation of a child to learn. Segregation with the sanction of law, therefore, has a tendency to retard the educational and mental development of Negro children and to deprive them of some of the benefits they would receive in a racially integrated school system.

Whatever may have been the extent of psychological knowledge at the time of *Plessy v. Ferguson,* this finding is amply supported by modern authority.*

. . . Any language in *Plessy v. Ferguson* contrary to this finding is rejected.

We conclude that in the field of public education the doctrine of "separate but equal" has no place. Separate educational facilities are inherently unequal. Therefore, we hold that the plaintiffs and others similarly situated for whom the actions have been brought are, by reason of the segregation complained of, deprived of the equal protection of the laws guaranteed by the Fourteenth Amendment. This disposition makes unnecessary any discussion whether such segregation also violates the Due Process clause of the Fourteenth Amendment.

Because these are class actions, because of the wide applicability of this decision, and because of the great variety of local conditions, the formulation of decrees in these cases presents problems of considerable complexity. On reargument, the consideration of appropriate relief was necessarily subordinated to the primary question—the constitutionality of segregation in public education.

We have now announced that such segregation is a denial of the equal protection of the laws. In order that we may have the full assistance of the parties in formulating decrees the cases will be restored to the docket, and the parties are requested to present further argument on Questions 4 and 5 previously propounded by the Court for the reargument this term [these related to the form of decrees to be issued where segregated schools were outlawed].

The Attorney General of the United States is again invited to participate. The Attorneys General of the States requiring or permitting segregation in public education will also be permitted to appear as *amici curiae* upon request to do so by September 15, 1954, and submission of briefs by October 1, 1954.

It is so ordered.

* Citing: K. B. Clark, *Effect of Prejudice and Discrimination on Personality Development* (Mid-Century White House Conference on Children and Youth, 1950); Witmer and Kotinsky, *Personality in the Making* (1952), Ch. VI; Deutscher and Chein, "The Psychological Effects of Enforced Segregation: A Survey of Social Science Opinion," 26 *J. Psychology,* 259 (1948); Chein, "What are the Psychological Effects of Segregation Under Conditions of Equal Facilities?" *Int. J. Opinion and Attitude Res.* 229 (1949); Brameld, "Educational Costs," in *Discrimination and National Welfare* (MacIver, ed., 1949), 44-48; Frazier, *The Negro in the United States* (1949), 674-681. And Myrdal, *An American Dilemma* (1944).

22b. *BOLLING v. SHARPE (District of Columbia:* 1954)

MR. JUSTICE WARREN DELIVERED THE OPINION OF THE COURT:

This case challenges the validity of segregation in the public schools of the District of Columbia. The petitioners, minors of the Negro race, allege that such segregation deprives them of due process of law under the Fifth Amendment. They were refused admission to a public school attended by white children solely because of their race.

They sought the aid of the District Court for the District of Columbia in obtaining admission. That court dismissed their complaint. We granted a writ of certiorari before judgment in the Court of Appeals because of the importance of the constitutional question presented.

We have this day held that the Equal Protection clause of the Fourteenth Amendment prohibits the States from maintaining racially segregated public schools.

The legal problem in the District of Columbia is somewhat different, however. The Fifth Amendment, which is applicable in the District of Columbia, does not contain an Equal Protection clause as does the Fourteenth Amendment which applies only to the States.

But the concepts of equal protection and due process, both stemming from our American ideal of fairness, are not mutually exclusive. The "equal protection of the laws" is a more explicit safeguard of prohibited unfairness than "due process of law," and, therefore, we do not imply that the two are always interchangeable phrases.

But, as this court has recognized, discrimination may be so unjustifiable as to be violative of due process. Classifications based solely upon race must be scrutinized with particular care, since they are contrary to our traditions and hence constitutionally suspect.

As long ago as 1896, this court declared the principle "that the Constitution of the United States, in its present form, forbids, so far as civil and political rights are concerned, discrimination by the general Government, or by the States, against any citizen because of his race."

And in *Buchanan v. Warley* [1917], the Court held that a statute which limited the right of a property owner to convey his property to a person of another race was, as an unreasonable discrimination, a denial of due process of law.

Although the Court has not assumed to define "liberty" with any great precision, that term is not confined to mere freedom from bodily restraint. Liberty under law extends to the full range of conduct which the individual is free to pursue, and it cannot be restricted except for a proper governmental objective.

Segregation in public education is not reasonably related to any proper governmental objective, and thus it imposes on Negro children of the District of Columbia a burden that constitutes an arbitrary deprivation of their liberty in violation of the Due Process clause.

In view of our decision that the Constitution prohibits the States from maintaining racially segregated public schools, it would be unthinkable that the same Constitution would impose a lesser duty on the Federal Government. We hold that racial segregation in the public schools of the District of Columbia is a denial of the Due Process of Law guaranteed by the Fifth Amendment to the Constitution.

For the reasons set out in *Brown v. Board of Education,* this case will be restored to the docket for reargument on Questions 4 and 5 previously propounded by the Court.

It is so ordered.

22c. *BROWN v. BOARD OF EDUCATION* (Second Case: 1955)

[In 1955, after its decision in *Brown v. Board of Education* in 1954, the Supreme Court issued the following decree to guide lower courts in future desegregation litigations:]

MR. CHIEF JUSTICE WARREN DELIVERED THE OPINION OF THE COURT:

These cases were decided on May 17, 1954. The opinions of that date, declaring the fundamental principle that racial discrimination in public education is unconstitutional, are incorporated herein by reference. All provisions of federal, state, or local law requiring or permitting such discrimination must yield to this principle. There remains for consideration the manner in which relief is to be accorded. . . .

Full implementation of these constitutional principles may require solution of varied local school problems. School authorities have the primary responsibility of elucidating, assessing, and solving these problems; courts will have to consider whether the action of school authorities constitutes good faith implementation of the governing constitutional principles. Because of their proximity to local conditions and the possible need for further hearings, the courts which originally heard these cases can best perform this judicial appraisal. Accordingly, we believe it appropriate to remand the cases to those courts.

In fashioning and effectuating the decrees, the courts will be guided by equitable principles. Traditionally, equity has been characterized by a practical flexibility in shaping its remedies and by a facility for adjusting and reconciling public and private needs. These cases call for the exercise of these traditional attributes of equity power. At stake is the personal interest of the plaintiffs in admission to public schools as soon as practicable on a nondiscriminatory basis. To effectuate this interest may call for elimination of a variety of obstacles in making the transition to school systems operated in accordance with the constitutional principles set forth in our May 17, 1954, decision. Courts of equity may properly take into account the public interest in the elimination of such obstacles in a systematic and effective manner. But it should go without saying that the vitality of these constitutional principles cannot be allowed to yield simply because of disagreement with them.

While giving weight to these public and private considerations, the courts will require that the defendants make a prompt and reasonable start toward full compliance with our May 17, 1954, ruling. Once such a start has been made, the courts may find that additional time is necessary to carry out the ruling in an effective manner. The burden rests upon the defendants to establish that such time is necessary in the public interest and is consistent with good faith compliance at the earliest practicable date. To that end, the courts may consider problems related to administration, arising from the physical condition of the school plant, the school transportation system, personnel, revision of school districts and attendance areas into compact units to achieve a system of determining admission to the public schools on a nonracial basis, and revision of local laws and regulations which may be necessary in solving the foregoing problems. They will also consider the adequacy of any plans the defendants may propose to meet these problems and to effectuate a transition to a racially nondiscriminatory school system. During this period of transition, the courts will retain jurisdiction of these cases. . . .

It is so ordered.

The right of students not to be segregated on racial grounds is fundamental.

23. *COOPER v. AARON* (1958)

The decision of Brown v. Board of Education *met with opposition in the States practicing school segregation. In many parts of the South, the mandate of the Court was either evaded or directly opposed. It led to conflicts between federal and state power, one of the most sensational of which took place in Little Rock, Arkansas, where the Governor called out the National Guard to prevent Negro children from entering Central High School.*

In Cooper v. Aaron, *a follow-up of* Brown, *the Supreme Court, again speaking unanimously, condemned the recalcitrant State: "No state legislator or executive or judicial officer can war against the Constitution . . ." It also ringingly reaffirmed the* Brown *decision as "indispensable for the protection of the freedoms guaranteed by our fundamental charter for all of us."*

Background: *The facts of the case are stated in the opinion of the Court.*

Some Related Cases

(On Anti-Negro Discrimination):

Gayle v. Browder (1956)
Detroit Housing Commission v. Lewis (1955)
Baltimore v. Dawson (1955)
Holmes v. Atlanta (1955)
Garner et al. *v. Louisiana* (1961)
Edwards v. South Carolina (1963)
Bell v. Maryland (1964)
Greenwood v. Peacock (1966)

OPINION OF THE COURT BY THE CHIEF JUSTICE, MR. JUSTICE BLACK, MR. JUSTICE FRANKFURTER, MR. JUSTICE DOUGLAS, MR. JUSTICE BURTON, MR. JUSTICE CLARK, MR. JUSTICE HARLAN, MR. JUSTICE BRENNAN, AND MR. JUSTICE WHITTAKER:

As this case reaches us it raises questions of the highest importance to the maintenance of our federal system of government. It necessarily involves a claim by the Governor and legislature of a State that there is no duty on state officials to obey federal court orders resting on this court's considered interpretation of the United States Constitution. Specifically it involves actions by the Governor and legislature of Arkansas upon the premise that they are not bound by our holding in *Brown v. Board of Education,* 347 U.S. 483. That holding was that the Fourteenth Amendment forbids States to use their governmental powers to bar children on racial grounds from attending schools where there is state participation through any arrangement, management, funds or property. We are urged to uphold a suspension of the Little Rock School Board's plan to do away with segregated public schools in Little Rock until state laws and efforts to upset and nullify our holding in *Brown v. Board of Education* have been further challenged and tested in the courts. We reject these contentions. . . .

The following are the facts and circumstances so far as necessary to show how the legal questions are presented.

On May 17, 1954, this court decided that enforced racial segregation in the public schools of a State is a denial of the equal protection of the laws enjoined by the Fourteenth Amendment. *Brown v. Board of Education* (U.S.), *supra.* The Court postponed, pending further argument, formulation of a decree to effectuate this decision. That decree was rendered May 31, 1955. *Brown v. Board of Education* 349 U.S. 294, ... In the formulation of that decree the Court recognized that good faith compliance with the principles declared in *Brown* might in some situations "call for elimination of a variety of obstacles in making the transition to school systems operated in accordance with the constitutional principles set forth in our May 17, 1954, decision." [*Brown v. Board of Education.*]

. . . It was made plain that delay in any guise in order to deny the constitutional rights of Negro children could not be countenanced, and that only a prompt start, diligently and earnestly pursued, to eliminate racial segregation from the public schools could constitute good faith compliance. State authorities were thus duty bound to devote every effort toward initiating desegregation and bringing about the elimination of racial discrimination in the public school system.

On May 21, 1954, three days after the first *Brown* opinion, the Little Rock District School Board adopted, and on May 23, 1954, made public, a statement of policy entitled "Supreme Court Decision—Segregation in Public Schools." In this statement the Board recognized that

"It is our responsibility to comply with Federal Constitutional Requirements and we intend to do so when the Supreme Court of the United States outlines the method to be followed."

Thereafter the Board undertook studies of the administrative problems confronting the transition to a desegregated public school system at Little Rock. It instructed the superintendent of schools to prepare a plan for desegregation, and approved such a plan on May 24, 1955, seven days before the second *Brown* opinion. The plan provided for desegregation at the senior high school level (grades 10 through 12) as the first stage. Desegregation at the junior high and elementary levels was to follow. It was contemplated that desegregation at the high school level would commence in the fall of 1957, and the expectation was that complete desegregation of the school system would be accomplished by 1963. Following the adoption of this plan, the Superintendent of Schools discussed it with a large number of citizen groups in the city. As a result of these discussions, the Board reached the conclusion that "a large majority of the residents" of Little Rock were of "the belief . . . that the Plan, although objectionable in principle," from the point of view of those supporting segregated schools, "was still the best for the interests of all pupils in the District."

Upon challenge by a group of Negro plaintiffs desiring more rapid completion of the desegregation process, the District Court upheld the School Board's plan. . . .

While the School Board was thus going forward with its preparation for desegregating the Little Rock school system, other state authorities, in contrast, were actively pursuing a program designed to perpetuate in Arkansas the system of racial segregation which this court had held violated the Fourteenth Amendment. First came, in November 1956, an amendment to the State Constitution flatly commanding the Arkansas General Assembly to oppose "in every Constitutional manner the unconstitutional desegregation decisions of May 17, 1954 and May 31, 1955 of the United States Supreme Court. . . ." Pursuant to this state constitutional command, a law relieving school children from compulsory attendance at racially mixed schools, and a law establishing a State Sovereignty Commission, were enacted by the General Assembly in February 1957.

The School Board and the Superintendent of Schools nevertheless continued with preparations to carry out the first stage of the desegregation program. Nine Negro children were scheduled for admission in September 1957 to Central High School, which has more than two thousand students. Various administrative measures, designed to assure the smooth transition of this first stage of desegregation, were undertaken.

On September 2, 1957, the day before these Negro students were to enter Central High, the school authorities were met with drastic opposing action on the part of the Governor of Arkansas who dispatched units of the Arkansas National Guard to the Central High School grounds, and placed the school "off limits" to colored students. As found by the District Court in subsequent proceedings, the Governor's action had not been requested by the school authorities, and was entirely unheralded. The findings were these:

> Up to this time [September 2], no crowds had gathered about Central High School and no acts of violence or threats of violence in connection with the carrying out of the plan had occurred. Nevertheless, out of an abundance of caution, the school authorities had frequently conferred with the Mayor and Chief of Police of Little Rock about taking appropriate steps by the Little Rock police to prevent any possible disturbances or acts of violence in connection with the attendance of the nine colored students at Central High School. The Mayor considered that the Little Rock police force could adequately cope with any incidents which might arise at the opening of school. The Mayor, the Chief of Police, and the school authorities made no request to the Governor or any representative of his for State assistance in maintaining peace and order at Central High School. Neither the Governor nor any other official of the State Government consulted with

the Little Rock authorities about whether the Little Rock police were prepared to cope with any incidents which might arise at the school, about any need for State assistance in maintaining peace and order, or about stationing the Arkansas National Guard at Central High School. . . .

The Board's petition for postponement in this proceeding states: "The effect of that action [of the Governor] was to harden the core of opposition to the Plan and cause many persons who theretofore had reluctantly accepted the Plan to believe that there was some power in the State of Arkansas which, when exerted, could nullify the Federal law and permit disobedience of the decree of this [District] Court, and from that date hostility to the Plan was increased and criticism of the officials of the [School] District has become more bitter and unrestrained." The Governor's action caused the School Board to request the Negro students on September 2 not to attend the high school "until the legal dilemma was solved." The next day, September 3, 1957, the Board petitioned the District Court for instructions, and the court, after a hearing, found that the Board's request of the Negro students to stay away from the high school had been made because of the stationing of the military guards by the state authorities. The court determined that this was not a reason for departing from the approved plan, and ordered the School Board and Superintendent to proceed with it.

On the morning of the next day, September 4, 1957, the Negro children attempted to enter the high school but, as the District Court later found, units of the Arkansas National Guard "acting pursuant to the Governor's order, stood shoulder to shoulder at the school grounds and thereby forcibly prevented the nine Negro students . . . from entering," as they continued to do every school day during the following three weeks.

The same day, September 4, 1957, the United States Attorney for the Eastern District of Arkansas was requested by the District Court to begin an immediate investigation in order to fix responsibility for the interference with the orderly implementation of the District Court's direction to carry out the desegregation program. Three days later, September 7, the District Court denied a petition of the School Board and the Superintendent of Schools for an order temporarily suspending continuance of the program.

Upon completion of the United States Attorney's investigation, he and the Attorney General of the United States, at the District Court's request, entered the proceedings and filed a petition on behalf of the United States, as *amicus curiae,* to enjoin the Governor of Arkansas and officers of the Arkansas National Guard from further attempts to prevent obedience to the Court's order. After hearings on the petition, the District Court found that the School Board's plan had been obstructed by the

Governor through the use of National Guard troops, and granted a preliminary injunction on September 20, 1957, enjoining the Governor and the officers of the Guard from preventing the attendance of Negro children at Central High School, and from otherwise obstructing or interfering with the orders of the court in connection with the plan. 156 F. Supp. 220, affirmed *Faubus v. United States*. . . . The National Guard was then withdrawn from the school.

The next school day was Monday, September 23, 1957. The Negro children entered the high school that morning under the protection of the Little Rock Police Department and members of the Arkansas State Police. But the officers caused the children to be removed from the school during the morning because they had difficulty controlling a large and demonstrating crowd which had gathered at the high school. On September 25, however, the President of the United States dispatched federal troops to Central High School and admission of the Negro students to the school was thereby effected. Regular army troops continued at the high school until November 27, 1957. They were then replaced by federalized National Guardsmen who remained throughout the balance of the school year. Eight of the Negro students remained in attendance at the school throughout the school year.

We come now to the aspect of the proceedings presently before us. On February 20, 1958, the School Board and the Superintendent of Schools filed a petition in the District Court seeking a postponement of their program for desegregation. Their position in essence was that because of extreme public hostility, which they stated had been engendered largely by the official attitudes and actions of the Governor and the legislature, the maintenance of a sound educational program at Central High School, with the Negro students in attendance, would be impossible. The Board therefore proposed that the Negro students already admitted to the school be withdrawn and sent to segregated schools, and that all further steps to carry out the Board's desegregation program be postponed for a period later suggested by the Board to be two and one-half years.

After a hearing the District Court granted the relief requested by the Board. Among other things the court found that the past year at Central High School had been attended by conditions of "chaos, bedlam, and turmoil"; that there were "repeated incidents of more or less serious violence directed against the Negro students and their property"; that there was "tension and unrest among the school administrators, the classroom teachers, the pupils, and the latters' parents, which inevitably had an adverse effect upon the educational program"; that a school official was threatened with violence; that a "serious financial burden" had been cast on the School District; that the education of the students had suffered "and under existing conditions will continue to suffer"; that the Board would continue to need "military assistance or its equivalent"; that the local police department would not be able "to detail enough men to afford the necessary protection"; and that the situation was "intolerable." . . .

The District Court's judgment was dated June 20, 1958. The Negro respondents appealed to the Court of Appeals for the Eighth Circuit and also sought there a stay of the District Court's judgment. At the same time they filed a petition for certiorari in this court asking us to review the District Court's judgment without awaiting the disposition of their appeal to the Court of Appeals, or of their petition to that court for a stay. That we declined to do. . . . The Court of Appeals did not act on the petition for a stay but on August 18, 1958, after convening in special session on August 4 and hearing the appeal, reversed the District Court. . . . On August 21, 1958, the Court of Appeals stayed its mandate to permit the School Board to petition this Court for certiorari. . . . The petition for certiorari, duly filed, was granted in open Court on September 11, 1958. . . . , and further arguments were had, the Solicitor General again urging the correctness of the judgment of the Court of Appeals. On September 12, 1958, as already mentioned, we unanimously affirmed the judgment of the Court of Appeals in the *per curiam* opinion set forth in the margin at the outset of this opinion.

In affirming the judgment of the Court of Appeals which reversed the District Court we have accepted without reservation the position of the School Board, the Superintendent of Schools, and their counsel that they displayed entire good faith in the conduct of these proceedings and in dealing with the unfortunate and distressing sequence of events which has been outlined. We likewise have accepted the findings of the District Court as to the conditions at Central High School during the 1957–1958 school year, and also the findings that the educational progress of all the students, white and colored, of that school has suffered and will continue to suffer if the conditions which prevailed last year are permitted to continue.

The significance of these findings, however, is to be considered in the light of the fact, indisputably revealed by the record before us, that the conditions they depict are directly traceable to the actions of legislators and executive officials of the State of Arkansas, taken in their official capacities, which reflect their own determination to resist this Court's decision in the *Brown* case and which have brought about violent resistance to that decision in Arkansas.

One may well sympathize with the position of the Board in the face of the frustrating conditions which have confronted it, but, regardless of the Board's good faith, the actions of the other state agencies responsible for those conditions compel us to reject the Board's legal position. Had Central High School been under the direct management of the State itself, it could hardly be suggested that those immediately in charge of the school should be heard to assert their own good faith as a legal excuse for delay in implementing the constitutional rights of these respondents, when vindication of those rights was rendered difficult or impossible by the actions of other state officials. The situation here is in no different posture because the members of the School Board and the Superintendent of Schools are local officials; from the point of view of the Fourteenth Amendment, they stand in this litigation as the agents of the State.

The constitutional rights of respondents are not to be sacrificed or yielded to the violence and disorder which have followed upon the actions of the Governor and legislature. As this court said some forty-one years ago in a unanimous opinion in a case involving another aspect of racial segregation: "It is urged that this proposed segregation will promote the public peace by preventing race conflicts. Desirable as that is, and important as is the preservation of the public peace, this aim cannot be accomplished by laws or ordinances which deny rights created or protected by the Federal Constitution." *Buchanan v. Warley* 245 U.S. 60. Thus law and order are not here to be preserved by depriving the Negro children of their constitutional rights. The record before us clearly established that the growth of the Board's difficulties, as counsel for the Board forthrightly conceded on the oral argument in this court, can also be brought under control by state action.

The controlling legal principles are plain. The command of the Fourteenth Amendment is that no "State" shall deny to any person within its jurisdiction the equal protection of the laws. . . .

. . . In short, the constitutional rights of children not to be discriminated against in school admission on grounds of race or color declared by this court in the *Brown* case can neither be nullified openly and directly by state legislators or state executive or judicial officers, nor nullified indirectly by them through evasive schemes for segregation whether attempted "ingeniously or ingenuously." *Smith v. Texas* . . . [1940].

What has been said, in the light of the facts developed, is enough to dispose of the case. However, we should answer the premise of the actions of the Governor and legislature that they are not bound by our holding in the *Brown* case. It is necessary only to recall some basic constitutional propositions which are settled doctrine.

Article VI of the Constitution makes the Constitution the "supreme law of the land." In 1803, Chief Justice Marshall, speaking for a unanimous Court, referring to the Constitution as "the fundamental and paramount law of the nation," declared in the notable case of *Marbury v. Madison* . . . that "It is emphatically the province and duty of the judicial department to say what the law is." This decision declared the basic principle that the federal judiciary is supreme in the exposition of the law of the Constitution, and that principle has ever since been respected by this court and the country as a permanent and indispensable feature of our constitutional system. It follows that the interpretation of the Fourteenth Amendment enunciated by this court in the *Brown* case is the supreme law of the land, and Article VI of the Constitution makes it of binding effect on the States "any thing in the Constitution or laws of any state to the contrary notwithstanding." Every state legislator and executive and judicial officer is solemnly committed by oath taken pursuant to Article VI, Section 3 "to support this Constitution." Chief Justice Taney, speaking for a unanimous Court in 1859, said that this requirement reflected the Framers' "anxiety to preserve it [the Constitution] in full force, in all its powers, and to guard against resistance to or evasion of its authority, on the part of a State. . . ." *Ableman v. Booth* . . . [1859].

No state legislator or executive or judicial officer can war against the Constitution without violating his undertaking to support it. Chief Justice Marshall spoke for a unanimous Court in saying that: "If the legislatures of the several states may, at will, annul the judgments of the courts of the United States, and destroy the rights acquired under those judgments, the Constitution itself becomes a solemn mockery. . . ." *United States v. Peters*. . . . A Governor who asserts a power to nullify a federal court order is similarly restrained. If he had such power, said Chief Justice Hughes, in 1932, also for a unanimous Court, "it is manifest that the fiat of a State Governor, and not the Constitution of the United States, would be the supreme law of the land; that the restrictions of the Federal Constitution upon the exercise of state power would be but impotent phrases. . . ." *Sterling v. Constantin* . . . [1932].

It is, of course, quite true that the responsibility for public education is primarily the concern of the States, but it is equally true that such responsibilities, like all other state activity, must be exercised consistently with federal constitutional requirements as they apply to state action. The Constitution created a government dedicated to equal justice under law. The Fourteenth Amendment embodied and emphasized that ideal. State support of segregated schools through any arrangement, management, funds, or property cannot be squared with the Amendment's command that no State shall deny to any person within its jurisdiction the equal protection of the laws. The right of a student not to be segregated on racial grounds in schools so maintained is indeed so fundamental and pervasive that it is embraced in the concept of due process of law. *Bolling v. Sharpe*. . . . The basic decision in *Brown* was unanimously reached by this court only after the case had been briefed and twice argued and the issues had been given the most serious consideration. Since the first *Brown* opinion three new Justices have come to the Court. They are at one with the Justices still on the Court who participated in the basic decision as to its correctness, and that decision is now unanimously reaffirmed. The principles announced in that decision and the obedience of the States to them, according to the command of the Constitution, are indispensable for the protection of the freedoms guaranteed by our fundamental charter for all of us. Our constitutional idea of equal justice under law is thus made a living truth.

Affirmed.

Chapter XV

Civil Liberties—First Amendment Freedoms

"Congress shall make no law respecting an establishment of religion, or prohibiting the free exercise thereof; or abridging the freedom of speech, or of the press; or the right of the people peaceably to assemble, and to petition the government for a redress of grievances."—Art. I (First Amendment)

In this Chapter:

Schenck v. United States (1919)
{*Minersville School District v. Gobitis* (1940)
{*W. Va. State Board of Education v. Barnette* (1943)
Dennis et al. v. United States (1951)
Roth v. United States and Alberts v. California (1957)
NAACP v. Alabama (1958)
{*School District of Abington Township, Pa. v. Schempp* (1963)
{*Murray v. Curlett* (1963)
New York Times Co. v. Sullivan (1964)
Griswold v. Connecticut (1965)

Free speech must be restrained if there is a "clear and present danger" to the country.

24. *SCHENCK v. UNITED STATES* (1919)

In this famous case, the Court attempted to draw a line between the constitutionally guaranteed freedom of speech, and security of the Nation in wartime.

Background: *Schenck, secretary of the Socialist Party, printed and sent through the mails pacifist literature, de-*

signed to obstruct military recruitment and enlistment. Indicted under the Espionage Act of June 15, 1917, he claimed that the Act violated the First Amendment. Speaking for a unanimous Court, Justice Holmes upheld the Espionage Act on the ground that when there was a "clear and present danger" to the country, restraints on free speech must be invoked. "When a nation is at war," Justice Holmes stated, "many things that might be said in time of peace . . . will not be endured so long as men fight . . ." It is interesting to note that he completely reversed himself in a subsequent case, Abrams v. United States *(1919), where he wrote a dissenting opinion upholding free speech.*

Some Related Cases

(On Freedom and Free Speech in Wartime):

Firth et al. v. United States (1918)
Debs v. United States (1919)
Sugarman v. United States (1919)
Frohwerk v. United States (1919)
Schaefer v. United States (1919)
Gilbert v. Minnesota (1920)
Hirabayashi v. United States (1943)
Korematsu v. United States (1944)
Terminiello v. Chicago (1949)

(On Free Speech, including Public and Outdoor Meetings):

Robertson v. Baldwin (1897)
Davis v. Massachusetts (1897)
Gompers v. United States (1914)
Hague v. C.I.O. (1939)
Thornhill v. Alabama (1940)
Bridges v. California (1941)
Pennekamp v. Florida (1945)
Thomas v. Collins (1945)
Kovacs v. Cooper (1949)
Feiner v. New York (1951)

MR. JUSTICE HOLMES DELIVERED THE OPINION OF THE COURT:

This is an indictment in three counts. The first charges a conspiracy to violate the Espionage Act of June 15, 1917 . . . by causing and attempting to cause insubordination, etc., in the military and naval forces of the United States, and to obstruct the recruiting and enlistment service of the United States, when the United States was at war with the German Empire, to wit, that the defendant wilfully conspired to have printed and circulated to men who had been called and accepted for military service under the Act of May 18, 1917, a document set forth. The second count alleges a conspiracy to commit an offense against the United States, to wit, to use the mails for the transmission of matter declared to be nonmailable by . . . the Act of June 15, 1917, to wit, the above mentioned document, with an averment of the same overt acts. The third count charges an unlawful use of the mails for the transmission of the same matter and otherwise above. The defendants were found guilty on all the counts. They set up the First Amendment to the Constitution forbidding Congress to make any law abridging the freedom of speech, or of the press, and bringing the case here on that ground have argued some other points also of which we must dispose.

It is argued that the evidence, if admissible, was not sufficient to prove that the defendant Schenck was concerned in sending the documents. According to the testimony Schenck said he was general secretary of the Socialist Party and had charge of the Socialist headquarters from which the documents were sent. He identified a book found there as the minutes of the Executive Committee of the party. The book showed a resolution of August 13, 1917, that 15,000 leaflets should be printed on the other side of one of them in use, to be mailed to men who had passed exemption boards, and for distribution. Schenck personally attended to the printing. On August 20 the general secretary's report said, "Obtained new leaflets from printer and started work addressing envelopes," etc.; and there was a resolve that Comrade Schenck be allowed $125 for sending leaflets through the mail. He said that he had about fifteen or sixteen thousand printed. There were files of the circular in question in the inner office which he said were printed on the other side of the one-sided circular and were there for distribution. Other copies were proved to have been sent through the mails to drafted men. Without going into confirmatory details that were proved, no reasonable man could doubt that the defendant Schenck was largely instrumental in sending the circulars about. As to the defendant Baer there was evidence that she was a member of the Executive Board and that the minutes of its transactions were hers. The argument as to the sufficiency of the evidence that the defendants conspired to send the documents only impairs the seriousness of the real defense. . . .

The document in question upon its first printed side recited the first section of the Thirteenth Amendment, said that the idea embodied in it was violated by the Conscription Act and that a conscript is little better than a convict. In impassioned language it intimated that conscription was despotism in its worst form and a monstrous wrong against humanity in the interest of Wall Street's chosen few. It said, "Do not submit to intimidation," but in form at least confined itself to peaceful measures such as a petition for the repeal of the act. The other and later-printed side of the sheet was headed "Assert Your Rights." It stated reasons for alleging that anyone violated the Constitution when he refused to recognize "your right to assert opposition to the draft," and went on, "If you do not assert and support your rights, you are helping to deny or disparage rights which it is the solemn duty of all citizens and residents of the United States to retain." It described the arguments on the other side as coming from cunning politicians and a mercenary capitalist press, and even silent consent to the conscription law as helping to support an infamous conspiracy. It denied the power to send our citizens away tc foreign shores to shoot up the people of other lands, and added that words could not express the condemnation such cold-blooded ruthlessness deserves, . . . winding up, "You must do your share to maintain, support and uphold the rights of the people of this country." Of course the document would not have been sent unless it had been intended to have some effect, and we do not see what effect it could be expected to have upon persons subject to the draft except to influence them to obstruct the carrying of it out. The defendants do not deny that the jury might find against them on this point.

But it is said, suppose that that was the tendency of this circular, it is protected by the First Amendment to the Constitution. Two of the strongest expressions are said to be quoted respectively from well-known public men. It well may be that the prohibition of laws abridging the freedom of speech is not confined to previous restraints, although to prevent them may have been the main purpose, as intimated in *Paterson v. Colorado,* 205 U.S. 454, 462. We admit that in many places and in ordinary times the defendants in saying all that was said in the circular would have been within their constitutional rights. But the character of every act depends upon the circumstances in which it is done. . . . The most stringent protection of free speech would not protect a man in falsely shouting fire in a theatre and causing a panic. It does not even protect a man from an injunction against uttering words that may have all the effect of force. . . . The question in every case is whether the words are used in such circumstances and are of such a nature as to create a clear and present danger that they will bring about the substantive evils that Congress has a right to prevent. It is a question of proximity and degree. When a nation is at war many things that might be said in time of peace are such a hindrance to its effort that their utterance will not be endured so long as men fight and that no court could regard them as protected by any constitutional right. It seems to be admitted that if an actual obstruction of the recruiting service were proved, liability for words that produced that effect might be enforced. The statute of 1917 . . . punishes conspiracies to obstruct as well as actual obstruction. If the act (speaking, or circulating a paper), its tendency and the intent with which it is done, are the same, we perceive no ground for saying that success alone warrants making the act a crime. . . .

Judgments affirmed.

Can restraints be put on religious beliefs and exercises?

25a. *MINERSVILLE SCHOOL DISTRICT v. GOBITIS* (1940)

25b. *WEST VIRGINIA STATE BOARD OF EDUCATION v. BARNETTE* (1943)

Both of these cases deal with the same problem—namely, whether the law can compel school children to salute the flag despite their religious convictions. Specifically, the cases involved Jehovah's Witnesses, a sect which considers saluting the flag as contrary to Scripture, as interpreted by the Watch Tower Bible and Tract Society. In the Minersville decision, the Supreme Court ruled that children can be forced to salute the flag; in the West Virginia decision, it ruled the opposite.

Background: *The two children of Walter Gobitis, a member of Jehovah's Witnesses, were expelled from the Minersville, Pennsylvania, public schools for refusing to salute the flag, as required by the Board of Education. Gobitis brought suit against the Board of Education and won his case in the Pennsylvania District and Circuit Courts. The Minersville School Board appealed to the United States Supreme Court, which, by a vote of eight to one, ruled against Gobitis. The argument of the Court, as formulated by Justice Frankfurter, was that the "flag is the symbol of our national unity" and that it was, therefore, legitimate for the State to train children in "patriotic impulses."*

In the case of West Virginia, the situation was practically identical, but the judicial decision was different. After the West Virginia State Board of Education ordered that the ceremony of flag saluting be made compulsory, Jehovah's Witnesses brought successful suit in the District Court, whereupon West Virginia appealed to the United States Supreme Court. This time, by a vote of six to three, the Court ruled that the flag-saluting ceremony was unconstitutional in that it violated the spirit of the First Amendment. In the words of Justice Jackson, speaking for the Court's majority: "If there is any fixed star in our constitutional constellation, it is that no official, high or petty, can describe what shall be orthodox in politics, nationalism, religion, or other matters of opinion or force citizens to confess by word or act their faith therein."

The dramatic reversal of the Court between 1940 and 1943 may have been due in part to an addition of two new members—Justices Jackson and Rutledge—and in part to a change of opinion by Justices Black, Douglas, and Murphy in favor of more liberalism. This new viewpoint is also evidenced in Abington . . . v. Schempp, *which was decided by the Court twenty years after* West Virginia . . . v. Barnette.

Some Related Cases

(On Various Religious Practices):

Reynolds v. United States (1879)
Hamilton v. Regents (1934)
Jones v. Opelika (1942) reversed in *Jones v. Opelika* (1943)
Murdock v. Pennsylvania (1943)
Martin v. Struthers (1943)
Prince v. Massachusetts (1944)
Kunz v. New York (1951)
Niemotko v. Maryland (1951)

25a. *MINERSVILLE SCHOOL DISTRICT v. GOBITIS* (1940)

MR. JUSTICE FRANKFURTER DELIVERED THE OPINION OF THE COURT:

A grave responsibility confronts this court whenever in course of litigation it must reconcile the conflicting claims of liberty and authority. But when the liberty invoked is liberty of conscience, and the authority is authority to safeguard the Nation's fellowship, judicial conscience is put to its severest test. Of such a nature is the present controversy.

Lillian Gobitis, aged twelve, and her brother William, aged ten, were expelled from the public schools of Minersville, Pennsylvania, for refusing to salute the national flag as part of a daily school exercise. . . .

The Gobitis children were of an age for which Pennsylvania makes school attendance compulsory. Thus they were denied a free education, and their parents had to put them into private schools. To be relieved of the financial burden thereby entailed, their father, on behalf of the children and in his own behalf, brought this suit. He sought to enjoin the authorities from continuing to exact participation in the flag-salute ceremony as a condition of his children's attendance at the Minersville school. . . .

We must decide whether the requirement of participation in such a ceremony, exacted from a child who refuses upon sincere religious grounds, infringes without due process of law the liberty guarantied by the Fourteenth Amendment.

Centuries of strife over the erection of particular dogmas as exclusive or all-comprehending faiths led to the inclusion of a guaranty for religious freedom in the Bill of Rights. The First Amendment, and the Fourteenth through its absorption of the First, sought to guard against repetition of those bitter religious struggles by prohibiting the establishment of a state religion and by securing to every sect the free exercise of its faith. So pervasive is the acceptance of this precious right that its scope is brought into question, as here, only when the conscience of individuals collides with the felt necessities of society.

Certainly the affirmative pursuit of one's convictions about the ultimate mystery of the universe and man's relation to it is placed beyond the reach of law. Government may not interfere with organized or individual expression of belief or disbelief. Propagation of belief—or even of disbelief in the supernatural—is protected, whether in church or chapel, mosque or synagogue, tabernacle or meeting-house. . . .

But the manifold character of man's relations may bring his conception of religious duty into conflict with the secular interests of his fellow-men. When does the constitutional guaranty compel exemption from doing what society thinks necessary for the promotion of some great common end, or from a penalty for conduct which appears dangerous to the general good? To state the problem is to recall the truth that no single principle can answer all of life's complexities. The right to freedom of religious belief, however dissident and however obnoxious to the cherished beliefs of others—even of a majority—is itself the denial of an absolute. But to affirm that the freedom to follow conscience has itself no limits in the life of a society would deny that very plurality of principles which, as a matter of history, underlies protection of religious toleration. . . . Our present task then, as is so often the case with courts, is to reconcile two rights in order to prevent either from destroying the other. But, because in safeguarding conscience we are dealing with interests so subtle and so dear, every possible leeway should be given to the claims of religious faith. . . .

The religious liberty which the Constitution protects has never excluded legislation of general scope not directed against doctrinal loyalties of particular sects. Judicial nullification of legislation cannot be justified by attributing to the Framers of the Bill of Rights views for which there is no historic warrant. Conscientious scruples have not, in the course of the long struggle for religious toleration, relieved the individual from obedience to a general law not aimed at the promotion or restriction of religious beliefs. The mere possession of religious convictions which contradict the relevant concerns of a political society does not relieve the citizen from the discharge of political responsibilities. The necessity for this adjustment has again and again been recognized. In a number of situations the exertion of political authority has been sustained, while basic considerations of religious freedom have been left inviolate. . . . Nor does the freedom of speech assured by Due Process move in a more absolute circle of immunity than that enjoyed by religious freedom. Even if it were assumed that freedom of speech goes beyond the historic concept of full opportunity to utter and to disseminate views, however heretical or offensive to dominant opinion, and includes freedom from conveying what may be deemed an implied but rejected affirmation, the question remains whether school children, like the Gobitis children, must be excused from conduct required of all the other children in the promotion of national cohesion. We are dealing with an interest inferior to none in the hierarchy of legal values. National unity is the basis of national security. To deny the legislature the right to select appropriate means for its attainment presents a totally different order of problem from that of the propriety of subordinating the possible ugliness of littered streets to the free expression of opinion through distribution of handbills. Compare *Schneider v. State,* 308 U.S. 147.

Situations like the present are phases of the profoundest problem confronting a democracy—the problem which Lincoln cast in memorable dilemma: "Must a government of necessity be too *strong* for the liberties of its people, or too *weak* to maintain its own existence?" No mere textual reading or logical talisman can solve the dilemma. And when the issue demands judicial determination, it is not the personal notion of judges of what wise adjustment requires which must prevail.

Unlike the instances we have cited, the case before us is not concerned with an exertion of legislative power for the promotion of some specific need or interest of secular society—the protection of the family, the promotion of health, the common defense, the raising of public revenues to defray the cost of government. But all these specific activities of government presuppose the existence of an organized political society. The ultimate foundation of a free society is the binding ties of cohesive sentiment. Such a sentiment is fostered by all these agencies of the mind and spirit which may serve to gather up the traditions of a people, transmit them from generation to generation, and thereby create that continuity of a treasured common life which constitutes a civilization. "We live by symbols." The flag is the symbol of our national unity, transcending all internal differences, however large, within the framework of the Constitution. . . .

The precise issue, then, for us to decide is whether the legislatures of the various States and the authorities in a thousand counties and school districts of this country are barred from determining the appropriateness of various means to evoke that unifying sentiment without which there can ultimately be no liberties, civil or religious. To stigmatize legislative judgment in providing for this universal gesture of respect for the symbol of our national life in the setting of the common school as a lawless inroad on that freedom of conscience which the Constitution protects, would amount to no less than the pronouncement of pedagogical and psychological dogma in a field where courts possess no marked and certainly no controlling competence. The influences which help toward a common feeling for the common country are manifold. Some may seem harsh and others no doubt are foolish. Surely, however, the end is legitimate. And the effective means for its attainment are still so uncertain and so unauthenticated by science as to preclude us from putting the widely prevalent belief in flag-saluting beyond the pale of legislative power. It mocks reason and denies our whole history to find in the allowance of a requirement to salute our flag on fitting occasions the seeds of sanction for obeisance to a leader.

The wisdom of training children in patriotic impulses by those compulsions which necessarily pervade so much of the educational process is not for our independent judgment. Even were we convinced of the folly of such a measure, such belief would be no proof of its unconstitutionality. For ourselves, we might be tempted to say that the deepest patriotism is best engendered by giving unfettered scope to the most crotchety beliefs. Perhaps it is best, even from the standpoint of those interests which ordinances like the one under review seek to promote, to give to the least popular sect leave from conformities like those here in issue. But the courtroom is not the arena for debating issues of educational policy. It is not our province to choose among competing considerations in the subtle process of securing effective loyalty to the traditional ideals of democracy, while respecting at the same time individual idiosyncrasies among a people so diversified in racial origins and religious allegiances. So to hold would in effect make us the school board for the country. That authority has not been given to this court, nor should we assume it. . . .

Judicial review, itself a limitation on popular government, is a fundamental part of our constitutional scheme. But to the legislature no less than to courts is committed the guardianship of deeply-cherished liberties. . . . Where all the effective means of inducing political changes are left free from interference, education in the abandonment of foolish legislation is itself a training in liberty. To fight out the wise use of legislative authority in the forum of public opinion and before legislative assemblies rather than to transfer such a contest to the judicial arena, serves to vindicate the self-confidence of a free people.

Reversed.

[Mr. Justice McReynolds concurs in the result.]

Mr. Justice Stone, dissenting:

Concededly the constitutional guaranties of personal liberty are not always absolutes. Government has a right to survive and powers conferred upon it are not necessarily set at naught by the express prohibitions of the Bill of Rights. . . . But it is a long step, and one which I am unable to take, to the position that government may, as a supposed educational measure and as a means of disciplining the young, compel public affirmations which violate their religious conscience. . . .

The guaranties of civil liberty are but guaranties of freedom of the human mind and spirit and of reasonable freedom and opportunity to express them. They presuppose the right of the individual to hold such opinions as he will and to give them reasonably free expression, and his freedom, and that of the state as well, to teach and persuade others by the communication of ideas. The very essence of the liberty which they guaranty is the freedom of the individual from compulsion as to what he shall think and what he shall say, at least where the compulsion is to bear false witness to his religion. If these guarantees are to have any meaning they must, I think, be deemed to withhold from the state any authority to compel belief or the expression of it where that expression violates religious convictions, whatever may be the legislative view of the desirability of such compulsion.

History teaches us that there have been but few infringements of personal liberty by the state which have not been justified, as they are here, in the name of righteousness and the public good, and few which have not been directed, as they are now, at politically helpless minorities. The Framers were not unaware that under the system which they created most governmental curtailments of personal liberty would have the support of a legislative judgment that the public interest would be better served by its curtailment than by its constitutional protection. I cannot conceive that in prescribing, as limitations upon the powers of government, the freedom of the mind and spirit secured by the explicit guaranties of freedom of speech and religion, they intended or rightly could have left any latitude for a legislative judgment that the compulsory expression of belief which violates religious convictions would better serve the public interest than their protection. The Constitution may well elicit expressions of loyalty to it and to the government which it created, but it does not command such expressions or otherwise give any indication that compulsory expressions of loyalty play any such part in our scheme of government as to override the constitutional protection of freedom of speech and religion. And while such expressions of loyalty, when voluntarily given, may promote national unity, it is quite another matter to say that their compulsory expression by children in violation of their own and their parents' religious convictions can be regarded as playing so important a part in our national unity as to leave school boards free to exact it despite the constitutional guaranty of freedom of religion. The very terms of the Bill of Rights preclude, it seems to me, any reconciliation of such compulsions with the constitutional guaranties by a legislative declaration that they are more important to the public welfare than the Bill of Rights.

But even if this view be rejected and it is considered that there is some scope for the determination by legislatures whether the citizen shall be compelled to give public expression of such sentiments contrary to his religion, I am not persuaded that we should refrain from passing upon the legislative judgment "as long as the remedial channels of the democratic process remain open and unobstructed." This seems to me no more than the surrender of the constitutional protection of the liberty of small minorities to the popular will. We have previously pointed to the importance of a searching judicial inquiry into the legislative judgment in situations where prejudice against discrete and insular minorities may tend to curtail the operation of those political processes ordinarily to be relied on to protect minorities. See *United States v. Carolene Products Co.,* 304 U.S. 144, 152, note 4. And until now we have not hesitated similarly to scrutinize legislation restricting the civil liberty of racial and religious minorities although no political process was affected. . . . Here we have such a small minority entertaining in good faith a religious belief, which is such a departure from the usual course of human conduct, that most persons are disposed to regard it with little toleration or concern. In such circumstances careful scrutiny of legislative efforts to secure conformity of belief and opinion by a compulsory affirmation of the desired belief, is especially needful if civil rights are to receive any protection. Tested by this standard, I am not prepared to say that the right of this small and helpless minority, including children having a strong religious conviction, whether they understand its nature or not, to refrain from an expression obnoxious to their religion, is to be overborne by the interest of the State in maintaining discipline in the schools.

The Constitution expresses more than the conviction of the people that democratic processes must be preserved at all costs. It is also an expression of faith and a command that freedom of mind and spirit must be preserved, which government must obey, if it is to adhere to that justice and moderation without which no free government can exist. For this reason it would seem that legislation which operates to repress the religious freedom of small minorities, which is admittedly within the scope of the protection of the Bill of Rights, must at least be subject to the same judicial scrutiny as legislation which we have recently held to infringe the constitutional liberty of religious and racial minorities.

With such scrutiny I cannot say that the inconveniences which may attend some sensible adjustment of school discipline in order that the religious convictions of these children may be spared, presents a problem so momentous or pressing as to outweigh the freedom from compulsory violation of religious faith which has been thought worthy of constitutional protection.

25b. *WEST VIRGINIA STATE BOARD OF EDUCATION v. BARNETTE* (1943)

MR. JUSTICE JACKSON DELIVERED THE OPINION OF THE COURT:

This case calls upon us to reconsider a precedent decision, as the Court throughout its history often has been required to do. Before turning to the Gobitis case, however, it is desirable to notice certain characteristics by which this controversy is distinguished.

The freedom asserted by these appellees does not bring them into collision with rights asserted by any other individual. It is such conflicts which most frequently require intervention of the State to determine where the rights of one end and those of another begin. But the refusal of these persons to participate in the ceremony does not interfere with or deny rights of others to do so. Nor is there any question in this case that their behavior is peaceable and orderly. The sole conflict is between authority and rights of the individual. The State asserts power to condition access to public education on making a prescribed sign and profession and at the same time to coerce attendance by punishing both parent and child. The latter stand on a right of self-determination in matters that touch individual opinion and personal attitude. . . .

There is no doubt that, in connection with the pledges, the flag salute is a form of utterance. Symbolism is a primitive but effective way of communicating ideas. . . .

It is also to be noted that the compulsory flag salute and pledge requires affirmation of a belief and an attitude of mind. It is not clear whether the regulation contemplates that pupils forego any contrary convictions of their own and become unwilling converts to the prescribed ceremony or whether it will be acceptable if they simulate assent by words without belief and by a gesture barren of meaning. It is now a commonplace that censorship or suppression of expression of opinion is tolerated by our Constitution only when the expression presents a clear and present danger of action of a kind the state is empowered to prevent and punish. It would seem that involuntary affirmation could be commanded only on even more immediate and urgent grounds than silence. But here the power of compulsion is invoked without any allegation that remaining passive during a flag salute ritual creates a clear and present danger that would justify an effort even to muffle expression. To sustain the compulsory flag salute we are required to say that a Bill of Rights which guards the individual's right to speak his own mind, left it open to public authorities to compel him to utter what is not in his mind.

Whether the First Amendment to the Constitution will permit officials to order observance of ritual of this nature does not depend upon whether as a voluntary exercise we would think it to be good, bad or merely innocuous. . . .

Nor does the issue as we see it turn on one's possession of particular religious views or the sincerity with which they are held. While religion supplies appellees' motive for enduring the discomforts of making the issue in this case, many citizens who do not share these religious views hold such a compulsory rite to infringe constitutional liberty of the individual. It is not necessary to inquire whether nonconformist beliefs will exempt from the duty to salute unless we first find power to make the salute a legal duty.

The Gobitis decision, however, *assumed,* as did the argument in that case and in this, that power exists in the State to impose the flag salute discipline upon school children in general. The Court only examined and rejected a claim based on religious beliefs of immunity from an unquestioned general rule. The question which underlies the flag salute controversy is whether such a ceremony so touching matters of opinion and political attitude may be imposed upon the individual by official authority under powers committed to any political organization under our Constitution. . . .

In weighing arguments of the parties it is important to distinguish between the Due Process clause of the Fourteenth

Amendment as an instrument for transmitting the principles of the First Amendment and those cases in which it is applied for its own sake. The test of legislation which collides with the Fourteenth Amendment because it also collides with the principles of the First, is much more definite than the test when only the Fourteenth is involved. Much of the vagueness of the Due Process clause disappears when the specific prohibitions of the First become its standard. The right of a State to regulate, for example, a public utility may well include, so far as the due process test is concerned, power to impose all of the restrictions which a legislature may have a "rational basis" for adopting. But freedoms of speech and of press, of assembly, and of worship may not be infringed on such slender grounds. They are susceptible of restriction only to prevent grave and immediate danger to interests which the State may lawfully protect. It is important to note that while it is the Fourteenth Amendment which bears directly upon the State it is the more specific limiting principles of the First Amendment that finally govern this case.

Nor does our duty to apply the Bill of Rights to assertions of official authority depend upon our possession of marked competence in the field where the invasion of rights occurs. True, the task of translating the majestic generalities of the Bill of Rights, conceived as part of the pattern of liberal government in the eighteenth century, into concrete restraints on officials dealing with the problems of the twentieth century, is one to disturb self-confidence. These principles grew in soil which also produced a philosophy that the individual was the center of society, that his liberty was attainable through mere absence of governmental restraints, and that government should be entrusted with few controls and only the mildest supervision over men's affairs. We must transplant these rights to a soil in which the *laissez-faire* concept or principle of non-interference has withered at least as to economic affairs, and social advancements are increasingly sought through closer integration of society and through expanded and strengthened governmental controls. These changed conditions often deprive precedents of reliability and cast us more than we would choose upon our own judgment. But we act in these matters not by authority of our competence but by force of our commissions. We cannot, because of modest estimates of our competence in such specialties as public education, withhold the judgment that history authenticates as the function of this court when liberty is infringed. . . .

The case is made difficult not because the principles of its decision are obscure but because the flag involved is our own. Nevertheless, we apply the limitations of the Constitution with no fear that freedom to be intellectually and spiritually diverse or even contrary will disintegrate the social organization. To believe that patriotism will not flourish if patriotic ceremonies are voluntary and spontaneous instead of a compulsory routine is to make an unflattering estimate of the appeal of our institutions to free minds. We can have intellectual individualism and the rich cultural diversities that we owe to exceptional minds only at the price of occasional eccentricity and abnormal attitudes. When they are so harmless to others or to the State as those we deal with here, the price is not too great. But freedom to differ is not limited to things that do not matter much. That would be a mere shadow of freedom. The test of its substance is the right to differ as to things that touch the heart of the existing order.

If there is any fixed star in our constitutional constellation, it is that no official, high or petty, can prescribe what shall be orthodox in politics, nationalism, religion, or other matters of opinion or force citizens to confess by word or act their faith therein. If there are any circumstances which permit an exception, they do not now occur to us.

We think the action of the local authorities in compelling the flag salute and pledge transcends constitutional limitations on their power and invades the sphere of intellect and spirit which it is the purpose of the First Amendment to our Constitution to reserve from all official control.

The decision of this Court in *Minersville School District v. Gobitis* and the holdings of those few *per curiam* decisions which preceded and foreshadowed it are overruled, and the judgment enjoining enforcement of the West Virginia regulation is

Affirmed.

The First and Fifth Amendments do not protect advocacy to overthrow the Government.

26. *DENNIS et al. v. UNITED STATES* (1951)

The Court held that advocacy of revolution was a criminal offense, even where no tangible action was proven. Such advocacy, which could be inferred also from discussion, is not protected by the First and Fifth Amendments.

Background: *In 1949, Dennis and other Communists were tried under the Smith Act of 1940 for conspiracy to overthrow the Government. Found guilty, they appealed to the Supreme Court on the ground that the Smith Act violated the First and Fifth Amendments. The Court rejected their ap-*

peal. It revived the so-called "bad tendency" test, which had been formerly criticized by Justice Holmes, when he wrote: "The leaders of the Communist Party . . . were unwilling to work within our framework of democracy, but intended to initiate a violent revolution. . . ."

Justices Black and Douglas dissented, the former because no "overt acts" were proven and the latter because the Court's decision violated the First Amendment guaranty of free speech. In his book, The Right of the People *(1958), Justice William O. Douglas wrote in reference to the Communists on trial in the Dennis case:*

> *But there was no evidence that these defendants had conspired to overthrow the Government. . . . In the United States in the early 1950's there was no remote possibility that the Government or existing economic structure would then, or in the foreseeable future, be overturned by violent or illegal means. Then, as now, Communists in the United States were the peddlers of unwanted ideas. They were more thoroughly investigated and exposed than any group in our history. They were the most unpopular people in the land, incapable of commanding enough votes to get elected to any office, no matter how lowly. Yet the Court sanctioned the suppression of speech which Congress had determined to be "dangerous."*

Some Related Cases
(On Communist and Radical Opinions):

Gitlow v. New York (1925)
Fiske v. Kansas (1927)
Whitney v. California (1927)
Stromberg v. California (1927)
Herndon v. Lowry (1937)
Blau v. United States (1950)
Rogers v. United States (1951)
Anti-Fascist Committee v. McGrath (1951)
Garner v. Board of Education (1951)
Sacher v. United States (1952)
United States v. Rumeley (1953)
Pennsylvania v. Nelson (1956) (see p. 135)
Slochower v. Board of Education (1956)
Watkins v. United States (1957)
Beilan v. Board of Education (1958)
Lerner v. Casey (1958)
Communist Party . . . v. Subversive Activities Control Board (1961)

MR. CHIEF JUSTICE VINSON ANNOUNCED THE JUDGMENT OF THE COURT AND AN OPINION IN WHICH MR. JUSTICE REED, MR. JUSTICE BURTON, AND MR. JUSTICE MINTON JOIN:

Sections 2 and 3 of the Smith Act, provide as follows:

"Sec. 2

(a) It shall be unlawful for any person—

(1) to knowingly or willfully advocate, abet, advise, or teach the duty, necessity, desirability, or propriety of overthrowing or destroying any government in the United States by force or violence, or by the assassination of any officer of such government;

(2) with the intent to cause the overthrow or destruction of any government in the United States, to print, publish, edit, issue, circulate, sell, distribute, or publicy display any written or printed matter advocating, advising, or teaching the duty, necessity, desirability, or propriety of overthrowing or destroying any government in the United States by force or violence;

(3) to organize or help to organize any society, group, or assembly of persons who teach, advocate, or encourage the overthrow or destruction of any government in the United States by force or violence; or to be or become a member of, or affiliate with, any such society, group, or assembly of persons, knowing the purposes thereof.

(b) For the purposes of this section, the term "government in the United States" means the Government of the United States, the government of any State, Territory, or possession of the United States, the government of the District of Columbia, or the government of any political subdivision of any of them.

Sec. 3. It shall be unlawful for any person to attempt to commit, or to conspire to commit, any of the acts prohibited by the provisions of . . . this title."

. . . Whether . . . petitioners did in fact advocate the overthrow of the Government by force and violence is not before us, and we must base any discussion of this point upon the conclusions stated in the opinion of the Court of Appeals, which treated the issue in great detail. The court held that the record in this case amply supports the necessary findings of the jury that petitioners, the leaders of the Communist Party in this country, were unwilling to work within our framework of democracy, but intended to initiate a violent revolution whenever the propitious occasion appeared. Petitioners dispute the meaning to be drawn from the evidence, contending that the Marxist-Leninist doctrine they advocated taught that force and violence to achieve a Communist form of government in an existing democratic state would be necessary only because the ruling classes of that state would never permit the transformation to be accomplished peacefully, but would use force and violence to defeat any peaceful political and economic gain the Communists could achieve. But the Court of Appeals held that the record supports the following broad conclusions: By virtue of their control over the political apparatus of the Communist Political Association, petitioners were able to transform that organization into the Communist Party; that the policies of the Association were changed from peaceful cooperation with the United States and its economic and political structure to a policy which had existed before the United States and the Soviet Union were fighting a common enemy, namely, a policy which worked for the overthrow of the Government by force and violence; that the Communist Party is a highly disciplined organization, adept at infiltration into strategic positions, use of aliases, and double-meaning language; that the Party is rigidly controlled; that Communists, unlike other political parties, tolerate no dissension from the policy laid down by the guiding forces, but that the approved program is slavishly followed by the members of the Party; that the literature of the Party and the statements and activities of its leaders, petitioners here, advocate, and the general goal of the Party was, during the period in question, to achieve a successful overthrow of the existing order by force and violence. . . .

The obvious purpose of the statute is to protect existing government, not from change by peaceable, lawful and constitutional means, but from change by violence, revolution and terrorism. That it is within the *power* of the Congress to protect the Government of the United States from armed rebellion is a proposition which requires little discussion. Whatever theoretical merit there may be to the argument that there is a "right" to rebellion against dictatorial governments is without force where the existing structure of the government provides for peaceful and orderly change. We reject any principle of governmental helplessness in the face of preparation for revolution, which principle, carried to its logical conclusion, must lead to anarchy. No one could conceive that it is not within the power of Congress to prohibit acts intended to overthrow the Government by force and violence. The question with which we are concerned here is not whether Congress has such *power,* but whether the *means* which it has employed conflict with the First and Fifth Amendments to the Constitution.

One of the bases for the contention that the means which Congress has employed are invalid takes the form of an attack on the face of the statute on the grounds that by its terms it prohibits academic discussion of the merits of Marxism-Leninism, that it stifles ideas and is contrary to all concepts of a free speech and a free press. . . .

The very language of the Smith Act negates the interpretation which petitioners would have us impose on that Act. It is directed at advocacy, not discussion. Thus, the trial judge properly charged the jury that they could not convict if they found that petitioners did "no more than pursue peaceful studies and discussions or teaching and advocacy in the realm of ideas." He further charged that it was not unlawful "to conduct in an American college or university a course explaining the philosophical theories set forth in the books which have been placed in evidence." Such a charge is in strict accord with the statutory language, and illustrates the meaning to be placed on those words. Congress did not intend to eradicate the free discussion of political theories, to destroy the traditional rights of Americans to discuss and evaluate ideas without fear of governmental sanction. Rather Congress was concerned with the very kind of activity in which the evidence showed these petitioners engaged. . . .

We pointed out in Douds, *supra,* that the basis of the First Amendment is the hypothesis that speech can rebut speech, propaganda will answer propaganda, free debate of ideas will result in the wisest governmental policies. It is for this reason that this court has recognized the inherent value of free discourse. An analysis of the leading cases in this court which have involved direct limitations on speech, however, will demonstrate that both the majority of the Court and the dissenters in particular cases have recognized that this is not an unlimited, unqualified right, but that the societal value of speech must, on occasion, be subordinated to other values and considerations. . . .

The rule we deduce from these cases is that where an offense is specified by a statute in nonspeech or nonpress terms, a conviction relying upon speech or press as evidence of violation may be sustained only when the speech or publication created a "clear and present danger" of attempting or accomplishing the prohibited crime, *e.g.,* interference with enlistment. The dissents, we repeat, in emphasizing the value of speech, were addressed to the argument of the sufficiency of the evidence.

The next important case before the Court in which free speech was the crux of the conflict was *Gitlow v. New York* . . . (1925). There New York had made it a crime to "advocate . . . the necessity or propriety of overthrowing . . . the government by force. . . ." The evidence of violation of the statute was that the defendant had published a manifesto attacking the Government and capitalism. The convictions were sustained, Justices Holmes and Brandeis dissenting. The majority refused to apply the "clear and present danger" test to the specific utterance. Its reasoning was as follows: The "clear and present danger" test was applied to the utterance itself in Schenck because the question was merely one of sufficiency of evidence under an admittedly constitutional statute. Gitlow, however, presented a different question. There a legislature had found that a certain kind of speech was, itself, harmful and unlawful. The constitutionality of such a state statute had to be adjudged by this court just as it determined the constitutionality of any state statute, namely, whether the statute was "reasonable." Since it was entirely reasonable for a State to attempt to protect itself from violent overthrow the statute was perforce reasonable. The only question remaining in the case became whether there was evidence to support the conviction, a question which gave the majority no difficulty. Justices Holmes and Brandeis refused to accept this approach, but insisted that wherever speech was the evidence of the violation, it was necessary to show that the speech created the "clear and present danger" of the substantive evil which the legislature had the right to prevent. Justices Holmes and Brandeis, then, made no distinction between a federal statute which made certain acts unlawful, the evidence to support the conviction being speech, and a statute which made speech itself the crime. This approach was emphasized in *Whitney v. California* . . . (1927), where the Court was confronted with a conviction under the California Criminal Syndicalist statute. The Court sustained the conviction, Justices Brandeis and Holmes concurring in the result. In their concurrence they repeated that even though the legislature had designated certain speech as criminal, this could not prevent the defendant from showing that there was no danger that the substantive evil would be brought about.

Although no case subsequent to Whitney and Gitlow has expressly overruled the majority opinions in those cases, there is little doubt that subsequent opinions have inclined toward the Holmes-Brandeis rationale. . . .

In this case we are squarely presented with the application of the "clear and present danger" test, and must decide what that phrase imports. We first note that many of the cases in which this court has reversed convictions by use of this or similar tests have been based on the fact that the interest which the State was attempting to protect was itself too insubstantial to warrant restriction of speech. In this category we may put such cases as *Schneider v. State,* 308 U.S. 147 (1939); *Cantwell v. Connecticut,* 310 U.S. 296 (1940); *Martin v. Struthers,* 319 U.S. 141 (1943); *West Virginia Board of Education v. Barnette,* 319 U.S. 624 (1943); *Thomas v. Collins,* 323 U.S. 516 (1945); *Marsh v. Alabama,* 326 U.S. 501 (1946); but cf. *Prince v. Massachusetts,* 321 U.S. 158 (1944); *Cox v. New Hampshire,* 312 U.S. 569 (1941). Overthrow of the Government by force and violence is certainly a substantial enough interest for the Government to limit speech. Indeed, this is the ultimate value of any society, for if a society cannot protect its very structure from armed internal attack, it must follow that no subordinate value can be protected. If, then, this interest may be protected, the literal problem which is presented is what has been meant by the use of the phrase "clear and present danger" of the utterances bringing about the evil within the power of Congress to punish.

Obviously, the words cannot mean that before the Government may act, it must wait until the putsch is about to be executed, the plans have been laid and the signal is awaited. If Government is aware that a group aiming at its overthrow is attempting to indoctrinate its members and to commit them to a course whereby they will strike when the leaders feel the circumstances permit, action by the Government is required. The argument that there is no need for Government to concern itself, for Government is strong, it possesses ample powers to put down a rebellion, it may defeat the revolution with ease, needs no answer. For that is not the question. Certainly an attempt to overthrow the Government by force, even though doomed from the outset because of inadequate numbers or power of the revolutionists, is a sufficient evil for Congress to prevent. The damage which such attempts create both physically and politically to a nation makes it impossible to measure the validity in terms of the probability of success, or the immediacy of a successful attempt. In the instant case the trial judge charged the jury that they could not convict unless they found that petitioners intended to overthrow the Government "as speedily as circumstances would permit." This does not mean, and could not properly mean, that they would not strike until there was certainty of success. What was meant was that the revolutionists would strike when they thought the time was ripe. We must therefore reject the contention that success or probability of success is the criterion.

The situation with which Justices Holmes and Brandeis were concerned in Gitlow was a comparatively isolated event, bearing little relation in their minds to any substantial threat to the safety of the community. Such also is true of cases like *Fiske v. Kansas,* 274 U.S. 380 . . . (1927), and *De Jonge v. Oregon,* 299 U.S. 353 . . . (1937); but cf. *Lazar v. Pennsylvania,* 286 U.S. 532 . . . (1932). They were not confronted with any situation comparable to the instant one—the development of an apparatus designed and dedicated to the overthrow of the Government, in the context of world crisis after crisis.

Chief Judge Learned Hand, writing for the majority below, interpreted the phrase as follows: "In each case [courts] must ask whether the gravity of the 'evil,' discounted by its improbability, justifies such invasion of free speech as is necessary to avoid the danger." We adopt this statement of the rule. As articulated by Chief Judge Hand, it is as succinct and inclusive as any other we might devise at this time. It takes into consideration those factors which we deem relevant, and relates their significance. More we cannot expect from words.

Likewise, we are in accord with the court below, which affirmed the trial court's finding that the requisite danger existed. The mere fact that from the period 1945 to 1948 petitioners' activities did not result in an attempt to overthrow the Government by force and violence is of course no answer to the fact that there was a group that was ready to make the attempt. The formation by petitioners of such a highly organized conspiracy, with rigidly disciplined members subject to call when the leaders, these petitioners, felt that the time had come for action, coupled with the inflammable nature of world conditions, similar uprisings in other countries, and the touch-and-go nature of our relations with countries with whom petitioners were in the very least ideologically attuned, convince us that their convictions were justified on this score. And this analysis disposes of the contention that a conspiracy to advocate, as distinguished from the advocacy itself, cannot be constitutionally restrained, because it comprises only the preparation. It is the existence of the conspiracy which creates the danger. . . . If the ingredients of the reaction are present, we cannot bind the Government to wait until the catalyst is added.

Although we have concluded that the finding that there was a sufficient danger to warrant the application of the statute was justified on the merits, there remains the problem of whether the trial judge's treatment of the issue was correct. He charged the jury, in relevant part, as follows:

> In further construction and interpretation of the statute I charge you that it is not the abstract doctrine of overthrowing or destroying organized government by unlawful means which is denounced by this law, but the teaching and advocacy of action for the accomplishment of that purpose, by language reasonably and ordinarily calculated to incite persons to such actions. . . .
>
> If you are satisfied that the evidence establishes beyond a reasonable doubt that the defendants, or any of them, are guilty of a violation of the statute, as I have interpreted it to you, I find as a matter of law that there is sufficient danger of a substantive evil that the Congress has a right to prevent to justify the application of the statute under the First Amendment of the Constitution.
>
> This is a matter of law about which you have no concern. It is a finding on a matter of law which I deem essential to support my ruling that the case should be submitted to you to pass upon the guilt or innocence of the defendants. . . .

It is thus clear that he reserved the question of the existence of the danger for his own determination, and the question becomes whether the issue is of such a nature that it should have been submitted to the jury. . . .

. . . The argument that the action of the trial court is erroneous, in declaring as a matter of law that such violation shows sufficient danger to justify the punishment despite the First Amendment, rests on the theory that a jury must decide a question of the application of the First Amendment. We do not agree.

When facts are found that establish the violation of a statute the protection against conviction afforded by the First Amendment is a matter of law. The doctrine that there must be a clear and present danger of a substantive evil that Congress has a right to prevent is a judicial rule to be applied as a matter of law by the courts. The guilt is established by proof of facts. Whether the First Amendment protects the activity which constitutes the violation of the statute must depend upon a judicial determination of the scope of the First Amendment applied to the circumstances of the case. . . .

There remains to be discussed the question of vagueness—whether the statute as we have interpreted it is too vague, not sufficiently advising those who would speak of the limitations upon their activity. It is urged that such vagueness contravenes the First and Fifth Amendments. This argument is particularly nonpersuasive when presented by petitioners, who, the jury found, intended to overthrow the Government as speedily as circumstances would permit. . . .

We agree that the standard as defined is not a neat, mathematical formulary. Like all verbalizations it is subject to criticism on the score of indefiniteness. But petitioners themselves contend that the verbalization, "clear and present danger" is the proper standard. We see no difference from the standpoint of vagueness, whether the standard of "clear and present danger" is one contained in haec verba within the statute, or whether it is the judicial measure of constitutional applicability. We have shown the indeterminate standard the phrase necessarily connotes. We do not think we have rendered that standard any more indefinite by our attempt to sum up the factors which are included within its scope. We think it well serves to indicate to those who would advocate constitutionally prohibited conduct that there is a line beyond which they may not go—a line, which they, in full knowledge of what they intend and the circumstances in which their activity takes place, will well appreciate and understand. . . .

Affirmed.

Mr. Justice Clark took no part in the consideration or decision of this case.

MR. JUSTICE FRANKFURTER, CONCURRING IN AFFIRMANCE OF THE JUDGMENT:

The language of the First Amendment is to be read not as barren words found in a dictionary but as symbols of historic experience illumined by the presuppositions of those who employed them. Not what words did Madison and Hamilton use, but what was it in their minds which they conveyed? Free speech is subject to prohibition of those abuses of expression which a civilized society may forbid. As in the case of every other provision of the Constitution that is not crystallized by the nature of its technical concepts, the fact that the First Amendment is not self-defining and self-enforcing neither impairs its usefulness nor compels its paralysis as a living instrument. . . .

. . . The demands of free speech in a democratic society as well as the interest in national security are better served by candid and informed weighing of the competing interests, within the confines of the judicial process, than by announcing dogmas too inflexible for the non-Euclidian problems to be solved.

But how are competing interests to be assessed? Since they are not subject to quantitative ascertainment, the issue necessarily resolves itself into asking, who is to make the adjustment? —who is to balance the relevant factors and ascertain which interest is in the circumstances to prevail? Full responsibility for the choice cannot be given to the courts. Courts are not representative bodies. They are not designed to be a good reflex of a democratic society. Their judgment is best informed, and therefore most dependable, within narrow limits. Their essential quality is detachment, founded on independence. History teaches that the independence of the judiciary is jeopardized when courts become embroiled in the passions of the day and assume primary responsibility in choosing between competing political, economic and social pressures.

Primary responsibility for adjusting the interests which compete in the situation before us of necessity belongs to the Congress. The nature of the power to be exercised by this court has been delineated in decisions not charged with the emotional appeal of situations such as that now before us. . . .

. . . A survey of the relevant decisions indicates that the results which we have reached are on the whole those that would ensue from careful weighing of conflicting interests. The complex issues presented by regulation of speech in public places, by picketing, and by legislation prohibiting advocacy of crime have been resolved by scrutiny of many factors besides the imminence and gravity of the evil threatened. The matter has been well summarized by a reflective student of the Court's work. "The truth is that the clear-and-present-danger test is an oversimplified judgment unless it takes account also of a number of other factors: the relative seriousness of the danger in comparison with the value of the occasion for speech or political activity; the availability of more moderate controls than those which the State has imposed; and perhaps the specific intent with which the speech or activity is launched. No matter how rapidly we utter the phrase 'clear and present danger,' or how closely we hyphenate the words, they are not a substitute for the weighing of values. They tend to convey a delusion of certitude when what is most certain is the complexity of the strands in the web of freedoms which the judge must disentangle." Freund, *On Understanding the Supreme Court,* 27-28. . . .

Bearing in mind that Mr. Justice Holmes regarded questions under the First Amendment as questions of "proximity and degree," *Schenck v. United States,* it would be a distortion, indeed a mockery, of his reasoning to compare the "puny anonymities," to which he was addressing himself in the Abrams case in 1919 or the publication that was "futile and too remote from possible consequences," 268 U.S. at 673, in the Gitlow case in 1925 with the setting of events in this case in 1950. . . .

Throughout our decisions there has recurred a distinction between the statement of an idea which may prompt its hearers to take unlawful action, and advocacy that such action be taken. . . .

It is true that there is no divining rod by which we may locate "advocacy." Exposition of ideas readily merges into advocacy. The same Justice who gave currency to application of the incitement doctrine in this field dissented four times from what he thought was its misapplication. As he said in the Gitlow dissent, "Every idea is an incitement." . . . Even though advocacy of overthrow deserves little protection, we should hesitate to prohibit it if we thereby inhibit the interchange of rational ideas so essential to representative government and free society.

But there is underlying validity in the distinction between advocacy and the interchange of ideas, and we do not discard a useful tool because it may be misused. That such a distinction could be used unreasonably by those in power against hostile or unorthodox views does not negate the fact that it may be used reasonably against an organization wielding the power of the centrally controlled international Communist movement. The object of the conspiracy before us is clear enough that the chance of error in saying that the defendants conspired to advocate rather than to express ideas is slight. Mr. Justice Douglas quite properly points out that the conspiracy before us is not a conspiracy to overthrow the Government. But it would be equally wrong to treat it as a seminar in political theory. . . .

It is not for us to decide how we would adjust the clash of interests which this case presents were the primary responsibility for reconciling it ours. Congress has determined that the danger created by advocacy of overthrow justifies the ensuing restriction on freedom of speech. The determination was made after due deliberation, and the seriousness of the congressional purpose is attested by the volume of legislation passed to effectuate the same ends.

Can we then say that the judgment Congress exercised was denied it by the Constitution? Can we establish a constitutional doctrine which forbids the elected representatives of the people to make this choice? Can we hold that the First Amendment deprives Congress of what it deemed necessary for the Government's protection?

To make validity of legislation depend on judicial reading of events still in the womb of time—a forecast, that is, of the outcome of forces at best appreciated only with knowledge of the topmost secrets of nations—is to charge the judiciary with duties beyond its equipment. We do not expect courts to pronounce historic verdicts on bygone events. Even historians have conflicting views to this day on the origin and conduct of the French Revolution. It is as absurd to be confident that we can measure the present clash of forces and their outcome as to ask us to read history still enveloped in clouds of controversy. . . .

Civil liberties draw at best only limited strength from legal guaranties. Preoccupation by our people with the constitutionality, instead of with the wisdom of legislation or of executive action, is preoccupation with a false value. Even those who would most freely use the judicial brake on the democratic process by invalidating legislation that goes deeply against their grain, acknowledge, at least by paying lip service, that constitutionality does not exact a sense of proportion or the sanity of humor or an absence of fear. Focusing attention on constitutionality tends to make constitutionality synonymous with wisdom. When legislation touches freedom of thought and freedom of speech, such a tendency is a formidable enemy of the free spirit. Much that should be rejected as illiberal, because repressive and envenoming, may well be not unconstitutional. The ultimate reliance for the deepest needs of civilization must be found outside their vindication in courts of law; apart from all else, judges, howsoever they may conscientiously seek to discipline themselves against it, unconsciously are too apt to be moved by the deep undercurrents of public feeling. A persistent, positive translation of the liberating faith into the feelings and thoughts and actions of men and women is the real protection against attempts to strait-jacket the human mind. Such temptations will have their way, if fear and hatred are not exorcised. The mark of a truly civilized man is confidence in the strength and security derived from the inquiring mind. We may be grateful for such honest comforts as it supports, but we must be unafraid of its uncertitudes. Without open minds there can be no open society. And if society be not open the spirit of man is mutilated and becomes enslaved. . . .

Mr. Justice Jackson, concurring:

What really is under review here is a conviction of conspiracy, after a trial for conspiracy, on an indictment charging conspiracy, brought under a statute outlawing conspiracy. With due respect to my colleagues, they seem to me to discuss anything under the sun except the law of conspiracy. One of the dissenting opinions even appears to chide me for "invoking the law of conspiracy." As that is the case before us, it may be more amazing that its reversal can be proposed without even considering the law of conspiracy. . . .

I do not suggest that Congress could punish conspiracy to advocate something, the doing of which it may not punish. Advocacy or exposition of the doctrine of communal property ownership, or any political philosophy unassociated with advocacy of its imposition by force or seizure of government by unlawful means could not be reached through conspiracy prosecution. But it is not forbidden to put down force or violence, it is not forbidden to punish its teaching or advocacy, and the end being punishable, there is no doubt of the power to punish conspiracy for the purpose. . . .

The law of conspiracy has been the chief means at the Government's disposal to deal with the growing problems created by such organizations. I happen to think it is an awkward and inept remedy, but I find no constitutional authority for taking this weapon from the Government. There is no constitutional right to "gang up" on the Government.

While I think there was power in Congress to enact this statute and that, as applied in this case, it cannot be held unconstitutional, I add that I have little faith in the long-range effectiveness of this conviction to stop the rise of the Communist movement. Communism will not go to jail with these Communists. No decision by this court can forestall revolution whenever the existing government fails to command the respect and loyalty of the people and sufficient distress and discontent is allowed to grow up among the masses. Many failures by fallen governments attest that no government can long prevent revolution by outlawry. Corruption, ineptitude, inflation, oppressive taxation, militarization, injustice, and loss of leadership capable of intellectual initiative in domestic or foreign affairs are allies on which the Communists count to bring opportunity knocking to their door. Sometimes I think they may be mistaken. But the Communists are not building just for today—the rest of us might profit by their example.

MR. JUSTICE BLACK, DISSENTING:

At the outset I want to emphasize what the crime involved in this case is, and what it is not. These petitioners were not charged with an attempt to overthrow the Government. They were not charged with overt acts of any kind designed to overthrow the Government. They were not even charged with saying anything or writing anything designed to overthrow the Government. The charge was that they agreed to assemble and to talk and publish certain ideas at a later date: The indictment is that they conspired to organize the Communist Party and to use speech or newspapers and other publications in the future to teach and advocate the forcible overthrow of the Government. No matter how it is worded, this is a virulent form of prior censorship of speech and press, which I believe the First Amendment forbids. I would hold section 3 of the Smith Act authorizing this prior restraint unconstitutional on its face and as applied. . . .

So long as this court exercises the power of judicial review of legislation, I cannot agree that the First Amendment permits us to sustain laws suppressing freedom of speech and press on the basis of Congress' or our own notions of mere "reasonableness." Such a doctrine waters down the First Amendment so that it amounts to little more than an admonition to Congress. The Amendment as so construed is not likely to protect any but those "safe" or orthodox views which rarely need its protection. I must also express my objection to the holding because as Mr. Justice Douglas' dissent shows, it sanctions the determination of a crucial issue of fact by the judge rather than by the jury. Nor can I let this opportunity pass without expressing my objection to the severely limited grant of certiorari in this case which precluded consideration here of at least two other reasons for reversing these convictions: (1) the record shows a discriminatory selection of the jury panel which prevented trial before a representative cross-section of the community; (2) the record shows that one member of the trial jury was violently hostile to petitioners before and during the trial.

Public opinion being what it now is, few will protest the conviction of these Communist petitioners. There is hope, however, that in calmer times, when present pressures, passions and fears subside, this or some later court will restore the First Amendment liberties to the high preferred place where they belong in a free society.

MR. JUSTICE DOUGLAS, DISSENTING:

If this were a case where those who claimed protection under the First Amendment were teaching the techniques of sabotage, the assassination of the President, the filching of documents from public files, the planting of bombs, the art of street warfare, and the like, I would have no doubts. The freedom to speak is not absolute; the teaching of methods of terror and other seditious conduct should be beyond the pale along with obscenity and immorality. This case was argued as if those were the facts. The argument imported much seditious conduct into the record. That is easy and it has popular appeal, for the activities of Communists in plotting and scheming against the free world are common knowledge. But the fact is that no such evidence was introduced at the trial. There is a statute which makes a seditious conspiracy unlawful. Petitioners, however, were not charged with a "conspiracy to overthrow" the Government. They were charged with a conspiracy to form a party and groups and assemblies of people who teach and advocate the overthrow of our Government by force or violence and with a conspiracy to advocate and teach its overthrow by force and violence. It may well be that indoctrination in the techniques of terror to destroy the Government would be indictable under either statute. But the teaching which is condemned here is of a different character. . . .

The vice of treating speech as the equivalent of overt acts of a treasonable or seditious character is emphasized by a concurring opinion, which by invoking the law of conspiracy makes speech do service for deeds which are dangerous to society. The doctrine of conspiracy has served divers and oppressive purposes and in its broad reach can be made to do great evil. But never until today has anyone seriously thought that the ancient law of conspiracy could constitutionally be used to turn speech into seditious conduct. Yet that is precisely what is suggested. I repeat that we deal here with speech alone, not with speech *plus* acts of sabotage or unlawful conduct. Not a single seditious act is charged in the indictment. To make a lawful speech unlawful because two men conceive it is to raise the law of conspiracy to appalling proportions. That course is to make a radical break with the past and to violate one of the cardinal principles of our constitutional scheme. . . .

There comes a time when even speech loses its constitutional immunity. Speech innocuous one year may at another time fan such destructive flames that it must be halted in the interests of the safety of the Republic. That is the meaning of the clear and present danger test. When conditions are so critical that there will be no time to avoid the evil that the speech threatens, it is time to call a halt. Otherwise, free speech which is the strength of the Nation will be the cause of its destruction.

Yet free speech is the rule, not the exception. The restraint to be constitutional must be based on more than fear, on more than passionate opposition against the speech, on more than a revolted dislike for its contents. There must be some immediate injury to society that is likely if speech is allowed. . . .

I had assumed that the question of the clear and present danger, being so critical an issue in the case, would be a matter for submission to the jury. It was squarely held in *Pierce v. United States,* 252 U.S. 239, 244, to be a jury question. . . .

Yet, whether the question is one for the Court or the jury, there should be evidence of record on the issue. This record, however, contains no evidence whatsoever showing that the acts charged, viz., the teaching of the Soviet theory of revolution with the hope that it will be realized, have created any clear and present danger to the Nation. The Court, however, rules to the contrary. It says, "The formation by petitioners of such a highly organized conspiracy, with rigidly disciplined members subject to call when the leaders, these petitioners, felt that the time had come for action, coupled with the inflammable nature of world conditions, similar uprisings in other countries, and the touch-and-go nature of our relations with countries with whom petitioners were in the very least ideologically attuned, convince us that their convictions were justified on this score."

That ruling is in my view not responsive to the issue in the case. We might as well say that the speech of petitioners is outlawed because Soviet Russia and her Red Army are a threat to world peace. . . .

The First Amendment provides that "Congress shall make no law . . . abridging the freedom of speech." The Constitution provides no exception. This does not mean, however, that the Nation need hold its hand until it is in such weakened condition that there is no time to protect itself from incitement to revolution. Seditious conduct can always be punished. But the command of the First Amendment is so clear that we should not allow Congress to call a halt to free speech except in the extreme case of peril from the speech itself. The First Amendment makes confidence in the common sense of our people and in their maturity of judgment, the great postulate of our democracy. Its philosophy is that violence is rarely, if ever, stopped by denying civil liberties to those advocating resort to force. The First Amendment reflects the philosophy of Jefferson "that it is time enough for the rightful purposes of civil government for its officers to interfere when principles break out into overt acts against peace and good order." The political censor has no place in our public debates. Unless and until extreme and necessitous circumstances are shown, our aim should be to keep speech unfettered and to allow the processes of law to be invoked only when the provocateurs among us move from speech to action.

Vishinsky wrote in 1948 in *The Law of the Soviet State,* "In our state, naturally there can be no place for freedom of speech, press, and so on for the foes of socialism."

Our concern should be that we accept no such standard for the United States. Our faith should be that our people will never give support to these advocates of revolution, so long as we remain loyal to the purposes for which our Nation was founded.

Obscenity is not protected by the First or Fourteenth Amendment.

27. *ROTH v. UNITED STATES* and *ALBERTS v. CALIFORNIA* (1957)

In this dual decision, the Supreme Court for the first time considered the question of whether the distribution of obscene material was a basic freedom protected by the First and Fourteenth Amendments. It decided that obscenity was "not within the area of constitutionally protected speech or press"; hence those who produce and mail obscene literature may be punished by existing laws.

Background: *Roth, in New York, was found guilty of*

mailing "obscene, lewd and lascivious" material; Alberts, in California, was found guilty of a similar offense, that of producing and advertising indecent literature. The Supreme Court, deciding both cases together, ruled against the appellants. It argued that there was a difference between sex, the expression of which had constitutional protection, and filth, which could claim no such protection. Justices Douglas and Black dissented: They held that the First Amendment protected even offensive utterances.

Some Related Cases
(On Obscenity):

Ex Parte Jackson (1878)
Hannegan v. Esquire (1946)
Winters v. New York (1948)
Commonwealth v. Gordon (1949)
Beauharnais v. Illinois (1952)
Teitel Film Corp. (1968)

MR. JUSTICE BRENNAN DELIVERED THE OPINION OF THE COURT:

The dispositive question is whether obscenity is utterance within the area of protected speech and press. Although this is the first time the question has been squarely presented to this court, either under the First Amendment or under the Fourteenth Amendment, expressions found in numerous opinions indicate that this court has always assumed that obscenity is not protected by the freedoms of speech and press. *Ex parte* Jackson, 96 U.S. 727. . . .

The guaranties of freedom of expression in effect in ten of the fourteen States which by 1792 had ratified the Constitution, gave no absolute protection for every utterance. Thirteen of the fourteen States provided for the prosecution of libel, and all of those States made either blasphemy or profanity, or both, statutory crimes. As early as 1712, Massachusetts made it criminal to publish "any filthy, obscene, or profane song, pamphlet, libel or mock sermon" in imitation or mimicking of religious services. . . .

All ideas having even the slightest redeeming social importance—unorthodox ideas, controversial ideas, even ideas hateful to the prevailing climate of opinion—have the full protection of the guaranties, unless excludable because they encroach upon the limited area of more important interests. But implicit in the history of the First Amendment is the rejection of obscenity as utterly without redeeming social importance. This rejection for that reason is mirrored in the universal judgment that obscenity should be restrained, reflected in the international agreement of over fifty nations, in the obscenity laws of all of the forty-eight States, and in the twenty obscenity laws enacted by the Congress from 1842 to 1956. . . .

We hold that obscenity is not within the area of constitutionally protected speech or press.

It is strenuously urged that these obscenity statutes offend the constitutional guaranties because they punish incitation to impure sexual *thoughts,* not shown to be related to any overt antisocial conduct which is or may be incited in the persons stimulated to such *thoughts.* In Roth, the trial judge instructed the jury: "The words, 'obscene, lewd and lascivious' as used in the law, signify that form of immorality which has relation to sexual impurity and has a tendency to excite lustful *thoughts.*" (Emphasis added.) In Alberts, the trial judge applied the test . . . whether the material has "a substantial tendency to deprave or corrupt its readers by inciting lascivious *thoughts* or arousing lustful desires." (Emphasis added.) It is insisted that the constitutional guaranties are violated because convictions may be had without proof either that obscene material will perceptibly create a clear and present danger of antisocial conduct, or will probably induce its recipients to such conduct. But, in light of our holding that obscenity is not protected speech, the complete answer to this argument is in the holding of this court in *Beauharnais v. Illinois, supra* (343 U.S. at 266):

> Libelous utterances not being within the area of constitutionally protected speech, it is unnecessary, either for us or for the state courts, to consider the issues behind the phrase "clear and present danger." Certainly no one would contend that obscene speech, for example, may be punished only upon a showing of such circumstances. Libel, as we have seen, is in the same class.

However, sex and obscenity are not synonymous. Obscene material is material which deals with sex in a manner appealing to prurient interest. The portrayal of sex, e.g., in art, literature and scientific works, is not itself sufficient reason to deny material the constitutional protection of freedom of speech and press. Sex, a great and mysterious motive force in human life, has indisputably been a subject of absorbing interest to mankind through the ages; it is one of the vital problems of human interest and public concern. . . .

The fundamental freedoms of speech and press have contributed greatly to the development and well-being of our free society and are indispensable to its continued growth. Ceaseless vigilance is the watchword to prevent their erosion by Congress or by the States. The door barring federal and state intrusion into this area cannot be left ajar; it must be kept tightly closed and opened only the slightest crack necessary to prevent encroachment upon more important interests. It is therefore vital that the standards for judging obscenity safeguard the protection of freedom of speech and press for material which does not treat sex in a manner appealing to prurient interest.

The early leading standard of obscenity allowed material to be judged merely by the effect of an isolated excerpt upon particularly susceptible persons. *Regina v. Hicklin* [1868] L.R. 3 Q.B. 360. Some American courts adopted this standard but later decisions have rejected it and substituted this test: whether to the average person, applying contemporary community standards, the dominant theme of the material taken as a whole appeals to prurient interest. . . .

It is argued that the statutes do not provide reasonably ascertainable standards of guilt and therefore violate the constitutional requirements of due process. *Winters v. New York,* 333 U.S. 507. . . . The federal obscenity statute makes punishable the mailing of material that is "obscene, lewd, lascivious, or filthy . . . or other publication of an indecent character." The California statute makes punishable, *inter alia,* the keeping for sale or advertising material that is "obscene or indecent." The thrust of the argument is that these words are not sufficiently precise because they do not mean the same thing to all people, all the time, everywhere.

Many decisions have recognized that these terms of obscenity statutes are not precise. This court, however, has consistently held that lack of precision is not itself offensive to the requirements of due process. ". . . The Constitution does not require impossible standards"; all that is required is that the language "conveys sufficiently definite warning as to the proscribed conduct when measured by common understanding and practices." . . .

In summary, then, we hold that these statutes, applied according to the proper standard for judging obscenity, do not offend constitutional safeguards against convictions based upon protected material, or fail to give men in acting adequate notice of what is prohibited. . . .

Affirmed.

[Mr. Chief Justice Warren, concurring in the result. . . .]

MR. JUSTICE HARLAN, CONCURRING IN THE RESULT IN NO. 61 [ALBERTS], AND DISSENTING IN NO. 582 [ROTH]:

I regret not to be able to join the Court's opinion. I cannot do so because I find lurking beneath its disarming generalizations a number of problems which not only leave me with serious misgivings as to the future effect of today's decisions, but which also, in my view, call for different results in these two cases.

My basic difficulties with the Court's opinion are threefold. First, the opinion paints with such a broad brush that I fear it may result in a loosening of the tight reins which state and federal courts should hold upon the enforcement of obscenity statutes. Second, the Court fails to discriminate between the different factors which, in my opinion, are involved in the constitutional adjudication of state and federal obscenity cases. Third, relevant distinctions between the two obscenity statutes here involved, and the Court's own definition of "obscenity," are ignored. . . .

I concur in the judgment of the Court in No. 61, *Alberts v. California.*

The question in this case is whether the defendant was deprived of liberty without due process of law when he was convicted for selling certain materials found by the judge to be obscene because they would have a "tendency to deprave or corrupt readers by exciting lascivious thoughts or arousing lustful desire."

In judging the constitutionality of this conviction, we should remember that our function in reviewing state judgments under the Fourteenth Amendment is a narrow one. We do not decide whether the policy of the State is wise, or whether it is based on assumptions scientifically substantiated. We can inquire only whether the state action so subverts the fundamental liberties implicit in the Due Process clause that it cannot be sustained as a rational exercise of power. . . . The States' power to make printed words criminal is, of course, confined by the Fourteenth Amendment, but only insofar as such power is inconsistent with our concepts of "ordered liberty." *Palko v. Connecticut,* 302 U.S. 319, 324. . . .

What, then, is the purpose of this California statute? Clearly the state legislature has made the judgment that printed words *can* "deprave or corrupt" the reader—that words can incite to antisocial or immoral action. The assumption seems to be that the distribution of certain types of literature will induce criminal or immoral sexual conduct. It is well known, of course, that the validity of this assumption is a matter of dispute among critics, sociologists, psychiatrists, and penologists. There is a large school of thought, particularly in the scientific community, which denies any causal connection between the reading of pornography and immorality, crime, or delinquency. Others disagree. Clearly it is not our function to decide this question. That function belongs to the state legislature. Nothing in the Constitution requires California to accept as truth the most advanced and sophisticated psychiatric opinion. It seems to me clear that it is not irrational, in our present state of knowledge, to consider that pornography can induce to a type of sexual conduct which a State may deem obnoxious to the moral fabric of society. In fact the very division of opinion on the subject counsels us to respect the choice made by the State. . . .

What has been said, however, does not dispose of the case. It still remains for us to decide whether the state court's determination that this material should be suppressed is consistent with the Fourteenth Amendment; and that, of course, presents a federal question as to which we, and not the state court, have the ultimate responsibility. And so, in the final analysis, I concur in the judgment because, upon an independent perusal of the material involved, and in light of the considerations discussed above, I cannot say that its suppression would so interfere with the communication of "ideas" in any proper sense of that term that it would offend the Due Process clause. I therefore agree with the Court that the appellant's conviction must be affirmed.

I dissent in No. 582, *Roth v. United States.*

We are faced here with the question whether the federal obscenity statute, as construed and applied in this case, violates the First Amendment to the Constitution. To me, this question is of quite a different order than one where we are dealing with state legislation under the Fourteenth Amendment. I do not think it follows that state and federal powers in this area are the same, and that just because the State may suppress a particular utterance, it is automatically permissible for the Federal Government to do the same. I agree with Mr. Justice Jackson that the historical evidence does not bear out the claim that the Fourteenth Amendment "incorporates" the First in any literal sense. See *Beauharnais v. Illinois* (U.S.), *supra.* But laying aside any consequences which might flow from that conclusion, cf. Mr. Justice Holmes in *Gitlow v. New York,* 268 U.S. 652, 672, . . . I prefer to rest my views about this case on broader and less abstract grounds.

The Constitution differentiates between those areas of human conduct subject to the regulation of the States and those subject to the power of the Federal Government. The substantive powers of the two governments, in many instances, are distinct. And in every case where we are called upon to balance the interest in free expression against other interests, it seems to me important that we should keep in the forefront the question of whether those other interests are state or federal. Since under our constitutional scheme the two are not necessarily equivalent, the balancing process must needs often produce different results. Whether a particular limitation on speech or press is to be upheld because it subserves a paramount governmental interest must, to a large extent, I think, depend on whether that government has, under the Constitution, a direct substantive interest, that is, the power to act, in the particular area involved. . . .

Not only is the federal interest in protecting the Nation against pornography attenuated, but the dangers of federal censorship in this field are far greater than anything the States may do. It has often been said that one of the great strengths of our federal system is that we have, in the forty-eight States, forty-eight experimental social laboratories. "State statutory law reflects predominantly this capacity of a legislature to introduce novel techniques of social control. The federal system has the immense advantage of providing forty-eight separate centers for such experimentation." Different States will have different attitudes toward the same work of literature. The same book which is freely read in one State might be classed as obscene in another. And it seems to me that no overwhelming danger to our freedom to experiment and to gratify our tastes in literature is likely to result from the suppression of a borderline book in one of the States, so long as there is no uniform nationwide suppression of the book, and so long as other States are free to experiment with the same or bolder books.

Quite a different situation is presented, however, where the Federal Government imposes the ban. The danger is perhaps not great if the people of one State, through their legislature, decide that *Lady Chatterley's Lover* goes so far beyond acceptable standards of candor that it will be deemed offensive and non-sellable, for the State next door is still free to make its own choice. At least we do not have one uniform standard. But the dangers to free thought and expression are truly great if the Federal Government imposes a blanket ban over the Nation on such a book. The prerogative of the States to differ on their ideas of morality will be destroyed, the ability of States to experiment will be stunted. The fact that the people of one State cannot read some of the works of D. H. Lawrence seems to me, if not wise or desirable, at least acceptable. But that no person in the United States should be allowed to do so seems to me to be intolerable, and violative of both the letter and spirit of the First Amendment. . . .

MR. JUSTICE DOUGLAS, WITH WHOM MR. JUSTICE BLACK CONCURS, DISSENTING:

The standard of what offends "the common conscience of the community" conflicts, in my judgment, with the command of the First Amendment that "Congress shall make no law . . . abridging the freedom of speech, or of the press." Certainly that standard would not be an acceptable one if religion, economics, politics or philosophy were involved. How does it become a constitutional standard when literature treating with sex is concerned?

Any test that turns on what is offensive to the community's standards is too loose, too capricious, too destructive of freedom of expression to be squared with the First Amendment. Under that test, juries can censor, suppress, and punish what they don't like, provided the matter relates to "sexual impurity" or has a tendency "to excite lustful thoughts." This is community censorship in one of its worst forms. It creates a regime where in the battle between the literati and the Philistines, the Philistines are certain to win. If experience in this field teaches anything, it is that "censorship of obscenity has almost always been both irrational and indiscriminate." . . . The test adopted here accentuates that trend.

I assume there is nothing in the Constitution which forbids Congress from using its power over the mails to proscribe *conduct* on the grounds of good morals. No one would suggest that the First Amendment permits nudity in public places, adultery, and other phases of sexual misconduct. . . .

Freedom of expression can be suppressed if, and to the extent that, it is so closely brigaded with illegal action as to be an inseparable part of it. . . . As a people, we cannot afford to relax that standard. For the test that suppresses a cheap tract today can suppress a literary gem tomorrow. All it need do is to incite a lascivious thought or arouse a lustful desire. The list of books that judges or juries can place in that category is endless.

I would give the broad sweep of the First Amendment full support. I have the same confidence in the ability of our people to reject noxious literature as I have in their capacity to sort out the true from the false in theology, economics, politics, or any other field.

Membership lists of private associations are immune from state scrutiny.

28. *NATIONAL ASSOCIATION FOR THE ADVANCEMENT OF COLORED PEOPLE* [*NAACP*] *v. ALABAMA* (1958)

This case must be viewed as part of the struggle for Negro rights. In an effort to hinder the NAACP's activities on behalf of Negroes, the State of Alabama demanded that the Association reveal the names and addresses of its Alabama members. In this decision, the Supreme Court ruled against Alabama on the ground that the right of private association was protected by the Fourteenth Amendment, and hence immune from state meddling.

Background: *Alabama claimed that the NAACP, a membership corporation chartered in New York, had failed to comply with the State's statute requiring foreign corporations to register with the Alabama Secretary of State. The Ala-*

bama Circuit Court enjoined the NAACP from engaging in further activities in the State and required that it produce the names and addresses of its local members and agents. The NAACP complied, submitting all data, except its membership list, and for the omission of the latter, the Circuit Court held the Association in contempt and imposed a fine of $100,000. After the Supreme Court of Alabama twice refused to review the case, the NAACP appealed to the United States Supreme Court, which reversed the Alabama verdict and nullified the fine.

Some Related Cases
(On Association):
De Jonge v. Oregon (1937)
Thomas v. Collins (1945)
American Communications Assoc. v. Douds (1950)
Osman v. Douds (1950)
Schware v. Board of Bar Examiners (1957)
Griswold v. Connecticut (1965) (see p. 320)

MR. JUSTICE HARLAN DELIVERED THE OPINION OF THE COURT:

. . . The question presented is whether Alabama, consistently with the Due Process clause of the Fourteenth Amendment, can compel petitioner to reveal to the State's Attorney General the names and addresses of all its Alabama members and agents, without regard to their positions or functions in the Association. . . .

The Association both urges that it is constitutionally entitled to resist official inquiry into its membership lists, and that it may assert, on behalf of its members, a right personal to them to be protected from compelled disclosure by the State of their affiliation with the Association as revealed by the membership lists. We think that petitioner argues more appropriately the rights of its members, and that its nexus with them is sufficient to permit that it act as their representative before this court. In so concluding, we reject respondent's argument that the Association lacks standing to assert here constitutional rights pertaining to the members, who are not of course parties to the litigation.

To limit the breadth of issues which must be dealt with in particular litigation, this court has generally insisted that parties rely only on constitutional rights which are personal to themselves. . . . This rule is related to the broader doctrine that constitutional adjudication should where possible be avoided.

See *Ashwander v. Tennessee Valley Authority,* 297 U.S. 288, (concurring opinion). The principle is not disrespected where constitutional rights of persons who are not immediately before the Court could not be effectively vindicated except through an appropriate representative before the Court. See *Barrows v. Jackson,* 346 U.S. 249; *Joint Anti-Fascist Refugee Committee v. McGrath,* 341 U.S. 123 (concurring opinion).

If petitioner's rank-and-file members are constitutionally entitled to withold their connection with the Association despite the production order, it is manifest that this right is properly assertable by the Association. To require that it be claimed by the members themselves would result in nullification of the right at the very moment of its assertion. Petitioner is the appropriate party to assert these rights, because it and its members are in every practical sense identical. The Association, which provides in its constitution that "any person who is in accordance with [its] principles and policies . . ." may become a member, is but the medium through which its individual members seek to make more effective the expression of their own views. The reasonable likelihood that the Association itself through diminished financial support and membership may be adversely affected if production is compelled is a further factor pointing toward our holding that petitioner has standing to complain of the production order on behalf of its members. Cf. *Pierce v. Society of Sisters.* . . .

We . . . reach petitioner's claim that the production order in the state litigation trespasses upon fundamental freedoms protected by the Due Process clause of the Fourteenth Amendment. Petitioner argues that in view of the facts and circumstances shown in the record, the effect of compelled disclosure of the membership lists will be to abridge the rights of its rank-and-file members to engage in lawful association in support of their common beliefs. It contends that governmental action which, although not directly suppressing association, nevertheless carries this consequence, can be justified only upon some overriding valid interest of the State.

Effective advocacy of both public and private points of view, particularly controversial ones, is undeniably enhanced by group association, as this court has more than once recognized by remarking upon the close nexus between the freedoms of speech and assembly. *De Jonge v. Oregon* . . . *Thomas v. Collins* . . . It is beyond debate that freedom to engage in association for the advancement of beliefs and ideas is an inseparable aspect of the "liberty" assured by the Due Process clause of the Fourteenth Amendment, which embraces freedom of speech. . . . Of course, it is immaterial whether the beliefs sought to be advanced by association pertain to political, economic, religious or cultural matters, and state action which may have the effect of curtailing the freedom to associate is subject to the closest scrutiny. . . .

It is hardly a novel perception that compelled disclosure of affiliation with groups engaged in advocacy may constitute as effective a restraint on freedom of association as the forms of governmental action in the cases above were thought likely to produce upon the particular constitutional rights there involved. This court has recognized the vital relationship between freedom to associate and privacy in one's associations. . . . *American Communications Asso. v. Douds. . . .*

We think that the production order, in the respects here drawn in question, must be regarded as entailing the likelihood of a substantial restraint upon the exercise by petitioner's members of their right to freedom of association. Petitioner has made an uncontroverted showing that on past occasions revelation of the identity of its rank-and-file members has exposed these members to economic reprisal, loss of employment, threat of physical coercion, and other manifestations of public hostility. Under these circumstances, we think it apparent that compelled disclosure of petitioner's Alabama membership is likely to affect adversely the ability of petitioner and its members to pursue their collective effort to foster beliefs which they admittedly have the right to advocate, in that it may induce members to withdraw from the Association and dissuade others from joining it because of fear of exposure of their beliefs shown through their associations and of the consequences of this exposure.

It is not sufficient to answer, as the State does here, that whatever repressive effect compulsory disclosure of names of petitioner's members may have upon participation by Alabama citizens in petitioner's activities follows not from *state* action but from *private* community pressures. The crucial factor is the interplay of governmental and private action, for it is only after the initial exertion of state power represented by the production order that private action takes hold.

We turn to the final question whether Alabama has demonstrated an interest in obtaining the disclosures it seeks from petitioner which is sufficient to justify the deterrent effect which we have concluded these disclosures may well have on the free exercise by petitioner's members of their constitutionally protected right of association. . . . It is not of moment that the State has here acted solely through its judicial branch, for whether legislative or judicial, it is still the application of state power which we are asked to scrutinize.

It is important to bear in mind that petitioner asserts no right to absolute immunity from state investigation, and no right to disregard Alabama's laws. As shown by its substantial compliance with the production order, petitioner does not deny Alabama's right to obtain from it such information as the State desires concerning the purposes of the Association and its activities within the State. Petitioner has not objected to divulging the identity of its members who are employed by or hold official positions with it. It has urged the rights solely of its ordinary rank-and-file members. This is therefore not analogous to a case involving the interest of a State in protecting its citizens in their dealings with paid solicitors or agents of foreign corporations by requiring identification. See *Cantwell v. Connecticut* . . . *Thomas v. Collins*. . . .

We hold that the immunity from state scrutiny of membership lists which the Association claims on behalf of its members is here so related to the right of the members to pursue their lawful private interest privately and to associate freely with others in so doing as to come within the protection of the Fourteenth Amendment. And we conclude that Alabama has fallen short of showing a controlling justification for the deterrent effect on the free enjoyment of the right to associate which disclosure of membership lists is likely to have. Accordingly, the judgment of civil contempt and the $100,000 fine which resulted from petitioner's refusal to comply with the production order in this respect must fall. . . .

Reversed.

State and local rules requiring prayers and other religious exercises in public schools violate the First Amendment.

29. *SCHOOL DISTRICT OF ABINGTON TOWNSHIP (Pa.) v. SCHEMPP* (1963) and *MURRAY v. CURLETT* (Md.) (1963)

In this decision, the Supreme Court made a searching inquiry into the meaning and intent of the First Amendment's Establishment clause, which provides for the separation of church and state. Reviewing the above-mentioned cases, one in Pennsylvania and one in Maryland, involving compulsory religious exercises in public schools, the Court ruled that such practices were in violation of the First Amendment.

Background: *In Pennsylvania, Mr. and Mrs. Schempp, Unitarians whose children attended Abington Senior High School, brought suit enjoining enforcement of a Pennsylvania statute which required Bible reading in classroom daily. The District Court of Pennsylvania upheld the Schempps, and the Abington School District appealed to the Supreme Court. In Maryland, Mrs. Murray, a professed atheist, brought a similar suit against Baltimore, whose schools, one of which her son attended, opened with Bible reading or the Lord's Prayer, as re-*

quired by state law. After the Maryland Court of Appeals upheld the State's statute, Mrs. Murray appealed to the Supreme Court.

In this dual decision, in which only Justice Stewart dissented, the Court held that such compulsory religious exercises as were practiced in Pennsylvania and Maryland were unconstitutional. Specifically, it ruled that the judgment in the case of Schempp was to be affirmed and that in the case of Murray was to be reversed. In other words, the District Court of Pennsylvania was constitutionally right, and the Court of Appeals of Maryland was constitutionally wrong.

Some Related Cases
(On Church-State Separation):

Davis v. Beason (1890)
Cantwell v. Connecticut (1940)
Everson v. Board of Education (1947)
McCollum v. Board of Education (1948)
Doremus v. Board of Education (1952)
Zorach v. Clauson (1952)
Torcaso v. Watkins (1961)
Engel v. Vitale (1962)

MR. JUSTICE CLARK DELIVERED THE OPINION OF THE COURT:

Once again we are called upon to consider the scope of the provision of the First Amendment to the United States Constitution which declares that "Congress shall make no law respecting an establishment of religion or prohibiting the free exercise thereof. . . ." These companion cases present the issues in the context of state action requiring that schools begin each day with readings from the Bible. While raising the basic questions under slightly different factual situations, the cases permit of joint treatment. In light of the history of the First Amendment and of our cases interpreting and applying its requirements, we hold that the practices at issue and the laws requiring them are unconstitutional under the Establishment clause, as applied to the States through the Fourteenth Amendment.

. . . It is true that religion has been closely identified with our history and government. As we said in *Engel v. Vitale,* 370 U.S. 421, 434, . . . "The history of man is inseparable from the history of religion. And . . . since the beginning of that history many people have devoutly believed that 'More things are wrought by prayer than this world dreams of.'" In *Zorach v. Clauson,* 343 U.S. 306, 313 . . . we gave specific recognition to the proposition that "[w]e are a religious people whose institutions presuppose a Supreme Being." The fact that the Founding Fathers believed devotedly that there was a God and that the unalienable rights of man were rooted in Him is clearly evidenced in their writings, from the Mayflower Compact to the Constitution itself. This background is evidenced today in our public life through the continuance in our oaths of office from the presidency to the alderman of the final supplication, "So help me God." Likewise each House of the Congress provides through its chaplain an opening prayer, and the sessions of this court are declared open by the crier in a short ceremony, the final phrase of which invokes the grace of God. Again, there are such manifestations in our military forces, where those of our citizens who are under the restrictions of military service wish to engage in voluntary worship. Indeed, only last year an official survey of the country indicated that 64 per cent of our people have church membership. . . . It can be truly said, therefore, that today, as in the beginning, our national life reflects a religious people who, in the words of Madison, are "earnestly praying, as . . . in duty bound, that the Supreme Lawgiver of the Universe . . . guide them into every measure which may be worthy of his . . . blessing. . . ."

. . . This is not to say, however, that religion has been so identified with our history and government that religious freedom is not likewise as strongly imbedded in our public and private life. . . . This freedom to worship was indispensable in a country whose people came from the four quarters of the earth and brought with them a diversity of religious opinion. Today authorities list eighty-three separate religious bodies, each with memberships exceeding 50,000, existing among our people, as well as innumerable smaller groups. . . .

Almost a hundred years ago in *Minor v. Board of Education of Cincinnati,* Judge Alphonso Taft, father of the revered Chief Justice, in an unpublished opinion stated the ideal of our people as to religious freedom as one of "absolute equality before the law of all religious opinion and sects. . . .

"The government is neutral, and while protecting all, it prefers none, and it disparages none."

. . . Finally, these principles were so universally recognized that the Court without the citation of a single case and over the sole dissent of Mr. Justice Stewart reaffirmed them. The Court found the twenty-two-word prayer used in "New York's program of daily classroom invocation of God's blessing as prescribed in the Regents' prayer . . . [to be] a religious activity." . . . It held that "it is no part of the business of government to compose official prayers for any group of the American people to recite as a part of a religious program carried on by the government." . . . In discussing the reach of the Establishment and Free Exercise clauses of the First Amendment the Court said:

> Although these two clauses may in certain instances overlap, they forbid two quite different kinds of governmental encroachment upon religious freedom. The Establishment clause, unlike the Free Exercise clause, does not depend upon any showing of direct governmental compulsion and is violated by the enactment of laws which establish an official religion whether those laws operate directly to coerce nonobserving individuals or not. This is not to say, of course, that laws officially prescribing a particular form of religious worship do not involve coercion of such individuals. When the power, prestige and financial support of government is placed behind a particular religious belief, the indirect coercive pressure upon religious minorities to conform to the prevailing officially approved religion is plain. [*Id.*, 370 U.S. at 430, 431.]

And in further elaboration the Court found that the "first and most immediate purpose [of the Establishment clause] rested on a belief that a union of government and religion tends to destroy government and to degrade religion." *Id.*, 370 U.S. at 431. When government, the Court said, allies itself with one particular form of religion, the inevitable result is that it incurs "the hatred, disrespect and even contempt of those who held contrary beliefs." *Ibid.*

The wholesome "neutrality" of which this court's cases speak thus stems from a recognition of the teachings of history that powerful sects or groups might bring about a fusion of governmental and religious functions or a concert or dependency of one upon the other to the end that official support of the State or Federal Government would be placed behind the tenets of one or of all orthodoxies. This the Establishment clause prohibits. And a further reason for neutrality is found in the Free Exercise clause, which recognizes the value of religious training, teaching and observance and, more particularly, the right of every person to freely choose his own course with reference thereto, free of any compulsion from the state. This the Free Exercise clause guaranties. Thus, as we have seen, the two clauses may overlap. As we have indicated, the Establishment clause has been directly considered by this court eight times in the past score of years and, with only one Justice dissenting on the point, it has consistently held that the clause withdrew all legislative power respecting religious belief or the expression thereof. The test may be stated as follows: What are the purpose and the primary effect of the enactment? If either is the advancement or inhibition of religion then the enactment exceeds the scope of legislative power as circumscribed by the Constitution. That is to say that to withstand the strictures of the Establishment clause there must be a secular legislative purpose and a primary effect that neither advances nor inhibits religion. . . . The Free Exercise clause, likewise considered many times here, withdraws from legislative power, state and federal, the exertion of any restraint on the free exercise of religion. Its purpose is to secure religious liberty in the individual by prohibiting any invasions thereof by civil authority. Hence it is necessary in a free exercise case for one to show the coercive effect of the enactment as it operates against him in the practice of his religion. The distinction between the two clauses is apparent —a violation of the Free Exercise clause is predicated on coercion while the Establishment clause violation need not be so attended.

Applying the Establishment clause principles to the cases at bar we find that the States are requiring the selection and reading at the opening of the school day of verses from the Holy Bible and the recitation of the Lord's Prayer by the students in unison. These exercises are prescribed as part of the curricular activities of students who are required by law to attend school. They are held in the school buildings under the supervision and with the participation of teachers employed in those schools. . . . The trial court . . . has found that such an opening exercise is a religious ceremony and was intended by the State to be so. We agree with the trial court's finding as to the religious character of the exercises. Given that finding the exercises and the law requiring them are in violation of the Establishment clause.

. . . The conclusion follows that in both cases the laws require religious exercises and such exercises are being conducted in direct violation of the rights of the appellees and petitioners. Nor are these required exercises mitigated by the fact that individual students may absent themselves upon parental request, for that fact furnishes no defense to a claim of unconstitutionality under the Establishment clause. See *Engel v. Vitale, supra* (370 U.S. at 430). Further, it is no defense to urge that the religious practices here may be relatively minor encroachments on the First Amendment. The breach of neutrality that is today a trickling stream may all too soon become a raging torrent and, in the words of Madison, "it is proper to take alarm at the first experiment on our liberties." . . .

It is insisted that unless these religious exercises are permitted a "religion of secularism" is established in the schools. We agree of course that the State may not establish a "religion of secularism" in the sense of affirmatively opposing or showing hostility to religion, thus "preferring those who believe in no religion over those who do believe." *Zorach v. Clauson, supra* (343 U.S. at 314). We do not agree, however, that this decision in any sense has that effect. In addition, it might well be said that one's education is not complete without a study of comparative religion or the history of religion and its relationship to the advancement of civilization. It certainly may be said that the Bible is worthy of study for its literary and historic qualities. Nothing we have said here indicates that such study of the Bible or of religion, when presented objectively as part of a secular program of education, may not be effected consistent with the First Amendment. But the exercises here do not fall into those categories. They are religious exercises, required by the States in violation of the command of the First Amendment that the Government maintain strict neutrality, neither aiding nor opposing religion.

. . . The place of religion in our society is an exalted one, achieved through a long tradition of reliance on the home, the church and the inviolable citadel of the individual heart and mind. We have come to recognize through bitter experience that it is not within the power of government to invade that citadel, whether its purpose or effect be to aid or oppose, to advance or retard. In the relationship between man and religion, the state is firmly committed to a position of neutrality. Though the application of that rule requires interpretation of a delicate sort, the rule itself is clearly and concisely stated in the words of the First Amendment. . . .

MR. JUSTICE BRENNAN, CONCURRING:

. . . The First Amendment forbids both the abridgment of the free exercise of religion and the enactment of laws "respecting an establishment of religion." The two clauses, although distinct in their objectives and their applicability, emerged together from a common panorama of history. The inclusion of both restraints upon the power of Congress to legislate concerning religious matters shows unmistakably that the Framers of the First Amendment were not content to rest the protection of religious liberty exclusively upon either clause. "In assuring the free exercise of religion," Mr. Justice Frankfurter has said, "the Framers of the First Amendment were sensitive to the then recent history of those persecutions and impositions of civil disability with which sectarian majorities in virtually all of the Colonies had visited deviation in the matter of conscience. This protection of unpopular creeds, however, was not to be the full extent of the Amendment's guarantee of freedom from governmental intrusion in matters of faith. . . ."

It is true that the Framers' immediate concern was to prevent the setting up of an official federal church of the kind which England and some of the Colonies had long supported. But nothing in the text of the Establishment clause supports the view that the prevention of the setting up of an official church was meant to be the full extent of the prohibitions against official involvements in religion. . . .

But an awareness of history and an appreciation of the aims of the Founding Fathers do not always resolve concrete problems. The specific question before us has, for example, aroused vigorous dispute whether the architects of the First Amendment —James Madison and Thomas Jefferson particularly—understood the prohibition against any "law respecting an establishment of religion" to reach devotional exercises in the public schools. It may be that Jefferson and Madison would have held such exercises to be permissible—although even in Jefferson's case serious doubt is suggested by his admonition against "putting the Bible and Testament into the hands of the children at an age when their judgments are not sufficiently matured for religious inquiries. . . ." But I doubt that their view, even if perfectly clear one way or the other, would supply a dispositive answer to the question presented by these cases. A more fruitful inquiry, it seems to me, is whether the practices here challenged threaten those consequences which the Framers deeply feared; whether, in short, they tend to promote that type of interdependence between religion and state which the First Amendment was designed to prevent. Our task is to translate "the majestic generalities of the Bill of Rights, conceived as part of the pattern of liberal government in the eighteenth century, into concrete restraints on officials dealing with the problems of the twentieth century. . . ." *West Virginia State Board of Education v. Barnette. . . .*

A too literal quest for the advice of the Founding Fathers upon the issues of these cases seems to me futile and misdirected for several reasons: First, on our precise problem the historical record is at best ambiguous, and statements can readily be found to support either side of the proposition. The ambiguity of history is understandable if we recall the nature of the problems uppermost in the thinking of the statesmen who fashioned the religious guaranties; they were concerned with far more flagrant intrusions of government into the realm of religion than any that our century has witnessed. While it is clear to me that the Framers meant the Establishment clause to prohibit more than the creation of an established federal church such as existed in England, I have no doubt that, in their preoccupation with the imminent question of established churches, they gave no distinct consideration to the particular question whether the clause also forbade devotional exercises in public institutions.

Second, the structure of American education has greatly changed since the First Amendment was adopted. In the context of our modern emphasis upon public education available to all citizens, any views of the eighteenth century as to whether the exercises at bar are an "establishment" offer little aid to decision. Education, as the Framers knew it, was in the main confined to private schools more often than not under strictly sectarian supervision. Only gradually did control of education pass largely to public officials. It would, therefore, hardly be significant if the fact was that the nearly universal devotional exercises in the schools of the young Republic did not provoke criticism; even today religious ceremonies in church-supported private schools are constitutionally unobjectionable.

Third, our religious composition makes us a vastly more diverse people than were our forefathers. They knew differences

chiefly among Protestant sects. Today the Nation is far more heterogeneous religiously, including as it does substantial minorities not only of Catholics and Jews but as well of those who worship according to no version of the Bible and those who worship no God at all. See *Torcaso v. Watkins,* 367 U.S. 488, 495, 6 L.Ed. 2d 982, 987, 81 S.Ct. 1680. In the face of such profound changes, practices which may have been objectionable to no one in the time of Jefferson and Madison may today be highly offensive to many persons, the deeply devout and the nonbelievers alike.

Whatever Jefferson or Madison would have thought of Bible reading or the recital of the Lord's Prayer in what few public schools existed in their day, our use of the history of their time must limit itself to broad purposes, not specific practices. By such a standard, I am persuaded, as is the Court, that the devotional exercises carried on in the Baltimore and Abington schools offend the First Amendment because they sufficiently threaten in our day those substantive evils the fear of which called forth the Establishment clause of the First Amendment. It is "*a constitution* we are expounding," and our interpretation of the First Amendment must necessarily be responsive to the much more highly charged nature of religious questions in contemporary society.

. . . Attendance at the public schools has never been compulsory; parents remain morally and constitutionally free to choose the academic environment in which they wish their children to be educated. The relationship of the Establishment clause of the First Amendment to the public school system is pre-eminently that of reserving such a choice to the individual parent, rather than vesting it in the majority of voters of each State or school district. The choice which is thus preserved is between a public secular education with its uniquely democratic values, and some form of private, or sectarian education, which offers values of its own. In my judgment the First Amendment forbids the State to inhibit that freedom of choice by diminishing the attractiveness of either alternative—either by restricting the liberty of the private schools to inculcate whatever values they wish, or by jeopardizing the freedom of the public school from private or sectarian pressures. The choice between these very different forms of education is one—very much like the choice of whether or not to worship—which our Constitution leaves to the individual parent. It is no proper function of the state or local government to influence or restrict that election. The lesson of history—drawn more from the experiences of other countries than from our own—is that a system of free public education forfeits its unique contribution to the growth of democratic citizenship when that choice ceases to be freely available to each parent.

MR. JUSTICE GOLDBERG, WITH WHOM MR. JUSTICE HARLAN JOINS, CONCURRING:

The First Amendment's guaranties, as applied to the States through the Fourteenth Amendment, foreclose not only laws "respecting an establishment of religion" but also those "prohibiting the free exercise thereof." These two proscriptions are to be read together, and in light of the single end which they are designed to serve. The basic purpose of the First Amendment is to promote and assure the fullest possible scope of religious liberty and tolerance for all and to nurture the conditions which secure the best hope of attainment of that end.

The fullest realization of true religious liberty requires that government neither engage in nor compel religious practices, that it effect no favoritism among sects or between religion and nonreligion, and that it work deterrence of no religious belief. But devotion even to these simply stated objectives presents no easy course, for the unavoidable accommodations necessary to achieve the maximum enjoyment of each and all of them are often difficult of discernment. There is for me no simple and clear measure which by precise application can readily and invariably demark the permissible from the impermissible.

It is said, and I agree, that the attitude of the State toward religion must be one of neutrality. But untutored devotion to the concept of neutrality can lead to invocation or approval of results which partake not simply of that noninterference and noninvolvement with the religious which the Constitution commands, but of a brooding and pervasive devotion to the secular and a passive, or even active, hostility to the religious. Such results are not only not compelled by the Constitution, but, it seems to me, are prohibited by it.

Neither the State nor this court can or should ignore the significance of the fact that a vast portion of our people believe in and worship God and that many of our legal, political and personal values derive historically from religious teachings. Government must inevitably take cognizance of the existence of religion and, indeed, under certain circumstances the First Amendment may require that it do so. And it seems clear to me from the opinions in the present and past cases that the Court would recognize the propriety of providing military chaplains and of the teaching *about* religion, as distinguished from the teaching of religion, in the public schools. The examples could readily be multiplied, for both the required and the permissible accommodations between state and church frame the relation as one free of hostility or favor and productive of religious and political harmony, but without undue involvement of one in the concerns or practices of the other. To be sure, the judgment in each case is a delicate one, but it must be made if we are to do loyal service as judges to the ultimate First Amendment objective of religious liberty.

The practices here involved do not fall within any sensible or acceptable concept of compelled or permitted accommodation and involve the state so significantly and directly in the realm of the sectarian as to give rise to those very divisive influences and inhibitions of freedom which both religion clauses of the First Amendment preclude. The State has ordained and has utilized its facilities to engage in unmistakably religious exercises —the devotional reading and recitation of the Holy Bible—in a manner having substantial and significant import and impact. That it has selected, rather than written, a particular devotional liturgy seems to me without constitutional import. The pervasive religiosity and direct governmental involvement inhering in the prescription of prayer and Bible reading in the public schools, during and as part of the curricular day, involving young impressionable children whose school attendance is statutorily compelled, and utilizing the prestige, power, and influence of school administration, staff, and authority, cannot realistically be termed simply accommodation, and must fall within the interdiction of the First Amendment. I find nothing in the opinion of the Court which says more than this. And, of course, today's decision does not mean that all incidents of government which import of the religious are therefore and without more banned by the strictures of the Establishment clause. . . .

MR. JUSTICE STEWART, DISSENTING:

The First Amendment declares that "Congress shall make no law respecting an establishment of religion, or prohibiting the free exercise thereof. . . ." It is, I think, a fallacious oversimplification to regard these two provisions as establishing a single constitutional standard of "separation of church and state," which can be mechanically applied in every case to delineate the required boundaries between government and religion. We err in the first place if we do not recognize, as a matter of history and as a matter of the imperatives of our free society, that religion and government must necessarily interact in countless ways. Secondly, the fact is that while in many contexts the Establishment clause and the Free Exercise clause fully complement each other, there are areas in which a doctrinaire reading of the Establishment clause leads to irreconcilable conflict with the Free Exercise clause.

A single obvious example should suffice to make the point. Spending federal funds to employ chaplains for the armed forces might be said to violate the Establishment clause. Yet a lonely soldier stationed at some faraway outpost could surely complain that a government which did *not* provide him the opportunity for pastoral guidance was affirmatively prohibiting the free exercise of his religion. And such examples could readily be multiplied. The short of the matter is simply that the two relevant clauses of the First Amendment cannot accurately be reflected in a sterile metaphor which by its very nature may distort rather than illumine the problems involved in a particular case. . . .

That the central value embodied in the First Amendment—and, more particularly, in the guaranty of "liberty" contained in the Fourteenth—is the safeguarding of an individual's right to free exercise of his religion has been consistently recognized. . . .

It is this concept of constitutional protection embodied in our decisions which makes the cases before us such difficult ones for me. For there is involved in these cases a substantial free exercise claim on the part of those who affirmatively desire to have their children's school day open with the reading of passages from the Bible. . . .

What seems to me to be of paramount importance, then, is recognition of the fact that the claim advanced here in favor of Bible reading is sufficiently substantial to make simple reference to the constitutional phrase "establishment of religion" as inadequate an analysis of the cases before us as the ritualistic invocation of the nonconstitutional phrase "separation of church and state." What these cases compel, rather, is an analysis of just what the "neutrality" is which is required by the interplay of the Establishment and Free Exercise clauses of the First Amendment, as imbedded in the Fourteenth.

. . . The dangers both to government and to religion inherent in official support of instruction in the tenets of various religious sects are absent in the present cases, which involve only a reading from the Bible unaccompanied by comments which might otherwise constitute instruction. Indeed, since, from all that appears in either record, any teacher who does not wish to do so is free not to participate, it cannot even be contended that some infinitesimal part of the salaries paid by the State are made contingent upon the performance of a religious function.

In the absence of evidence that the legislature or school board intended to prohibit local schools from substituting a different set of readings where parents requested such a change, we should not assume that the provisions before us—as actually administered—may not be construed simply as authorizing religious exercises, nor that the designations may not be treated simply as indications of the promulgating body's view as to the community's preference. We are under a duty to interpret these provisions so as to render them constitutional if reasonably possible. . . .

It is clear that the dangers of coercion involved in the holding of religious exercises in a schoolroom differ qualitatively from those presented by the use of similar exercises or affirmations in ceremonies attended by adults. Even as to children, however, the duty laid upon government in connection with religious exercises in the public schools is that of refraining from so structuring the school environment as to put any kind of pressure on a child to participate in those exercises; it is not that of providing an atmosphere in which children are kept scrupulously insulated from any awareness that some of their fellows may want to open the school day with prayer, or of the fact that there exist in our pluralistic society differences of religious belief. . . .

To be specific, it seems to me clear that certain types of exercises would present situations in which no possibility of coercion on the part of secular officials could be claimed to exist. Thus, if such exercises were held either before or after the official school day, or if the school schedule were such that participation were merely one among a number of desirable alternatives, it could hardly be contended that the exercises did anything more than to provide an opportunity for the voluntary expression of religious belief. On the other hand, a law which provided for religious exercises during the school day and which contained no excusal provision would obviously be unconstitutionally coercive upon those who did not wish to participate. And even under a law containing an excusal provision, if the exercises were held during the school day, and no equally desirable alternative were provided by the school authorities, the likelihood that children might be under at least some psychological compulsion to participate would be great. In a case such as the latter, however, I think we would err if we *assumed* such coercion in the absence of any evidence.

. . . What our Constitution indispensably protects is the freedom of each of us, be he Jew or Agnostic, Christian or Atheist, Buddhist or Freethinker, to believe or disbelieve, to worship or not worship, to pray or keep silent, according to his own conscience, uncoerced and unrestrained by government. It is conceivable that these school boards, or even all school boards, might eventually find it impossible to administer a system of religious exercises during school hours in such a way as to meet this constitutional standard—in such a way as completely to free from any kind of official coercion those who do not affirmatively want to participate. But I think we must not assume that school boards so lack the qualities of inventiveness and good will as to make impossible the achievement of that goal.

I would remand both cases for further hearings.

Political advertisements in newspapers, unless specifically libelous, are protected by the freedom guarantied in the Constitution.

30. *NEW YORK TIMES CO. v. SULLIVAN* (1964)

In this decision, the Supreme Court extended the protection of freedom of the press to include political advertisements in newspapers. The Court held that such ads, unless specifically and maliciously libelous, are a means of political expression and communication. As such, their freedom is guarantied by the First and Fourteenth Amendments.

Background: *The facts of the case are fully stated in the decision. Briefly, during the civil rights struggle in Montgomery, Alabama, in 1960,* The New York Times *carried an ad attacking brutality against Negroes. Commissioner Sullivan, in charge of the Montgomery police, considered himself personally libeled, sued the* Times *and won an award of $500,000 in damages. The Alabama Supreme Court upheld the verdict, and* The New York Times *appealed to the United States Supreme Court.*

The Supreme Court reversed the Alabama decision. Apart from the fact that the Court did not think that Sullivan was specifically or intentionally libeled, it ruled that political advertisements came under the constitutionally protected freedom of the press. In a concurring opinion, Justice Goldberg added a further note—namely, that the First and Fourteenth Amendment freedoms gave to both citizens and press the "unconditional privilege to criticize official conduct."

Some Related Cases

(On Freedom of the Press):

Patterson v. Colorado (1907)
Coleman v. MacLennan (1908)
Gompers v. Bucks Stone Range Co. (1911)
Toledo Newspaper Co. v. United States (1918)
City of Chicago v. Tribune Co. (1923)
Near v. Minnesota (1931)
Associated Press v. National Labor Relations Board (1937)
Lovell v. City of Griffin (1938)

Schneider v. State (1939)
Nye v. United States (1941)
Valentine v. Chrestensen (1942)
Chaplinsky v. New Hampshire (1942)
Associated Press v. United States (1945)
Oklahoma Press Publishing Co. v. Walling (1946)
Craig v. Harney (1947)
Winters v. New York (1948)
United States v. C.I.O. (1948)
Beauharnais v. Illinois (1952)
Mills v. Alabama (1966)

MR. JUSTICE BRENNAN DELIVERED THE OPINION OF THE COURT:

We are required in this case to determine for the first time the extent to which the constitutional protections for speech and press limit a State's power to award damages in a libel action brought by a public official against critics of his official conduct.

Respondent L. B. Sullivan is one of the three elected Commissioners of the city of Montgomery, Alabama. . . . He brought this civil libel action against the four individual petitioners, who are Negroes and Alabama clergymen, and against petitioner the New York Times Company, a New York corporation which publishes *The New York Times,* a daily newspaper. A jury in the Circuit Court of Montgomery County awarded him damages of $500,000, the full amount claimed, against all the petitioners, and the Supreme Court of Alabama affirmed. . . .

Respondent's complaint alleged that he had been libeled by statements in a full-page advertisement that was carried in *The New York Times* on March 29, 1960. Entitled "Heed Their Rising Voices," the advertisement began by stating that "As the whole world knows by now, thousands of Southern Negro students are engaged in widespread nonviolent demonstrations in positive affirmation of the right to live in human dignity as guaranteed by the U.S. Constitution and the Bill of Rights." It went on to charge that "in their efforts to uphold these guarantees, they are being met by an unprecedented wave of terror by those who would deny and negate that document which the whole world looks upon as setting the pattern for modern freedom. . . ."

The text appeared over the names of sixty-four persons, many widely known for their activities in public affairs, religion, trade unions, and the performing arts. . . .

Of the ten paragraphs of text in the advertisement, the third and a portion of the sixth were the basis of the respondent's claim of libel. They read as follows:

> Third paragraph:
>
> In Montgomery, Alabama, after students sang "My Country, 'Tis of Thee" on the State Capitol steps, their leaders were expelled from school, and truckloads of police armed with shotguns and tear-gas ringed the Alabama State College Campus. . . .
>
> Sixth paragraph:
>
> Again and again the Southern violators have answered Dr. King's peaceful protests with intimidation and violence. They have bombed his home almost killing his wife and child. They have assaulted his person. They have arrested him seven times—for "speeding," "loitering" and similar "offenses." And now they have charged him with "perjury" —a *felony* under which they could imprison him for *ten years*. . . .

Although neither of these statements mentions respondent by name, he contended that the word "police" in the third paragraph referred to him as the Montgomery Commissioner who supervised the police department. . . .

It is uncontroverted that some of the statements contained in the two paragraphs were not accurate descriptions of events which occurred in Montgomery. . . .

On the premise that the charges in the sixth paragraph could be read as referring to him, respondent was allowed to prove that he had not participated in the events described. Although Dr. King's home had in fact been bombed twice when his wife and child were there, both of these occasions antedated respondent's tenure as commissioner . . . Three of Dr. King's four [not seven] arrests took place before respondent became commissioner. Although Dr. King had in fact been indicted (he was subsequently acquitted) on two counts of perjury, each of which carried a possible five-year sentence, respondent had nothing to do with procuring the indictment.

Respondent made no effort to prove that he suffered actual pecuniary loss as a result of the alleged libel. . . .

Alabama law denies a public officer recovery of punitive damages in a libel action brought on account of a publication concerning his official conduct unless he first makes a written demand for a public retraction and the defendant fails or refuses to comply. . . . Respondent served such a demand upon each of the petitioners. None of the individual petitioners responded to the demand. . . . The *Times* did not publish a retraction to the demand, but wrote respondent a letter stating, among other things, that "we . . . are somewhat puzzled as to how you think the statements in any way reflect on you. . . ." Respondent filed this suit a few days later without answering the letter. The *Times* did, however, subsequently publish a retraction of the advertisement upon the demand of Governor John Patterson of Alabama. . . .

The trial judge submitted the case to the jury under instructions that the statements in the advertisement were "libelous per se" and were not privileged, so that petitioners might be held liable if the jury found that they had published the advertisement and that the statements were made "of and concerning" respondent. The jury was instructed that, because the statements were libelous per se, "the law . . . implies legal injury from the bare fact of publication itself. . . ." An award of punitive damages—as distinguished from "general" damages, which are compensatory in nature—apparently requires proof of actual malice under Alabama law, and the judge charged that "mere negligence or carelessness is not evidence of actual malice or malice in fact, and does not justify an award of exemplary or punitive damages." He refused to charge, however, that the jury must be "convinced" of malice . . . to make such an award, and he also refused to require that a verdict for respondent differentiate between compensatory and punitive damages. The judge rejected petitioners' contention that his rulings abridged the freedoms of speech and of the press that are guarantied by the First and Fourteenth Amendments.

In affirming the judgment, the Supreme Court of Alabama sustained the trial judge's rulings and instructions in all respects. . . .

Because of the importance of the constitutional issues involved, we granted the separate petitions for certiorari of the individual petitioners and of the *Times* . . . We reverse the judgment. We hold that the rule of law applied by the Alabama courts is constitutionally deficient for failure to provide the safeguards for freedom of speech and of the press that are required by the First and Fourteenth Amendments in a libel action brought by a public official against critics of his official conduct. We further hold that under the proper safeguards the evidence presented in this case is constitutionally insufficient to support the judgment for respondent.

We may dispose at the outset of two grounds asserted to insulate the judgment of the Alabama courts from constitutional scrutiny. The first is the proposition relied on by the State Supreme Court—that "The Fourteenth Amendment is directed against state action and not private action." That proposition has no application to this case. . . .

The second contention is that the constitutional guaranties of freedom of speech and of the press are inapplicable here, at least so far as the *Times* is concerned, because the allegedly libelous statements were published as part of a paid, "commercial" advertisement. The argument relies on *Valentine v. Chrestensen* . . . where the Court held that a city ordinance forbidding street distribution of commercial and business advertising matter did not abridge the First Amendment freedoms, even as applied to a handbill having a commercial message on one side but a protest against certain official action on the other. The reliance is wholly misplaced. The Court in Chrestensen reaffirmed the constitutional protection for "the freedom of communicating information and disseminating opinion." . . .

The publication here was not a "commercial" advertisement in the sense in which the word was used in Chrestensen. It communicated information, expressed opinion, recited grievances, protested claimed abuses, and sought financial support on behalf of a movement whose existence and objectives are matters of the highest public interest and concern . . . That the *Times* was paid for publishing the advertisement is as immaterial in this connection as is the fact that newspapers and books are sold . . . Any other conclusion would discourage newspapers from carrying "editorial advertisements" of this type, and so might shut off an important outlet for the promulgation of information and ideas by persons who do not themselves have access to publishing facilities—who wish to exercise their freedom of speech even though they are not members of the press. . . . The effect would be to shackle the First Amendment in its attempt to secure "the widest possible dissemination of information from diverse and antagonistic sources." To avoid placing such a handicap upon the freedoms of expression, we hold that if the allegedly libelous statements would otherwise be constitutionally protected from the present judgment, they do not forfeit that protection because they were published in the form of a paid advertisement. . . .

Thus we consider this case against the background of a profound national commitment to the principle that debate on public issues should be uninhibited, robust, and wide-open, and that it may well include vehement, caustic, and sometimes unpleasantly sharp attacks on government and public officials. . . . The present advertisement, as an expression of grievance and protest on one of the major public issues of our time, would seem clearly to qualify for the constitutional protection. The question is whether it forfeits that protection by the falsity of some of its factual statements and by its alleged defamation of respondent.

Authoritative interpretations of the First Amendment guaranties have consistently refused to recognize an exception for any test of truth, whether administered by judges, juries, or administrative officials—and especially not one that puts the burden of proving truth on the speaker. . . . The constitutional protection does not turn upon "the truth, popularity, or social utility of the ideas and beliefs which are offered." *NAACP v. Button*. . . .

Just as factual error affords no warrant for repressing speech that would otherwise be free, the same is true of injury to official reputation. Where judicial officers are involved, this court has held that concern for the dignity and reputation of the courts does not justify the punishment as criminal contempt of criticism of the judge or his decision. . . .

What a State may not constitutionally bring about by means of a criminal statute is likewise beyond the reach of its civil law of libel. The fear of damage awards under a rule such as that invoked by the Alabama courts here may be markedly more inhibiting than the fear of prosecution under a criminal statute. . . .

We hold today that the Constitution delimits a State's power to award damages for libel in actions brought by public officials against critics of their official conduct. Since this is such an action, the rule requiring proof of actual malice is applicable. While Alabama law apparently requires proof of actual malice for an award of punitive damages, where general damages are concerned malice is "presumed." Such a presumption is inconsistent with the federal rule. . . . Since the trial judge did not instruct the jury to differentiate between general and punitive damages, it may be that the verdict was wholly an award of one or the other. But it is impossible to know, in view of the general verdict returned. Because of this uncertainty, the judgment must be reversed and the case remanded. . . .

We also think the evidence [presented in the Alabama courts] was constitutionally defective in another respect: it was incapable of supporting the jury's finding that the allegedly libelous statements were made "of and concerning" respondent. . . . There was no reference to respondent in the advertisement, either by name or official position. . . . Although the statements may be taken as referring to the police, they did not on their face make even an oblique reference to respondent as an individual. Support for the asserted reference must, therefore, be sought in the testimony of respondent's witnesses. But none of them suggested any basis for the belief that respondent himself was attacked in the advertisement beyond the bare fact that he was in overall charge of the Police Department and thus bore official responsibility for police conduct. . . . This reliance on the bare fact of respondent's official position was made explicit by the Supreme Court of Alabama. That court . . . based its ruling on the proposition that:

> We think it common knowledge that the average person knows that municipal agents, such as police and firemen, and others, are under the control and direction of the city governing body, and more particularly under the direction and control of a single commissioner. In measuring the performance or deficiencies of such groups, praise or criticism is usually attached to the official in complete control of the body. . . .

This proposition has disquieting implications for criticism of governmental conduct. For good reason, "no court of last resort in this country has ever held, or even suggested, that prosecutions for libel on government have any place in the American system of jurisprudence." *City of Chicago v. Tribune Co.* [1923] . . . The present proposition would sidestep this obstacle by transmuting criticism of government, however impersonal it may seem on its face, into personal criticism, and hence potential libel, of the officials of whom the government is composed. There is no legal alchemy by which a State may thus create the cause of action that would otherwise be denied for a publication which, as respondent himself said of the advertisement, "reflects not only on me but on the other Commissioners and the community." Raising as it does the possibility that a good-faith critic of government will be penalized for his criticism, the proposition relied on by the Alabama courts strikes at the very center of the constitutionally protected area of free expression. We hold that such a proposition may not constitutionally be utilized to establish that an otherwise impersonal attack on governmental operations was a libel of an official responsible for those operations. Since it was relied on exclusively here, and there was no other evidence to connect the statements with respondent, the evidence was constitutionally insufficient to support a finding that the statements referred to respondent.

The judgment of the Supreme Court of Alabama is reversed and the case is remanded to that court for further proceedings not inconsistent with this opinion.

Reversed and remanded.

[Justice Black, with whom Justice Douglas concurred, wrote a separate concurring opinion. Justice Goldberg, joined by Justice Douglas, also wrote a separate concurring opinion.]

Marital privacy, including the right to seek birth-control information, is protected by the Constitution.

31. *GRISWOLD v. CONNECTICUT* (1965)

This is a landmark decision, in which the Supreme Court ruled that States cannot prohibit married couples from seeking birth-control information. The Connecticut statute invalidated here was so severe that it penalized not merely those who used birth-control devices but also those (doctors, for example) who gave advice on the subject. The Supreme Court held that the Connecticut law infringed on every Amendment in the Bill of Rights that guarantied personal freedom. In particular, to quote from the concurring opinion of Justice Goldberg, it violated "the right to privacy in the marital relation [*which*] *is fundamental and basic."*

Background: *The background of the case is given in the first three paragraphs of the decision listed below.*

The decision was seven to two, with Justices Black and Stewart dissenting.

Some Related Cases
(On the Right to Privacy):

Boyd v. United States (1886)
Goldman v. United States (1942)
Johnson v. United States (1948)

MR. JUSTICE DOUGLAS DELIVERED THE OPINION OF THE COURT:

Appellant Griswold is Executive Director of the Planned Parenthood League of Connecticut. Appellant Buxton is a licensed physician and a professor at the Yale Medical School who served as Medical Director for the League at its Center in New Haven—a center open and operating from November 1 to November 10, 1961, when appellants were arrested.

They gave information, instruction, and medical advice to *married persons* as to the means of preventing conception. They examined the wife and prescribed the best contraceptive device or material for her use. Fees were usually charged, although some couples were serviced free. . . .

The appellants were found guilty as accessories and fined $100 each, against the claim that the accessory statute [of Connecticut] as so applied violated the Fourteenth Amendment. The Appellate Division of the Circuit affirmed. The Supreme Court of Errors affirmed that judgment. . . .

We think that appellants have standing to raise the constitutional rights of the married people with whom they had a professional relationship. . . .

Coming to the merits, we are met with a wide range of questions that implicate the Due Process clause of the Fourteenth Amendment. Overtones of some arguments suggested that *Lochner v. New York* [1905] . . . should be our guide. But we decline that invitation as we did in *West Coast Hotel Co. v. Parrish*. . . . We do not sit as a super-legislature to determine the wisdom, need, and propriety of laws that touch economic problems, business affairs, or social conditions. This law, however, operates directly on an intimate relation of husband and wife and their physician's role in one aspect of that relation.

The association of people is not mentioned in the Constitution nor in the Bill of Rights. The right to educate a child in a school of the parents' choice—whether public or private or parochial—is also not mentioned. Nor is the right to study any particular subject or any foreign language. Yet the First Amendment has been construed to include certain of those rights. . . .

In other words, the State may not, consistently with the spirit of the First Amendment, contract the spectrum of available knowledge. The right of freedom of speech and press includes not only the right to utter or to print, but the right to distribute, the right to receive, the right to read . . . and freedom of inquiry, freedom of thought, and freedom to teach . . . indeed the freedom of the entire university community. . . . Without those peripheral rights the specific rights would be less secure. . . .

In *NAACP v. Alabama* . . . we protected the "freedom to associate and privacy in one's associations," noting that freedom of association was a peripheral First Amendment right. . . . In other words, the First Amendment has a penumbra where privacy is protected from governmental intrusion. In like context, we have protected forms of "association" that are not political in the customary sense but pertain to the social, legal, and economic benefit of the members. . . .

The right of "association," like the right of belief (*Board of Education v. Barnette* . . .), is more than the right to attend a meeting; it includes the right to express one's attitudes or philosophies by membership in a group or by affiliation with it or by other lawful means. Association in that context is a form of expression of opinion; and while it is not expressly included in the First Amendment its existence is necessary in making the express guaranties fully meaningful.

The foregoing cases suggest that specific guaranties in the Bill of Rights have penumbras, formed by emanations from those guaranties that help give them life and substance. . . . Various guaranties create zones of privacy. [Here Justice Douglas refers to the First, Third, Fourth, Fifth, and Ninth Amendments] . . .

The Fourth and Fifth Amendments were described in *Boyd v. United States* . . . as protection against all governmental invasions "of the sanctity of a man's home and the privacies of life." We recently referred in *Mapp v. Ohio* . . . to the Fourth Amendment as creating a "right to privacy, no less important than any other right carefully and particularly reserved to the people." . . .

The present case, then, concerns a relationship lying within the zone of privacy created by several fundamental constitutional guaranties. And it concerns a law which, in forbidding the *use* of contraceptives rather than regulating their manufacture or sale, seeks to achieve its goals by means having a maximum destructive impact upon that relationship. Such a law cannot stand in light of the familiar principle, so often applied by this court, that a "governmental purpose to control or prevent activities constitutionally subject to state regulation may not be achieved by means which sweep unnecessarily broadly and thereby invade the area of protected freedoms." *NAACP v. Alabama*. . . . Would we allow the police to search the sacred precincts of marital bedrooms for telltale signs of the use of contraceptives? The very idea is repulsive to the notions of privacy surrounding the marriage relationship.

We deal with a right of privacy older than the Bill of Rights—older than our political parties, older than our school system. Marriage is a coming together for better or for worse, hopefully enduring, and intimate to the degree of being sacred. It is an association that promotes a way of life, not causes; a harmony in living, not political faiths; a bilateral loyalty, not commercial or social projects. Yet it is an association for as noble a purpose as any involved in our prior decisions.

Reversed.

[Concurring opinion by Justice Goldberg, Chief Justice Warren, and Justice Brennan; another concurring opinion by Justice Harlan; still another by Justice White. Justice Stewart and Justice Black dissenting.]

Chapter XVI

Civil Liberties—Procedures

"The privilege of the writ of *habeas corpus* shall not be suspended, unless when in cases of rebellion or invasion the public safety may require it."—Art. I, Sec. 9

"The right of the people to be secure in their persons, houses, papers, and effects, against unreasonable searches and seizures, shall not be violated, and no warrants shall issue but upon probable cause, supported by oath or affirmation, and particularly describing the place to be searched, and the persons or things to be seized."—Art. IV (Fourth Amendment)

"No person shall be held to answer for a capital or other infamous crime unless on a presentment or indictment of a grand jury . . . nor shall any person be subject for the same offence to be twice put in jeopardy of life or limb; nor shall be compelled in any criminal case to be a witness against himself, nor be deprived of life, liberty, or property, without due process of law; nor shall private property be taken for public use, without just compensation."—Art. V (Fifth Amendment)

"In all criminal prosecutions, the accused shall enjoy the right to a speedy and public trial, by an impartial jury of the state and district wherein the crime shall have been committed, which district shall have been previously ascertained by law, and to be informed of the nature and cause of the accusation; to be confronted with the witnesses against him; to have the compulsory process for obtaining witnesses in his favor, and to have the assistance of counsel for his defence."—Art. VI (Sixth Amendment)

"Excessive bail shall not be required, nor excessive fines imposed, nor cruel and unusual punishments inflicted."—Art. VIII (Eighth Amendment)

In this Chapter:
Ex Parte Milligan (1866)
Palko v. Connecticut (1937)
Mapp v. Ohio (1961)
Gideon v. Wainwright (1963)

Martial rule cannot operate where civil courts are open.

32. *EX PARTE MILLIGAN* (1866)

The significance of this case lies in its rejection of military tribunals of justice in areas where civilian courts were in operation. The case is, therefore, basic to civil liberties. It is an eloquent reaffirmation of the rights of Americans under the Constitution.

Background: *On October 15, 1863, President Lincoln, after authorization by Congress, suspended the writ of habeas corpus in cases of persons arrested for military offenses. Under this authority, the Army jailed Lambain P. Milligan, a pro-Southern Indiana lawyer and teacher, tried him by a Military Commission for disloyalty, and condemned him to be hanged. Milligan petitioned the United States Circuit Court for a writ of habeas corpus, and that court decided that the case was so important that it should be heard by the Supreme Court. The Supreme Court, in the following opinion read by Justice Davis (a friend of Lincoln's), reversed the military sentence and ruled that Milligan should have been given a civilian trial with all the constitutional safeguards.*

Some Related Cases
(On Civil Justice in War Situations):
Luther v. Borden (1849)
Ex Parte Merryman (1861)
Duncan v. Kahanomoku (1946)
In re Yamashita (1946)
Reid v. Covert (1957)
Kinsella v. Krueger (1957)
Kinsella v. Singleton (1960)

MR. JUSTICE DAVIS DELIVERED THE OPINION OF THE COURT:

The importance of the main question presented by this record cannot be overstated; for it involves the very framework of the government and the fundamental principles of American liberty. . . .

The controlling question in the case is this: Upon the *facts* stated in Milligan's petition, and the exhibits filed, had the military commission mentioned in it *jurisdiction,* legally, to try and sentence him? Milligan, not a resident of one of the rebellious States, or a prisoner of war, but a citizen of Indiana for twenty years past, and never in the military or naval service, is, while at his home, arrested by the military power of the United States, imprisoned, and, on certain criminal charges preferred against him, tried, convicted, and sentenced to be hanged by a military commission, organized under the direction of the military commander of the military district of Indiana. Had this tribunal the legal power and authority to try and punish this man?

No graver question was ever considered by this court, nor one which more nearly concerns the rights of the whole people; for it is the birthright of every American citizen when charged with crime, to be tried and punished according to law. The power of punishment is alone through the means which the laws have provided for that purpose, and if they are ineffectual, there is an immunity from punishment no matter how great an offender the individual may be, or how much his crimes may have shocked the sense of justice of the country, or endangered its safety. By the protection of the law human rights are secured; withdraw that protection, and they are at the mercy of wicked rulers, or the clamor of an excited people. If there was law to justify this military trial, it is not our province to interfere; if there was not, it is our duty to declare the nullity of the whole proceedings. The decision of this question does not depend on argument or judicial precedents, numerous and highly illustrative as they are. These precedents inform us of the extent of the struggle to preserve liberty, and to relieve those in civil life from military trials. The founders of our government were familiar with the history of that struggle, and secured in a written Constitution every right which the people had wrested from power during a contest of ages. By that Constitution and the laws authorized by it this question must be determined. The provisions of that instrument on the administration of criminal justice are too plain and direct to leave room for misconstruction or doubt of their true meaning. Those applicable to this case are found in that clause of the original Constitution which says, "That the trial of all crimes, except in case of impeachment, shall be by jury"; and in the Fourth, Fifth, and Sixth Articles of the Amendments. . . .

Time has proven the discernment of our ancestors; for even these provisions, expressed in such plain English words, that it would seem the ingenuity of man could not evade them, are *now,* after the lapse of more than seventy years, sought to be avoided. . . . The Constitution of the United States is a law for rulers and people, equally in war and in peace, and covers with the shield of its protection all classes of men, at all times, and under all circumstances. No doctrine involving more pernicious consequences was ever invented by the wit of man than that any of its provisions can be suspended during any of the great exigencies of government. Such a doctrine leads directly to anarchy or despotism, but the theory of necessity on which it is based is false; for the government, within the Constitution, has all the powers granted to it which are necessary to preserve its existence; as has been happily proved by the result of the great effort to throw off its just authority.

Have any of the rights guarantied by the Constitution been violated in the case of Milligan? and if so, what are they?

Every trial involves the exercise of judicial power; and from what source did the military commission that tried him derive their authority? Certainly no part of the judicial power of the country was conferred on them; because the Constitution expressly vests it "in one Supreme Court and such inferior courts as the Congress may from time to time ordain and establish," and it is not pretended that the commission was a court ordained and established by Congress. They cannot justify on the mandate of the President, because he is controlled by law, and has his appropriate sphere of duty, which is to execute, not to make, the laws; and there is "no written criminal code to which resort can be had as a source of jurisdiction."

But it is said that the jurisdiction is complete under the "laws and usages of war."

It can serve no useful purpose to inquire what those laws and usages are, whence they originated, where found, and on whom they operate; they can never be applied to citizens in States which have upheld the authority of the Government, and where the courts are open and their process unobstructed. This court has judicial knowledge that in Indiana the federal authority was always unopposed, and its courts always open to hear criminal accusations and redress grievances; and no usage of war could sanction a military trial there for any offense whatever of a citizen in civil life, in nowise connected with the military service. Congress could grant no such power; and to the honor of our national legislature be it said, it has never been provoked by the state of the country even to attempt its exercise. One of the plainest constitutional provisions was, therefore, infringed when Milligan was tried by a court not ordained and established by

Congress, and not composed of judges appointed during good behavior.

Why was he not delivered to the Circuit Court of Indiana to be proceeded against according to law? No reason of necessity could be urged against it; because Congress had declared penalties against the offenses charged, provided for their punishment, and directed that court to hear and determine them. And soon after this military tribunal was ended, the Circuit Court met, peacefully transacted its business, and adjourned. It needed no bayonets to protect it, and required no military aid to execute its judgments. It was held in a State, eminently distinguished for patriotism, by judges commissioned during the rebellion who were provided with juries, upright, intelligent, and selected by a marshal appointed by the President. The Government had no right to conclude that Milligan, if guilty, would not receive in the court merited punishment; for its records disclose that it was constantly engaged in the trial of similar offenses, and was never interrupted in its administration of criminal justice. If it was dangerous, in the distracted condition of affairs, to leave Milligan unrestrained of his liberty, because he "conspired against the Government, afforded aid and comfort to rebels, and incited the people to insurrection," the *law* said, arrest him, confine him closely, render him powerless to do further mischief; and then present his case to the grand jury of the district, with proofs of his guilt, and, if indicted, try him according to the course of the common law. If this had been done, the Constitution would have been vindicated, the law of 1863 enforced, and the securities for personal liberty preserved and defended.

Another guaranty of freedom was broken when Milligan was denied a trial by jury. The great minds of the country have differed on the correct interpretation to be given to the various provisions of the Federal Constitution; and judicial decision has been often invoked to settle their true meaning; but until recently no one ever doubted that the right of trial by jury was forfeited in the organic law against the power of attack. It is *now* assailed; but if ideas can be expressed in words and language has any meaning, *this right*—one of the most valuable in a free country—is preserved to every one accused of crime who is not attached to the army, or navy, or militia in actual service.

It is claimed that martial law covers with its broad mantle the proceedings of this military commission. The proposition is this: that in a time of war the commander of an armed force (if, in his opinion, the exigencies of the country demanded it, and of which he is to judge) has the power, within the lines of his military district, to suspend all civil rights and their remedies, and subject citizens as well as soldiers to the rule of *his will;* and in the exercise of his lawful authority cannot be restrained, except by his superior officer or the President of the United States.

If this position is sound to the extent claimed, then when war exists, foreign or domestic, and the country is subdivided into military departments for mere convenience, the commander of one of them can, if he chooses, within his limits, on the plea of necessity, with the approval of the Executive, substitute military force for, and to the exclusion of, the laws, and punish all persons, as he thinks right and proper, without fixed or certain rules.

The statement of this proposition shows its importance; for, if true, republican government is a failure, and there is an end of liberty regulated by law. Martial law, established on such a basis, destroys every guarantee of the Constitution, and effectually renders the "military independent of, and superior to, the civil power",—the attempt to do which by the king of Great Britain was deemed by our fathers such an offense, that they assigned it to the world as one of the causes which impelled them to declare their independence. Civil liberty and this kind of martial law cannot endure together; the antagonism is irreconcilable; and, in the conflict, one or the other must perish.

This Nation, as experience has proved, cannot always remain at peace, and has no right to expect that it will always have wise and humane rulers, sincerely attached to the principles of the Constitution. Wicked men, ambitious of power, with hatred of liberty and contempt of law, may fill the place once occupied by Washington and Lincoln; and if this right is conceded, and the calamities of war again befall us, the dangers to human liberty are frightful to contemplate. If our fathers had failed to provide for just such a contingency, they would have been false to the trust reposed in them. They knew—the history of the world told them—the nation they were founding, be its existence short or long, would be involved in war; how often or how long continued, human foresight could not tell; and that unlimited power, wherever lodged at such a time, was especially hazardous to freemen. For this, and other equally weighty reasons, they secured the inheritance they had fought to maintain, by incorporating in a written Constitution the safeguards which time had proved were essential to its preservation. Not one of these safeguards can the President, or Congress, or the judiciary disturb, except the one concerning the writ of habeas corpus.

It is essential to the safety of every government that, in a great crisis like the one we have just passed through, there should be a power somewhere of suspending the writ of habeas corpus. In every war, there are men of previously good character, wicked enough to counsel their fellow-citizens to resist the measures deemed necessary by a good government to sustain its just authority and overthrow its enemies; and their influence may lead to dangerous combinations. In the emergency of the times, an immediate public investigation according to law may not be possible; and yet the peril to the country may be too imminent to suffer such persons to go at large. Unquestionably, there is then an exigency which demands that the Government, if it should see fit, in the exercise of a proper discretion, to make arrests, should not be required to produce the persons arrested in answer to a writ of habeas corpus. The Constitution goes no further. It does not say after a writ of habeas corpus is denied a citizen, that he shall be tried otherwise than by the course of the common law; if it had intended this result, it was easy by the use of direct words to have accomplished it. The illustrious men who framed that instrument were guarding the foundations of civil liberty against the abuses of unlimited power; they were full of wisdom, and the lessons of history informed them that a trial by an established court, assisted by an impartial jury, was the only sure way of protecting the citizens against oppression and wrong. Knowing this, they limited the suspension to one great right, and left the rest to remain forever inviolable. But, it is insisted that the safety of the country in time of war demands that this broad claim for martial law shall be sustained. If this were true, it could be well said that a country, preserved at the sacrifice of all the cardinal principles of liberty, is not worth the cost of preservation. Happily, it is not so.

It will be borne in mind that this is not a question of the power to proclaim martial law, when war exists in a community and the courts and civil authorities are overthrown. Nor is it a question what rule a military commander, at the head of his army, can impose on States in rebellion to cripple their resources and quell the insurrection. The jurisdiction claimed is much more extensive. The necessities of the service, during the late rebellion, required that the loyal States should be placed within the limits of certain military districts and commanders appointed in them; and, it is urged, that this, in a military sense, constituted them the theatre of military operations; and, as in this case, Indiana had been and was again threatened with invasion by the enemy, the occasion was furnished to establish martial law. The conclusion does not follow from the premises. If armies were collected in Indiana, they were to be employed in another locality, where the laws were obstructed and the national authority disputed. On *her* soil there was no hostile foot; if once invaded, that invasion was at an end, and with it all pretext for martial law. Martial law cannot arise from a *threatened* invasion. The necessity must be actual and present; the invasion real, such as effectually closes the courts and deposes the civil administration.

It is difficult to see how the *safety* of the country required martial law in Indiana. If any of her citizens were plotting treason, the power of arrest could secure them, until the Government was prepared for their trial, when the courts were open and ready to try them. It was as easy to protect witnesses before a civil as a military tribunal; and as there could be no wish to convict, except on sufficient legal evidence, surely an ordained and established court was better able to judge of this than a military tribunal composed of gentlemen not trained to the profession of the law.

It follows, from what has been said on this subject, that there are occasions when martial rule can be properly applied. If, in foreign invasion or civil war, the courts are actually here closed, and it is impossible to administer criminal justice according to law, *then,* in the theatre of active military operations, where war really prevails, there is a necessity to furnish a substitute for the civil authority, thus overthrown, to preserve the safety of the army and society; and as no power is left but the military, it is allowed to govern by martial rule until the laws can have their free course. As necessity creates the rule, so it limits its duration; for, if this government is continued *after* the courts are reinstated, it is a gross usurpation of power. Martial rule can never exist where the courts are open, and in the proper and unobstructed exercise of their jurisdiction. It is also confined to the locality of actual war. Because, during the late rebellion it could have been enforced in Virginia, where the national authority was overturned and the courts driven out, it does not follow that it should obtain in Indiana, where that authority was never disputed, and justice was always administered. . . .

[Mr. Chief Justice Chase, for himself and Mr. Justice Wayne, Mr. Justice Swayne, and Mr. Justice Miller, delivered an opinion in which he differed from the Court in several important points, but concurred in the judgment of the case.]

The "double jeopardy" immunity of the Fifth Amendment is not applicable to the States.

33. *PALKO v. CONNECTICUT* (1937)

Does the Fifth Amendment's immunity from "double jeopardy" always protect a person from being tried for the same crime twice? In this decision, Justice Cardozo, speaking for a virtually unanimous Court (only Justice Butler dissented), said "no."

Background: *Palko, convicted in Connecticut for second-degree murder, made a successful appeal to the state court. Retried, he was convicted of first-degree murder and sentenced to death. Palko appealed to the United States Supreme Court on the ground that he had been placed in double jeopardy, in violation of the Fifth Amendment. The Supreme*

Court rejected his appeal on the ground that the Fifth Amendment granted him no immunity since it was "not directed to the States, but solely to the Federal Government."

Some Related Cases
(On "Double Jeopardy"):
United States v. Perez (1824)
Ex Parte Lange (1874)
Dreyer v. Illinois (1902)
Kepner v. United States (1904)
Burton v. United States (1906)
Shoener v. Pennsylvania (1907)
Louisiana ex rel. Francis v. Resweber (1947)
Bartkus v. Illinois (1966)

MR. JUSTICE CARDOZO DELIVERED THE OPINION OF THE COURT:

The argument for appellant is that whatever is forbidden by the Fifth Amendment is forbidden by the Fourteenth Amendment also. The Fifth Amendment, which is not directed to the States, but solely to the Federal Government, creates immunity from double jeopardy. No person shall be "subject for the same offense to be twice put in jeopardy of life or limb." The Fourteenth Amendment ordains, "nor shall any state deprive any person of life, liberty, or property without due process of law." To retry a defendant, though under one indictment and only one, subjects him, it is said, to double jeopardy in violation of the Fifth Amendment, if the prosecution is one on behalf of the United States. From this the consequence is said to follow that there is a denial of life or liberty without due process of law, if the prosecution is one on behalf of the people of a State. . . .

The thesis is even broader. Whatever would be a violation of the original Bill of Rights (Amendments I to VIII) if done by the Federal Government is now equally unlawful by force of the Fourteenth Amendment if done by a State. There is no such general rule.

The Fifth Amendment provides, among other things, that no person shall be held to answer for a capital or otherwise infamous crime unless on presentment or indictment of a grand jury. This court has held that, in prosecutions by a State, presentment or indictment by a grand jury may give way to informations at the instance of a public officer. . . . The Fifth Amendment provides also that no person shall be compelled in any criminal case to be a witness against himself. This court has said that, in prosecutions by the State, the exemption will fail if the State elects to end it. . . . The Sixth Amendment calls for a jury trial in criminal cases and the Seventh for a jury trial in civil cases at common law where the value in controversy shall exceed twenty dollars. This court has ruled that consistently with those amendments trial by jury may be modified by a State or abolished altogether. . . .

On the other hand, the Due Process clause of the Fourteenth Amendment may make it unlawful for a State to abridge by its statutes the freedom of speech which the First Amendment safeguards against encroachment by the Congress . . . or the like freedom of the press . . . or the right of peaceable assembly, without which speech would be unduly trammeled. . . .

The line of division may seem to be wavering and broken if there is a hasty catalogue of the cases on the one side and the other. Reflection and analysis will induce a different view. There emerges the perception of a rationalizing principle which gives to discrete instances a proper order and coherence. The right to trial by jury and the immunity from prosecution except as the result of an indictment may have value and importance. Even so, they are not of the very essence of a scheme of ordered liberty. To abolish them is not to violate a "principle of justice so rooted in the traditions and conscience of our people as to be ranked as fundamental." . . . Few would be so narrow or provincial as to maintain that a fair and enlightened system of justice would be impossible without them. What is true of jury trials and indictments is true also, as the cases show, of the immunity from compulsory self-incrimination. . . . This too might be lost, and justice still be done. Indeed, today as in the past there are students of our penal system who look upon the immunity as a mischief rather than a benefit, and who would limit its scope, or destroy it altogether. No doubt there would remain the need to give protection against torture, physical or mental. . . . Justice, however, would not perish if the accused were subject to a duty to respond to orderly inquiry. The exclusion of these immunities and privileges from the privileges and immunities protected against the action of the States has not been arbitrary or casual. It has been dictated by a study and appreciation of the meaning, the essential implications, of liberty itself.

We reach a different plane of social and moral values when we pass to the privileges and immunities that have been taken over from the earlier articles of the Federal Bill of Rights and brought within the Fourteenth Amendment by a process of absorption. These in their origin were effective against the Federal Government alone. If the Fourteenth Amendment has absorbed them, the process of absorption has had its source in the belief that neither liberty nor justice would exist if they were sacrificed. . . . This is true, for illustration, of freedom of thought and speech. Of that freedom one may say that it is the matrix, the indispensable condition, of nearly every other form of freedom.

With rare aberrations a pervasive recognition of that truth can be traced in our history, political and legal. So it has come about that the domain of liberty, withdrawn by the Fourteenth Amendment from encroachment by the States, has been enlarged by latter-day judgments to include liberty of the mind as well as liberty of action. . . .

Our survey of the cases serves, we think, to justify the statement that the dividing line between them, if not unfaltering throughout its course, has been true for the most part to a unifying principle. On which side of the line the case made out by the appellant has appropriate location must be the next inquiry and the final one. Is that kind of double jeopardy to which the statute has subjected him a hardship so acute and shocking that our polity will not endure it? Does it violate those "fundamental principles of liberty and justice which lie at the base of all our civil and political institutions?" . . . The answer surely must be "no."

The judgment is

Affirmed.

[Mr. Justice Butler dissents.]

Illegally seized or acquired evidence is not admissible in any court.

34. *MAPP v. OHIO* (1961)

Under the Fourth Amendment, prohibiting unreasonable searches and seizures, the so-called "exclusionary rule" forbade the use of illegally seized evidence in federal courts. Did this prohibition also apply to state courts? In the case of Wolf v. Colorado *(1949), the Court ruled in the negative, presumably on the ground that the Due Process clause of the Fourteenth Amendment offered sufficient protection.* Mapp v. Ohio, *however, overturned that decision and declared that the Fourth Amendment extended also to state courts.*

Background: *Cleveland police, acting without a search warrant, forced their way into the house of Mrs. Mapp, and found there obscene material, for possession of which she was indicted and convicted. The Ohio Supreme Court upheld the conviction, on the ground that state law did not exclude evidence obtained illegally. The United States Supreme Court, in this case, overruled the Ohio court, stating, by a vote of six to three, that illegal evidence (by extension, this includes information obtained by bugging and other electronic devices) was inadmissible and that the "right to privacy embodied in the Fourth Amendment is enforceable against the States. . . ."*

Some Related Cases

(On Illegal Searches and Seizures):

Weeks v. United States (1914)
Burdeau v. McDowell (1921)
Gouled v. United States (1921)
Carroll v. United States (1925)
Byars v. United States (1927)
Nathanson v. United States (1933)
Harris v. United States (1947)
McDonald v. United States (1948)
Trupiano v. United States (1948)
Johnson v. United States (1948)
United States v. Rabinowitz (1950)
Irvine v. California (1954)
Frank v. Maryland (1959)
Ohio ex rel. Eaton v. Price (1960)

(On Wiretapping and Electronic Eavesdropping):

Olmstead v. United States (1928)
Nardone v. United States (1937)
Nardone v. United States (1939)
Goldman v. United States (1942)
Lee v. United States (1952)
Silverman v. United States (1961)
Lopez v. United States (1963)
Katz v. United States (1967)
Kolod v. United States (1968)

MR. JUSTICE CLARK DELIVERED THE OPINION OF THE COURT:

In 1949 . . . this court, in *Wolf v. Colorado,* 338 U.S. 25 . . . discussed the effect of the Fourth Amendment upon the States through the operation of the Due Process clause of the Fourteenth Amendment. It said: "We have no hesitation in saying that were a State affirmatively to sanction such police incursion into privacy it would run counter to the guaranty of the Fourteenth Amendment."

. . . The Court's reasons for not considering essential to the right to privacy, as a curb imposed upon the States by the Due Process clause, that which decades before had been posited as part and parcel of the Fourth Amendment's limitation upon federal encroachment of individual privacy, were bottomed on factual considerations.

While they are not basically relevant to a decision that the exclusionary rule is an essential ingredient of the Fourth Amendment as the right it embodies is vouchsafed against the States by the Due Process clause, we will consider the current validity of the factual grounds upon which *Wolf* was based.

The Court in *Wolf* first stated that "[t]he contrariety of views of the States" on the adoption of the exclusionary rule of Weeks was "particularly impressive" (at p. 29); and, in this connection, that it could not "brush aside the experience of States which deem the incidence of such conduct by the police too slight to call for a deterrent remedy . . . by overriding the [States'] relevant rules of evidence." At pp. 31, 32. While in 1949, prior to the *Wolf* case, almost two-thirds of the States were opposed to the use of the exclusionary rule, now, despite the *Wolf* case, more than half of those since passing upon it, by their own legislative or judicial decision, have wholly or partly adopted or adhered to the *Weeks* rule. . . . Significantly, among those now following the rule is California which, according to its highest court, was "compelled to reach that conclusion because other remedies have completely failed to secure compliance with the constitutional provisions." . . . In connection with this California case, we note that the second basis elaborated in *Wolf* in support of its failure to enforce the exclusionary doctrine against the States was that "other means of protection" have been afforded "the right to privacy." 338 U.S. at 30. The experience of California that such other remedies have been worthless and futile is buttressed by the experience of other States. The obvious futility of relegating the Fourth Amendment to the protection of other remedies has, moreover, been recognized by this court since Wolf. . . .

Likewise, time has set its face against what *Wolf* called the "weighty testimony" of *People v. Defore,* 242 N.Y. 13, 150 N.E. 585 (1926). There Justice (then Judge) Cardozo, rejecting adoption of the *Weeks* exclusionary rule in New York, had said that "the Federal rule as it stands is either too strict or too lax." However, the force of that reasoning has been largely vitiated by later decisions of this court. These include the recent discarding of the "silver platter" doctrine which allowed federal judicial use of evidence seized in violation of the Constitution by state agents, *Elkins v. United States,* 364 U.S. 206; the relaxation of the formerly strict requirements as to standing to challenge the use of evidence thus seized, so that now the procedure of exclusion, "ultimately referable to constitutional safeguards," is available to anyone even "legitimately on the premises" unlawfully searched, *Jones v. United States,* 362 U.S. 257; and, finally, the formulation of a method to prevent State use of evidence unconstitutionally seized by federal agents, *Rea v. United States,* 350 U.S. 214. Because there can be no fixed formula, we are admittedly met with "recurring questions of the reasonableness of searches," but less is not to be expected when dealing with a Constitution, and, at any rate, "reasonableness is in the first instance for the [trial court] . . . to determine." *United States v. Rabinowitz,* 339 U.S. 56.

It, therefore, plainly appears that the factual considerations supporting the failure of the *Wolf* Court to include the Weeks exclusionary rule when it recognized the enforceability of the right to privacy against the States in 1949, while not basically relevant to the constitutional consideration, could not, in any analysis, now be deemed controlling. . . .

. . . Today we once again examine *Wolf*'s constitutional documentation of the right to privacy free from unreasonable state intrusion, and, after its dozen years on our books, are led by it to close the only courtroom door remaining open to evidence secured by official lawlessness in flagrant abuse of that basic right, reserved to all persons as a specific guaranty against that very same unlawful conduct. We hold that all evidence obtained by searches and seizures in violation of the Constitution is, by that same authority, inadmissible in a state court.

Since the Fourth Amendment's right of privacy has been declared enforceable against the States through the Due Process clause of the Fourteenth, it is enforceable against them by the same sanction of exclusion as is used against the Federal Government. Were it otherwise, then just as without the *Weeks* rule the assurance against unreasonable federal searches and seizures would be "a form of words," valueless and undeserving of mention in a perpetual charter of inestimable human liberties, so too, without that rule the freedom from state invasions of privacy would be so ephemeral and so neatly severed from its conceptual nexus with the freedom from all brutish means of coercing evidence as not to merit this court's high regard as a freedom "implicit in the concept of ordered liberty." At the time that the Court held in *Wolf* that the Amendment was applicable to the States through the Due Process clause, the cases of this court, as we have seen, had steadfastly held that as to federal officers the Fourth Amendment included the exclusion of the evidence seized in violation of its provisions. Even *Wolf* "stoutly adhered" to that proposition. The right to privacy, when conceded operatively enforceable against the States, was not susceptible of destruction by avulsion of the sanction upon which its protection and enjoyment had always been deemed dependent under the *Boyd, Weeks* and *Silverthorne* cases. Therefore, in extending the substantive protections of due process to all constitutionally unreasonable searches—state or federal—it was logically and constitutionally necessary that the exclusion doctrine—an essential part of the right to privacy—be also insisted upon as an essential ingredient of the right newly recognized by the *Wolf* case. In short, the admission of the new constitutional right by *Wolf* could not consistently tolerate denial of its most important constitutional privilege, namely, the exclusion of the evidence which an accused had been forced to give by reason of the unlawful seizure. To hold otherwise is to grant the right but in reality to withhold its privilege and enjoyment. . . .

Indeed, we are aware of no restraint, similar to that rejected today, conditioning the enforcement of any other basic constitutional right. The right to privacy, no less important than any other right carefully and particularly reserved to the people, would stand in marked contrast to all other rights declared as "basic to a free society." *Wolf v. Colorado, supra* (338 U.S. at 27). This court has not hesitated to enforce as strictly against the States as it does against the Federal Government the rights of free speech and of a free press, the rights to notice and to a fair, public trial, including, as it does, the right not to be convicted by use of a coerced confession, however logically relevant it be, and without regard to its reliability. . . . And nothing could be more certain than that when a coerced confession is involved, "the relevant rules of evidence" are overridden without regard to "the incidence of such conduct by the police," slight or frequent. Why should not the same rule apply to what is tantamount to coerced testimony by way of unconstitutional seizure of goods, papers, effects, documents, etc.? . . .

The ignoble shortcut to conviction left open to the State tends to destroy the entire system of constitutional restraints on which the liberties of the people rest. Having once recognized that the right to privacy embodied in the Fourth Amendment is enforceable against the States, and that the right to be secure against rude invasions of privacy by state officers is, therefore, constitutional in origin, we can no longer permit that right to remain an empty promise. Because it is enforceable in the same manner and to like effect as other basic rights secured by the Due Process clause, we can no longer permit it to be revocable at the whim of any police officer who, in the name of law enforcement itself, chooses to suspend its enjoyment. Our decision, founded on reason and truth, gives to the individual no more than that which the Constitution guaranties him, to the police officer no less than that to which honest law enforcement is entitled, and, to the courts, that judicial integrity so necessary in the true administration of justice. . . .

Reversed and remanded.

MR. JUSTICE BLACK, CONCURRING:

I am still not persuaded that the Fourth Amendment, standing alone, would be enough to bar the introduction into evidence against an accused of papers and effects seized from him in violation of its commands. For the Fourth Amendment does not itself contain any provision expressly precluding the use of such evidence, and I am extremely doubtful that such a provision could properly be inferred from nothing more than the basic command against unreasonable searches and seizures. Reflection on the problem, however, in the light of cases coming before the Court since *Wolf*, has led me to conclude that when the Fourth Amendment's ban against unreasonable searches and seizures is considered together with the Fifth Amendment's ban against compelled self-incrimination, a constitutional basis emerges which not only justifies but actually requires the exclusionary rule. . . .

[Mr. Justice Douglas wrote a separate concurring opinion.]

Mr. Justice Harlan, whom Mr. Justice Frankfurter and Mr. Justice Whittaker join, dissenting:

In overruling the *Wolf* case the Court, in my opinion, has forgotten the sense of judicial restraint which, with due regard for *stare decisis*, is one element that should enter into deciding whether a past decision of this court should be overruled. Apart from that I also believe that the *Wolf* rule represents sounder constitutional doctrine than the new rule which now replaces it.

From the Court's statement of the case one would gather that the central, if not controlling, issue on this appeal is whether illegally state-seized evidence is constitutionally admissible in a state prosecution, an issue which would of course face us with the need for re-examining *Wolf*. However, such is not the situation. For, although that question was indeed raised here and below among appellant's subordinate points, the new and pivotal issue brought to the Court by this appeal is whether Section 2905.34 of the Ohio Revised Code making criminal the *mere* knowing possession or control of obscene material, and under which appellant has been convicted, is consistent with the rights of free thought and expression assured against state action by the Fourteenth Amendment. That was the principal issue which was decided by the Ohio Supreme Court, which was tendered by appellant's jurisdictional statement, and which was briefed and argued in this court.

In this posture of things, I think it fair to say that five members of this court have simply "reached out" to overrule Wolf. With all respect for the views of the majority, and recognizing that *stare decisis* carries different weight in constitutional adjudication than it does in nonconstitutional decision, I can perceive no justification for regarding this case as an appropriate occasion for re-examining *Wolf*. . . .

At the heart of the majority's opinion in this case is the following syllogism: (1) the rule excluding in federal criminal trials evidence which is the product of an illegal search and seizure is a "part and parcel" of the Fourth Amendment; (2) *Wolf* held that the "privacy" assured against federal action by the Fourth Amendment is also protected against state action by the Fourteenth Amendment; and (3) it is therefore "logically and constitutionally necessary" that the Weeks exclusionary rule should also be enforced against the States.

This reasoning ultimately rests on the unsound premise that because *Wolf* carried into the States, as part of "the concept of ordered liberty" embodied in the Fourteenth Amendment . . . it must follow that whatever configurations of the Fourth Amendment have been developed in the particularizing federal precedents are likewise to be deemed a part of "ordered liberty," and as such are enforceable against the States. For me, this does not follow at all.

It cannot be too much emphasized that what was recognized in *Wolf* was not that the Fourth Amendment *as such* is enforceable against the States as a facet of due process, a view of the Fourteenth Amendment which, as *Wolf* itself pointed out . . . has long since been discredited, but the principle of privacy "which is at the core of the Fourth Amendment." . . . It would not be proper to expect or impose any precise equivalence, either as regards the scope of the right or the means of its implementation, between the requirements of the Fourth and Fourteenth Amendments. For the Fourth, unlike what was said in *Wolf* of the Fourteenth, does not state a general principle only; it is a particular command, having its setting in a pre-existing legal context on which both interpreting decisions and enabling statutes must at least build. . . .

The preservation of a proper balance between State and federal responsibility in the administration of criminal justice demands patience on the part of those who might like to see things move faster among the States in this respect. Problems of criminal law enforcement vary widely from State to State. One State, in considering the totality of its legal picture, may conclude that the need for embracing the *Weeks* rule is pressing because other remedies are unavailable or inadequate to secure compliance with the substantive constitutional principle involved. Another, though equally solicitous of constitutional rights, may choose to pursue one purpose at a time, allowing all evidence relevant to guilt to be brought into a criminal trial, and dealing with constitutional infractions by other means. Still another may consider the exclusionary rule too rough and ready a remedy, in that it reaches only unconstitutional intrusions which eventuate in criminal prosecution of the victims. Further, a State after experimenting with the *Weeks* rule for a time may, because of unsatisfactory experience with it, decide to revert to a nonexclusionary rule. And so on. From the standpoint of constitutional permissibility in pointing a State in one direction or another, I do not see at all why "time has set its face against" the considerations which led Mr. Justice Cardozo, then chief judge of the New York Court of Appeals, to reject for New York in *People v. Defore, . . .* the *Weeks* exclusionary rule. For us the question remains, as it has always been, one of state power, not one of passing judgment on the wisdom of one state course or another. In my view this court should continue to forbear from fettering the States with an adamant rule which may embarrass them in coping with their own peculiar problems in criminal law enforcement. . . .

MEMORANDUM OF MR. JUSTICE STEWART:

Agreeing fully with Part I of Mr. Justice Harlan's dissenting opinion, I express no view as to the merits of the constitutional issue which the Court today decides. I would, however, reverse the judgment in this case, because I am persuaded that the provision of Section 2905.34 of the Ohio Revised Code, upon which the petitioner's conviction was based, is, in the words of Mr. Justice Harlan, not "consistent with the rights of free thought and expression assured against state action by the Fourteenth Amendment."

The right to counsel is absolute and applies to state courts equally with the federal courts.

35. *GIDEON v. WAINWRIGHT* (1962)

The Supreme Court, particularly in the case of Betts v. Brady *(1942), had taken the position that the Sixth Amendment's guaranty of the right to counsel did not apply to state courts. In this case of* Gideon v. Wainwright *the Court reversed itself and threw out the Betts decision so thoroughly that Justice Harlan, who concurred in the reversal, complained wryly that it was not even given "respectful burial." Justices Douglas, Clark, and Harlan wrote separate concurring opinions.*

Background: *Gideon, a Florida indigent, was tried for breaking into a poolroom in order to commit a felony. Denied counsel, he acted as his own lawyer, and was found guilty. The Supreme Court reversed the Florida court's decision on the ground that Gideon had been denied a fair trial, and that under the Sixth Amendment the right to counsel was absolute, applicable everywhere, in all the courts of the land.*

Some Related Cases

(On the Right to Counsel and other Rights of the Accused):

Powell v. Alabama (1932)
Johnson v. Zerbst (1938)
Avery v. Alabama (1940)
White v. Texas (1940)
Smith v. O'Grady (1941)
Ward v. Texas (1942)
McNabb v. United States (1943)
Ashcraft v. Tennessee (1944)
House v. Mayo (1945)
Gayes v. New York (1947)
Marino v. Ragen (1947)
In re Oliver (1947)
Uveges v. California (1948)
Wade v. Mayo (1948)
Watts v. Indiana (1949)
Rochin v. California (1952)
Mallory v. United States (1957)
Jencks v. United States (1957)
Fikes v. Alabama (1957)
Crooker v. California (1958)
Payne v. Arkansas (1958)
Coulombe v. Connecticut (1961)
Rogers v. Richmond (1961)
Douglas v. California (1963)
Lynumn v. Illinois (1963)
Malloy v. Hogan (1964)
Escobedo v. Illinois (1964)
Miranda v. Arizona (1966)
Johnson v. New Jersey (1966)
Davis v. North Carolina (1966)
Schmerber v. California (1966)
Smith v. Illinois (1968)

(On Self-Incrimination and Forced Confessions):

Pierce v. United States (1896)
Wilson v. United States (1896)
Brown v. Walker (1896)
Jack v. Kansas (1905)
Burdick v. United States (1915)
McCarthy v. Arndstein (1923)
McCarthy v. Arndstein (1924)

United States v. Murdock (1931)
Snyder v. Massachusetts (1934)
Brown v. Mississippi (1936)
Chambers v. Florida (1940)
Lisenba v. California (1941)
Feldman v. United States (1944)
Lyons v. Oklahoma (1944)
United States v. Mitchell (1944)
Malinski v. New York (1945)
Adamson v. California (1947)
Shapiro v. United States (1948)
Malloy v. Hogan (1965)

MR. JUSTICE BLACK DELIVERED THE OPINION OF THE COURT:

Petitioner was charged in a Florida state court with having broken and entered a poolroom with intent to commit a misdemeanor. This offense is a felony under Florida law. Appearing in court without funds and without a lawyer, petitioner asked the court to appoint counsel for him, whereupon the following colloquy took place:

> The COURT: Mr. Gideon, I am sorry, but I cannot appoint Counsel to represent you in this case. Under the laws of the State of Florida, the only time the Court can appoint Counsel to represent a Defendant is when that person is charged with a capital offense. I am sorry, but I will have to deny your request to appoint Counsel to defend you in this case.
>
> The DEFENDANT: The United States Supreme Court says I am entitled to be represented by Counsel.

Put to trial before a jury, Gideon conducted his defense about as well as could be expected from a layman. He made an opening statement to the jury, cross-examined the State's witnesses, presented witnesses in his own defense, declined to testify himself, and made a short argument "emphasizing his innocence to the charge contained in the Information filed in this case." The jury returned a verdict of guilty, and petitioner was sentenced to serve five years in the state prison. Later, petitioner filed in the Florida Supreme Court this habeas corpus petition attacking his conviction and sentence on the ground that the trial court's refusal to appoint counsel for him denied him rights "guarantied by the Constitution and the Bill of Rights by the United States Government." Treating the petition for habeas corpus as properly before it, the State Supreme Court, "upon consideration thereof" but without an opinion, denied all relief. Since 1942, when *Betts v. Brady*, 316 U.S. 455, was decided by a divided Court, the problem of a defendant's federal constitutional right to counsel in a state court has been a continuing source of controversy and litigation in both state and federal courts. To give this problem another review here, we granted certiorari. 370 U.S. 908. Since Gideon was proceeding *in forma pauperis,* we appointed counsel to represent him and requested both sides to discuss in their briefs and oral arguments the following: "Should this Court's holding in *Betts v. Brady,* 316 U.S. 455, be reconsidered?"

The facts upon which Betts claimed that he had been unconstitutionally denied the right to have counsel appointed to assist him are strikingly like the facts upon which Gideon here bases his federal constitutional claim. . . . Like Gideon, Betts sought release by habeas corpus, alleging that he had been denied the right to assistance of counsel in violation of the Fourteenth Amendment. Betts was denied any relief, and on review this court affirmed. It was held that a refusal to appoint counsel for an indigent defendant charged with a felony did not necessarily violate the Due Process clause of the Fourteenth Amendment, which for reasons given the Court deemed to be the only applicable federal constitutional provision. The Court said:

> "Asserted denial [of due process] is to be tested by an appraisal of the totality of facts in a given case. That which may, in one setting, constitute a denial of fundamental fairness, shocking to the universal sense of justice, may, in other circumstances, and in the light of other considerations, fall short of such denial." 316 U.S., at 462.

. . . Since the facts and circumstances of the two cases are so nearly indistinguishable, we think the *Betts v. Brady* holding if left standing would require us to reject Gideon's claim that the Constitution guarantees him the assistance of counsel. Upon full reconsideration we conclude that *Betts v. Brady* should be overruled. . . .

We accept *Betts v. Brady*'s assumption, based as it was on our prior cases, that a provision of the Bill of Rights which is "fundamental and essential to a fair trial" is made obligatory upon the States by the Fourteenth Amendment. We think the Court in *Betts* was wrong, however, in concluding that the Sixth Amendment's guaranty of counsel is not one of these fundamental rights. Ten years before *Betts v. Brady,* this court, after full consideration of all the historical data examined in Betts, had unequivocally declared that "the right to the aid of counsel is of this fundamental character." *Powell v. Alabama,* 287 U.S. 45, 68 (1932). While the Court at the close of its Powell opinion did by its language, as this court frequently does, limit its holding to the particular facts and circumstances of that case, its conclusions about the fundamental nature of the right to counsel are unmistakable. Several years later, in

1936, the Court reemphasized what it had said about the fundamental nature of the right to counsel. . . .

In light of these and many other prior decisions of this court, it is not surprising that the Betts Court, when faced with the contention that "one charged with crime, who is unable to obtain counsel, must be furnished counsel by the State," conceded that "expressions in the opinions of this court lend color to the argument . . ." 316 U.S., at 462-463. The fact is that in deciding as it did—that "appointment of counsel is not a fundamental right, essential to the fair trial"—the Court in *Betts v. Brady* made an abrupt break with its own well-considered precedents. In returning to these old precedents, sounder we believe than the new, we but restore constitutional principles established to achieve a fair system of justice. Not only these precedents but also reason and reflection require us to recognize that in our adversary system of criminal justice, any person haled into court, who is too poor to hire a lawyer, cannot be assured a fair trial unless counsel is provided for him. This seems to us to be an obvious truth. Governments, both state and federal, quite properly spend vast sums of money to establish machinery to try defendants accused of crime. Lawyers to prosecute are everywhere deemed essential to protect the public's interest in an orderly society. Similarly, there are few defendants charged with crime, few indeed, who fail to hire the best lawyers they can get to prepare and present their defenses. That government hires lawyers to prosecute and defendants who have the money hire lawyers to defend are the strongest indications of the widespread belief that lawyers in criminal courts are necessities, not luxuries. The right of one charged with crime to counsel may not be deemed fundamental and essential to fair trials in some countries, but it is in ours. From the very beginning, our state and national constitutions and laws have laid great emphasis on procedural and substantive safeguards designed to assure fair trials before impartial tribunals in which every defendant stands equal before the law. This noble ideal cannot be realized if the poor man charged with crime has to face his accusers without a lawyer to assist him. . . . The Court in *Betts v. Brady* departed from the sound wisdom upon which the Court's holding in *Powell v. Alabama* rested. Florida, supported by two other States, has asked that *Betts v. Brady* be left intact. Twenty-two States, as friends of the Court, argue that *Betts* was "an anachronism when handed down" and that it should now be overruled. We agree. . . .

Reversed.

[Justices Douglas and Clark wrote separate concurring opinions.]

MR. JUSTICE HARLAN, CONCURRING:

I agree that *Betts v. Brady* should be overruled, but consider it entitled to a more respectful burial than has been accorded, at least on the part of those of us who were not on the Court when that case was decided.

I cannot subscribe to the view that *Betts v. Brady* represented "an abrupt break with its own well-considered precedents." . . . In 1932, in *Powell v. Alabama,* 287 U.S. 45, a capital case, this court declared that under the particular facts there presented . . . the state court had a duty to assign counsel for the trial as a necessary requisite of due process of law. It is evident that these limiting facts were not added to the opinion as an afterthought; they were repeatedly emphasized . . . and were clearly regarded as important to the result.

Thus when this court, a decade later, decided *Betts v. Brady,* it did no more than to admit of the possible existence of special circumstances in noncapital as well as capital trials, while at the same time to insist that such circumstances be shown in order to establish a denial of due process. The right to appointed counsel had been recognized as being considerably broader in federal prosecutions, see *Johnson v. Zerbst,* 304 U.S. 458, but to have imposed these requirements on the States would indeed have been "an abrupt break" with the almost immediate past. The declaration that the right to appointed counsel in state prosecutions, as established in *Powell v. Alabama,* was not limited to capital cases was in truth not a departure from, but an extension of, existing precedent.

The principles declared in *Powell* and in *Betts,* however, had a troubled journey throughout the years that have followed first the one case and then the other. Even by the time of the Betts decision, dictum in at least one of the Court's opinions [*Avery v. Alabama*] had indicated that there was an absolute right to the services of counsel in the trial of state capital cases. . . .

In noncapital cases, the "special circumstances" rule has continued to exist in form while its substance has been substantially and steadily eroded. In the first decade after Betts, there were cases in which the Court found special circumstances to be lacking, but usually by a sharply divided vote. However, no such decision has been cited to us, and I have found none, after *Quicksall v. Michigan,* 339 U.S. 660, decided in 1950. At the same time, there have been not a few cases in which special circumstances were found in little or nothing more than the "complexity" of the legal questions presented, although those questions were often of only routine difficulty. The Court has come to recognize, in other words, that the mere existence of a serious criminal charge constituted in itself special circumstances requiring the services of counsel at trial. In truth the *Betts v. Brady* rule is no longer a reality.

This evolution, however, appears not to have been fully recognized by many state courts, in this instance charged with the front-line responsibility for the enforcement of constitutional rights. To continue a rule which is honored by this court only with lip service is not a healthy thing and in the long run will do disservice to the federal system.

The special circumstances rule has been formally abandoned in capital cases, and the time has now come when it should be similarly abandoned in noncapital cases, at least as to offenses which, as the one involved here, carry the possibility of a substantial prison sentence. (Whether the rule should extend to *all* criminal cases need not now be decided.) This indeed does no more than to make explicit something that has long since been foreshadowed in our decisions.

In agreeing with the Court that the right to counsel in a case such as this should now be expressly recognized as a fundamental right embraced in the Fourteenth Amendment, I wish to make a further observation. When we hold a right or immunity, valid against the Federal Government, to be "implicit in the concept of ordered liberty" and thus valid against the States, I do not read our past decisions to suggest that by so holding, we automatically carry over an entire body of federal law and apply it in full sweep to the States. Any such concept would disregard the frequently wide disparity between the legitimate interests of the States and of the Federal Government, the divergent problems that they face, and the significantly different consequences of their actions. Cf. *Roth v. United States,* 354 U.S. 476, 496–508 (separate opinion of this writer). In what is done today I do not understand the Court to depart from the principles laid down in *Palko v. Connecticut,* 302 U.S. 319, or to embrace the concept that the Fourteenth Amendment "incorporates" the Sixth Amendment as such.

On these premises I join in the judgment of the Court.

Appendix A

List of Supreme Court Decisions

a. In Chronological Order

1793 *Chisholm v. Georgia*
1796 *Hylton v. United States*
1798 *Calder v. Bull*
1803 *Marbury v. Madison*
1819 *Dartmouth College v. Woodward*
1819 *McCulloch v. Maryland*
1821 *Cohens v. Virginia*
1824 *Gibbons v. Ogden*
1857 *Dred Scott v. Sandford*
1866 *Ex parte Milligan*
1873 *Slaughterhouse Cases*
1883 *Civil Rights Cases*
1919 *Schenck v. United States*
1920 *Missouri v. Holland*
1926 *Myers v. United States*
1936 *United States v. Curtiss-Wright Export Corp.*
1937 *National Labor Relations Board v. Jones & Laughlin Steel Corp.*
1937 *West Coast Hotel Co. v. Parrish*
1937 *Palko v. Connecticut*
1940 *Minersville School District v. Gobitis*
1942 *Wickard v. Filburn*
1943 *West Virginia State Board of Education v. Barnette*
1951 *Dennis et al. v. United States*
1952 *Youngstown Sheet and Tube Co. v. Sawyer*
1952 *United States v. Kahriger*
1954 *Brown v. Board of Education of Topeka* (First Case)
1954 *Bolling v. Sharpe*
1955 *Brown v. Board of Education of Topeka* (Second Case)
1956 *Pennsylvania v. Nelson*
1957 *Roth v. United States*
1957 *Alberts v. California*
1958 *Cooper v. Aaron*

b. In Alphabetical Order

United States v. Kahriger
West Coast Hotel Co. v. Parrish
West Virginia State Board of Education v. Barnette
Wickard v. Filburn
Youngstown Sheet and Tube Co. v. Sawyer

Appendix B

Justices of the United States Supreme Court

(In Alphabetical Order)

a. CHIEF JUSTICES

	Appointed from:	*Term of Service*
Chase, Salmon P. (1808-1873)	Ohio	1864-1873
Ellsworth, Oliver (1745-1807)	Conn.	1796-1799*
Fuller, Melville, W. (1833-1910)	Ill.	1888-1910
Hughes, Charles E. (1862-1948)	N.Y.	1930-1941†
Jay, John (1745-1829)	N.Y.	1790-1795*
Marshall, John (1755-1835)	Va.	1801-1835
Rutledge, John (1739-1800)	S.C.	1795 ‡
Stone, Harlan F. (1872-1946)	N.Y.	1941-1946
Taft, William H. (1857-1930)	Conn.	1921-1930†
Taney, Roger B. (1777-1864)	Md.	1836-1864
Vinson, Frederick M. (1890-1953)	Ky.	1946-1953
Waite, Morrison R. (1816-1888)	Ohio	1874-1888
Warren, Earl (1891-)	Cal.	1953-
White, Edward D. (1845-1921)	La.	1910-1921

* Resigned.
† Retired.
‡ Rejected by the Senate, Dec. 15, 1795.

b. ASSOCIATE JUSTICES

	Appointed from:	*Term of Service*
Baldwin, Henry (1780-1844)	Conn.	1830-1844
Barbour, Philip P. (1783-1841)	Va.	1836-1841
Black, Hugo L. (1886-)	Ala.	1937-
Blair, John (1732-1800)	Va.	1789-1796*
Blatchford, Samuel (1820-1893)	N.Y.	1882-1893
Bradley, Joseph P. (1813-1892)	N.Y.	1870-1892
Brandeis, Louis D. (1856-1941)	Mass.	1916-1939†
Brennan, William J. (1906-)	N.J.	1956-
Brewer, David J. (1837-1910)	Kan.	1890-1910
Brown, Henry B. (1836-1913)	Mass.	1890-1906†
Burton, Harold H. (1888-1964)	Ohio	1945-1958†
Butler, Pierce (1866-1939)	Minn.	1922-1939
Byrnes, James F. (1879-)	S.C.	1941-1942*
Campbell, John A. (1811-1889)	Ala.	1853-1861*
Cardozo, Benjamin N. (1870-1938)	N.Y.	1932-1938
Catron, John (1786-1865)	Tenn.	1837-1865
Chase, Samuel (1741-1811)	Md.	1796-1811
Clark, Tom C. (1899-)	Texas	1949-1967*
Clarke, John H. (1857-1945)	Ohio	1916-1922
Clifford, Nathan (1803-1881)	Maine	1858-1881
Curtis, Benjamin R. (1809-1874)	Mass.	1851-1857*
Cushing, William (1732-1810)	Mass.	1790-1810
Daniel, Peter V. (1784-1860)	Va.	1841-1860
Davis, David (1815-1886)	Ill.	1862-1877*
Day, William R. (1849-1923)	Ohio	1903-1922†
Douglas, William O. (1898-)	Conn.	1939-
Duvall, Gabriel (1752-1844)	Md.	1811-1835*
Field, Stephen J. (1816-1899)	Cal.	1863-1897†
Fortas, Abe (1910-)	Tenn.	1965-
Frankfurter, Felix (1882-1965)	Mass.	1939-1962†
Goldberg, Arthur (1908-)	Ill.	1962-1965*
Gray, Horace (1828-1902)	Mass.	1881-1902
Grier, Robert C. (1794-1870)	Pa.	1846-1870
Harlan, John M. (1833-1911)	Ky.	1877-1911

* Resigned.
† Retired.

	Appointed from:	*Term of Service*
Holmes, Oliver W. (1841-1935)	Mass.	1902-1932†
Hunt, Ward (1810-1886)	N.Y.	1872-1882‡
Iredell, James (1751-1799)	N.C.	1790-1799
Jackson, Howell E. (1835-1895)	Tenn.	1893-1895
Jackson, Robert H. (1892-1954)	N.Y.	1941-1954
Johnson, Thomas (1732-1819)	Md.	1791-1793*
Johnson, William (1771-1834)	S.C.	1804-1834
Lamar, Lucius Q. C. (1825-1893)	Miss.	1888-1893
Livingston, Henry B. (1753-1823)	N.Y.	1807-1823
Lurton, Horace H. (1844-1914)	Tenn.	1910-1914
Marshall, Thurgood (1908-)	Md.	1967-
McKenna, Joseph (1843-1926)	Cal.	1898-1925†
McKinley, John (1780-1852)	Ala.	1837-1852
McLean, John (1785-1861)	Ohio	1829-1861
McReynolds, James C. (1862-1946)	Tenn.	1914-1941†
Miller, Samuel F. (1816-1890)	Iowa	1862-1890
Minton, Sherman (1890-1965)	Ind.	1949-1956†
Moody, William H. (1853-1917)	Mass.	1906-1910**
Moore, Alfred (1755-1810)	N.C.	1799-1804*
Murphy, Frank (1890-1949)	Mich.	1940-1949
Nelson, Samuel (1792-1873)	N.Y.	1845-1872†
Paterson, William (1745-1806)	N.J.	1793-1806
Peckham, Rufus W. (1838-1909)	N.Y.	1896-1909
Pitney, Mahlon (1858-1924)	N.J.	1912-1922**
Reed, Stanley F. (1884-)	Ky.	1938-1957†
Roberts, Owen J. (1875-1955)	Pa.	1930-1945*
Rutledge, Wiley B. (1894-1949)	Iowa	1943-1949
Sanford, Edward T. (1865-1930)	Tenn.	1923-1930
Shiras, George (1832-1924)	Pa.	1892-1903†
Stewart, Potter (1915-)	Ohio	1958-
Stone, Harlan F. (1872-1946) (1941-1946 Chief Justice)	N.Y.	1925-1941
Story, Joseph (1779-1845)	Mass.	1811-1845
Strong, William (1808-1895)	Pa.	1870-1880*
Sutherland, George (1862-1942)	Utah	1922-1938†
Swayne, Noah H. (1804-1884)	Ohio	1862-1881†
Thompson, Smith (1768-1843)	N.Y.	1823-1843
Todd, Thomas (1765-1826)	Ky.	1803-1826
Trimble, Robert (1777-1828)	Ky.	1826-1828
Van Devanter, Willys (1859-1941)	Wyo.	1911-1937†
Washington, Bushrod (1762-1829)	Va.	1798-1829
Wayne, James M. (1790-1867)	Ga.	1835-1867
White, Byron R. (1917-)	Colo.	1962-

* Resigned.
† Retired.
** Disabled.
‡ Disabled and pensioned.

	Appointed from:	Term of Service
White, Edward D. (1845-1921) (1910-1921, Chief Justice)	La.	1894-1910
Whittaker, Charles E. (1901-)	Mo.	1957-1962†
Wilson, James (1742-1798)	Pa.	1789-1798
Woodbury, Levi (1789-1851)	N.H.	1845-1851
Woods, William B. (1824-1887)	Ga.	1881-1887

† Retired.

Part III

Indexed Guide to the Constitution and Supreme Court Decisions

Indexed Guide to the Constitution and Supreme Court Decisions

Post offices, Congressional power to establish (Art. 1, sec. 8, 7), 73